CHILTON'S
REPAIR & TUNE-UP GUIDE
TOYOTA CELICA/SUPRA 1971-83
All Models

Y0-BOD-089

President LAWRENCE A. FORNASIERI
Vice President and General Manager JOHN P. KUSHNERICK
Executive Editor KERRY A. FREEMAN, S.A.E.
Senior Editor RICHARD J. RIVELE, S.A.E.
Editor A. Lindsay Brooke

CHILTON BOOK COMPANY
Radnor, Pennsylvania
19089

SAFETY NOTICE

Proper service and repair procedures are vital to the safe, reliable operation of all motor vehicles, as well as the personal safety of those performing repairs. This book outlines procedures for servicing and repairing vehicles using safe, effective methods. The procedures contain many NOTES, CAUTIONS and WARNINGS which should be followed along with standard safety procedures to eliminate the possibility of personal injury or improper service which could damage the vehicle or compromise its safety.

It is important to note that repair procedures and techniques, tools and parts for servicing motor vehicles, as well as the skill and experience of the individual performing the work vary widely. It is not possible to anticipate all of the conceivable ways or conditions under which vehicles may be serviced, or to provide cautions as to all of the possible hazards that may result. Standard and accepted safety precautions and equipment should be used when handling toxic or flammable fluids, and safety goggles or other protection should be used during cutting, grinding, chiseling, prying, or any other process that can cause material removal or projectiles.

Some procedures require the use of tools specially designed for a specific purpose. Before substituting another tool or procedure, you must be completely satisfied that neither your personal safety, nor the performance of the vehicle will be endangered.

Although information in this guide is based on industry sources and is as complete as possible at the time of publication, the possibility exists that the manufacturer made later changes which could not be included here. While striving for total accuracy, Chilton Book Company cannot assume responsibility for any errors, changes, or omissions that may occur in the compilation of this data.

PART NUMBERS

Part numbers listed in this reference are not recommendations by Chilton for any product by brand name. They are references that can be used with interchange manuals and aftermarket supplier catalogs to locate each brand supplier's discrete part number.

SPECIAL TOOLS

Special tools are recommended by the vehicle manufacturer to perform their specific job. Use has been kept to a minimum, but where absolutely necessary, are they referred to in the text by the part number of the tool manufacturer. These tools can be purchased, under the appropriate part number, from Toyota dealers or Toyota Motor Sales, U.S.A. (address below) or an equivalent tool can be purchased locally from a tool supplier or parts outlet. Before substituting any tool for the one recommended, read the SAFETY NOTICE at the top of this page.

ACKNOWLEDGMENTS

The Chilton Book Company expresses appreciation to Toyota Motor Sales, U.S.A., Inc., 2055 W. 190th Street, Torrance, California 90504, Biscotte Toyota, 2062 W. Main Street, Norristown, Pennsylvania 19401 and Speedcraft Enterprises, Inc., Devon, Pennsylvania 19333 for their generous assistance.

Copyright © 1983 by Chilton Book Company
All Rights Reserved
Published in Radnor, Pennsylvania 19089, by Chilton Book Company

Manufactured in the United States of America
    4567890   21098765

Chilton's Repair & Tune-Up Guide: Toyota Celica/Supra 1971–83
ISBN 0-8019-7314-7 pbk.
Library of Congress Catalog Card No. 82-72936

CONTENTS

Quick Reference Specifications For Your Vehicle

Fill in this chart with the most commonly used specifications for your vehicle. Specifications can be found in Chapters 1 through 3 or on the tune-up decal under the hood of the vehicle.

 ## Tune-Up

Firing Order_____

Spark Plugs:

    Type_____

    Gap (in.)_____

Point Gap (in.)_____

Dwell Angle (°)_____

Ignition Timing (°)_____

    Vacuum (Connected/Disconnected)_____

Valve Clearance (in.)

    Intake_____   Exhaust_____

Capacities

Engine Oil (qts)

    With Filter Change_____

    Without Filter Change_____

Cooling System (qts)_____

Manual Transmission (pts)_____

    Type_____

Automatic Transmission (pts)_____

    Type_____

Front Differential (pts)_____

    Type_____

Rear Differential (pts)_____

    Type_____

Transfer Case (pts)_____

    Type_____

FREQUENTLY REPLACED PARTS

Use these spaces to record the part numbers of frequently replaced parts.

PCV VALVE

Manufacturer_____

Part No._____

OIL FILTER

Manufacturer_____

Part No._____

AIR FILTER

Manufacturer_____

Part No._____

General Information and and Maintenance

HOW TO USE THIS BOOK

Chilton's Repair and Tune-Up Guide for the Toyota Celica and Supra is intended to teach you more about the inner workings of your automobile and save you money on its upkeep. Chapters 1 and 2 will probably be most frequently used in the book. The first chapter contains all the information that may be required at a moment's notice. Aside from giving the location of various serial numbers and the proper towing instructions, it also contains all the information on basic day-to-day maintenance that you will need to ensure good performance and long component life. Chapter 2 covers the necessary tune-up procedures which will assist you not only in keeping the engine running properly and at peak performance levels, but also in restoring some of the more delicate components to operating condition in the event of a failure. Chapters 3 through 10 cover repairs (rather than maintenance) for various portions of the car, with each chapter covering either one separate system or two related systems. The mechanics data then lists general information which may be useful in rebuilding the engine or performing some other operation on any car.

When using the Table of Contents, refer to the bold listings for the subject of the chapter and the smaller listings (or the index) for information on a particular component.

In general, there are three things a proficient mechanic has which must be allowed for when a non-professional does work on his/her car. These are:

1. A sound knowledge of the construction of the parts he is working with, their order of assembly, etc.

2. A knowledge of potentially hazardous situations; particularly how to prevent them.

3. Manual dexterity.

This book provides step-by-step instructions and illustrations whenever possible. Use them carefully and wisely—don't just jump headlong into disassembly. When there is doubt about being able to readily reassemble something, make a careful drawing of the component before taking it apart. Assembly always looks simple when everything is still assembled.

"CAUTIONS," "WARNINGS" and "NOTES" will be provided where appropriate to help prevent you from injuring yourself or damaging your car. Consequently, you should always read through the entire procedure before beginning the work so as to familiarize yourself with any special problems which may occur during the given procedure. Since no number of warnings could cover every possible situation, you should work slowly and try to envision what is going to happen in each operation ahead of time.

When it comes to tightening things, there is generally a slim area between too loose to properly seal or resist vibration and so tight as to risk damage or warping. When dealing with major engine parts, or with any aluminum component, it pays to buy a torque wrench and go by the recommended figures.

When reference is made in this book to the "right side" or the "left side" of the car, it should be understood that the positions are always to be viewed from the front seat. This means that the left side of the car is the driver's side and the right side is the passenger's side. This will hold true throughout the book, regardless of how you might be looking at the car at the time.

We have attempted to eliminate the use of special tools whenever possible, substituting more readily available hand tools. However, in some cases, the special tools are necessary. These can usually be purchased from your local Toyota dealer or from an automotive parts store.

Always be conscious of the need for safety in your work. Never get under a car unless it is firmly supported by jackstands or ramps. Never smoke near, or allow flame to get near the battery or the fuel system. Keep your clothing, hands and hair clear of the fan and all pulleys when working near the engine if it is running. Most importantly, try to be patient; even in the midst of an argument with a stubborn bolt, reaching for the largest hammer in the garage is usually a cause for later regret and more extensive repair. As you gain confidence and experience, working on your car will become a source of pride and satisfaction.

TOOLS AND EQUIPMENT

The service procedures in this book presuppose a familiarity with hand tools and their proper use. However, it is possible that you may have a limited amount of experience with the sort of equipment needed to work on an automobile. This section is designed to help you assemble a basic set of tools that will handle most of the jobs you may undertake.

In addition to the normal assortment of screwdrivers and pliers, automotive service work requires an investment in wrenches, sockets and the handles needed to drive them, and various measuring tools such as torque wrenches and feeler gauges.

You will find that virtually every nut and bolt on your Toyota is metric. Therefore, despite a few close size similarities, standard inch-size tools will not fit and must not be used. You will need a set of metric wrenches as your most basic tool kit, ranging from about 6 mm to 17 mm in size. High quality forged wrenches are available in three styles: open end, box end, and combination open/box end. The combination tools are generally the most desirable as a starter set; the wrenches shown in the accompanying illustration are of the combination type.

The other set of tools inevitably required is a ratchet handle and socket set. This set should have the same size range as your wrench set. The ratchet, extension, and flex drives for the sockets are available in many sizes; it is advisable to choose a ⅜ inch drive set initially. One break in the inch/metric sizing war is that metric-sized sockets sold in the U.S. have inch-sized drive (¼, ⅜, ½, etc.). Thus, if you already have an inch-sized socket set, you need only buy new metric sockets in the sizes needed. Sockets are available in six and twelve point versions; six point types are stronger and are a good choice for a first set. The choice of a drive handle for the sockets should be made with some care. If this is your first set, take the plunge and invest in a flex-head ratchet; it will get into many places otherwise accessible only through a long chain of universal joints, extensions, and adapters. An alternative is a flex handle, which lacks the ratcheting feature but has a head which pivots 180°; such a tool

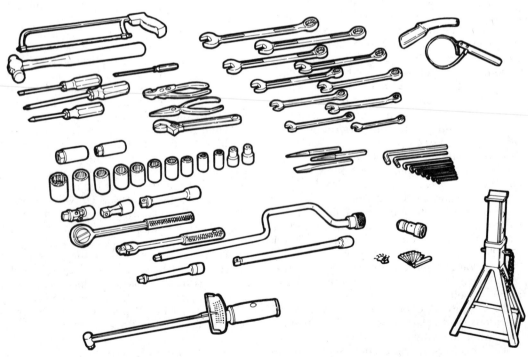

A basic collection of hand tools is necessary for automotive service

is shown below the ratchet handle in the illustration. In addition to the range of sockets mentioned, a rubber-lined spark plug socket should be purchased.

The most important thing to consider when purchasing hand tools is quality. Don't be misled by the low cost of "bargain tools. Forged wrenches, tempered screwdriver blades, and fine tooth ratchets are much better investments than their less expensive counterparts. The skinned knuckles and frustration inflicted by poor quality tools make any job an unhappy chore. Another consideration is that quality tools come with an unbeatable replacement guarantee—if the tool breaks, you get a new one, no questions asked.

Most jobs can be accomplished using the tools on the accompanying lists. There will be an occasional need for a special tool, such as snap ring pliers; that need will be mentioned in the text. It would not be wise to buy a large assortment of tools on the premise that someday they will be needed. Instead, the tools should be acquired one at a time, each for a specific job, both to avoid unnecessary expense and to be certain that you have the right tool.

The tools needed for basic maintenance jobs, in addition to the wrenches and sockets mentioned, include:

1. Jackstands, for support;
2. Oil filter wrench;
3. Oil filler spout or funnel;
4. Grease gun;
5. Battery post and clamp cleaner;
6. Container for draining oil;
7. Many rags for the inevitable spills.

In addition to these items there are several others which are not absolutely necessary, but handy to have around. These include a transmission funnel and filler tube, a drop (trouble) light on a long cord, an adjustable (crescent) wrench, and slip joint pliers.

A *hydraulic floor jack* is one of the best investments you can make if you are serious about repairing and maintaining your own car.

The bumper jack that comes with the car is simply not safe enough to use when doing anything more than changing a flat. The hydraulic floor jack (1½ ton is fine for the Toyota) will pay for itself quickly in convenience, utility and much greater safety.

A more advanced list of tools, suitable for tune-up work, can be drawn up easily. While the tools are slightly more sophisticated, they need not be outrageously expensive. The key to these purchases is to make them with an eye towards adaptability and wide range. A basic list of tune-up tools could include:

1. Tachometer/dwell meter;
2. Spark plug gauge and gapping tool;
3. Feeler gauges for valve adjustment;
4. Timing light.

You will need both wire-type and flat-type feeler gauges, the former for the spark plugs and the latter for the valves. The choice of a timing light should be made carefully. A light which works on the DC current supplied by the car battery is the best choice; it should have a xenon tube for brightness. Since many of the newer cars have electronic ignition, and since nearly all cars will have it in the future, the light should have an inductive pickup which

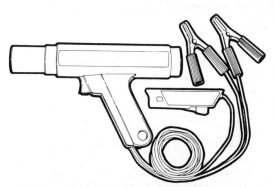

An inductive pickup simplifies timing light connection to the spark plug wire

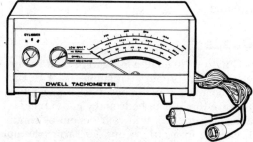

A dwell/tachometer is useful for tune-up work; you won't need a dwell meter if your car has electronic ignition

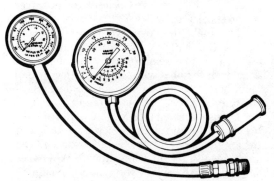

A compression gauge and a combination vacuum/fuel pressure gauge are handy for troubleshooting and tune-up work

clamps around the number one spark plug cable (the timing light illustrated has one of these pickups).

In addition to these basic tools, there are several other tools and gauges which you may find useful. These include:

1. A compression gauge. The screw-in type is slower to use, but eliminates the possibility of a faulty reading due to escaping pressure;

2. A manifold vacuum gauge;

3. A test light;

4. A combination volt/ohmmeter;

5. An induction meter, used to determine whether or not there is current flowing in a wire, an extremely helpful tool for electrical troubleshooting.

Finally, you will find a torque wrench necessary for all but the most basic of work. The beam-type models are perfectly adequate. The newer click-type (breakaway) torque wrenches are more accurate, but are much more expensive, and must be periodically recalibrated.

SERVICING YOUR CAR SAFELY

It is virtually impossible to anticipate all of the hazards involved with automotive maintenance and service, but care and common sense will prevent most accidents.

The rules of safety for mechanics range from "don't smoke around gasoline," to "use the proper tool for the job." The trick to avoiding injuries is to develop safe work habits and take every possible precaution.

Dos

• Do keep a fire extinguisher and first aid kit within easy reach.

• Do wear safety glasses or goggles when cutting, drilling, grinding or prying. If you wear glasses for the sake of vision, they should be made of hardened glass that can serve also as safety glasses, or wear safety goggles over your regular glasses.

• Do shield your eyes whenever you work around the battery. Batteries contain sulphuric acid. In case of contact with the eyes or skin, flush the area with water or a mixture of water and baking soda and get medical attention immediately.

• Do use safety stands for any undercar service. Jacks are for raising vehicles; safety stands are for making sure the vehicle stays raised until you want it to come down. Whenever the car is raised, block the wheels remaining on the ground and set the parking brake.

• Do use adequate ventilation when working with any chemicals or hazardous materials. Like carbon monoxide, the asbestos dust re-

Always support the car on jackstands when working under it

sulting from brake lining wear can be poisonous in sufficient quantities.

• Do disconnect the negative battery cable when working on the electrical system. The secondary ignition system can contain up to 40,000 volts.

• Do follow manufacturer's directions whenever working with potentially hazardous materials. Both brake fluid and antifreeze are poisonous if taken internally.

• Do properly maintain your tools. Loose hammerheads, mushroomed punches and chisels, frayed or poorly grounded electrical cords, excessively worn screwdrivers, spread open end wrenches, cracked sockets, slipping ratchets, or faulty droplight sockets can cause accidents.

• Do use the proper size and type of tool for the job being done.

• Do when possible, pull on a wrench handle rather than push on it, and adjust your stance to prevent a fall.

• Do be sure that adjustable wrenches are tightly closed on the nut or bolt and pulled so that the face is on the side of the fixed jaw.

• Do select a wrench or socket that fits the nut or bolt. The wrench or socket should sit straight, not cocked.

• Do strike squarely with a hammer; avoid glancing blows.

• Do set the parking brake and block the drive wheels if the work requires the engine running.

Don'ts

• Don't run an engine in a garage or anywhere else without proper ventilation—EVER! Carbon monoxide is poisonous; it takes a long time to leave the human body and you can build up a deadly supply of it in your system by simply breathing in a little every day. You may not realize you are slowly poisoning yourself. Always use power vents, windows, fans or open the garage doors.

• Don't work around moving parts while

wearing a necktie or other loose clothing. Short sleeves are much safer than long, loose sleeves; hard-toed shoes with neoprene soles protect your toes and give a better grip on slippery surfaces. Jewelry such as watches, fancy belt buckles, beads or body adornment of any kind is not safe working around a car. Long hair should be hidden under a hat or cap.

• Don't use pockets for toolboxes. A fall or bump can drive a screwdriver deep into your body. Even a wiping cloth hanging from the back pocket can wrap around a spinning shaft or fan.

• Don't use screwdrivers for anything other than driving screws! A screwdriver used as a prying tool or chisel can snap when least expected, causing bodily harm. Besides, you ruin a good tool when it is used for purposes other than those intended.

• Don't use a bumper jack (that little scissors or pantograph jack that comes with the car) for anything other than changing a flat tire! If you are serious about repairing and maintaining your own car, then one of the best investments you can make is in a hydraulic floor jack of at least 1½ ton capacity.

• Don't smoke when working around gasoline, cleaning solvent or other flammable material.

• Don't smoke when working around the battery. When the battery is being charged, it gives off explosive hydrogen gas.

• Don't use gasoline to wash your hands; there are excellent soaps available. Gasoline may contain lead, and lead can enter the body through a cut, accumulating in the body until you are very ill. Gasoline also removes all the natural oils from the skin so that bone dry hands will suck up oil and grease.

• *Don't service the air conditioning system unless you are equipped with the necessary tools and training.* The refrigerant, R-12, is extremely cold when compressed, and when released into the air will instantly freeze any surface it contacts, including your eyes. Although the refrigerant is normally non-toxic, R-12 becomes a deadly poisonous gas in the presence of an open flame. One good whiff of the vapors from burning refrigerant can be fatal.

SERIAL NUMBER IDENTIFICATION

Vehicle

All models have the vehicle identification number (VIN) stamped on a plate which is attached to the left side of the instrument panel. This plate is visible through the windshield.

VIN plate on the left-side of the instrument panel

Vehicle Identification

Model/Type	Year	Series Identification Number*
Celica 1900 (8R-C)	1971	RA20L
Celica 2000 (18R-C)	1972–74	RA21L
Celica 2200 (20R)	1975–77 1978–80	RA22L RA42L
Celica 2400 (22R)	1981	RA43L
Celica Supra 2600 (4M-E)	1979–80	MA46L
Celica Supra 2800	1981	MA47L
Celica 2400 (22R)	1982	RA64 RA65
Celica Supra 2800 (5M-GE)	1982	MA67
Celica 2400 (22R, 22R-E)	1983	RA63C RA64C RA65C RA64L RA65L
Celica Supra 2800 (5M-GE)	1983	MA67L

*The suffix L may not appear in the serial number; a typical serial number would look like this: MA46-132246

The VIN is also stamped on a plate on the firewall, in the engine compartment.

The serial number consists of a series identification number (see the chart below) followed by a six-digit production number.

VIN plate on the firewall

Engine

The engine serial number consists of an engine series identification number, followed by a six-digit production number.

The location of this serial number varies from one engine type to another. Serial numbers may be found in the following locations:

1900 cc (8R-C)

The serial number is stamped on the right side of the engine block, by the fuel pump.

2800 cc (5M-GE) Twin Cam

The engine serial number is stamped on the lower right hand side of the cylinder block, just above the oil pan.

All Others

The serial number is stamped on the left side of the engine block.

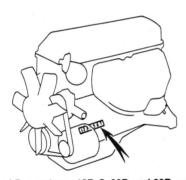

Engine I.D. numbers, 18R-C, 20R and 22R series

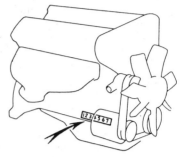

5M-GE Twin Cam engine I.D. stamping

ROUTINE MAINTENANCE

Air Cleaner

All of the dust present in the air is kept out of the engine by means of the air cleaner filter element. Proper maintenance is vital, as a clogged element not only restricts the air flow and thus the power, but can also cause premature engine wear.

The filter element should be cleaned every 7,500 miles, or more often if the car is driven under dry, dusty conditions. Remove the filter element and using low pressure compressed air, blow the dirt out.

NOTE: *The filter element used on Toyota vehicles is of the dry, disposable type. It should never be washed, soaked or oiled.*

The filter element should be replaced every 18,000 miles, (1970–72); every 24,000 miles, (1973–74); every 25,000 miles, (1975–77); and

Engine Identification

Year	Model	Displacement Cu. In. (cc)	Number of Cylinders	Type	Engine Series Identification
1971	1900	113.3 (1858)	4	SOHC	8R-C
1972–74	2000	120.7 (1980)	4	SOHC	18R-C
1975–80	2200	133.3 (2189)	4	SOHC	20R
1981–83	2400	144.4 (2367)	4	SOHC	22R ①
1979½–80	2600	156.4 (2563)	6	SOHC	4M-E
1981	2800	168.4 (2759)	6	SOHC	5M-E
1982–83	2800	168.4 (2759)	6	DOHC	5M-GE

SOHC Single Overhead Camshaft
DOHC Double Overhead Camshaft
① 22R-E on 1983 (fuel injected); carbureted 22-R also available

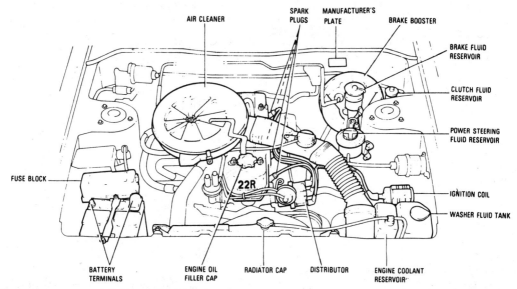

Engine compartment, 22R models. Other carbureted models similar (some components may be in different locations)

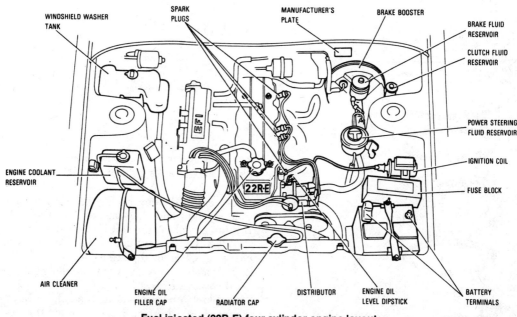

Fuel injected (22R-E) four cylinder engine layout

every 30,000 miles, (1978 and later); or more often under dry, dusty conditions. Be sure to use the correct one; all Toyota elements are of the same type but they come in a variety of sizes.

To replace:

1. Unfasten the wing nut(s) and clips (if so equipped) on top of the air cleaner housing and lift off the top.

2. Lift out the air filter element and clean it with compressed air or replace it.

3. Clean out the filter case with a rag.

4. Installation is in the reverse order of removal.

PCV Valve

The PCV valve regulates crankcase ventilation during various engine operating conditions. At high vacuum (idle speed and partial load range) it will open slightly and at low vacuum (full throttle) it will open fully. This causes vapor

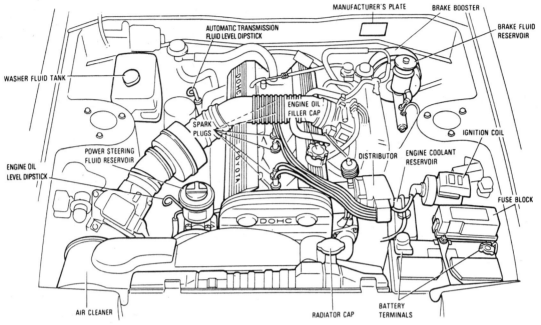

Twin-cam six cylinder (5M-GE) engine layout

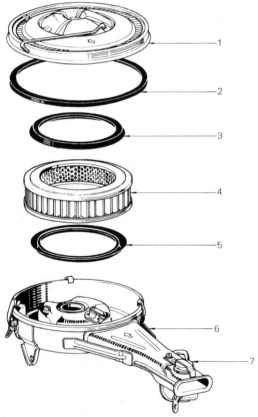

1. Air cleaner case cover
2. Gasket
3. Gasket
4. Cleaner element
5. Gasket
6. Case
7. Diaphragm

Air cleaner assembly

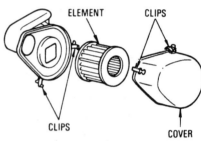

22R-E fuel injected four cylinder air cleaner assembly. Other fuel injected engines similar

to be removed from the crankcase by the engine vacuum and then sucked into the combustion chamber where it is dissipated.

1. Check the ventilation hoses for leaks or clogging. Clean or replace as necessary.

2. Locate the PCV valve in the cylinder head cover. Remove it.

3. Blow into the crankcase end of the valve. There should be free passage of air through the valve.

4. Blow into the intake manifold end of the valve. There should be little or no passage of air through the valve.

5. If the PCV valve failed either of the preceding two checks, it will require replacement.

6. Installation is in the reverse order of removal.

NOTE: *On models with fuel injection there is no PCV valve. Vapor passage in the ventilation lines is controlled by two orifices. To check the PCV system on these models in-*

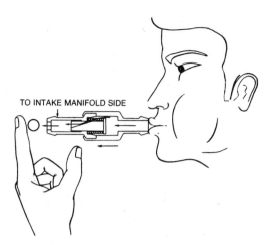

TO INTAKE MANIFOLD SIDE

Air should pass through the PCV valve when blowing into the crankcase side

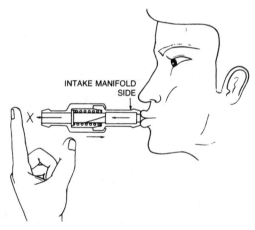

INTAKE MANIFOLD SIDE

Air should not pass through the PCV valve when blowing through the intake manifold side

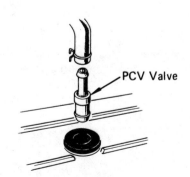

PCV Valve

PCV valves are located in the cam cover

spect the hoses for cracks, leaks or other damage. Blow through the orifices to make sure they are not blocked. Replace all components as necessary.

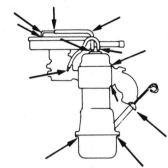

Check all PCV hoses, connections and gaskets for cracks, brittleness

Evaporative Emissions System

Check the evaporation control system every 15,000 miles. Check the fuel and vapor lines and the vacuum hoses for proper connections and correct routing, as well as condition. Replace clogged, damaged or deteriorated parts as necessary.

If the charcoal canister is clogged, it may be cleaned using low-pressure (no more than 43 psi.) compressed air. The entire canister should be replaced every 5 years/50,000 miles (60,000 miles for 1978 and later cars). The charcoal canister is located in the left, front of the engine compartment on the early Celicas and in the right rear on the later ones.

For more details on the canister and evaporative emissions system, refer to Chapter 4.

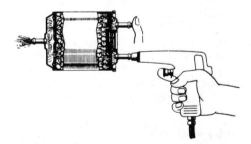

Using compressed air to clean the charcoal canister

Battery

SPECIFIC GRAVITY (EXCEPT "MAINTENANCE FREE" BATTERIES)

At least once a year, check the specific gravity of the battery. It should be between 1.20 and 1.26 at room temperature.

The scientific gravity can be checked with the use of an hydrometer, an inexpensive instrument available from many sources, including auto parts stores. The hydrometer has a squeeze bulb at one end and a nozzle at the other. Battery electrolyte is sucked into the

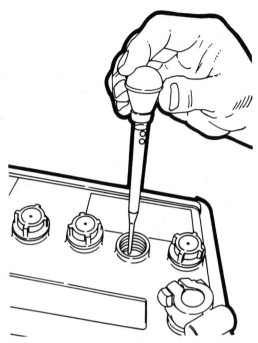

The specific gravity of the battery can be checked with a simple float-type hydrometer

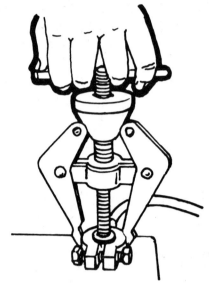

Special pullers are available to remove cable clamps

hydrometer until the float is lifted from its seat. The specific gravity is then read by noting the position of the float. Generally, if after charging, the specific gravity between any two cells varies more than 50 points (.050), the battery is bad and should be replaced.

It is not possible to check the specific gravity in this manner on sealed ("maintenance free") batteries. Instead, the indicator built into the top of the case must be relied on to display any signs of battery deterioration. If the indicator is dark, the battery can be assumed to be OK. If the indicator is light, the specific gravity is low, and the battery should be charged or replaced.

CABLES AND CLAMPS

Once a year, the battery terminals and the cable clamps should be cleaned. Loosen the clamps and remove the cables, negative cable first. On batteries with posts on top, the use of a puller specially made for the purpose is recommended. These are inexpensive, and available in auto parts stores. Side terminal battery cables are secured with a bolt.

Clean the cable clamps and the battery terminal with a wire brush, until all corrosion, grease, etc. is removed and the metal is shiny. It is especially important to clean the inside of the clamp thoroughly, since a small deposit of foreign material or oxidation there will prevent a sound electrical connection and inhibit either starting or charging. Special tools are

available for cleaning these parts, one type for conventional batteries and another type for side terminal batteries.

Before installing the cables, loosen the battery hold-down clamp or strap, remove the battery and check the battery tray. Clear it of

Clean the battery posts with a wire brush, or the special tool shown

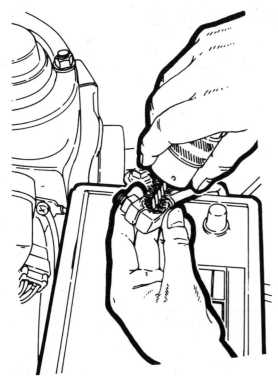

Clean the inside of the clamps with a wire brush, or the special tool

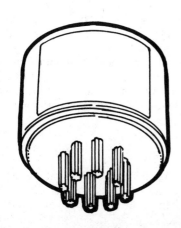

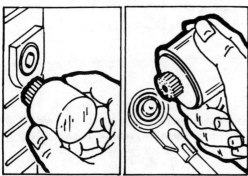

Special tools are also available for cleaning the posts and clamps on side terminal batteries

any debris, and check it for soundness. Rust should be wire brushed away, and the metal given a coat of anti-rust paint. Replace the battery and tighten the hold-down clamp or strap securely, but be careful not to overtighten, which will crack the battery case.

After the clamps and terminals are clean, reinstall the cables, negative cable last; do not hammer on the clamps to install. Tighten the clamps securely, but do not distort them. Give the clamps and terminals a thin external coat of grease after installation, to retard corrosion.

Check the cables at the same time that the terminals are cleaned. If the cable insulation is cracked or broken, or if the ends are frayed, the cable should be replaced with a new cable of the same length and gauge.

NOTE: *Keep flame or sparks away from the battery; it gives off explosive hydrogen gas. Battery electrolyte contains sulphuric acid. If you should splash any on your skin or in your eyes, flush the affected area with plenty of clear water; if it lands in your eyes, get medical help immediately.*

REPLACEMENT

When it becomes necessary to replace the battery, select a battery with a cold cranking power rating equal to or greater than the battery originally installed. Deterioration, embrittlement and just plain aging of the battery cables, starter motor, and associated wires makes the battery's job harder in successive years. The slow increase in electrical resistance over time makes it prudent to install a new battery with a greater capacity than the old. Details on battery removal and installation are covered in Chapter 3.

Belts

Check the condition of the drive belts and check and adjust the belt tension every 15,000 miles.

1. Inspect the belts for signs of glazing or cracking. A glazed belt will be perfectly smooth from slippage, while a good belt will have a slight texture of favric visible. Cracks will usually start at the inner edge of the belt and run outward. Replace the belt at the first sign of cracking or if the glazing is severe.

2. Belt tension does not refer to play or droop. By placing your thumb midway between the two pulleys, it should be possible to depress the belt between 1/4 and 1/2 an in. If any of the belts can be depressed more than this, or cannot be depressed this much, adjust the tension. Inadequate tension will result in slippage and wear, while excessive tension will

HOW TO SPOT WORN V-BELTS

V-Belts are vital to efficient engine operation—they drive the fan, water pump and other accessories. They require little maintenance (occasional tightening) but they will not last forever. Slipping or failure of the V-belt will lead to overheating. If your V-belt looks like any of these, it should be replaced.

This belt has deep cracks, which cause it to flex. Too much flexing leads to heat build-up and premature failure. These cracks can be caused by using the belt on a pulley that is too small. Notched belts are available for small diameter pulleys.

Cracking or weathering

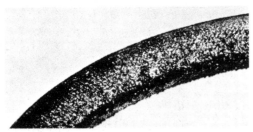

Oil and grease on a belt can cause the belt's rubber compounds to soften and separate from the reinforcing cords that hold the belt together. The belt will first slip, then finally fail altogether.

Softening (grease and oil)

Glazing is caused by a belt that is slipping. A slipping belt can cause a run-down battery, erratic power steering, overheating or poor accessory performance. The more the belt slips, the more glazing will be built up on the surface of the belt. The more the belt is glazed, the more it will slip. If the glazing is light, tighten the belt.

Glazing

The cover of this belt is worn off and is peeling away. The reinforcing cords will begin to wear and the belt will shortly break. When the belt cover wears in spots or has a rough jagged appearance, check the pulley grooves for roughness.

Worn cover

This belt is on the verge of breaking and leaving you stranded. The layers of the belt are separating and the reinforcing cords are exposed. It's just a matter of time before it breaks completely.

Separation

damage bearings and cause belts to fray and crack.

3. All drive belts should be replaced every 60,000 miles regardless of their condition.

ADJUSTMENT

Alternator

To adjust the tension of the alternator drive belt on all models, loosen the pivot and mounting bolts on the alternator. Using a wooden hammer handle, a broomstick or your hand, move the alternator one way or the other until the proper tension is achieved.

CAUTION: *Do not use a screwdriver or any other metal device such as a pry bar, as a lever.*

Tighten the mounting bolts securely. If a new belt has been installed, recheck the tension after about 200 miles of driving.

Air Conditioning Compressor

A/C compressor belt tension can be adjusted by turning the tension adjusting bolt which is located on the compressor tensioner bracket.

1. Loosen the pivot bolt

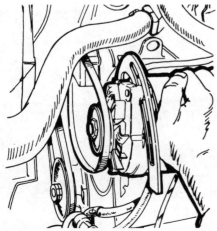

2. Push the component inwards

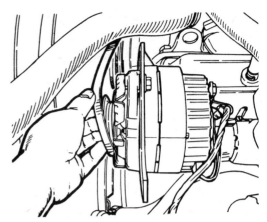

3. Slip the old belt off and the new one on

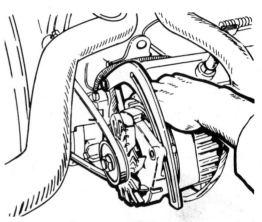

4. Pull outwards to tension the belt

Turn the bolt clockwise to tighten the belt and counterclockwise to loosen it.

Air Pump

To adjust the tension of the air pump drive belt, loosen the adjusting lever bolt and the pivot bolt. Move the pump in or out until the desired tension is felt.

NOTE: *The tension should be checked between the air pump and the crankshaft pulley on cars without air conditioning. On cars with A/C the tension should be checked between the A/C compressor and the crankshaft pulley.*

Power Steering Pump

Tension on the power steering belt is adjusted by means of an idler pulley. Turn the adjusting bolt on the idler pulley until the desired tension is felt and then retighten the lock bolt.

Hoses

Upper and lower radiator hoses and all heater hoses should be checked for deterioration,

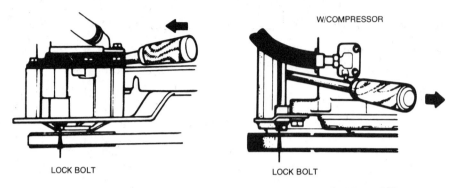

Moving the air pump to tension the drive belt (with and without A/C)

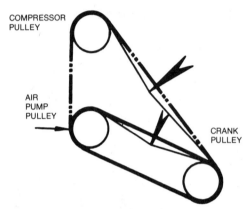

Air pump drive belt tension checking locations with and without A/C

leaks and loose hose clamps every 15,000 miles. To remove the hoses:

1. Drain the radiator.

2. Loosen the hose clamps at each end of the hose to be removed.

3. Working the hose back and forth, slide it off its connection and install the new hose if needed.

4. Position the hose clamps at least ¼ of an in. from the end of the hose and tighten them.

NOTE: *Make sure that the hose clamps are beyond the bead and placed in the center of the clamping surface before tightening them.*

Cooling System

Dealing with the cooling system can be a tricky matter unless the proper precautions are observed. It is best to check the coolant level in the radiator when the engine is cold. This is done by removing the radiator cap and seeing that the coolant is within ¾ of an in. of the bottom of the filler neck. On later models, the cooling system has, as one of its components, an expansion tank. If coolant is visible above the "Low" mark on the tank, the level is satisfactory. Always be certain that the filler caps

on both the radiator and the reservoir are tightly closed.

In the event that the coolant level must be checked when the engine is warm on engines without the expansion tank, place a thick rag over the radiator cap and slowly turn the cap counterclockwise until it reaches the first detent. Allow all the hot steam to escape. This will allow the pressure in the system to drop gradually, preventing an explosion of hot coolant. When the hissing noise stops, remove the cap the rest of the way.

If the coolant level is low, add equal amounts of ethylene glycol-based antifreeze and clean water. On models without an expansion tank, add coolant through the radiator filler neck. Fill the expansion tank to the "Full" level on cars with that system.

CAUTION: *Never add cold coolant to a hot engine unless the engine is running, to avoid cracking the engine block.*

If the coolant level is chronically low or rusty, refer to Chapter 11 for diagnosis of the problem.

The radiator hoses and clamps and the radiator cap should be checked at the same time as the coolant level. Hoses which are brittle,

On models without a coolant expansion tank, the coolant level should be ¾ of an inch below the filler neck (engine cold)

HOW TO SPOT BAD HOSES

Both the upper and lower radiator hoses are called upon to perform difficult jobs in an inhospitable environment. They are subject to nearly 18 psi at under hood temperatures often over 280°F., and must circulate nearly 7500 gallons of coolant an hour—3 good reasons to have good hoses.

Swollen hose

A good test for any hose is to feel it for soft or spongy spots. Frequently these will appear as swollen areas of the hose. The most likely cause is oil soaking. This hose could burst at any time, when hot or under pressure.

Cracked hose

Cracked hoses can usually be seen but feel the hoses to be sure they have not hardened; a prime cause of cracking. This hose has cracked down to the reinforcing cords and could split at any of the cracks.

Frayed hose end (due to weak clamp)

Weakened clamps frequently are the cause of hose and cooling system failure. The connection between the pipe and hose has deteriorated enough to allow coolant to escape when the engine is hot.

Debris in cooling system

Debris, rust and scale in the cooling system can cause the inside of a hose to weaken. This can usually be felt on the outside of the hose as soft or thinner areas.

Some radiator caps have pressure release levers

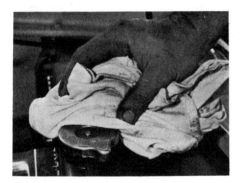

If the engine is hot, cover the radiator cap with a rag

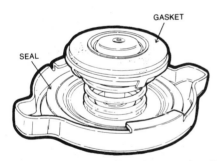

Check the radiator cap seal and gasket condition

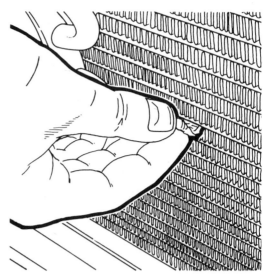

Clean the radiator fins of any debris which impedes air flow

bricant to the bearings and also helps to prevent the seals and hoses from drying out. To do this comfortably in the winter, turn the air conditioning "On," the temperature control lever to "Warm" or "Hi" and turn on the blower to the highest setting. This will engage the compressor, circulating lubricating oils within the system, but preventing the discharge of cold air. The system should also be checked for proper refrigerant charge using the procedure given below.

SYSTEMS CHECKS

CAUTION: *Do not attempt to charge or discharge the refrigerant system unless you are thoroughly familiar with its operation and the hazards involved. The compressed refrigerant (R-12) used in the air conditioning system expands and evaporates (boils) into the atmosphere at a temperature of −29.8°C (−21.7°F) or less. This will freeze any surface that it comes in contact with,*

cracked, or swollen should be replaced. Clamps should be checked for tightness (screwdriver tight only—do not allow the clamp to cut into the hose or crush the fitting). The radiator cap gasket should be checked for any obvious tears, cracks or swelling, or any signs of incorrect seating in the radiator neck.

Air Conditioning

Regular maintenance for the air conditioning system includes periodic checks of the drive belt tension. In addition, the system should be operated for *at least five minutes every month*. This ensures an adequate supply of lu-

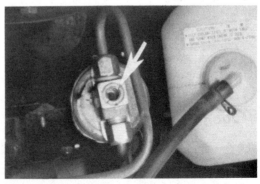

The receiver/drier has a sight glass (arrow)

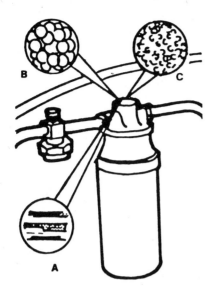

Oil streaks (A), constant bubbles (B) or foam (C) indicate there is not enough refrigerant in the system. Occasional bubbles during initial operation is normal. A clear sight glass indicates a proper charge of refrigerant or no refrigerant at all, which can be determined by the presence of cold air at the outlets in the car. If the glass is clouded with a milky white substance, have the receiver/drier checked professionally

including your eyes. In addition, the refrigerant decomposes into a poisonous gas in the presence of flame.

Factory installed Toyota air conditioners have a sight glass for checking the refrigerant charge. The sight glass is on top of the receiver/drier which is located in the front of the engine compartment, on the right or left side of the radiator depending upon the year of your car.

NOTE: *If your car is equipped with an aftermarket air conditioner, the following system check may not apply. Contact the manufacturer of the unit for instructions on system checks.*

This test works best if the outside air temperature is warm (above 70°F).

1. Place the automatic transmission in Park or the manual transmission in Neutral. Set the parking brake.

2. With the help of a friend, run the engine at a fast idle (about 1500 rpm).

3. Set the controls for maximum cold with the blower on high.

4. Look at the sight glass on top of the receiver/drier. If a steady stream of bubbles is present in the sight glass, the system is low on charge. Very likely there is a leak in the system.

5. If no bubbles are present, the system is either fully charged or empty. Feel the high

and low pressure lines at the compressor, if no appreciable temperature difference is felt, the system is empty, or nearly so.

6. If one hose is warm (high pressure) and the other is cold (low pressure), the system may be OK. However, you are probably making these tests because there is something wrong with the air conditioning, so proceed to the next step.

7. Either disconnect the compressor clutch wire or have an assistant in the car turn the fan control On and Off to operate the compressor clutch. Watch the sight glass.

8. If bubbles appear when the clutch is disengaged and disappear when it is engaged, the system is properly charged.

9. If the refrigerant takes more than 45 seconds to bubble when the clutch is disengaged, the system is most likely overcharged. This will usually result in poor cooling at low speeds.

NOTE: *If it is determined that the system has a leak, it should be repaired as soon as possible. Leaks may allow moisture to enter the system, causing an expensive rust problem.*

Windshield Wipers

For maximum effectiveness and longest element life, the windshield and wiper blades should be kept clean. Dirt, tree sap, road tar and so on will cause streaking, smearing and blade deterioration if left on the glass. It is advisable to wash the windshield carefully with a commercial glass cleaner at least once a month. Wipe off the rubber blades with the wet rag afterwards. Do not attempt to move the wipers back and forth by hand; damage to the motor and drive mechanism will result.

If the blades are found to be cracked, broken or torn, they should be replaced immediately. Replacement intervals will vary with usage, although ozone deterioration usually limits blade life to about one year. If the wiper pattern is smeared or streaked, or if the blade chatters across the glass, the blades should be replaced. It is easiest and most sensible to replace them in pairs.

There are basically three different types of wiper blade refills, which differ in their method of replacement. One type has two release buttons, approximately one-third of the way up from the ends of the blade frame. Pushing the buttons down releases a lock and allows the rubber blade to be removed from the frame. The new blade slides back into the frame and locks in place.

The second type of refill has two metal tabs which are unlocked by squeezing them together. The rubber blade can then be with-

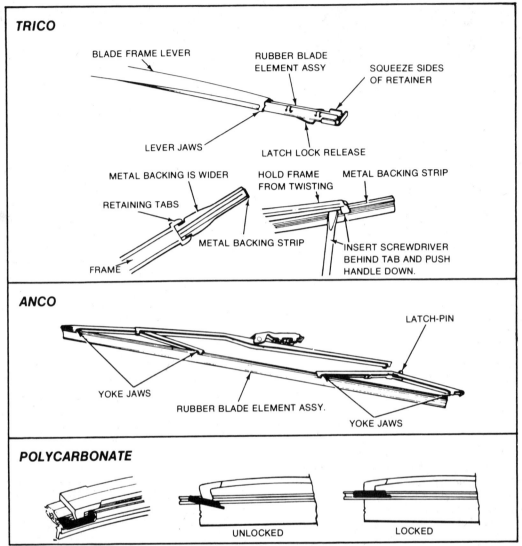

The three types of wiper element retention

drawn from the frame jaws. A new one is installed by inserting it into the front frame jaws and sliding it rearward to engage the remaining frame jaws. There are usually four jaws; when installing, be certain that the refill is engaged in all of them. At the end of its travel, the tabs will lock into place on the front jaws of the wiper blade frame.

The third type is a refill made from polycarbonate. The refill has a simple locking device at one end which flexes downward out of the groove into which the jaws of the holder fit, allowing easy release. By sliding the new refill through all the jaws and pushing through the slight resistance when it reaches the end of its travel, the refill will lock into position.

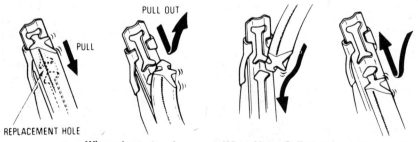

Wiper element replacement, '82 and later Celica and Supra

Regardless of the type of refill used, make sure that all of the frame jaws are engaged as the refill is pushed into place and locked. The metal blade holder and frame will scratch the glass if allowed to touch it.

Fluid Level Checks
ENGINE OIL

Every time you stop for fuel, check the engine oil as follows:

1. Park the car on level ground.
2. When checking the oil level it is best for the engine to be at operating temperature, although checking the oil immediately after stopping will lead to a false reading. Wait a few minutes after turning off the engine to allow the oil to drain back into the crankcase.
3. Open the hood and locate the dipstick which is on the right side of all engines but the 20R where it is on the left. Pull the dipstick from its tube, wipe it clean and reinsert it.

The dipstick for the 20R engine is on the left side

4. Pull the dipstick out again and, holding it horizontally, read the oil level. The oil should be between the "F" and "L" marks on the dipstick. If the oil is below the "L" mark, add oil of the proper viscosity through the capped opening on the top of the cylinder head cover. See the "Oil and Fuel Recommendations" chart in this chapter for the proper viscosity and rating of oil to use.

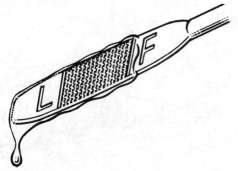

Oil level indicated on the dipstick should never be below the "LOW" line or above the "FULL" line

5. Replace the dipstick and check the oil level again after adding any oil. *Be careful not to overfill the crankcase.* Approximately one quart of oil will raise the level from the "L" to the "F". Excess oil will generally be consumed at an accelerated rate.

TRANSMISSION
Manual

The oil in the manual transmission should be checked at least every 15,000 miles and replaced every 25,000–30,000 miles.

1. With the car parked on a level surface, remove the filler plug from the side of the transmission housing.
2. If the lubricant begins to trickle out of the hole, there is enough. Otherwise, carefully insert your finger (watch out for sharp threads) and check to see if the oil is up to the edge of the hole.
3. If not, add oil through the hole until the level is at the edge of the hole. Most gear lubricants come in a plastic squeeze bottle with a nozzle; making additions simple. You can also use a common everyday kitchen baster. Use standard GL-4 hypoid type gear oil—SAE 80 or SAE 80/90.
4. Replace the filler plug, run the engine and check for leaks.

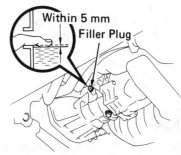

Manual transmission oil level should be up to the bottom of the filler (upper) plug

Automatic

Check the automatic transmission fluid level at least every 15,000 miles (more if possible). The dipstick is in the rear of the engine compartment. The fluid level should be checked only when the transmission is hot (normal operating temperature). The transmission is considered hot after about 20 miles of highway driving.

1. Park the car on a level surface with the engine idling. Shift the transmission into Neutral and set the parking brake.
2. Remove the dipstick, wipe it clean and reinsert it firmly. Be sure that it has been

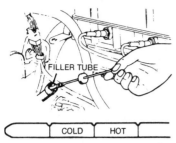

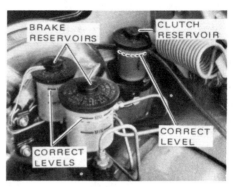

Check the automatic transmission dipstick with the engine hot and idling

Some models have two brake fluid reservoirs while others have only one

pushed all the way in. Remove the dipstick and check the fluid level while holding it horizontally. With the engine running, the fluid level should be between the second and third notches on the dipstick.

3. If the fluid level is below the second notch, add Type F automatic transmission fluid through the dipstick tube. This is easily done with the aid of a funnel. Check the level often as you are filling the transmission. Be extremely careful not to overfill it. Overfilling will cause slippage, seal damage and overheating. Approximately one pint of ATF will raise the level from one notch to the other.

NOTE: *Always use ATF Type F. The use of Dexron® ATF or any other will cause severe damage to the transmission.*

The fluid on the dipstick should always be a bright red color. It it is discolored (brown or black), or smells burnt, serious transmission troubles, probably due to overheating, should be suspected. The transmission should be inspected by a qualified service technician to locate the cause of the burnt fluid.

BRAKE AND CLUTCH MASTER CYLINDERS

The brake and clutch master cylinders are located under the hood, in the left rear section of the engine compartment. They are made of translucent plastic so that the levels may be checked without removing the tops. The fluid level in both reservoirs should be checked at least every 15,000 miles. The fluid level should be maintained at the upper most mark on the side of the reservoir. Any sudden decrease in the level indicates a possible leak in the system and should be checked out immediately.

NOTE: *Some models may have two reservoirs for the brake master cylinder. Automatic transmission cars, of course, do not have a clutch master cylinder.*

When making additions of brake fluid, use only fresh, uncontaminated brake fluid meeting or exceeding DOT 3 standards. *Be careful not to spill any brake fluid on painted sur-*

faces, *as it eats the paint.* Do not allow the brake fluid container or the master cylinder reservoir to remain open any longer than necessary; brake fluid absorbs moisture from the air, reducing its effectiveness and causing corrosion in the lines.

RADIATOR COOLANT

It's a good idea to check the coolant every time that you stop for fuel. If the engine is hot, let it cool for a few minutes and then check the

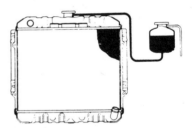

Check the coolant level in the expansion tank on models with a closed cooling system

The freezing protection rating can be checked with an antifreeze tester

level following the procedure given earlier in this chapter.

Check the freezing protection rating at least once a year, preferably just before the winter sets in. This can be done with an antifreeze tester (most service stations will have one on hand and will probably check it for you, if not, they are available at auto parts stores. The tester, shaped like a kitchen baster, has a float or balls inside which (when floating) indicate the strength of the coolant and the protection it will give. Be sure to draw only enough coolant into the tester to lift the float or balls; don't let it fill up all at once, or you will not have an accurate reading.

REAR AXLE

The oil in the differential should be checked at least every 15,000 miles and replaced every 25,000–30,000 miles.

1. With the car on a level surface, remove the filler plug from the back of the differential.

NOTE: *The plug on the bottom is the drain plug.*

2. If the oil begins to trickle out of the hole, there is enough. Otherwise, carefully insert

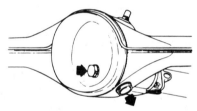

Filler (upper) plug and drain (lower) plug locations on the differential

Less than 5 mm (0.20 in.)

Correct fluid level, '82 and later independent rear axle

your finger (watch out for sharp threads) into the hole and check to see if the oil is up to the bottom edge of the filler hole.

3. If not, add oil through the hole until the level is at the edge of the hole. Most gear oils come in a plastic squeeze bottle with a nozzle, making additions simple. You can also use a common kitchen baster. Use standard GL-5 hypoid type gear oil—SAE 90 or SAE 80 if you live in a particularly cold area.

4. Replace the filler plug and drive the car for a while. Stop the car and check for leaks.

STEERING GEAR—1971–81

The non-rack and pinion steering gear oil level should be checked at least every 15,000 miles. The filler plug is on top of the gear housing. The oil level should be kept even with the bottom of the filler hole or slightly lower. Use standard GL-4 hypoid type gear oil—SAE 90. Rack and pinion steering systems (1982 and later) do not require an oil level check.

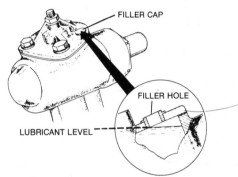

Fill the steering gear to the bottom of the filler hole

POWER STEERING RESERVOIR

The fluid level in the power steering reservoir should be checked at least every 15,000 miles. Remove the filler cap and check the level on the dipstick; it should be in between the edges of the cross-hatched area. If it is not, add Dexron® type automatic transmission fluid until the proper level is achieved.

Checking the power steering fluid; the level should be in the crosshatched area (inset)

BATTERY

Check the battery electrolyte level at least once a month, or more often in hot weather or during periods of extended car operation. The level can be checked through the case on

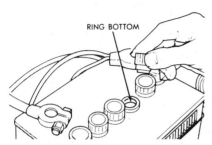

Fill each battery cell to the bottom of the split ring with distilled water

translucent polypropylene batteries; the cell caps must be removed on other models. The electrolyte level in each cell should be kept filled to the split ring inside, or the line marked on the outside of the case.

If the level is low, add only distilled water, or boiled drinking water, through the opening until the level is correct. Each cell is completely separate from the others, so each must be checked and filled individually.

If water is added in freezing whether, the car should be driven several miles to allow the water to mix with the electrolyte. Otherwise, the battery could freeze.

Tires

Tires should be checked weekly for proper air pressure. A chart, located either in the glove compartment or on the driver's or passenger's door, gives the recommended inflation pressures. Maximum fuel economy and tire life will result if the pressure is maintained at the highest figure given on the chart. Pressures should be checked before driving since pressure can increase as much as six pounds per square inch (psi) due to heat buildup. It is a good idea to have your own accurate pressure gauge, because not all gauges on service station air pumps can be trusted. When checking pressures, do not neglect the spare tire. Note that some spare tires require pressures considerably higher than those used in the other tires.

While you are about the task of checking air pressure, inspect the tire treads for cuts, bruises and other damage. Check the air valves to be sure that they are tight. Replace any missing valve caps.

Check the tires for uneven wear that might indicate the need for front end alignment or tire rotation. Tires should be replaced when a tread wear indicator appears as a solid band across the tread.

When buying new tires, give some thought to the following points, especially if you are considering a switch to larger tires or a different profile series:

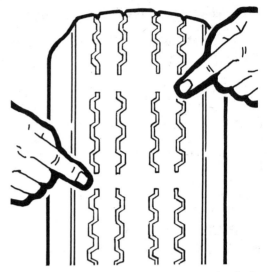

Tread wear indicators will appear when the tire is worn out

Tread depth can also be checked with an inexpensive gauge

A penny works as well as anything for checking tread depth; when the top of Lincoln's head is visible, it's time for new tires

1. All four tires must be of the same construction type. *This rule cannot be violated.* Radial, bias, and bias-belted tires must not be mixed.

2. The wheels should be the correct width for the tire. Tire dealers have charts of tire and rim compatibility. A mismatch will cause sloppy handling and rapid tire wear. The tread width should match the rim width (inside bead

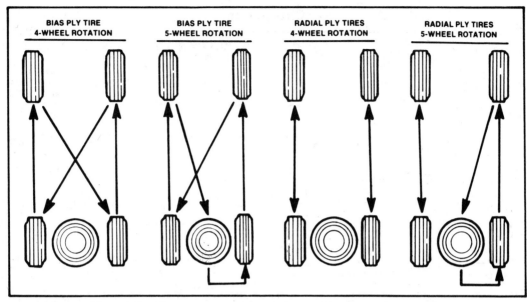

| BIAS PLY TIRE 4-WHEEL ROTATION | BIAS PLY TIRE 5-WHEEL ROTATION | RADIAL PLY TIRES 4-WHEEL ROTATION | RADIAL PLY TIRES 5-WHEEL ROTATION |

Tire rotation diagrams; note that radials should not be cross-switched

to inside bead) within an inch. For radial tires, the rim width should be 80% or less of the tire (not tread) width.

3. The height (mounted diameter) of the new tires can change speedometer accuracy, engine speed at a given road speed, fuel mileage, acceleration, and ground clearance. Tire manufacturers furnish full measurement specifications.

4. The spare tire should be usable, at least for short distance and low speed operation, with the new tires.

5. There shouldn't be any body interference when loaded, on bumps, or in turns.

TIRE ROTATION

Tire rotation is recommended every 6000 miles or so, to obtain maximum tire wear. The pattern you use depends on whether or not your car has a usable spare. Radial tires should not be cross-switched (from one side of the car to the other); they last longer if their direction of rotation is not changed. Snow tires sometimes have directional arrows molded into the side of the carcass; the arrow shows the direction of rotation. They will wear very rapidly if the rotation is reversed. Studded tires will lose their studs if their rotational direction is reversed.

NOTE: *Mark the wheel position or direction of rotation on radial tires or studded snow tires before removing them.*

STORAGE

Store the tires at the proper inflation pressure if they are mounted on wheels. Keep them in a cool dry place, laid on their sides. If the tires are stored in the garage or basement, do not let them stand on a concrete floor; set them on strips of wood.

Fuel Filter

All Celicas and Supras use the throwaway type fuel filter. It is located in the fuel line and must be completely removed in order to be replaced. The fuel filter on all models but the Supra can be found on the right side wheel arch. The Supra fuel filter is on the left side wheel arch.

The fuel filter should be replaced every 25,000–30,000 miles or sooner if it seems dirty or clogged. Removal and installation procedures differ slightly for certain years.

CAUTION: *Do not smoke or have open flame near the car when working on the fuel system.*

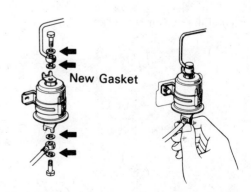

New Gasket

Always use new gaskets when installing fuel filters

Capacities

| Year | Model | Engine Displacement Cu. In. (cc) | Engine Crankcase (qts) | | Transmission (qts) | | | Drive Axle (qts) | Gasoline Tank (gals) | Cooling System (qts) |
| | | | With Filter | Without Filter | Manual | | Automatic | | | |
					4-spd	5-spd				
1971	1900	113.3 (1858)	5.3	4.3	2.1	—	—	1.0	13.0	8.4
1972–74	2000	120.7 (1980)	4.5	3.6	2.9	2.8	2.3 ①	1.3	13.0	8.4
1975–77	2200	133.6 (2189)	4.9	4.0	2.9	2.8	2.3 ①	1.3②	13.0②	8.5
1978–80	2200	133.6 (2189)	4.9	4.0	2.9	2.8	2.5 ①	1.3②	15.5④	8.9
1979½–80	2600	156.4 (2563)	4.9	4.3	—	2.8	2.5 ①	1.6	16.1	11.6
1981–83	2400	144.4 (2367)	4.9	4.0	—	2.5	2.5 ①	1.3②	16.1	8.9
1981	2800	168.4 (2759)	4.9	4.3	—	2.7	2.5 ①	1.6	16.1	9.5
1982–83	2800	168.4 (2759)	5.4	4.9	—	2.7	2.5 ①	1.3	16.1	8.5

① This figure is for a drain and refill.
② Figure given is for vehicles with a unitized-type rear; for vehicles with a banjo-type rear—1.4 qts.
③ 1977—14.6 gals.
④ 1980—16.1 gals.

1971–74

1. Unfasten the fuel intake line. Use a wrench to loosen the attachment nut and another wrench on the opposite side of the filter to keep the filter body from turning in its retaining bracket.
2. Remove the remaining fuel line from the fuel filter in the same manner as you did the first one.
3. Unbolt the fuel filter and remove it.
4. Installation is in the reverse order of removal.
NOTE: *The arrow on the fuel filter should always point toward the carburetor.*
5. Run the engine for a few minutes and check the filter for any leaks.

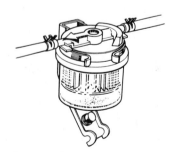

Throwaway-type fuel filter

1975 AND LATER (ALL BUT SUPRA)

1. Remove the hose clamps from the inlet and outlet hoses.
2. Work the hoses off of the filter necks.
3. Snap the filter out of its bracket and replace it with a new one.
NOTE: *The arrow on the fuel filter must always point toward the carburetor.*
4. Installation of the remaining components is in the reverse order of removal.
5. Run the engine for a few minutes and check the filter for any leaks.

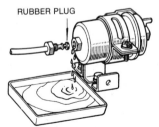

RUBBER PLUG

When removing the fuel lines it is always a good idea to place a pan underneath to catch any dripping fuel

SUPRA

1. Unbolt the retaining screws and remove the protective shield for the fuel filter.

2. Place a pan under the delivery pipe (large connection) to catch the dripping fuel and SLOWLY loosen the union bolt to bleed off the fuel pressure.

3. Remove the union bolt and drain the remaining fuel.

4. Disconnect and plug the inlet line.

5. Unbolt and remove the fuel filter.

NOTE: *When tightening the fuel line bolts to the fuel filter, you must use a torque wrench. The tightening torque is very important, as under or over tightening may cause fuel leakage. Insure that there is no fuel line interference and that there is sufficient clearance between it and any other parts.*

6. Coat the flare nut, union nut and bolt threads with engine oil.

7. Hand tighten the inlet line to the fuel filter.

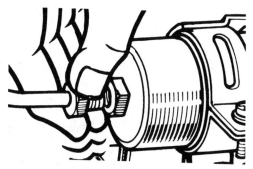

Hand tighten the fuel inlet line

8. Install the fuel filter and then tighten the inlet line bolt to 23–33 ft. lbs.

9. Reconnect the delivery pipe using new gaskets and then tighten the union bolt to 18–25 ft. lbs.

10. Run the engine for a few minutes and check for any fuel leaks.

11. Install the protective shield.

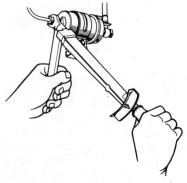

A torque wrench is essential when tightening the fuel lines to the Supra fuel filter

LUBRICATION

Oil and Fuel Recommendations

OIL

The SAE (Society of Automotive Engineers) grade number indicates the viscosity of the engine oil—its resistance to flow at a given temperature. The lower the SAE grade number, the lighter the oil. For example, the mono-grade oils begin with SAE 5 weight, which is a thin, light oil, and continue in viscosity up to SAE 80 or 90 weight, which are heavy gear lubricants. These oils are also known as "straight weight", meaning they are of a single viscosity, and do not vary with engine temperature.

Multi-viscosity oils offer the important advantage of being adaptable to temperature extremes. These oils have designations such as 10W-40, 20W-50, etc. The "10W-40" means that in winter (the "W" in the designation) the oil acts like a thin 10 weight oil, allowing the engine to spin easily when cold and offering rapid lubrication. Once the engine has warmed up, however, the oil acts like a straight 40 weight, maintaining good lubrication and protection for the engine's internal components. A 20W-50 oil would therefore be slightly heavier than and not as ideal in cold weather as the 10W-40, but would offer better protection at higher rpm and temperatures because when warm it acts like a 50 weight oil. Whichever oil viscosity you choose when changing the oil, make sure you are anticipating the temperatures your engine will be operating in until the oil is changed again. Refer to the oil viscosity chart for oil recommendations according to temperature.

The API (American Petroleum Institute) designation indicates the classification of engine oil used under certain given operating conditions. Only oils designated for use "Service SE" should be used. Oils of the SE type perform a variety of functions inside the engine in addition to the basic function as a lu-

The oil sequence test symbol must be found on the top of the can; all engines must use SE quality oil

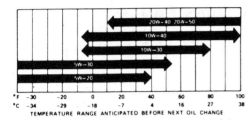

Oil viscosity chart

bricant. Through a balanced system of metallic detergents and polymeric dispersants, the oil prevents the formation of high and low temperature deposits and also keeps sludge and particles of dirt in suspension. Acids, particularly sulfuric acid, as well as other by-products of combustion, are neutralized. Both the SAE grade number and the API designation can be found on top of the oil can.

SYNTHETIC OIL

There are many excellent synthetic and fuel-efficient oils currently available that can provide better gas mileage, longer service life, and in some cases better engine protection. These benefits do not come without a few hitches, however—the main one being the price of synthetic oils, which is three or four times the price per quart of conventional oil.

Synthetic oil is not for every car and every type of driving, so you should consider your engine's condition and your type of driving. Also, check your car's warranty conditions regarding the use of synthetic oils.

Both brand new engines and older, high mileage engines are the wrong candidates for synthetic oil. The synthetic oils are so slippery that they can prevent the proper break-in of new engines; most manufacturers recommend that you wait until the engine is properly broken in (5,000 miles) before using synthetic oil. Older engines with wear have a different problem with synthetics: they "use" (consume during operation) more oil as they age. Slippery synthetic oils get past these worn parts easily—if your engine is "using" conventional oil, it will use synthetics much faster. Also, if your car is leaking oil past old seals you'll have a much greater leak problem with synthetics.

Consider your type of driving. If most of your accumulated mileage if high speed, highway type driving, the more expensive synthetic oils may be of benefit. Extended highway driving gives the engine a chance to warm up, accumulating less acids in the oil and putting less stress on the engine over the long run. Under these conditions, the oil change interval can be extended (as long as your oil filter can last the extended life of the oil) up to the advertised mileage claims of the synthet-

Recommended Lubricants

Lubricant	Classification
Engine Oil	API SE
Manual Transmission	API GL-4
Automatic Transmission	ATF Type F
Rear Axle ①	API GL-5
Ball Joints	NLGI #1 NLGI #2
Wheel Bearings	NLGI #2
Brake Fluid	DOT 3
Clutch Fluid	DOT 3
Steering Box	API GL-4
Power Steering Fluid	Dexron ATF
Antifreeze	Ethylene Glycol

① Limited Slip Differentials use LSD oil exclusively

ics. Cars with synthetic oils may show increased fuel economy in highway driving, due to less internal friction. However, many automotive experts agree that 50,000 miles is too long to keep any oil in your engine.

Cars used under harder circumstances, such as stop-and-go, city type driving, short trips, or extended idling, should be serviced more frequently. For the engines in these cars, the much greater cost of synthetic or fuel-efficient oils may not be worth the investment. Internal wear increases much quicker on these cars, causing greater oil consumption and leakage.

NOTE: *The mixing of conventional and synthetic oils is not recommended. If you are using synthetic oil, it might be wise to carry two or three quarts with you no matter where you drive, as not all service stations carry this type of lubricant.*

NOTE: *Non-detergent or straight mineral oils must never be used.*

FUEL

The 1971 Celica was designed to run on premium grade fuel (98 octane or higher). 1972–76 models are designed to operate on regular grade fuel (90 octane or higher). 1975–76 Celicas made for use in California and all cars made in 1977 or later are designed to run on unleaded fuel. The use of leaded fuel in a car requiring unleaded fuel will plug the catalytic converter, rendering it inoperative and will increase exhaust backpressure to the point where engine output will be severely reduced. In all cases, the minimum octane rating of the fuel used must be at least 91 RON (87 CLC). All unleaded fuels sold in the U.S. are required to meet this minimum octane rating.

The use of a fuel too low in octane (a measurement of anti-knock quality) will result in spark knock. Since many factors affect operating efficiency, such as altitude, terrain, air temperature and humidity, knocking may result even though the recommended fuel is being used. If persistent knocking occurs, it may be necessary to switch to a higher grade of fuel. Continuous or heavy knocking may result in engine damage.

NOTE: *Your engine's fuel requirement can change with time, mainly due to carbon buildup, which changes the compression ratio. If your engine pings, knocks, or runs on, switch to a higher grade of fuel. Sometimes just changing brands will cure the problem. If it becomes necessary to retard the timing from specifications, don't change it more than a few degrees. Retarded timing will reduce power output and fuel mileage and will increase the engine temperature.*

Fluid Changes

ENGINE OIL AND FILTER

The oil should be changed every 6,000 miles in Celicas built between 1971–77. All 1978 and later models should have the oil changed every 7,500 miles.

The oil drain plug is located on the bottom, rear of the oil pan (bottom of the engine, underneath the car). The oil filter is located on the right side of the engine on all models.

The mileage figures given are the Toyota

recommended intervals assuming normal driving and conditions. If your car is being used under dusty, polluted or off-road conditions, change the oil and filter more frequently than specified. The same goes for cars driven in stop-and-go traffic or only for short distances. Always drain the oil after the engine has been running long enough to bring it to normal operating temperature. Hot oil will flow easier and more contaminants will be removed along with the oil than if it were drained cold. To change the oil and filter:

1. Run the engine until it reaches normal operating temperature.

2. Jack up the front of the car and support it on safety stands.

3. Slide a drain pan of at least 6 quarts capacity under the oil pan.

4. Loosen the drain plug. Turn the plug out by hand. By keeping an inward pressure on the plug as you unscrew it, oil won't escape past the threads and you can remove it without being burned by hot oil.

5. Allow the oil to drain completely and then install the drain plug. *Don't overtighten the plug*, or you'll be buying a new pan or a trick replacement plug for stripped threads.

6. Using a strap wrench, remove the oil filter. Keep in mind that it's holding about one quart of dirty, hot oil.

Lubricate the gasket on the new filter with clean engine oil. A dry gasket may not make a good seal and will allow the filter to leak

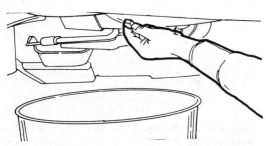

By keeping an inward pressure on the drain plug as you unscrew it, the oil won't escape past the threads

Remove the oil filter with a strap wrench

Install the new oil filter by hand

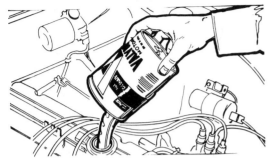

Add oil through the cylinder head cover only

7. Empty the old filter into the drain pan and dispose of the filter.

8. Using a clean rag, wipe off the filter adapter on the engine block. Be sure that the rag doesn't leave any lint which could clog an oil passage.

9. Coat the rubber gasket on the filter with fresh oil. Spin in onto the engine *by hand;* when the gasket touches the adapter surface give it another ½–¾ turn. No more, or you'll squash the gasket and it will leak.

10. Refill the engine with the correct amount of fresh oil. See the "Capacities" chart.

11. Check the oil level on the dipstick. It is normal for the level to be a bit above the full mark. Start the engine and allow it to idle for a few minutes.

CAUTION: *Do not run the engine above idle speed until it has built up oil pressure, indicated when the oil light goes out.*

12. Shut off the engine, allow the oil to drain for a minute, and check the oil level. Check around the filter and drain plug for any leaks, and correct as necessary.

TRANSMISSION

Manual

The manual transmission oil should be changed at least every 25,000 miles under normal conditions, or 15,000 miles under extreme (hot/cold weather, trailer pulling, etc.) conditions. To change, proceed as follows:

1. The oil must be hot before it is drained. If the car is driven until the engine is at normal operating temperature, the oil should be hot enough.

2. Remove the filler plug to provide a vent.

3. The drain plug is on the bottom of the transmission. Place a large container underneath the transmission and remove the plug.

4. Allow the oil to drain completely. Clean off the plug and replace it. Tighten it until it is just snug.

5. Fill the transmission with SAE 80 or SAE 80/90 gear oil. This usually comes in a plastic squeeze bottle with a long nozzle; otherwise

you can use a squeeze bulb or a kitchen baster to squirt the oil in. Refer to the "Capacities" chart for the proper amount of oil to put in.

6. The oil level should come up to the top of the filler hole.

7. Replace the filler plug, drive the car for a few minutes, stop, and check for any leaks.

Automatic

The automatic transmission fluid should be changed at least every 25,000–30,000 miles. If the car is normally used in severe service, such as stop-and-go driving, trailer towing or the like, the interval should be halved. The fluid should be hot before it is drained; a 20 minute drive will accomplish this.

Toyota automatic transmissions have a drain plug in them so that if you are in a hurry, you can simply remove the plug, drain the fluid, replace the plug and then refill the transmission. Although this method is fine, a more thorough procedure is recommended.

1. Remove the plug and drain the fluid. When the fluid stops coming out of the drain hole, loosen the pan retaining screws until the pan can be pulled down at one corner. Lower a corner of the pan and allow any remaining fluid to drain out.

2. After the pan has drained completely,

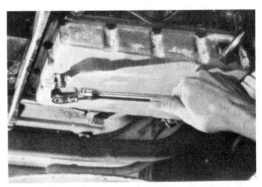

Removing the drain plug from bottom of automatic transmission pan

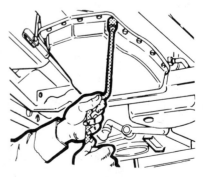

Removing the pan on the automatic transmission

Always replace the gasket when installing the pan

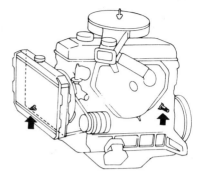

Drain plug locations for the four cylinder engine

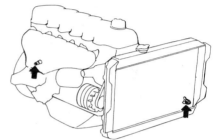

Drain plug locations for the 4M-E and 5M-E six cylinder engines

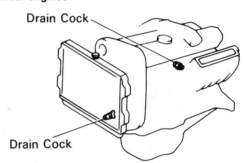

Coolant system drains, Twin Cam six

remove the pan retaining screws and then remove the pan and gasket.

3. Clean the pan thoroughly and allow it to air dry. If you wipe it out with a rag you run the risk of leaving bits of lint in the pan which will clog the tiny hydraulic passages in the transmission.

4. Install the pan using a new gasket.

5. Install the drain plug.

6. It is a good idea to measure the amount of fluid drained from the transmission to determine the correct amount of fresh fluid to add. This is because some parts of the transmission may not drain completely and using the dry refill amount specified in the "Capacities" chart could lead to overfilling. Fluid is added only through the dipstick tube. Use only Type F automatic transmission fluid; Do not overfill.

7. Replace the dipstick after filling. Start the engine and allow it to idle. DO NOT race the engine.

8. After the engine has idled for a few minutes, shift the transmission slowly through the gears and then return it to Park. With the engine still idling, check the fluid level on the dipstick. If necessary, add more fluid to raise the level to where it is supposed to be.

RADIATOR COOLANT

The cooling system should be drained, thoroughly flushed and refilled at least every 25,000–30,000 miles. This should be done with the engine cold.

1. Remove the radiator cap and the expansion tank cap (if so equipped).

2. Remove the two coolant drain plugs and drain the coolant. The drain plugs on all four cylinder engines are located on the bottom of the radiator and on the left side of the engine block. On the six cylinder engines, the plugs are on the bottom of the radiator and on the right side of the engine block (under the manifold).

3. Flush the cooling system (this should be done once in the spring and again in the fall) with a quality radiator flush. Follow instruc-

tions on the can. The drained coolant can be reused if it is still a strong mixture and is clean.

4. Replace the plugs and add a 50/50 mixture of ethylene glycol-type antifreeze and water. See the "Capacities" chart for the correct amount of coolant.

5. Run the engine for a few minutes and check the coolant level; if necessary, top it off.

REAR AXLE

The gear oil in the rear axle should be changed at least every 25,000–30,000 miles.

To drain and fill the rear axle, proceed as follows:

1. Park the vehicle on a level surface. Set the parking brake.

2. Remove the filler (upper) plug. Place a container which is large enough to catch all of the differential oil, under the drain plug.

3. Remove the drain (lower) plug and gas-

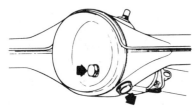

Filler (upper) and drain (lower) plug locations, all differentials

ket, if so equipped. Allow all of the oil to drain into the container.

4. Install the drain plug. Tighten it so that it will not leak, but do not overtighten.

5. Refill with the proper grade and viscosity of axle lubricant (See "Recommended Lubricants" chart). Be sure that the level reaches the bottom of the filler plug (or to within 5 mm of the plug on independent-type differentials). DO NOT overfill.

6. Install the filler plug and check for leakage.

Chassis Greasing

Chassis lubrication for the Celica is limited to greasing the front ball joints every 25,000–30,000 miles.

1. Remove the screw plug from the ball joint. Install a grease nipple.

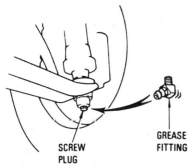

SCREW PLUG   GREASE FITTING

Remove the screw plug and fit a grease nipple; the nipple can then remain on the ball joint for later lubrication

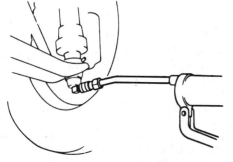

Pump grease into the ball joint until the excess just begins to swell from the ball joint boot

2. Using a *hand-operated* grease gun, lubricate the ball joint with NLGI #1 or NLGI #2 molybdenum-disulphide lithium-base grease.

CAUTION: *Do not use multipurpose or chassis grease.*

3. Remove the nipple and reinstall the screw plug.

4. Repeat for the other ball joint(s).

Body Lubrication

There is no set period recommended by Toyota for body lubrication. However, it is a good idea to lubricate the following body points at least once a year, especially in the fall before cold weather.

Lubricate with engine oil:
• Door lock latches
• Door lock rollers
• Door, hood, and hinge pivots
Lubricate with Lubriplate®:
• Trunk lid latch and hinge
• Glove box door latch
• Front seat slides
Lubricate with silicone spray:
• All rubber weather stripping
• Hood stops
When finished lubricating a body part, be sure that all the excess lubricant has been wiped off, especially in the areas of the car which may come in contact with clothing.

Wheel Bearings

Refer to the appropriate section in Chapter 9 for wheel bearing assembly and packing procedures. The front wheel bearings should be repacked every 24,000 miles on 1970–74 vehicles, 25,000 miles on 1975–77 vehicles, and 30,000 miles on 1978 and later vehicles, or every 24 months, whichever occurs first.

PUSHING AND TOWING

Pushing

All Celicas equipped with a manual transmission can be push started, although more than one car has received a dented fender or bumper from this operation. To push start the car; turn the ignition switch to the ON position, push in the clutch pedal, put the gear shift lever in second or third gear and partially depress the gas pedal. As the car begins to pick up momentum while being pushed, release the clutch pedal and give it gas.

CAUTION: *Never attempt to push start the car while it is in reverse.*

Celicas that are equipped with an automatic transmission can not be push started no matter how far or how fast they are pushed.

Towing

Cars with a manual transmission can be towed with either end up in the air or with all four wheels on the ground. You need only remember that the transmission must be in Neutral, the parking brake must be off and the ignition switch must be in the "ACC" position.

Cars with an automatic transmission have a few more restrictions when it comes to towing them. The transmission must always be in Neutral, the parking brake must be off and the ignition switch must be in the "ACC" position. Towing with the rear wheels in the air is fine, but remember that the steering column lock is not designed to hold the front wheels in the straight ahead position while the car is being towed.

With the exception of 1974–77 models, Celicas may be towed with the front wheels in the air, but for not more than 50 miles at speeds no greater than 30 mph. Anything more than this will require disconnecting the driveshaft. The same restriction applies when the car is being flat-towed.

1974–77 Celicas can not be towed with the rear wheels on the ground regardless of the circumstances. If the front end must be raised, either put dollies under the rear wheels or disconnect the driveshaft. The only way that the car can be flat-towed is if the driveshaft has been disconnected.

NOTE: *Most Celicas are equipped with tow hooks at the front and back of the car. If the car is to be flat-towed, use the hooks. Don't use an unsuspecting suspension member or the bumper.*

JACKING

There are certain safety precautions which should be observed when jacking the vehicle. They are as follows:

1. Always jack the car on a level surface.
2. Set the parking brake if the *front* wheels are to be raised. This will keep the car from rolling backward off the jack.
3. If the rear wheels are to be raised, block the front wheels to keep the car from rolling forward.
4. Block the wheel diagonally opposite the one which is being raised.

NOTE: *The tool kit which is supplied with most Toyota passenger cars includes a wheel block.*

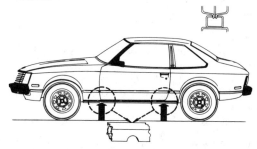

Jacking points for the scissors jack and jackstands

When jacking the rear of the car, always place the jack pad under the center of the axle housing

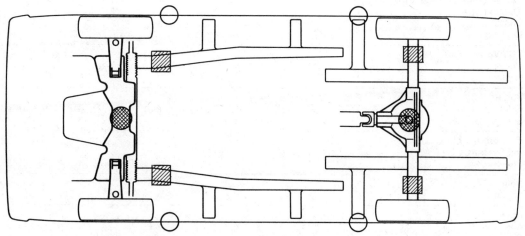

Jacking points, all solid rear axle cars. The four empty circles are pantograph jack points

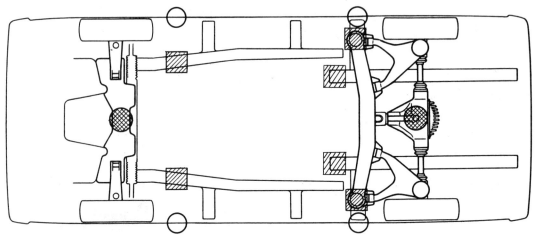

1982 and later Supra and Celica GT-S (IRS) jacking points. The four empty circles are pantograph jack points

5. If the vehicle is being raised in order to work underneath it, support it with jackstands. Do not place the jackstands against the sheet metal panels beneath the car or they will become distorted.

CAUTION: *Do not work beneath a vehicle supported only by a tire-changing jack. Use a hydraulic floor jack.*

6. Do not use a bumper jack to raise the vehicle; the bumpers are not designed for this purpose.

Maintenance Intervals Chart

Intervals are for thousands of miles or number of months, whichever comes first.

NOTE: *Heavy-duty operation (trailer towing, prolonged idling, severe stop-and-go driving and winter operation on salted roads) should be accompanied by a 50% increase in maintenance. Cut the interval in half for these conditons. Operation in extremely dirty or dusty conditions may require immediate changes of engine oil and all filters.*

Maintenance	7.5 (6)	15 (12)	22.5 (18)	30 (24)	37.5 (30)	45 (36)	52.5 (42)	60 (48)	See Chapter
Air Filter									
Check	x	x	x	x	x	x	x	x	1
Replace				x				x	
Vacuum Fittings, Hoses and Connections									
Check				x				x	1 & 4
Replace	①	①	①	①	①	①	①	①	
PCV Valve									
Check		x		x		x		x	1 & 4
Replace	①	①	①	①	①	①	①	①	
Battery									
Fluid Level	②	②	②	②	②	②	②	②	1
Specific Gravity		x		x		x		x	
Evaporative Emission Control System									
Check		x		x		x		x	1
Belts									
Adjust Tension		x		x		x		x	1
Hoses									
Check		x		x		x		x	1
Replace	①	①	①	①	①	①	①	①	

Maintenance Intervals Chart (cont.)

Intervals are for thousands of miles or number of months, whichever comes first.

NOTE: *Heavy-duty operation (trailer towing, prolonged idling, severe stop-and-go driving and winter operation on salted roads) should be accompanied by a 50% increase in maintenance. Cut the interval in half for these conditons. Operation in extremely dirty or dusty conditions may require immediate changes of engine oil and all filters.*

Maintenance	7.5 (6)	15 (12)	22.5 (18)	30 (24)	37.5 (30)	45 (36)	52.5 (42)	60 (48)	See Chapter
Engine Coolant									
Check	②	②	②	②	②	②	②	②	1
Freezing Protection Rating		x				x			
Change				x				x	
Engine Oil									
Check	②	②	②	②	②	②	②	②	1
Change③	x	x	x	x	x	x	x	x	
Oil Filter									
Replace	x	x	x	x	x	x	x	x	1
Manual Transmission Fluid									
Check		x		x		x		x	1
Change				x				x	
Automatic Transmission Fluid									
Check		x		x		x		x	1
Change				x				x	
Rear Axle									
Check		x		x		x		x	1
Change				x				x	
Brake Master Cylinder									
Check		x		x		x		x	1
Clutch Master Cylinder									
Check		x		x		x		x	1
Power Steering Fluid									
Check		x		x		x		x	1
Steering Gear									
Check		x		x		x		x	1
Wheels and Tires									
Check	②	②	②	②	②	②	②	②	1
Fuel Filter									
Check		x		x		x		x	1
Replace				x				x	
Wheel Bearing									
Grease				x				x	9
Ball Joints									
Grease				x				x	1 & 8
Body Lubrication		x		x		x		x	1
Valve Lash									
Check and Adjust		x		x		x		x	2
Clutch Pedal									
Check Play and Adjustment		x		x		x		x	6

① As necessary
② At least once a month
③ 1971–77; every 6,000 miles

JUMP STARTING A DEAD BATTERY

The chemical reaction in a battery produces explosive hydrogen gas. This is the safe way to jump start a dead battery, reducing the chances of an accidental spark that could cause an explosion.

Jump Starting Precautions

1. Be sure both batteries are of the same voltage.
2. Be sure both batteries are of the same polarity (have the same grounded terminal).
3. Be sure the vehicles are not touching.
4. Be sure the vent cap holes are not obstructed.
5. Do not smoke or allow sparks around the battery.
6. In cold weather, check for frozen electrolyte in the battery.
7. Do not allow electrolyte on your skin or clothing.
8. Be sure the electrolyte is not frozen.

Jump Starting Procedure

1. Determine voltages of the two batteries; they must be the same.
2. Bring the starting vehicle close (they must not touch) so that the batteries can be reached easily.
3. Turn off all accessories and both engines. Put both cars in Neutral or Park and set the handbrake.
4. Cover the cell caps with a rag—do not cover terminals.
5. If the terminals on the run-down battery are heavily corroded, clean them.
6. Identify the positive and negative posts on both batteries and connect the cables in the order shown.
7. Start the engine of the starting vehicle and run it at fast idle. Try to start the car with the dead battery. Crank it for no more than 10 seconds at a time and let it cool off for 20 seconds in between tries.
8. If it doesn't start in 3 tries, there is something else wrong.
9. Disconnect the cables in the reverse order.
10. Replace the cell covers and dispose of the rags.

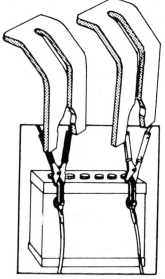

Side terminal batteries occasionally pose a problem when connecting jumper cables. There frequently isn't enough room to clamp the cables without touching sheet metal. Side terminal adaptors are available to alleviate this problem and should be removed after use.

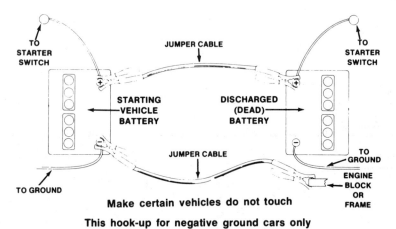

Make certain vehicles do not touch

This hook-up for negative ground cars only

Tune-Up and Performance Maintenance

2

TUNE-UP PROCEDURES

In order to extract the best performance and economy from your engine it is essential that it be properly tuned at regular intervals. A regular tune-up will keep your Toyota's engine running smoothly and will prevent the annoying minor breakdowns and poor performance associated with an untuned engine.

NOTE: *All Toyota Celicas use a conventional breaker points ignition system through 1974. In 1975 Toyota switched to a transistorized ignition system. This system was much like the previous system with one basic difference; instead of the breaker points switching the primary current to the coil on and off, they triggered a transistor which did it for them. In 1977, Celica GTs sold in California came equipped with a fully transistorized electronic ignition system. In 1978, this system became standard on all models.*

A complete tune-up should be performed every 15,000 miles or twelve months, whichever comes first. This interval should be halved if the car is operated under severe conditions, such as trailer towing, prolonged idling, continual stop and start driving, or if starting or running problems are noticed. It is assumed that the routine maintenance described in Chapter 1 has been kept up, as this will have a decided effect on the results of a tune-up. All of the applicable steps of a tune-up should be followed in order, as the result is a cumulative one.

If the specifications on the tune-up sticker in the engine compartment of your Toyota disagree with the "Tune-Up Specifications" chart in this chapter, the figures on the sticker must be used. The sticker often reflects changes made during the production run.

Spark Plugs

Spark plugs ignite the air and fuel mixture in the cylinder as the piston reaches the top of the compression stroke. The controlled explosion that results forces the piston down, turning the crankshaft and the rest of the drive train.

The average life of a spark plug is 15,000 miles. This is, however, dependent on a number of factors: the mechanical condition of the engine; the type of fuel; the driving conditions; and the driver.

When you remove the spark plugs, check their condition. They are a good indicator of the condition of the engine. It is a good idea to remove the spark plugs every 6,000 miles to keep an eye on the mechanical state of the engine.

A small deposit of light tan or gray material (or rust red with unleaded fuel) on a spark plug that has been used for any period of time is to be considered normal. Any other color, or abnormal amounts of deposit, indicates that there is something amiss in the engine.

The gap between the center electrode and the side or ground electrode can be expected to increase not more than 0.001 in. every 1,000 miles under normal conditions.

When a spark plug is functioning normally or, more accurately, when the plug is installed in an engine that is functioning properly, the plugs can be taken out, cleaned, regapped, and reinstalled in the engine without doing the engine any harm.

When, and if, a plug fouls and begins to misfire, you will have to investigate, correct the cause of the fouling, and either clean or replace the plug.

There are several reasons why a spark plug will foul and you can learn which is at fault by just looking at the plug. Refer to the color "Spark Plug Diagnosis" section in the center of this guide for illustrations of these problems and information on their cure.

Spark plugs suitable for use in your Toyota's engine are offered in a number of different heat ranges. The amount of heat which the plug ab-

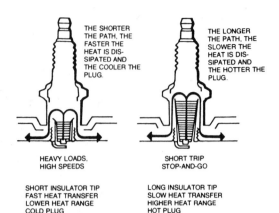

THE SHORTER THE PATH, THE FASTER THE HEAT IS DISSIPATED AND THE COOLER THE PLUG.

THE LONGER THE PATH, THE SLOWER THE HEAT IS DISSIPATED AND THE HOTTER THE PLUG.

HEAVY LOADS.
HIGH SPEEDS

SHORT TRIP
STOP-AND-GO

SHORT INSULATOR TIP
FAST HEAT TRANSFER
LOWER HEAT RANGE
COLD PLUG

LONG INSULATOR TIP
SLOW HEAT TRANSFER
HIGHER HEAT RANGE
HOT PLUG

Spark plug heat range

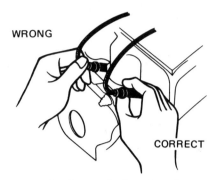

WRONG

CORRECT

When removing the spark plug wire, always grasp it by the rubber boot

sorbs is determined by the length of the lower insulator. The longer the insulator, the hotter the plug will operate; the shorter the insulator, the cooler it will operate. A spark plug that absorbs (or retains) little heat and remains too cool will accumulate deposits of lead, oil, and carbon, because it is not hot enough to burn them off. This leads to fouling and consequent misfiring. A spark plug that absorbs too much heat will have no deposits, but the electrodes will burn away quickly and, in some cases, preignition may result. Preignition occurs when the spark plug tips get so hot that they ignite the fuel/air mixture before the actual spark fires. This premature ignition will usually cause a pinging sound under conditions of low speed and heavy load. In severe cases, the heat may become high enough to start the fuel/air mixture burning throughout the combustion chamber rather than just to the front of the plug. In this case, the resultant explosion will be strong enough to damage pistons, rings, and valves.

In most cases the factory recommended heat range is correct; it is chosen to perform well under a wide range of operating conditions. However, if most of your driving is long distance, high speed travel, you may want to install a spark plug one step colder than standard. If most of your driving is of the short trip variety, when the engine may not always reach operating temperature, a hotter plug may help burn off the deposits normally accumulated under those conditions.

REMOVAL

1. Number the wires so that you won't cross them when you replace them.

2. Remove the wire from the end of the spark plug by grasping the wire by the rubber boot. If the boot sticks to the plug, remove it by twisting and pulling at the same time. *Do not pull the wire itself or you will damage the core.*

3. Use a $^{13}/_{16}$ in. spark plug socket to loosen all of the plugs about two turns.

NOTE: *The cylinder head is cast from aluminum. Remove the spark plugs when the engine is cold, if possible, to prevent damage to the threads.*

If removal of the plugs is difficult, apply a few drops of penetrating oil or silicone spray to the area around the base of the plug, and allow it a few minutes to work.

4. If compressed air is available, apply it to the area around the spark plug holes. Otherwise, use a rag or a brush to clean the area. Be careful not to allow any foreign material to drop into the spark plug holes.

5. Remove the plugs by unscrewing them the rest of the way from the engine.

INSPECTION

Check the plugs for deposits and wear (see the "Spark Plug Diagnosis" color section in the center of this book). If they are not going to be replaced, clean the plugs thoroughly. Remember that any kind of deposit will decrease the efficiency of the plug. Plugs can be cleaned on a spark plug cleaning machine, which can sometimes be found in service stations, or you can do an acceptable job of cleaning with a stiff brush. If the plugs are cleaned, the electrodes must be filed flat. Use an ignition points file, not an emery board or the like, which will leave deposits. The electrodes must be filed perfectly flat with sharp edges; rounded edges reduce the spark plug voltage by as much as 50%.

Check spark plug gap before installation. The ground electrode (the L-shaped one connected to the body of the plug) must be parallel to the center electrode and the specified size wire gauge (see "Tune-Up Specifications") should pass through the gap with a slight drag. Always check the gap on new plugs, too; they are not always set correctly at the factory. Do not use a flat feeler gauge when measuring the

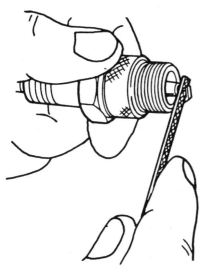

Plugs in good condition can be filed and re-used

Check the spark plug gap with a wire feeler gauge

Bend the side electrode to adjust the gap

gap, because the reading will be inaccurate. Wire gapping tools usually have a bending tool attached. Use that to adjust the side electrode until the proper distance is obtained. *Absolutely never bend the center electrode.* Also, be careful not to bend the side electrode too far or too often; it may weaken and break off within the engine, requiring removal of the cylinder head to retrieve it.

NOTE: *1983 and later Supras have platinum-tipped spark plugs as original equipment. They are designed to last longer than conventional plugs.*

INSTALLATION

1. Lubricate the threads of the spark plugs with a drop of oil. Install the plugs and tighten them hand-tight. Take care not to cross-thread them.

2. Tighten the spark plugs with the socket. Do not apply the same amount of force you would use for a bolt; just snug them in. If a torque wrench is available, tighten to 11–15 ft. lbs.

3. Install the wires on their respective plugs. Make sure the wires are firmly connected. You will be able to feel them click into place.

CHECKING AND REPLACING SPARK PLUG CABLES

At every tune-up, visually inspect the spark plug cables for burns, cuts, or breaks in the insulation. Check the boots and the nipples on the distributor cap and coil. Replace any damaged wiring.

Every 36,000 miles or so, the resistance of the wires should be checked with an ohmmeter. Wires with excessive resistance will cause misfiring, and may make the engine difficult to start in damp weather. Generally, the useful life of the cables is 36,000–50,000 miles.

To check resistance, remove the distributor cap, leaving the wires attached. Connect one lead of an ohmmeter to an electrode within the cap; connect the other lead to the corresponding spark plug terminal (remove it from the plug for this test). Replace any wire which

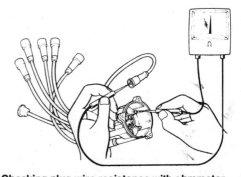

Checking plug wire resistance with ohmmeter

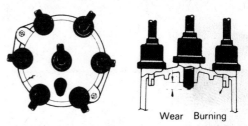

Check distributor cap for cracks; check cable ends for wear

Tune-Up Specifications

When analyzing compression test results, look for uniformity among cylinders, rather than specific pressures.

Year	Engine Type	Spark Plugs		Distributor		Ignition Timing (deg)▲		Compression Pressure (psi)**	Fuel Pump Pressure (psi)	Idle Speed (rpm)▲		Valve Clearance (in.)‡	
		Type	Gap (in.)	Point Dwell (deg)	Point Gap (in.)	MT	AT			MT	AT	In	Ex
1971	8R-C	W20EP	0.031	52	0.018	10° BTDC	10° BTDC	164	2.8–4.3	650	650	0.008	0.014
1971–74	18R-C	W20EO	0.031①	52	0.018	7° BTDC	7° BTDC	164②	2.8–4.3	650	650③	0.008	0.014
1975–76	20R	W16EP	0.030	52	0.018	8° BTDC	8° BTDC	156	2.2–4.2	850	850	0.008	0.012
1977	20R	W16EP	0.031	52	0.018	8° BTDC	8° BTDC	156	2.8–4.3	850	800	0.008	0.012
1978–80	20R	W16EXR-U	0.031④	⑤	0.012⑥	8° BTDC	8° BTDC	156	2.2–4.3	800	850	0.008	0.012⑦
1981–83	22R	W16EXR-U	0.031	⑤	0.012⑥	8° BTDC⑨	8° BTDC⑨	171	NA	700①	750⑧	0.008	0.012
1979½–80	4M-E	W16EXR-U	0.031	⑤	0.012⑥	12° BTDC	12° BTDC	156	33–38	800	800	0.011	0.014

Year												
1981	5M-E	W16EXR-U	0.031	⑤	0.012 ⑥	8° BTDC	8° BTDC	156	33–38	800	800	0.011	0.014
1982	5M-GE	W16EXR-U	0.031	⑤	0.012 ⑥	8° BTDC	8° BTDC	164	35–38	650	650	⑩	⑩
1983	5M-GE	P16R	0.043	⑤	0.012 ⑥	10° BTDC	10° BTDC	164	35–38	650	650	⑩	⑩

NOTE: The underhood specifications sticker often reflects tune-up specification changes made while the car is in production. Sticker figures must be used if they disagree with those in this chart.
① For California cars W/EGR—W16EP
② 1973–74— 156 psi
③ 1974—850 rpm
④ 1979—0.030 in.
⑤ Electronic ignition; dwell is pre-set at the factory and not adjustable
⑥ Electronic ignition; refers to air gap, not point gap
⑦ 1979—0.010 in.
⑧ Canada—850 rpm
⑨ 5° BTDC on 1983 models
⑩ Engine equipped with hydraulic lash adjusters; valves operate with zero clearance
⑪ 750 rpm on '83 models with fuel injection
▲With the manual transmission in Neutral and the automatic transmission in Drive (D)
**The difference between cylinders should not exceed 14 psi
‡Valve clearances checked with the engine HOT
NA—Not available at time of publication
MT—Manual transmission
AT—Automatic transmission
BTDC—Before top dead center

shows a resistance over 25,000 ohms. Test the high tension lead from the coil by connecting the ohmmeter between the center contact in the distributor cap and either of the primary terminals of the coil. If resistance is more than 25,000 ohms, remove the cable from the coil and check the resistance of the cable alone. Anything over 15,000 ohms is cause for replacement. It should be remembered that resistance is also a function of length; the longer the cable, the greater the resistance. Thus, if the cables on your car are longer than the factory originals, resistance will be higher, quite possibly outside these limits.

When installing new cables, replace them one at a time to avoid mixups. Start by replacing the longest one first. Install the boot firmly over the spark plug. Route the wire over the same path as the original. Insert the nipple firmly into the tower on the cap or the coil.

Breaker Points and Condenser

The points function as a circuit breaker for the primary circuit of the ignition system. The ignition coil must boost the 12 volts of electrical pressure supplied by the battery to as much as 25,000 volts in order to fire the plugs. To do this, the coil depends on the points and the condenser to make a clean break in the primary circuit.

The coil has both primary and secondary circuits. When the ignition is turned on, the battery supplies voltage through the coil and onto the points. The points are connected to ground, completing the primary circuit. As the current passes through the coil, a magnetic field is created in the iron center core of the coil. When the cam in the distributor turns, the points open, breaking the primary circuit. The magnetic field in the primary circuit of the coil then collapses and cuts through the secondary circuit windings around the iron core. Because of the physical principle called "electromagnetic induction," the battery voltage is increased to a level sufficient to fire the spark plugs.

When the points open, the electrical charge in the primary circuit tries to jump the gap created between the two open contacts of the points. If this electrical charge were not transferred elsewhere, the metal contacts of the points would start to change rapidly.

The function of the condenser is to absorb excessive voltage from the points when they open and thus prevent the points from becoming pitted or burned.

If you have ever wondered why it is necessary to tune-up your engine occasionally, consider the fact that the ignition system must complete the above cycle each time a spark plug fires. On a four-cylinder, four-cycle engine, two of the four plugs must fire once for every engine revolution. If the idle speed of your engine is 800 revolutions per minute (800 rpm), the breaker points open and close two times for each revolution. For every minute your engine idles, your points open and close 1,600 times $(2 \times 800 = 1,600)$. And that is just at idle. What about at 3000 rpm?

There are two ways to check breaker point gap: with a feeler gauge or with a dwell meter. Either way you set the points, you are adjusting the amount of time (in degrees of distributor rotation) that the points will remain open. If you adjust the points with a feeler gauge, you are setting the maximum amount the points will open when the rubbing block on the points is on a high point of the distributor cam. When you adjust the points with a dwell meter, you are measuring the number of degrees (of distributor cam rotation) that points will remain closed before they start to open as a high point of the distributor cam approaches the rubbing block of the points.

If you still do not understand how the points function, take a friend, go outside, and remove the distributor cap from your engine. Have your friend operate the starter (make sure that the transmission is not in gear) as you look at the exposed parts of the distributor.

There are two rules that should *always* be followed when adjusting or replacing points. *The points and condenser are a matched set; never replace one without replacing the other. If you change the point gap or dwell of the engine, you also change the ignition timing. Therefore, if you adjust the points, you must also adjust the timing.*

INSPECTION AND CLEANING

The breaker points should be inspected and cleaned at 6,000 mile intervals. To do so, perform the following steps:

1. Disconnect the high-tension lead from the coil.

2. Unsnap the two distributor cap retaining clips and lift the cap straight up. Leave the leads connected to the cap and position it out of the way.

3. Remove the rotor and dust cover by pulling them straight up.

4. Place a screwdriver against the breaker points and pry them open. Examine their condition. If they are excessively worn, burned, or pitted, they should be replaced.

5. Polish the points with a point file. *Do not use emery cloth or sandpaper; these may leave particles on the points causing them to arc.*

6. Clean the distributor cap and rotor with

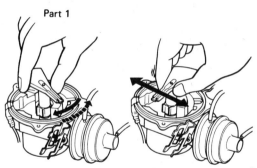

Part 1

The rotor should return to its original position when rotated slightly and then let go

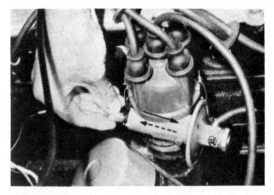

Checking the vacuum advance unit

alcohol. Inspect the cap terminals for looseness and corrosion. Check the rotor tip for excessive burning. Inspect both cap and rotor for cracks. Replace either if they show any of the above signs of wear or damage.

7. Check the operation of the centrifugal advance mechanism by turning the rotor clockwise. Release the rotor; it should return to its original position. If it doesn't, check for binding parts.

8. Check the vacuum advance unit, by removing the plastic cap and pressing on the octane selector. It should return to its original position. Check for binding if it doesn't.

9. If the points do not require replacement, proceed with the adjustment section below. Otherwise perform the point and condenser replacement procedures.

POINT REPLACEMENT 1971–77

The points should be replaced every 12,000 miles, or if they are badly pitted, worn, or burned. To replace them, proceed as follows:

1. If you have not already done so, perform Steps 1 through 3 of the preceding "Inspection and Cleaning" procedure.

2. Unfasten the point lead connector.

3. Remove the point retaining clip and unfasten the point hold-down screw(s). It is a good idea to use a magnetic or locking screwdriver

to remove the small screws inside the distributor, since they are almost impossible to find once they have been dropped.

4. Lift out the point set.

5. Install the new point set in the reverse order of removal. Adjust the points as detailed below, after completing installation.

CONDENSER REPLACEMENT 1971–74

Replace the condenser whenever the points are replaced, or if it is suspected of being defective. On Toyota passenger cars the condenser is located on the outside of the distributor. To replace it, proceed as follows:

1. Carefully remove the nut and washer from the condenser lead terminal.

2. Use a magnetic or locking screwdriver to remove the condenser mounting screw.

3. Remove the condenser.

Installation of a new condenser is performed in the reverse order of removal.

ADJUSTMENT

Perform the gap adjustment procedure whenever new points are installed, or as part of routine maintenance. If you are adjusting an old set of points, you must check the dwell as well, since the feeler gauge is really only accurate with a new point set. The points on 1975–77 Celicas are adjusted in a slightly different manner than you may be familiar with so make sure that you follow the correct adjustment procedure below.

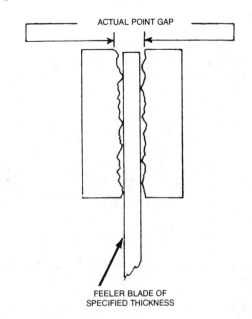

ACTUAL POINT GAP

FEELER BLADE OF SPECIFIED THICKNESS

The feeler gauge method of checking point gap is less accurate than the dwell meter method

1971–74

1. Rotate the engine by hand (with a wrench on the crankshaft pulley nut) or by using a remote starter switch, so that the rubbing block is on the high point of the cam lobe.

2. Insert a 0.018 in. feeler gauge between the points; a slight drag should be felt.

3. If no drag is felt or if the feeler gauge cannot be inserted at all, loosen, but do not remove, the point hold-down screw.

4. Insert a screwdriver into the adjustment slot. Rotate the screwdriver until the proper point gap is attained. The point gap is increased by rotating the screwdriver counterclockwise and decreased by rotating it clockwise.

5. Tighten the point hold-down screw.

Lubricate the cam lobes, breaker arm, rubbing block, arm pivot, and distributor shaft with special high-temperature distributor grease.

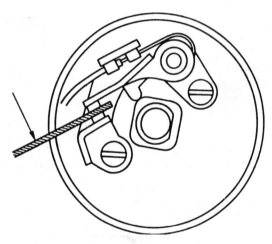

The arrow indicates the feeler gauge used to check the point gap (1971–74)

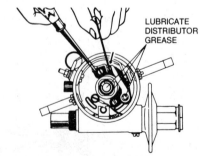

LUBRICATE DISTRIBUTOR GREASE

Adjustment of the points and distributor lubrication

1975–77

The point set on this ignition system is covered by a piece of protective plastic shielding.

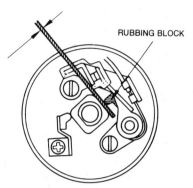

RUBBING BLOCK

Checking the point gap (1975–77)

Because of this, the gap must be checked between the point rubbing block and the distributor cam lobe instead of between the two points. Do not try to remove the plastic shielding as it will damage the point set.

1. Using your hands, a wrench on the crankshaft pulley nut, or a remote starter switch, rotate the engine so that the rubbing block is resting on the low point (flat side) of the cam lobe.

2. Insert a 0.018 in. flat feeler gauge between the rubbing block and the cam lobe; a slight drag should be felt.

3. If no drag can be felt or if the feeler gauge cannot be inserted at all, loosen, but do not remove, the point hold-down screw.

4. Insert a screwdriver into the point adjustment slot. Rotate the screwdriver until the proper gap is achieved. The gap is increased by rotating the screwdriver counterclockwise and decreased by rotating it clockwise.

5. Tighten the point hold-down screw. Lubricate the cam lobes, breaker arm, rubbing block, arm pivot and distributor shaft with special high temperature distributor grease.

Transistorized Ignition

In 1975 Toyota introduced its transistorized ignition system. This system works very much like the conventional system previously described. Regular breaker points are used, but instead of switching primary current to the coil off-and-on, they are used to trigger a switching transistor. The transistor, in turn, switches the coil primary current on and off.

Since only a very small amount of current is needed to operate the transistor, the points will not become burned or pitted, as they would if they had full primary current passing through them. This also allows the primary current to be higher than usual because the use of a higher current would normally cause the points to fail much more rapidly.

As already stated, the condenser is used to

absorb any extra high-voltage passing through the points. Since, in the transistorized system, there is no high current, no condenser is needed or used.

As a result of the lower stress placed on them, the points only have to be replaced every 24,000 miles instead of the usual 12,000 miles.

The Toyota transistorized ignition system may be quickly identified by the lack of a condenser on the outside of the distributor and by the addition of a control box, which is connected between the distributor and the primary side of the coil. This system was available on all 1975–77 Celicas (1975–76 California Celicas).

SERVICE PRECAUTIONS

Basically, the transistorized ignition is serviced just like its conventional counterpart. The points must be checked, adjusted, and replaced in the same manner. Point gap and dwell must be checked and set. The points should also be kept clean and should be replaced at 24,000 mile intervals. Of course, since there is no condenser, it does not have to be replaced when the points are.

However, there are several precautions to observe when servicing the transistorized ignition system:

1. Use only pure alcohol to clean the points. Shop solvent or an oily rag will leave a film on the points which will not allow the low current to pass.

2. Hook up a tachometer, dwell meter, or a combination dwell/tachometer to the *negative* (−) side of the coil; NOT to the distributor or the postive (+) side. Damage to the switching transistor will result if the meter is connected in the usual manner.

3. See the previous section for the remaining service procedures which are identical to those for the conventional ignition system.

Dwell Angle

The dwell angle is the number of degrees of distributor cam rotation through which the points remain closed (conducting electricity). Increasing the point gap decreases dwell, while decreasing the gap increases dwell.

The dwell angle may be checked with the distributor cap and rotor installed and the engine running, or with the cap and rotor removed and the engine cranking at starter speed. The meter gives a constant reading with the engine running. With the engine cranking, the meter will fluctuate between zero degrees dwell and the maximum figure for that setting. Never attempt to adjust the points

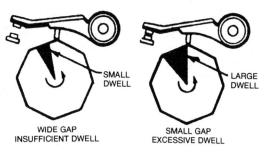

SMALL DWELL — LARGE DWELL
WIDE GAP INSUFFICIENT DWELL   SMALL GAP EXCESSIVE DWELL

Dwell as a function of point gap

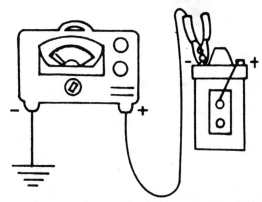

Dwell meter connections with transistorized ignition

when the ignition is on, or you may receive a shock.

NOTE: *On cars with electronic ignition, the dwell is pre-set at the factory and is not adjustable.*

ADJUSTMENT WITH A DWELL METER

1. Connect a dwell meter to the ignition system, according to the manufacturer's instructions.

   a. When checking the dwell on a conventional ignition system, connect one meter lead (usually black) to a metallic part of the car to ground the meter; the other lead (usually red) is connected to the coil primary post (the one with the small lead which runs to the distributor body).

   b. When checking dwell on a model with transistorized ignition, ground one meter lead (usually black) to a metallic part of the car; hook up the other lead (usually red) to the negative (−) coil terminal. Under no circumstances should the meter be connected to the distributor or the positive (+) side of the coil. (See the preceding "Service Precautions").

2. If the dwell meter has a set line, adjust the needle until it rests on the line.

3. Start the engine. It should be warmed-up and running at the specified idle speed.

It is not necessary to check the dwell on the transistorized system for Celica GT (California) models. It is set at the factory and requires no adjustment.

CAUTION: *Be sure to keep fingers, tools, clothes, hair, and wires clear of the engine fan. The transmission should be in Neutral (or Park), parking brake set, and running in a well-ventilated area.*

4. Check the reading on the dwell meter. If your meter doesn't have a four/cylinder scale, multiply the eight/cylinder reading by two.

5. If the meter reading is within the range specified in the "Tune-Up Specifications" chart, shut the engine off and disconnect the dwell meter.

6. If the dwell is not within specifications, shut the engine off and adjust the point gap as previously outlined. Increasing the point gap decreases the dwell angle and vice versa.

7. Adjust the points until dwell is within specifications, then disconnect the dwell meter. Adjust the timing; see the following section.

Electronic Ignition

Electronic ignition systems offer many advantages over the conventional breaker points ignition system. By eliminating the points, maintenance requirements are greatly reduced. An electronic ignition system is capable of producing much higher voltage which in turn aids in starting, reduces spark plug fouling and provides better emission control.

In 1977, Celica GTs made for California came equipped with electronic ignition. In 1978, Toyota decided to make electronic ignition standard equipment on all Celicas and that same basic system is still used on Celicas and Supras today.

The system Toyota uses consists of a distributor with a signal generator, an ignition coil and an electronic igniter. The signal generator is used to activate the electronic components of the igniter. It is located in the distributor and consists of three main components; the signal rotor, the pick-up coil and the permanent magnet. The signal rotor (not to be confused with the normal rotor) revolves with the distributor shaft, while the pickup coil and the permanent magnet are stationary. As the signal rotor spins, the teeth on it pass a projection leading from the pickup coil. When this happens, voltage is allowed to flow through the system, firing the spark plugs. There is no physical contact and no electrical arcing, hence no need to replace burnt or worn parts.

Service consists of inspection of the distributor cap, rotor and the ignition wires; replacing them as necessary. In addition, the air gap between the signal rotor and the projection on the pickup coil should be checked periodically.

1. Remove the distributor cap as detailed earlier. Inspect the cap for cracks, carbon tracks or a worn center contact. Replace it if necessary, transferring the wires one at a time from the old cap to the new one.

2. Pull the ignition rotor (not the signal rotor) straight up and remove it. Replace it if the contacts are worn, burned or pitted. Do not file the contacts.

3. Turn the engine over (you may use a socket wrench on the front pulley bolt to do this) until the projection on the pickup coil is *directly* opposite the signal rotor tooth.

4. Get a non-ferrous (paper, brass, or plastic) feeler gauge of .012 in., and insert it into the pickup air gap. DO NOT USE AN ORDINARY METAL FEELER GAUGE! The gauge should just touch either side of the gap (the permissible range is .008–.016 in.).

5. If the gap is either too wide or too narrow, loosen the two phillips screws mounting the pickup coil onto the distributor base plate. Then, wedge a screwdriver between the notch in the pickup coil assembly and the two dimples on the base plate, and turn the screwdriver back and forth until the pickup gap is correct.

6. Tighten the screws and recheck gap, readjusting if necessary.

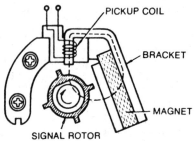

Components of the electronic ignition signal generator

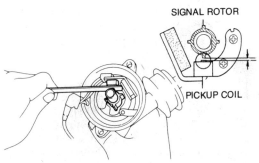

Use a non-ferrous feeler gauge when checking the air gap on the electronic ignition system

Ignition Timing

Ignition timing is the measurement in degrees of crankshaft rotation of the instant the spark plugs in the cylinders fire, in relation to the location of the piston, while the piston is on its compression stroke.

Ignition timing is adjusted by loosening the distributor locking device and turning the distributor in the engine.

Ideally, the air/fuel mixture in the cylinder will be ignited (by the spark plug) and just beginning its rapid expansion as the piston passes top dead center (TDC) of the compression stroke. If this happens, the piston will be beginning the power stroke just as the compressed (by the movement of the piston) and ignited (by the spark plug) air/fuel mixture starts to expand. The expansion of the air/fuel mixture will then force the piston down on the power stroke and turn the crankshaft.

It takes a fraction of a second for the spark from the plug to completely ignite the mixture in the cylinder. Because of this, the spark plug must fire before the piston reaches TDC, if the mixture is to be completely ignited as the piston passes TDC. This measurement is given in degrees (of crankshaft rotation) *before* the piston reaches *top dead center* (BTDC). If the ignition timing setting for your engine is seven degrees (7°) BTDC, this means that the spark plug must fire at a time when the piston for that cylinder is 7° before top dead center of its compression stroke. However, this only holds true while your engine is at idle speed.

As you accelerate from idle, the speed of your engine (rpm) increases. The increase in rpm means that the pistons are now traveling up and down much faster. Because of this, the spark plugs will have to fire even sooner if the mixture is to be completely ignited as the piston passes TDC. To accomplish this, the distributor incorporates means to advance the timing of the spark as engine speed increases.

The distributor in your Celica has two means of advancing the ignition timing. One is called centrifugal advance and is actuated by weights in the distributor. The other is called vacuum advance and is controlled by that larger circular housing on the side of the distributor.

In addition, some distributors have a vacuum-retard mechanism which is contained in the same housing on the side of the distributor as the vacuum advance. The function of this mechanism is to retard the timing of the ignition spark under certain engine conditions. This causes more complete burning of the air/fuel mixture in the cylinder and consequently lowers exhaust emissions.

Because these mechanisms change ignition timing, it is necessary to disconnect and plug the one or two vacuum lines from the distributor when setting the basic ignition timing.

If ignition timing is set too far advanced (BTDC), the ignition and expansion of the air/fuel mixture in the cylinder will try to force the piston down the cylinder while it is still traveling upward. This causes engine "ping," a sound which resembles marbles being dropped into an empty tin can. If the ignition timing is too far retarded (after, or ATDC), the piston will have already started down on the power stroke when the air/fuel mixture ignites and expands. This will cause the piston to be forced down only a portion of its travel. This will result in poor engine performance and lack of power.

Ignition timing adjustment is checked with a timing light. This instrument is connected to the number one (No. 1) spark plug of the engine. The timing light flashes every time an electrical current is sent from the distributor, through the No. 1 spark plug wire, to the spark plug. The crankshaft pulley and the front cover of the engine are marked with a timing pointer and a timing scale. When the timing pointer is aligned with the "0" mark on the timing scale, the piston in No. 1 cylinder is at TDC of its compression stroke. With the engine running, and the timing light aimed at the timing pointer and timing scale, the stroboscopic flashes from the timing light will allow you to check the ignition timing setting of the engine. The timing light flashes every time the spark plug in the No. 1 cylinder of the engine fires. Since the flash from the timing light makes the crankshaft pulley seem stationary for a moment, you will be able to read the exact position of the piston in the No. 1 cylinder on the timing scale on the front of the engine.

There are three basic types of timing light available. The first is a simple neon bulb with two wire connections (one for the spark plug and one for the plug wire, connecting the light in series). This type of light is quite dim, and must be held closely to the marks to be seen, but it is inexpensive. The second type of light operates from the car battery. Two alligator clips connect to the battery terminals, while a third wire connects to the spark plug with an adapter. This type of light is more expensive, but the xenon bulb provides a nice bright flash which can even be seen in sunlight. The third type replaces the battery source with 110 volt house current. Some timing lights have other functions built into them, such as dwell meters, tachometers, or remote starting switches. These are convenient, in that they reduce the tangle of wires under the hood, but may duplicate the functions of tools you already have.

If your Celica has electronic ignition, you should use a timing light with an inductive pickup. This pickup simply clamps onto the No. 1 plug wire, eliminating the adapter. It is not susceptible to crossfiring or false triggering, which may occur with a conventional light, due to the greater voltages produced by electronic ignition.

CHECKING AND ADJUSTMENT

All Engines Except 5M-GE

1. Warm-up the engine. Connect a tachometer and check the engine idle speed to be sure that it is within the specification given in the "Tune-Up Specifications" chart at the beginning of the chapter.

NOTE: *Before hooking up a tachometer to a 1975–77 car with a transistorized ignition system, see the preceeding "service precautions."*

2. If the timing marks are difficult to see, use a dab of paint or chalk to make them more visible.

3. Connect a timing light according to the manufacturer's instructions.

4. Disconnect the vacuum line(s) from the distributor vacuum unit. Plug it (them) with a pencil or golf tee(s).

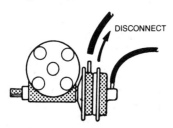

Disconnect the distributor vacuum hoses before adjusting timing

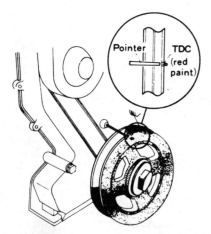

8R-C and 18R-C timing marks; 18R-C with A/C has white mark for TDC, non-A/C mark is longest of the four

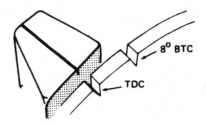

20R timing marks

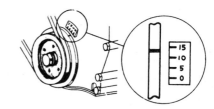

4M-E, 5M-E timing marks

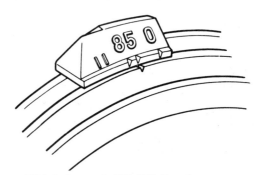

5° BTDC timing mark, 22R, 22R-E engines

1982 5M-GE Twin Cam 8° BTDC timing mark

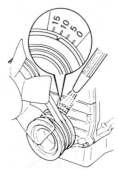

Timing marks, 1983 5M-GE Twin Cam. Shows 10° BTDC

5. Be sure that the timing light wires are clear of the fan and start the engine.

CAUTION: *Keep fingers, clothes, tools, hair, and leads clear of the spinning engine fan. Be sure that you are running the engine in a well-ventilated area.*

6. Allow the engine to run at the specified idle speed with the gearshift in Neutral with manual transmission and Drive (D) with automatic transmission.

CAUTION: *Be sure that the parking brake is set and that the front wheels are blocked to prevent the car from rolling forward, especially when Drive is selected with an automatic.*

7. Point the timing light at the marks indicated in the chart and illustrations below. With the engine at idle, timing should be at the specification given on the "Tune-Up Specifications" chart at the beginning of the chapter.

8. If the timing is not at the specification, loosen the pinch-bolt (hold-down bolt) at the base of the distributor just enough so that the distributor can be turned. Turn the distributor to advance or retard the timing as required. Once the proper marks are seen to align with the timing light, timing is correct.

9. Stop the engine and tighten the pinch-bolt. Start the engine and recheck timing. Stop the engine; disconnect the tachometer and timing light. Connect the vacuum line(s) to the distributor vacuum unit.

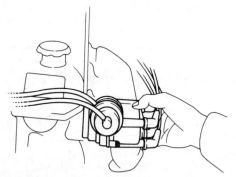

Loosen the pinch bolt and turn the distributor to adjust the timing

5M-GE Twin Cam Six

1. Connect a timing light to the engine following the manufacturer's instructions.

2. Start the engine and run it at idle.

3. Remove the rubber cap from the check connector and short the connector as shown.

4. Loosen the distributor pinch bolt just enough that the distributor can be turned. Aim the timing light at the timing marks on the crankshaft pulley and slowly turn the distrib-

utor until the timing mark on the pulley aligns with the 8° (1982) or 10° (1983) mark. Tighten the distributor pinch bolt.

5. Unshort the connector.

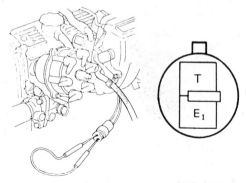

Short circuit the terminals of the timing check connector T—E$_1$; check and adjust timing, then unshort the connector

Octane Selector

The octane selector is used on some models as a fine adjustment to match the vehicle's ignition timing to the grade of gasoline being used. It is located near the distributor vacuum unit, beneath a plastic dust cover. Normally the octane selector should not require adjustment, however, adjustment is as follows:

1. Align the setting line with the threaded end of the housing and then align the center line with the setting mark on the housing.

2. Drive the car to the speed specified in the "Octane Selector Test Speeds" chart in High gear on a level road.

3. Depress the accelerator pedal all the way to the floor. A slight "pinging" sound should be heard. As the car accelerates, the sound should gradually go away.

4. If the pinging sound is loud or if it fails to disappear as the vehicle speed increases, retard the timing by turning the knob toward "R" (Retard).

5. If there is no pinging sound at all, advance the timing by turning the knob toward "A" (Advance).

NOTE: *On 1973–79 models, do not turn the*

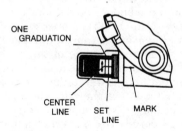

Octane selector

Octane Selector Test Speeds

Engine Type	Test Speeds (mph)
8R-C	16 – 22
18R-C	16 – 22
20R	19 – 22

octane selector more than ½ turn toward "R." Do not turn it toward "A" at all.

6. When the adjustment is completed, replace the plastic dust cover.

NOTE: *One graduation of the octane selector is equal to about ten degrees of crankshaft angle.*

Valve Lash

All Toyota Celica engines except the 5M-GE are equipped with a screw and locknut-type valve adjustment on their rocker arms. Valves on these engines should be adjusted at the factory-recommended intervals (1971–77, every 12,000 miles; 1978–83, every 15,000 miles).

The 5M-GE Twin Cam Six is equipped with hydraulic lash adjusters in the valve train. These adjusters maintain a zero clearance between the rocker arm and valve stem; no adjustment is possible or necessary.

Valve lash is one factor which determines how far the intake and exhaust valves will open into the cylinder.

If the valve clearance is too large, part of the lift of the camshaft will be used up in removing the excessive clearance, thus the valves will not be opened far enough. This condition has two effects, the valve train components will emit a tapping noise as they take up the excessive clearance, and the engine will perform poorly, since the less the intake valves open, the smaller the amount of air/fuel mixture admitted to the cylinders will be. The less the exhaust valves open, the greater the backpressure in the cylinder which prevents the proper air/fuel mixture from entering the cylinder.

If the valve clearance is too small, the intake and exhaust valves will not fully seat on the cylinder head when they close. When a valve seats on the cylinder head it does two things; it seals the combustion chamber so none of the gases in the cylinder can escape and it cools itself by transferring some of the heat it absorbed from the combustion process through the cylinder head and into the engine cooling system. Therefore, if the valve clearance is too small, the engine will run poorly (due to gases escaping from the combustion chamber), and the valves will overheat and warp (since they

cannot transfer heat unless they are touching the seat in the cylinder head).

While all valve adjustments must be as accurate as possible, it is better to have the valve adjustment slightly loose than slightly tight, as burnt valves may result from overly tight adjustments.

ADJUSTMENT

8R-C and 18R-C

1. Start the engine and allow it to run until it reaches normal operating temperature. NOTE:
Be careful not to touch the engine as it will be quite hot.

2. Turn the engine off and remove the air cleaner assembly; the housing, hoses and bracket.

3. Remove any other hoses, cables or wires which are attached to the cylinder head cover.

4. Check that the rocker arm bolts, the camshaft bearing cap bolts and the bearing cap union bolts are all tightened to the proper torque.

5. Set the No. 1 cylinder at TDC. Turn the crankshaft pulley until the pointer on the front cover lines up with the notch on the pulley.

NOTE: *Do not attempt to align the marks by cranking the engine with the starter. Valve clearances are checked with the engine stopped to prevent hot oil from being splashed out by the timing chain.*

6. Check that the rocker arms on the No.

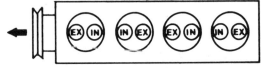

Valve arrangement for the 8R-C and 18R-C engines

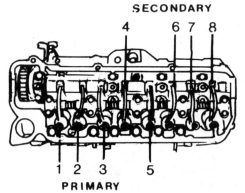

Valve adjusting sequence for the 8R-C and 18R-C engines

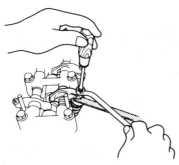

Measure the clearance between the valve stem and adjusting nut; there should be a slight drag on feeler gauge when properly adjusted.

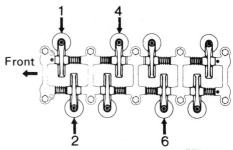

Adjust this set of valves first on the 20R and 22R engines

1 cylinder are loose and that the rockers on the No. 4 (No. 6 if you have a six cylinder engine) cylinder are tight. If not, rotate the crankshaft 360° until the marks line up again.

7. Valve clearance is checked between the end of the valve stem (it sticks out of the valve spring) and the bottom of the adjusting screw on the rocker arm.

8. Insert a feeler gauge and check for proper clearance on the No. 1 valve. To adjust, loosen the locknut on the end of the rocker arm and turn the adjusting screw until the clearance is in accordance with the figures given in the "Tune-Up Specifications" chart. Tighten the locknut and recheck the clearance; there should be a slight drag felt when the feeler gauge is pulled through the gap. Repeat the procedure for the Nos. 2, 3 and 5 valves.

9. Turn the crankshaft 360° until the marks align with each other again and repeat Step 8 for valves 4, 6, 7 and 8.

10. Installation of the remaining components is in the reverse order of removal.

20R and 22R

1. Disconnect the HAI and MC hoses, and follow Steps 1–7 of the 18R-C adjustment procedure. Disregard Step 5. When setting the No. 1 cylinder to TDC on the 20R engine, align the notch on the crankshaft pulley with the '0' mark on the pointer scale.

2. Insert a feeler gauge and check for proper clearance on the No. 1 valve. To adjust, loosen the locknut on the end of the rocker arm and turn the adjusting screw until the clearance is in accordance with the figures given in the "Tune-Up Specifications" chart. Tighten the

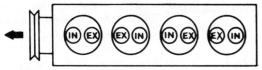

Valve arrangement for the 20R and 22R engines

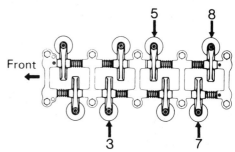

Turn the crankshaft 360° and then adjust this set of valves

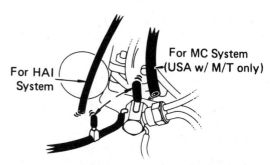

Disconnect and plug the Hot Air Intake and Mixture Control (if equipped) hoses on the 22R-E engine before adjusting valves. Located under carburetor

locknut and recheck the clearance; there should be a slight drag felt when the feeler gauge is pulled through the gap. Repeat the procedure for Nos. 2, 4 and 6 valves.

3. Turn the crankshaft 360° until the marks align with each other again and repeat Step 2 for valves 3, 5, 7 and 8.

4. Installation of the remaining components is in the reverse order of removal.

4M-E and 4M-E

1. Follow Steps 1–7 of the 18R-C adjustment procedure. Disregard Step 5. When setting the No. 1 cylinder to TDC on the 4M-E engine, align the notch on the crankshaft pulley with 'O' mark on the pointer scale.

2. Insert a feeler gauge to check for the proper clearance on the No. 1 valve. To ad-

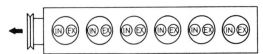

Valve arrangement for the 4M-E and 5M-E engines

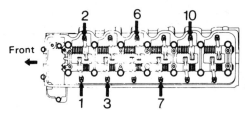

Adjust this set of valves first on the 4M-E and 5M-E engines

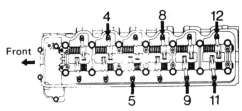

Turn the crankshaft 360° and then adjust this set of valves

just, loosen the locknut on the end of the rocker arm and turn the adjusting screw until the clearance is in accordance with the figures given in the "Tune-Up Specifications" chart. Tighten the locknut and recheck the clearance; there should be a slight drag felt when the feeler gauge is pulled through the gap. Repeat the procedure for Nos. 2, 3, 6, 7 and 10 valves.

3. Turn the crankshaft 360° until the marks align with each other again and repeat Step 2 for valves 4, 5, 8, 9, 11 and 12.

4. Installation is in the reverse order of removal.

Carburetor

This section contains only carburetor adjustments as they normally apply to engine tune-up. Descriptions of the carburetor and complete adjustment procedures can be found in Chapter 4.

When the engine in your Celica is running, air/fuel mixture from the carburetor is being drawn into the engine by a partial vacuum which is created by the downward movement of the pistons on the intake stroke of the four-stroke cycle of the engine. The amount of air/fuel mixture that enters the engine is controlled by throttle plates in the bottom of the carburetor. When the engine is not running, the throttle plates are closed, completely blocking off the bottom of the carburetor from

the inside of the engine. The throttle plates are connected, through the throttle linkage, to the gas pedal in the passenger compartment of the car. After you start the engine and put the transmission in gear, you depress the gas pedal to start the car moving. What you actually are doing when you depress the gas pedal is opening the throttle plate in the carburetor to admit more of the air/fuel mixture to the engine. The further you open the throttle plates in the carburetor, the higher the engine speed becomes.

As previously stated, when the engine is not running, the throttle plates in the carburetor are closed. When the engine is idling, it is necessary to open the throttle plates slightly. To prevent having to keep your foot on the gas pedal when the engine is idling, an idle speed adjusting screw was added to the carburetor. This screw has the same effect as keeping your foot slightly depressed on the gas pedal. The idle speed adjusting screw contacts a lever (the throttle lever) on the outside of the carburetor. When the screw is turned in, it opens the throttle plate on the carburetor, raising the idle speed of the engine. This screw is called the curb idle adjusting screw, and the procedures in this section tell you how to adjust it.

Since it is difficult for the engine to draw the air/fuel mixture from the carburetor with the small amount of throttle plate opening that is present when the engine is idling, an idle mixture passage is provided in the carburetor. This passage delivers air/fuel mixture to the engine from a hole which is located in the bottom of the carburetor below the throttle plates. This idle mixture passage contains an adjusting screw which restricts the amount of air/fuel mixture that enters the engine at idle.

IDLE SPEED AND MIXTURE

1971–74

NOTE: *Perform the following adjustments with the air cleaner in place. When adjusting the idle speed and mixture, the gear selector should be placed in Drive (D) on 1971–73 models equipped with an automatic transmission. Be sure to set the parking brake and block the front wheels. On all cars equipped with manual transmissions and all 1974 automatics, adjust the idle speed with the gearshift in Neutral (N).*

1. Run the engine until it reaches normal operating temperature. Stop the engine.

2. Connect a tachometer to the engine as detailed in the manufacturer's instructions.

3. Remove the plug and install a vacuum gauge in the manifold vacuum port by using a suitable metric adapter.

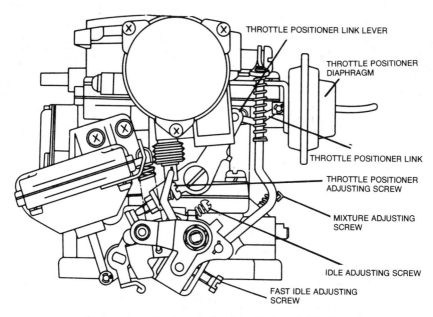

THROTTLE POSITIONER LINK LEVER

THROTTLE POSITIONER DIAPHRAGM

THROTTLE POSITIONER LINK

THROTTLE POSITIONER ADJUSTING SCREW

MIXTURE ADJUSTING SCREW

IDLE ADJUSTING SCREW

FAST IDLE ADJUSTING SCREW

Carburetor adjustments for the 8R-C and 18R-C engines

4. Start the engine and allow it to stabilize at idle.

5. Turn the mixture screw in or out, until the engine runs smoothly at the lowest possible engine speed without stalling.

6. Turn the idle speed screw until the vacuum gauge indicates the highest specified reading (see the "Vacuum At Idle" chart) at the specified idle speed. (See the "Tune-Up Specifications" chart at the beginning of the chapter.)

7. Tighten the idle speed screw to the point just before the engine rpm and vacuum readings drop off.

8. Remove the tachometer and the vacuum gauge. Install the plug back in the manifold vacuum port. Road-test the vehicle.

9. In some states, emission inspection is required. In such cases, you should take your car to a diagnostic center which has an HC/CO meter, and have the idle emission level checked to be sure that it is in accordance with state regulations. Starting 1974, CO levels at idle are given on the engine tune-up decal under the hood.

1975–77

The idle speed and mixture should be adjusted under the following conditions: the air cleaner must be installed, the choke fully opened, the transmission should be in Neutral (N), all accessories should be turned off, all vacuum lines should be connected, and the ignition timing should be set to specification.

1. Start the engine and allow it to reach normal operating temperature (180°F).

2. Check the float setting; the fuel level should be just about even with the spot on the sight glass. If the fuel level is too high or low, adjust the float level. (See Chapter 4).

3. Connect a tachometer in accordance with the manufacturer's instructions. However, connect the tachometer positive (+) lead to the coil Negative (−) terminal. Do NOT hook it up to the distributor or positive (+) side; damage to the transistorized ignition will result.

4. Adjust the speed to the highest rpm it

Vacuum At Idle
(in. Hg)

Year	Engine	Transmission	Minimum Vacuum Gauge Reading
1971	8R-C	All	15.7
1972–73	18R-C	MT	17.7
		AT	15.7
1974	18R-C	All	17.7

MT—Manual Transmission
AT—Automatic Transmission

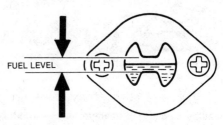

FUEL LEVEL

Checking the fuel level on the 20R engine

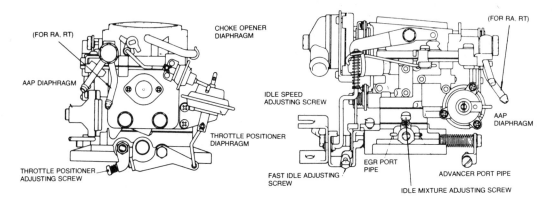

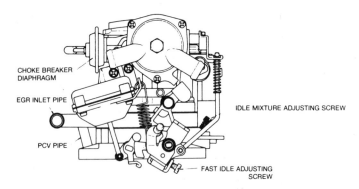

Carburetor adjustments for the 20R engine

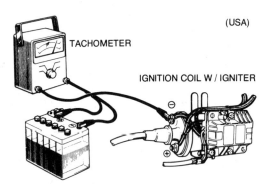

Tach hook-up, all U.S. models with electronic ignition

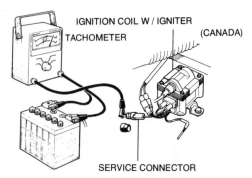

Canadian model tach hook-up for electronic ignition systems

will attain with the idle mixture adjusting screw.

5. Set the rpm to the idle mixture speed of 900 rpm, by turning the idle speed adjusting screw. You may have to repeat Steps 4 and 5 a few times until the highest idle reached in Step 4 will go no further.

6. Now set the speed to the initial idle speed of 850± 50 rpm, by turning the idle mixture adjusting screw in (clockwise).

7. Disconnect the tachometer.

1978–81

Use the same procedure described for 1975–77 models, described above. However, substitute different idle mixture and idle speeds as specified below:

NOTE: *Certain models may have an idle limiter cap on the idle adjusting screw; if so, use pliers to break it off. Be sure to install a new cap after adjustment.*

To meet U.S. emissions regulations, the idle mixture adjusting screw on the later models covered here is preadjusted and plugged by Toyota. When troubleshooting a rough idle, check all other possible causes before attempting to adjust the idle mixture; *the plug should not be removed and the adjusting screw tampered with in the course of a normal tune-up.*

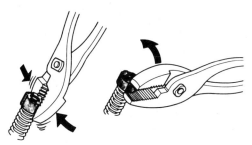

Carefully break off the idle limiter cap, if equipped

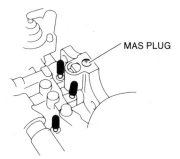

MAS PLUG

Cap or plug all vacuum ports before attempting to drill the plug. Carburetor shown on its side

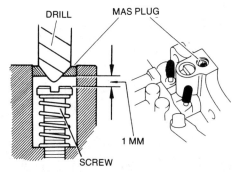

DRILL MAS PLUG

1 MM

SCREW

Use a variable-speed or hand drill on the plug—there is only 1mm clearance between the plug and top of screw

Toyota recommends all mixture adjustments be handled by a professional mechanic equipped with the proper emissions test equipment. If all other trouble causes have been checked, then the carburetor must be removed while the plug is removed from the mixture screw hole. Plug all vacuum ports to keep metal chips out before drilling. After the plug is removed, remove the mixture screw to inspect the tip for wear, and blow out the hole with compressed air. Reinstall the adjusting screw by screwing it in fully until it *just* seats, then unscrewing it 2½ full turns (4 turns on '83 models). Reinstall the carburetor and proceed with the mixture adjustment only if necessary.

    a. For idle mixture speeds (Step 5), use the following specifications:

- 1978 20R   850
- 1979 20R   870 Manual, 920 Automatic
- 1980 20R   700 (4 spd.) Manual, 800 (5 spd.) Manual, 850 Automatic
- 1981 22R   Not Adjustable
- 1982 22R   740 Manual, 790 U.S. Automatic, 890 Canadian Automatic
- 1983 22R   740 Manual, 790 Automatic

    b. For idle speed (step 6), use the following figures:

- 1978 20R   800
- 1979 20R   800 Manual, 850 Automatic
- 1980 20R   750 (4 spd.) Manual, 870 (5 spd.) Manual, 920 Automatic
- 1981–2 22R   700 All Manual, 750 Automatic (850 Canada)
- 1983 22R   700 All Manual, 750 All Automatics

Fuel Injection
IDLE SPEED AND MIXTURE
All Models

NOTE: *In order to complete this procedure you will need a voltmeter and an EFI idle adjusting wiring harness (Special Service Tool 09842-14010) which is available at your Toyota dealer. If you do not have these tools which are essential to this procedure, the car should be taken to a competent mechanic or dealership equipped for this procedure.*

    1. Behind the battery on the left front fender apron is a service connector. Remove the rubber caps from the connector and connect the EFI idle adjusting wiring harness.

    2. Connect the positive lead of the voltmeter to the red wire of the wiring harness

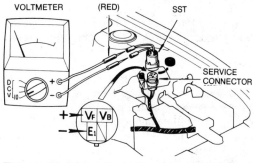

VOLTMETER   (RED)   SST

SERVICE CONNECTOR

The service connector is found on the left front fender apron; right front apron on '82 and later Supra

and then connect the negative lead to the black wire.

3. Hook up a tachometer as per the manufacturer's instructions.

4. Warm up the oxygen sensor by running the engine at 2,500 rpm for about two minutes. The needle of the voltmeter should be fluctuating at this time, if not, turn the idle mixture adjusting screw until it does.

5. Set the idle speed to specifications (see "Tune-Up Specifications" chart) by turning the idle speed adjusting screw.

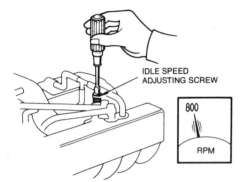

Setting the idle speed, 4M-E, 5M-E and 22R-E

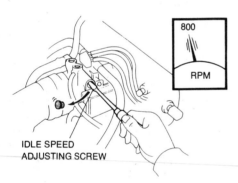

5M-GE Twin Cam six idle speed adjustment

NOTE: *The idle speed should be set immediately after warm-up while the needle of the voltmeter is fluctuating.*

6. The idle adjustment procedure for the 22R-E four cylinder and 5M-GE Twin Cam six cylinder engines is now complete. Follow the remaining steps for the 4M-E and 5M-E engines.

7. Remove the rubber cap from the idle adjusting connector and short both terminals of the connector with a wire.

8. While the connector is still shorted, run the engine at 2,500 rpm for two more minutes.

9. With the engine at idle and the connector still shorted, read and remember the voltage shown on the voltmeter.

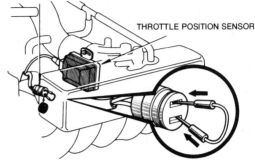

Short the idle adjusting connector

Idle adjusting harness Special Service Tool

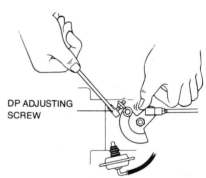

Loosen the locknut and turn the adjusting screw to set the dashpot

10. Remove the short circuit wire from the connector and then race the engine to 2,500 rpm once.

11. Adjust the idle mixture adjusting screw until the median of the indicated voltage range is the same as the reading taken in Step 8.

12. Replug the idle mixture adjusting screw hole. Disconnect the tachometer, the voltmeter and the special wiring harness. Replace the

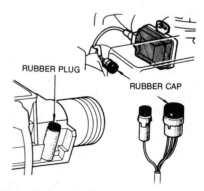

Replace all plugs and caps

rubber cap to the service connector and the idle adjusting connector.

DASHPOT ADJUSTMENT

4M-E and 5M-E Engines

1. Fully open and then return the throttle valve.

2. The throttle valve should return to the idle position in approximately 3.5 seconds.

3. To adjust the return time, loosen the lock nut and turn the adjusting bolt.

22R-E and 5M-GE Engines

1. Warm the engine up to operating temperature.

2. Connect a tachometer and check the idle speed. Adjust if necessary.

3. Have an assistant run the engine up to 2,500 rpm on the 22R-E, or 3,000 rpm on the 5M-GE and hold it there. Pinch the vacuum hose between the dashpot and the vacuum transmitting valve (VTV).

4. Release the throttle valve. See that the engine speed drops to 2,000 rpm and check that the dashpot is set. If the engine speed does not remain at 2,000 rpm, adjust the dashpot with the adjusting screw and locknut.

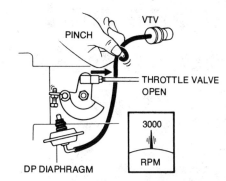

Pinch the vacuum hose between the VTV and dashpot

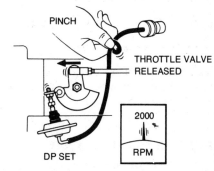

Engine speed should drop to 2000 rpm when throttle valve is released

Engine and Engine Rebuilding

3

UNDERSTANDING THE ENGINE ELECTRICAL SYSTEM

The engine electrical system can be broken down into three separate and distinct systems—(1) the starting system: (2) the charging system; (3) the ignition system.

Battery and Starting System

The battery is the first link in the chain of mechanisms which work together to provide cranking of the automobile engine. In most modern cars, the battery is a lead-acid electrochemical device consisting of six two-volt (2 V) subsections connected in series so the unit is capable of producing approximately 12 V of electrical pressure. Each subsection, or cell, consists of a series of positive and negative plates held a short distance apart in a solution of sulfuric acid and water. The two types of plates are of dissimilar metals. This causes a chemical reaction to be set up, and it is this reaction which produces current flow from the battery when its positive and negative terminals are connected to an electrical appliance such as a lamp or motor. The continued transfer of electrons would eventually convert the sulfuric acid in the electrolyte to water, and make the two plates identical in chemical composition. As electrical energy is removed from the battery, its voltage output tends to drop. Thus, measuring battery voltage and battery electrolyte composition are two ways of checking the ability of the unit to supply power. During the starting of the engine, electrical energy is removed from the battery. However, if the charging circuit is in good condition and the operating conditions are normal, the power removed from the battery will be replaced by the generator (or alternator) which will force electrons back through the battery, reversing the normal flow, and restoring the battery to its original chemical state.

The battery and starting motor are linked by very heavy electrical cables designed to minimize resistance to the flow of current. Generally, the major power supply cable that leaves the battery goes directly to the starter, while other electrical system needs are supplied by a smaller cable. During the starter operation, power flows from the battery to the starter and is grounded through the car's frame and the battery's negative ground strap.

The starting motor is a specially designed, direct current electric motor capable of producing a very great amount of power for its size. One thing that allows the motor to produce a great deal of power is its tremendous rotating speed. It drives the engine through a tiny pinion gear (attached to the starter's armature), which drives the very large flywheel ring gear at a greatly reduced speed. Another factor allowing it to produce so much power is that only intermittent operation is required of it. Thus, little allowance for air circulation is required, and the windings can be built into a very small space.

The starter solenoid is a magnetic device which employs the small current supplied by the starting switch circuit of the ignition switch. This magnetic action moves a plunger which mechanically engages the starter and electrically closes the heavy switch which connects it to the battery. The starting switch circuit consists of the starting switch contained within the ignition switch, a transmission neutral safety switch or clutch pedal switch, and the wiring necessary to connect these with the starter solenoid or relay.

A pinion, which is a small gear, is mounted to a one-way drive clutch. This clutch is splined to the starter armature shaft. When the ignition switch is moved to the "start" position, the solenoid plunger slides the pinion toward the flywheel ring gear via a collar and spring. If the teeth on the pinion and flywheel match properly, the pinion will engage the flywheel immediately. If the gear teeth butt one another, the spring will be compressed and will force the gears to mesh as soon as the starter turns far enough to allow them to do so. As the solenoid plunger reaches the end of its travel, it closes the contacts that connect the battery and starter and then the engine is cranked.

As soon as the engine starts, the flywheel ring gear begins turning fast enough to drive the pinion at an extremely high rate of speed. At this point, the one-way clutch begins allowing the pinion to spin faster than the starter shaft so that the starter will not operate at excessive speed. When the ignition switch is released from the starter position, the solenoid is de-energized, and a spring contained within the solenoid assembly pulls the gear out of mesh and interrupts the current flow to the starter.

Some starters employ a separate relay, mounted away from the starter, to switch the motor and solenoid current on and off. The relay thus replaces the solenoid electrical switch, but does not eliminate the need for a solenoid mounted on the starter used to mechanically engage the starter drive gears. The relay is used to reduce the amount of current the starting switch must carry.

The Charging System

The automobile charging system provides electrical power for operation of the vehicle's ignition and starting systems and all the electrical accessories. The battery serves as an electrical surge or storage tank, storing (in chemical form) the energy originally produced by the engine-driven generator. The system also provides a means of regulating generator output to protect the battery from being overcharged and to avoid excessive voltage to the accessories.

The storage battery is a chemical device incorporating parallel lead plates in a tank containing a sulfuric acid-water solution. Adjacent plates are slightly dissimilar, and the chemical reaction of the two dissimilar plates produces electrical energy when the battery is connected to a load such as the starter motor. The chemical reaction is reversible, so that when the generator is producing a voltage (electrical pressure) greater than that produced by the battery, electricity is forced into the battery, and the battery is returned to its fully charged state.

The vehicle's generator is driven mechanically, through V belts, by the engine crankshaft. It consists of two coils of fine wire, one stationary (the "stator"), and one movable (the "rotor"). The rotor may also be known as the "armature," and consists of fine wire wrapped around an iron core which is mounted on a shaft. The electricity which flows through the two coils of wire (provided initially by the battery in some cases) creates an intense magnetic field around both rotor and stator, and the interaction between the two fields creates voltage, allowing the generator to power the accessories and charge the battery.

There are two types of generators; the earlier is the direct current (DC) type. The current produced by the DC generator is generated in the armature and carried off the spinning armature by stationary brushes contacting the commutator. The commutator plates, which are separated from one another by a very short gap, are connected to the armature circuits so that the current will flow in one direction only in the wires carrying the generator output. The generator stator consists of two stationary coils of wire which draw some of the output current of the generator to form a powerful magnetic field and create the interaction of fields which generates the voltage. The generator field is wired in series with the regulator.

Newer automobiles use alternating current generators because they are more efficient, can be rotated at higher speeds, and have fewer brush problems. In an alternator, the field rotates while all the current produced passes only through the stator windings. The brushes bear against continuous slip rings rather than a commutator. This causes the current produced to periodically reverse the direction of its flow. Diodes (electrical one-way switches) block the flow of current from traveling in the wrong direction. A series of diodes is wired together to permit the alternating flow of the stator to be converted to a pulsating, but unidirectional flow at the alternator output. The alternator's field is wired in series with the voltage regulator.

The regulator consists of several circuits. Each circuit has a core, or magnetic coil of wire, which operates a switch. Each switch is connected to ground through one or more resistors. The coil of wire responds directly to system voltage. When the voltage reaches the required level, the magnetic field created by the winding of wire closes the switch and inserts a resistance into the generator field circuit, thus reducing the output. The contacts of the switch cycle open and close many times each second to precisely control voltage.

While alternators are self-limiting as far as maximum current is concerned, DC generators employ a current regulating circuit which responds directly to the total amount of current flowing through the generator circuit rather than to the output voltage. The current regulator is similar to the voltage regulator except that all system current must flow through the energizing coil on its way to the various accessories.

SAFETY PRECAUTIONS

Observing these precautions will ensure safe handling of the electrical system components and will avoid damage to the vehicle's electrical system:

A. Be *absolutely* sure of the polarity of a booster battery before making connections. *Connect the cables positive to positive, and negative to negative.* Connect positive cables first and then make the last connection to a ground on the body of the booster vehicle so that arcing cannot ignite hydrogen gas that may have accumulated near the battery. Even momentary connection of a booster battery with the polarity reversed will dammage alternator diodes.

B. Disconnect both vehicle battery cables before attempting to charge a battery.

C. Never ground the alternator or generator output or battery terminal. Be cautious when using metal tools around a battery to avoid creating a short circuit between the terminals.

D. Never ground the field circuit between the alternator and regulator.

E. Never run an alternator or generator without load unless the field circuit is disconnected.

F. Never attempt to polarize an alternator.

G. Keep the regulator cover in place when taking voltage and current limiter readings.

H. Use insulated tools when adjusting the regulator.

I. Whenever DC generator-to-regulator wires have been disconnected, the generator *must* be repolarized. To do this with an externally grounded, light duty generator, momentarily place a jumper wire between the battery terminal and the generator terminal of the regulator. With an internally grounded heavy duty unit, disconnect the wire to the regulator field terminal and touch the regulator battery terminal with it.

Troubleshooting the Fully Transistorized Electronic Ignition System

PRECAUTIONS

1. Do not allow the ignition switch to be ON for more than ten minutes if the engine will not start.

2. When a tachometer is connected to the system, always connect the tachometer positive lead to the ignition coil *negative* terminal. As some tachometers are not compatible with this system, it is recommended that you consult with the manufacturer.

3. NEVER allow the ignition coil terminals to touch ground as it could result in damage to the igniter and/or the ignition coil itself.

4. Do not disconnect the battery when the engine is running.

5. Make sure that the igniter is always properly grounded to the body.

TROUBLESHOOTING

Troubleshooting this system is easy, but you must have an accurate ohmmeter and voltmeter. The numbers in the diagram correspond to the numbers of the following troubleshooting steps. Be sure to perform each step in order.

1. Check for spark at the spark plugs by hooking up a timing light in the usual manner. If the light flashes, it can be assumed that voltage is reaching the plugs, which should then be inspected, along with the fuel system. If no flash is generated, go on to the following ignition checks.

2. Check all wiring and plastic connectors for tight and proper connections.

3. (1) With an ohmmeter, check between the positive (+) and negative (−) primary terminals of the ignition coil. The resistance (cold) should be 1.3–1.7 ohms. Between the (+) primary terminal and the high tension terminal, the resistance (cold) should be 12–16 kilo-ohms.

(2) The insulation resistance between the (+) primary terminal and the ignition coil case should be infinite.

4. The resistor wire (brown and yellow) resistance should be 1.2 ohms (cold). To measure, disconnect the plastic connector at the igniter and connect one wire of the ohmmeter to the yellow wire and one to the brown.

5. Remove the distributor cap and ignition rotor. (1) Check the air gap between the timing rotor spoke and the pick-up coil. When aligned, the air gap should be 0.008–0.016 in. You will probably have to "bump" the engine around with the starter to line up the timing rotor.

(2) Unplug the distributor connector at the distributor. Connect one wire of the ohmmeter to the white wire, and one wire to the pink wire. The resistance of the signal generator should be 130–190 ohms.

6. (1) Checking the igniter last, connect the (−) voltmeter wire to the (−) ignition coil primary terminal, and the (+) voltmeter wire to the yellow resistor wire at the connector un-

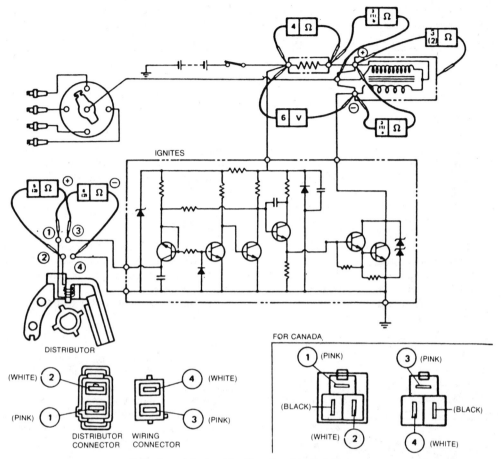

IGNITES

DISTRIBUTOR

(WHITE) 2
(PINK) 1

4 (WHITE)
3 (PINK)

DISTRIBUTOR   WIRING
CONNECTOR   CONNECTOR

FOR CANADA

1 (PINK)
(BLACK)
(WHITE) 2

3 (PINK)
(BLACK)
4 (WHITE)

Fully transistorized ignition troubleshooting

plugged in Step 4. With the ignition switch turned to "On" (not "Start") the voltage should measure 12 volts.

(2) Check the voltage between the (−) ignition coil primary terminal and the yellow resistor wire again, but this time use the ohmmeter as resistance. Using the igniter end of the distributor connector unplugged in Step 5, connect the positive (+) ohmmeter wire to the pink distributor wire, and the negative (−) ohmmeter wire to the white wire.

CAUTION: *Do not intermix the (+) and (−) terminals of the ohmmeter.*

Select either the 1 ohm or 10 ohm range of the ohmmeter. With the voltmeter connected as in Step 6 (1), and the ignition switch turned to "On" (not "Start"), the voltage should measure nearly zero.

Ignition Coil
PRIMARY RESISTANCE CHECK

In order to check the coil primary resistance, you must first disconnect all wires from the ignition coil terminals. Using an ohmmeter, check the resistance between the positive (15)

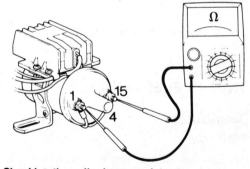

Checking the coil primary resistance

and the negative (1) terminals on the coil. The resistance should be:

- 18R-C and 20R up to 1979—1.3–1.7 ohms
- 20R 1980—0.5–0.6 ohms
- 4M-E—0.5–0.7 ohms
- 22R 1981—0.8–1.0 ohms
    1982–83—0.8–1.1 ohms;
    Canada 0.4–0.5 ohms
- 5M-E—0.5–0.6 ohms
- 5M-GE—0.4–0.5 ohms

If the resistance is not within these tolerances, the coil will require replacement.

For further information on this testing procedure, refer to Chapter 11; test 3.6.

SECONDARY RESISTANCE CHECK

In order to check the coil secondary resistance, you must first disconnect all wires from the ignition coil terminals. Using an ohmmeter, check the resistance between the positive (15) terminal and the coil wire (4) terminal. The resistance should be:

1. 18R-C and 20R up to 1979—6,500–10,500 ohms.
2. 20R 1980—11,500–15,500 ohms
3. 4M-E—11,500–15,500 ohms
4. 22R 1981—11,500–15,500 ohms
   1982–83—8,500–11,500 ohms
   Canada 8,500—11,500–11,500 ohms
5. 5M-E—11,500–15,500 ohms
6. 5M-GE—8,500–11,500 ohms

If the resistance is not within these tolerances, the coil will require replacement.

For further information on this testing procedure, refer to Chapter 11; test 4.4.

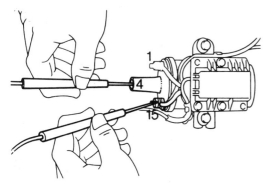

Checking the coil secondary resistance

ENGINE ELECTRICAL

Distributor

REMOVAL

Ona all four-cylinder engines except the 20R, the distributor is on the right (passenger's) side. On the 20R engines and all sixes, the distributor is located at the front of the engine on the left (driver's) side. To remove the distributor, proceed in the following order:

1. Unfasten the retaining clips and lift the distributor cap straight up. It will be easier to install the distributor if the wiring is left connected to the cap. If the wires must be removed from the cap, mark their positions to aid in installation.
2. Remove the dust cover and mark the position of the rotor relative to the distributor body; then mark the position of the body relative to the block.
3. Disconnect the coil primary wire and the vacuum line(s). If the distributor vacuum unit has two vacuum lines, mark which is which for installation.
4. Remove the pinch-bolt and lift the distributor straight out, away from the engine. The rotor and body are marked so that they can be returned to the position from which they were removed. *Do not turn or disturb the engine* (unless absolutely necessary, such as for engine rebuilding), after the distributor has been removed.

INSTALLATION—TIMING NOT DISTURBED

1. Insert the distributor in the block and align the matchmarks made during removal.
2. Engage the distributor driven gear with the distributor drive.
3. Install the distributor clamp and secure it with the pinch-bolt.
4. Install the cap, primary wire, and vacuum line(s).
5. Install the spark plug leads. Consult the marks made during removal to be sure that the proper lead goes to each plug. Install the high-tension wire if it was removed.
6. Start the engine. Check the timing and adjust it and the octane selector (if equipped), as outlined in chapter 2.

INSTALLATION—TIMING LOST

All Engines Except Twin Cam Six

If the engine has been cranked, dismantled, or the timing otherwise lost, proceed as follows:

1. Determine top dead center (TDC) of the No. 1 cylinder's compression stroke by removing the spark plug from the No. 1 cylinder and placing your finger on a vacuum gauge over the spark plug hole. This is important because the timing marks will also line up with the last cylinder in the firing order in its exhaust stroke. CAUTION: *On engines which have the spark plugs buried in the exhaust manifold, use a compression gauge or a screwdriver handle, not your finger, if the manifold is still hot.* Crank the engine until compression pressure starts to build up. Continue cranking the engine until the timing marks indicate TDC (or "0").
2. Next, align the timing marks to the specifications given in the "Ignition Timing" column of the "Tune-Up Specifications" chart at the beginning of Chapter 2.
3. Temporarily install the rotor in the dis-

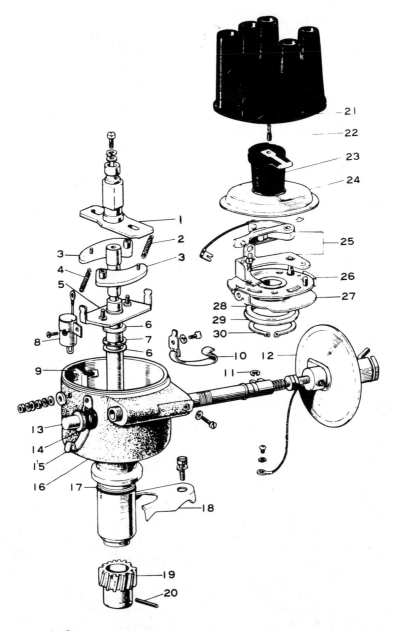

1. Cam	16. Distributor housing
2. Governor spring	17. O-ring
3. Governor weight	18. Distributor clamp
4. Governor spring	19. Spiral gear
5. Distributor shaft	20. Pin
6. Metal washer	21. Distributor cap
7. Bakelite washer	22. Spring
8. Condenser (not used	23. Rotor
w/transistor ignition)	24. Dust cover
9. Insulator	25. Breaker point assembly
10. Cap spring clip	26. Movable plate
11. Snap-ring	27. Stationary plate
12. Vacuum advance unit	28. Adjusting washer
13. Octane selector assembly	29. Wave washer
14. Rubber washer	30. Snap-ring
15. Cap spring clip	

An exploded view of the breaker points distributor

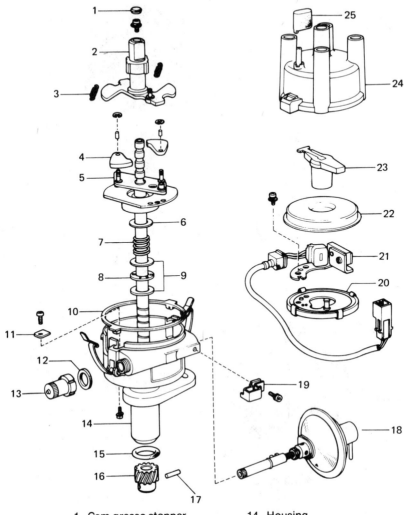

1. Cam grease stopper
2. Signal rotor
3. Governor spring
4. Governor weight
5. Governor shaft
6. Plate washer
7. Compression coil spring
8. Thrust bearing
9. Washer
10. Dustproof packing
11. Steel plate washer
12. Rubber washer
13. Octane selector cap
14. Housing
15. O ring
16. Spiral gear
17. Pin
18. Vacuum advancer
19. Cord clamp
20. Breaker plate
21. Signal generator
22. Dustproof cover
23. Distributor rotor
24. Distributor cap
25. Rubber cap

An exploded view of a distributor with the fully transistorized ignition system

tributor without the dust cover. Turn the distributor shaft so that the rotor is pointing toward the No. 1 terminal in the distributor cap. The points should just be about to open.

4. Use a small screwdriver to align the slot on the distributor drive (oil pump driveshaft) with the key on the bottom of the distributor shaft.

5. Align the matchmarks on the distributor body and the block which were made dur-

ing the removal. Install the distributor in the block by rotating it slightly (no more than one gear tooth in either direction) until the driven gear meshes with the drive.

NOTE: *Oil the distributor spiral gear and the oil pump driveshaft end before distributor installation.*

6. Rotate the distributor, once it is installed, so that the points are just about to open or the projection on the pickup coil is almost

opposite the signal rotor tooth. Temporarily tighten the pinchbolt.

7. Remove the rotor and install the dust cover. Replace the rotor and the distributor cap.

8. Install the primary wire and the vacuum line(s).

9. Install the No. 1 spark plug. Connect the cables to the spark plugs in the proper order by using the marks made during removal. Install the high-tension lead if it was removed.

10. Start the engine. Adjust the ignition timing and the octane selector (if equipped), as outlined in Chapter 2.

5M-GE Twin Cam Six

1. Follow Step 1 of the above procedure for "All Engines Except Twin Cam."

2. Remove the oil filler cap. Looking into the camshaft housing with the aid of a flashlight, check to make sure that the match hole on the second (No. 2) journal of the camshaft housing is aligned with the hole in the No. 2 journal of the camshaft. If the holes are not aligned, rotate the camshaft one full turn.

3. Install a new O-ring on the distributor shaft. Make sure the distributor cap is still removed at this time.

4. Align the matchmark on the distributor spiral gear with that of the distributor housing as shown.

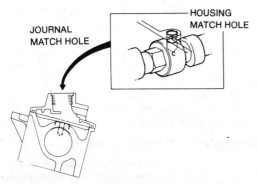

Align the camshaft and camshaft housing matchmarks through the oil filler hole

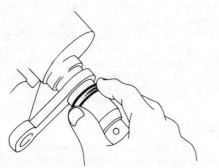

Always install a new O-ring on the distributor shaft

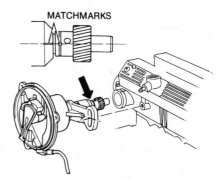

Align the matchmarks on the distributor gear and housing

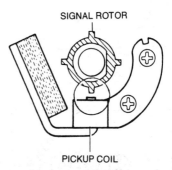

Rotor tooth-to-pickup coil alignment

5. Insert the distributor into the camshaft housing, aligning the center of the mounting flange with that of the bolt hole in the side of the housing.

6. Align the rotor tooth in the distributor with the pickup coil. Temporarily install the distributor pinch bolt.

7. Install the distributor cap, and install the oil filler cap.

8. Follow steps 9 and 10 of the above procedure, adjusting ignition timing as outlined in Chapter 2.

FIRING ORDER

To avoid confusion, replace the spark plug wires one at a time.

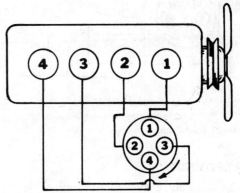

8R-C and 18R-C

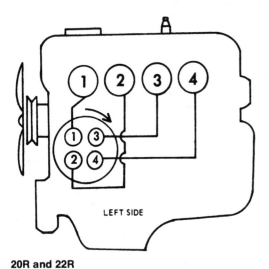

20R and 22R

4M-E and 5M-E

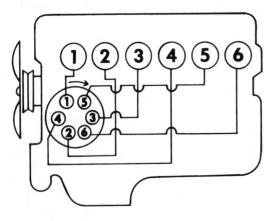

5M-GE Twin Cam

Alternator

All Celicas and Supras use a 12 volt alternator. Amperage ratings vary according to the year

and model. 1971–79 models utilize a separate, adjustable regulator, while 1980–83 have a transistorized, nonadjustable regulator, integral with the alternator.

ALTERNATOR PRECAUTIONS

To prevent damage to the alternator and regulator, the following precautionary measures must be taken when working with the electrical system.

1. Never reverse battery connections. Always check the battery polarity visually. This is to be done before any connections are made to ensure that all of the connections correspond to the battery ground polarity of the car.

2. Booster batteries must be connected properly. *Make sure the positive cable of the booster battery is connected to the positive terminal of the battery* which is getting the boost.

3. Disconnect the battery cables before using a fast charger; the charger has a tendency to force current through the diodes in the opposite direction for which they were designed.

4. Never use a fast charger as a booster for starting the car.

5. Never disconnect the voltage regulator while the engine is running, unless as noted for testing purposes.

6. Do not ground the alternator output terminal.

7. Do not operate the alternator on an open circuit with the field energized.

8. Do not attempt to polarize the alternator.

9. Disconnect the battery cables and remove the alternator before using an electric arc welder on the car.

10. Protect the alternator from excessive moisture. If the engine is to be steam cleaned, cover or remove the alternator.

REMOVAL AND INSTALLATION

1. Disconnect the negative battery cable.

2. Remove the alternator pivot bolt. Push the alternator in and remove the drive belt.

3. Pull back the rubber boots and disconnect the wiring from the back of the alternator.

4. Remove the alternator mounting bolt and then withdraw the alternator from its bracket.

5. Installation is in the reverse order of removal. After installation, adjust the belt tension as detailed in Chapter 1.

Regulator

All 1971–79 models are equipped with a separate, adjustable regulator. 1980 and later models are equipped with a transistorized reg-

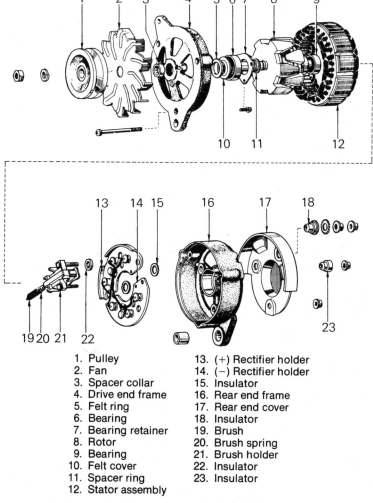

1. Pulley
2. Fan
3. Spacer collar
4. Drive end frame
5. Felt ring
6. Bearing
7. Bearing retainer
8. Rotor
9. Bearing
10. Felt cover
11. Spacer ring
12. Stator assembly
13. (+) Rectifier holder
14. (−) Rectifier holder
15. Insulator
16. Rear end frame
17. Rear end cover
18. Insulator
19. Brush
20. Brush spring
21. Brush holder
22. Insulator
23. Insulator

An exploded view of a typical alternator; 1971–79

ulator which is attached to the brush assembly on the side of the alternator housing. If faulty, it must be replaced; there are no adjustments which can be made.

REMOVAL AND INSTALLATION

1971–79

1. Disconnect the negative battery cable.
2. Disconnect the wiring harness connector at the back of the regulator.
3. Remove the regulator mounting bolts.
4. Remove the regulator.
5. Installation is in the reverse order of removal.

1980 and Later

1. Remove the alternator as detailed earlier.
2. Remove the two screws on the back of the alternator housing and then remove the regulator end cover.
3. Underneath the end cover there are three terminal screws, remove them.
4. Remove the two regulator mounting screws and remove the regulator.
5. Using a small screwdriver, pry out the plastic housing and the rubber seal around the regulator terminals.
6. Installation is in the reverse order of removal.

VOLTAGE ADJUSTMENT 1971–79

1. Connect a voltmeter up to the battery terminals. Negative (black) lead to the negative (−) terminal; positive (red) lead to positive (+) terminal.
2. Start the engine and gradually increase its speed to about 1,500 rpm.
3. At this speed, the voltage reading should

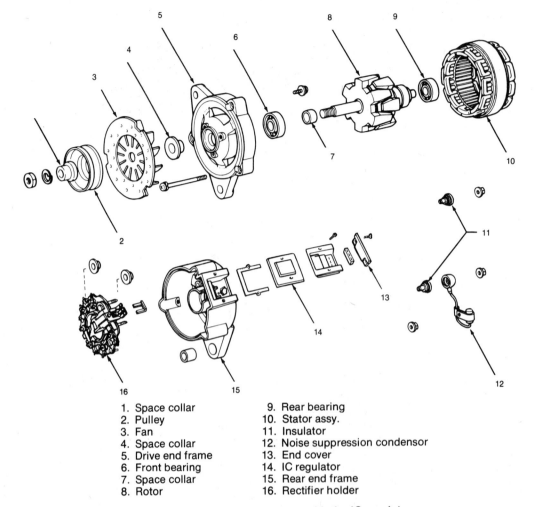

1. Space collar
2. Pulley
3. Fan
4. Space collar
5. Drive end frame
6. Front bearing
7. Space collar
8. Rotor
9. Rear bearing
10. Stator assy.
11. Insulator
12. Noise suppression condensor
13. End cover
14. IC regulator
15. Rear end frame
16. Rectifier holder

An exploded view of an alternator with the IC regulator

fall within the range specified in the "Alternator and Regulator Specifications" chart.

4. If the voltage does not fall within the specifications, remove the cover from the regulator and adjust it by bending the adjusting arm.

5. Repeat Steps 2 and 3 if the voltage cannot be brought to specification, proceed with the mechanical adjustments which follow.

MECHANICAL ADJUSTMENTS 1971–79

NOTE: *Perform the voltage adjustment outlined above, before beginning the mechanical adjustments.*

Field Relay

1. Remove the cover from the regulator assembly.

2. Use a feeler gauge to check the amount that the contact spring is deflected while the armature is being depressed.

3. If the measurement is not within speci-

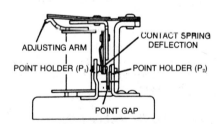

Field relay adjustments

fications (see the "Alternator and Regulator Specifications" chart), adjust the regulator by bending the point holder P_2 (see the illustration).

4. Check the point gap with a feeler gauge against the specifications in the chart.

5. Adjust the point gap, as required, by bending the point holder P_1 (see the illustration).

6. Clean off the points with emery cloth if they are dirty and wash them with solvent.

Alternator and Regulator Specifications

Engine Type	Alternator			Regulator						
					Field Relay			Regulator		
	Manufacturer	Output (amps)	Manufacturer	Contact Spring Deflection (in.)	Point Gap (in.)	Volts to Close	Air Gap (in.)	Point Gap (in.)	Volts
8R-C	Nippondenso	40	Nippondenso	0.008– 0.000	0.016– 0.047	4.5– 5.8	0.008	0.0010– 0.018	13.8– 14.8
18R-C	Nippondenso	45	Nippondenso	0.008– 0.024	0.016– 0.047	4.5– 5.8	0.012	0.0118– 0.0177	13.8– 14.8
20R 1975–79	Nippondenso	40 ①	Nippondenso	0.008– 0.024	0.016– 0.047	4.5– 5.8	0.012	0.0118– 0.0177	13.8– 14.8 ②
20R 1980	Nippondenso	40 ①	Nippondenso	③	③	③	③	③	14.0– 14.7
22R 1981	Nippondenso	40 ① ④	Nippondenso	③	③	③	③	③	14.0– 14.7
22R 1982–83	Nippondenso	55 ④	Nippondenso	③	③	③	③	③	13.8– 14.4
4M-E	Nippondenso	55 ④	Nippondenso	③	③	③	③	③	14.3– 14.9
5M-E	Nippondenso	60 ⑤	Nippondenso	③	③	③	③	③	14.3– 14.9
5M-GE	Nippondenso	65	Nippondenso	③	③	③	③	③	13.8– 14.4

① Optional 55 amp
② W/55 amp alternator — 14.0–14.7
③ Regulator not adjustable
④ Optional 60 amp
⑤ Optional 65 amp

Voltage Regulator

1. Use a feeler gauge to measure the air (armature) gap. If it is not within the specifications (see the "Alternator and Regulator Specifications" Chart), adjust it by bending the *low*-speed point holder (see the illustration).

2. Check the point gap with a feeler gauge. If it is not within specifications, adjust it by bending the *high*-speed point holder (see the illustration). Clean the points with emery cloth and wash them off with solvent.

3. Check the amount of contact spring deflection while depressing the armature. The specification should be the same as that for the contact spring on the field relay.

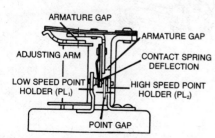

Voltage regulator adjustments

Starter

REMOVAL AND INSTALLATION

NOTE: *In the following text there are two types of starters covered. The direct drive type is used on the 8R-C, some 1972 18R-C, and some 20R engines. The other engines covered here including most of the 18R-Cs have the gear-reduction starters.*

1. Disconnect the negative battery cable.
2. Tag and disconnect all wiring leading from the starter.
3. Unscrew the two starter mounting bolts.
4. Remove the starter.
5. Installation is in the reverse order of removal.

STARTER OVERHAUL

Solenoid Replacement—Direct Drive Type

1. Remove the starter.
2. Unscrew the two solenoid switch (magnetic switch) retaining screws.
3. Remove the solenoid. In order to unhook the solenoid from the starter drive lever, lift it up at the same time that you are pulling it out of the starter housing.

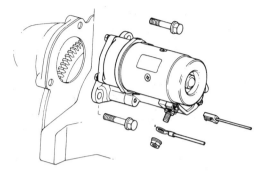

Starter mounting, all models similar

4. Installation is in the reverse order of removal. Make sure that the solenoid switch is properly engaged with the drive lever before tightening the mounting screws.

Brush Replacement—Direct Drive Type

1. Remove the starter.
2. Remove the solenoid (magnetic switch).
3. Remove the two end frame cap mounting bolts and remove the end frame cap.
4. Remove the O-ring and the lock plate from the armature shaft groove and then slide the shims off the shaft.
5. Unscrew the two long housing screws

(they are found at the front of the starter) and carefully pull off the end plate.

6. Using a screwdriver, separate the brushes and the brush springs and then remove the brushes from the brush holder.
7. Slide the brush holder off of the armature shaft.
8. Crush the old brushes off of the copper braid and file away any remaining solder.
9. Fit the new brushes to the braid and spread the braid slightly.

NOTE: *Use a soldering iron of at least 250 watts.*

10. Using radio-grade solder, solder the brush to the braid. *Grip the copper braid with flat pliers to prevent the solder from flowing down its length.*
11. File off any extra solder and then repeat the procedure for the remaining three brushes.
12. Installation is in the reverse order of removal.

NOTE: *When installing the brush holder, make sure that the brushes line up properly.*

Brush Replacement—Reduction Gear Type

1. Remove the starter.
2. Disconnect the lead from the solenoid (magnetic switch) terminal.

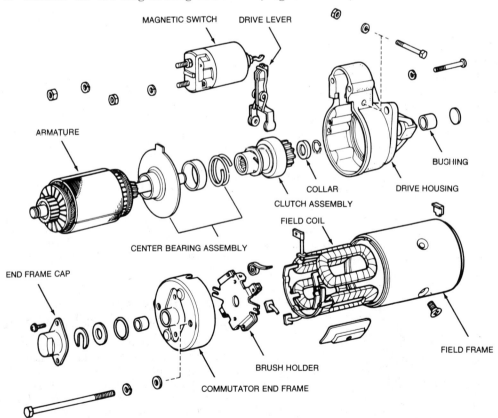

An exploded view of a direct drive starter

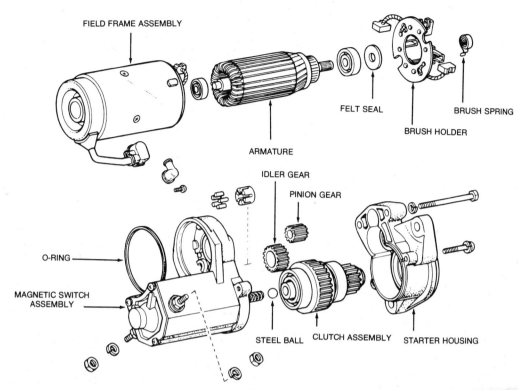

FIELD FRAME ASSEMBLY

FELT SEAL

BRUSH SPRING

BRUSH HOLDER

ARMATURE

IDLER GEAR

PINION GEAR

O-RING

MAGNETIC SWITCH
ASSEMBLY

STEEL BALL   CLUTCH ASSEMBLY   STARTER HOUSING

An exploded view of a reduction gear starter

3. Unscrew the two mounting bolts and remove the field frame assembly from the solenoid housing.

4. Remove the O-ring and the felt seal.

5. Unscrew the mounting screws and remove the starter housing from the solenoid housing.

6. Pull out the clutch assembly and then remove the pinion and idler gears.

7. Remove the steel ball from the clutch shaft hole.

8. Using a screwdriver, separate the brush and brush spring and remove the brush from the brush holder.

9. Install the four new brushes onto the brush holder using a screwdriver to hold the brush spring back.

NOTE: *Make sure that the positive lead wires are not grounded.*

10. To reassemble, apply a dab of grease to the steel ball and insert it into the clutch shaft hole. Reverse the disassembly procedure starting with Step 6. Apply grease to the idler gears before assembly, and make sure the gears mesh during assembly.

Starter Drive Replacement—Direct Drive Type

1. Perform Steps 1–7 of the "Brush Replacement—Direct Drive Type" procedure.

MAGNET

Remove the steel ball from the clutch shaft hole with a magnet; when reinstalling, dab the ball with grease

2. Pull the field frame away from the drive housing and remove it.

3. Remove the drive lever pivot bolt from the drive housing.

4. Pull the armature from the drive housing.

5. Take a 14 mm socket and slide it over the armature shaft until it rests on the stop collar.

6. Tap the stop collar down with a hammer.

7. Pry off the exposed stop ring and then remove the stop collar from the shaft.

8. Remove the starter drive clutch assembly.

9. Installation is in the reverse order of removal.

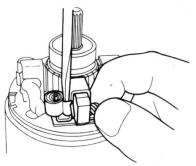

Separate the starter brush and brush spring with a screwdriver

Battery

Refer to Chapter 1 for details on battery maintenance.

REMOVAL AND INSTALLATION

1. Disconnect the negative cable from the terminal, then disconnect the positive cable. Special pullers are available to remove the clamps.

NOTE: *To avoid sparks, always disconnect the negative cable first and reconnect it last.*

2. Unscrew and remove the battery hold-down clamp.

3. Remove the battery, being careful not to spill any of the acid.

NOTE: *Spilled acid can be neutralized with a baking soda and water solution. If you somehow get acid into your eyes, flush it out with lots of clean water and get to a doctor as quickly as possible.*

4. Clean the battery posts thoroughly before reinstalling or when installing a new one.

5. Clean the cable clamps using the special tools or a wire brush, both inside and out.

6. Install the battery and the hold-down clamp. Connect the positive and then the negative cable. *Do not hammer them into place.* The terminals should be coated with grease to prevent corrosion.

CAUTION: *Make absolutely sure that the battery is connected properly before you turn on the ignition switch. Reversed polarity can burn out your alternator and regulator in a matter of seconds.*

ENGINE MECHANICAL

Checking Engine Compression

A noticeable lack of engine power, excessive oil consumption and/or poor fuel mileage measured over an extended period are all indicators of internal engine wear. Worn piston rings, scored and worn cylinder bores, blown head gaskets, sticking or burnt valves and worn valve seats are all possible culprits here. A check of each cylinder's compression will help you locate the problems.

As mentioned in the "Tools and Equipment" section of Chapter 1, a screw-in compression gauge is more accurate than the type you simply hold against the spark plug hole, although it takes slightly longer to use (it's worth it). To check compression:

1. Warm the engine up to operating temperature.

2. Remove all four or all six spark plugs.

3. Disconnect the high tension wire from the ignition coil.

4. Screw the compression gauge into the No. 1 spark plug hole until the fitting is snug. *Be very careful not to crossthread the hole, as the head is aluminum.*

5. Fully open the throttle either by operating the carburetor throttle linkage by hand, or on fuel injected cars having an assistant "floor" the accelerator pedal.

6. Ask the assistant to crank the engine a few times using the ignition switch.

7. Record the highest reading on the gauge, and compare it to the compression specifications in the "Tune-Up Specifications" chart in this chapter. The specs listed are maximum, and a cylinder is usually acceptable if its

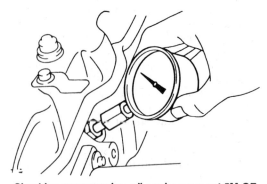

Checking compression, all engines except 5M-GE

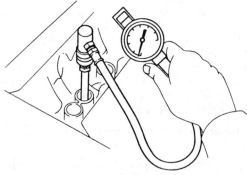

An adaptor may be needed to check compression on the 5M-GE six

compression is within about 20 pounds of maximum.

8. Repeat the procedure for the remaining cylinders, recording each cylinder's compression. The difference between each cylinder should be no more than 14 pounds. If a cylinder is unusually low, pour a tablespoon of clean engine oil into the cylinder through the spark plug hole and repeat the compression test. If the compression comes up after adding the oil, it appears that that cylinder's piston rings or bore are damaged or worn. If the pressure remains low, the valves may not be seating properly (a valve job is needed) or the head gasket may be blown near that cylinder.

Design

The 8R-C/18R-C family of four cylinder engines was used in the Celica from 1971–74.

The engine is an overhead cam design with an aluminum head and a cast iron cylinder block. In 1971 it had a displacement of 1858cc (8R-C); at the beginning of 1972 it was enlarged to 1980cc (18R-C).

In 1975, a new engine, the 20R replaced the 18R-C. About the only similarity between these two engines is the cylinder block; the head and front cover are completely different. The 20R has a single overhead camshaft, cross-flow heads (intake valves on one side of the head, exhausts on the other) and hemispherical combustion chambers. A new gear-type oil pump is used, and is similar in design to the one used on cars with an automatic transmission.

Because it was designed as an emission control engine, most of the EGR and air injection passages on the 20R are cast right into the head.

In 1981 the size was increased from 2189cc to 2367cc and will be known as the 22R. Other than the larger size and a single-row cam chain, the 22R is still basically the same as the 20R. A fuel-injection option was added for 1983.

The Supra has been equipped with three different engines since the car's introduction in 1979. The 1979 and 1980 powerplant was the 4M-E, a fuel-injected inline six based on the 20R four cylinder. In 1981, the 2563cc 4M-E was enlarged to 2759cc, becoming the 5M-

Battery and Starter Specifications

All cars use 12 volt, negative ground electrical systems

Year	Model	Battery Amp Hour Capacity	Starter							Brush Spring Tension (oz)	Min. Brush Length (in.)
			Lock Test			No Load Test					
			Amps	Volts	Torque (ft. lbs.)	Amps	Volts	RPM			
1971	8R-C	35–38 ①	550	7.7	10	45	11	6,000	2.3–3.0	0.47
1972–74	18R-C	50 ②	600	7.0	13	50	11	5,000	2.76–3.42	0.47
1975–77	20R ③	50 ④	Not Recommended			50	11	5,000	NA	0.47
1975–77	20R ⑤	50 ④	Not Recommended			80	11.5	3,500	NA	0.30
1978–80	20R ③	150 ⑥	Not Recommended			50	11	5,000	NA	0.4
1978–80	20R ⑤	150 ⑥	Not Recommended			90	11.5	3,500	NA	0.4
1981–83	22R	⑧	Not Recommended			90	11.5	3,500	NA	0.39 ⑦
1983	22R-E		Not Recommended			90	11.5	3,500	NA	0.57
1979–80	4M-E ③	⑧	Not Recommended			50	11	5,000	NA	0.39
1979–80	4M-E ⑤	⑧	Not Recommended			90	11.5	3,500	NA	0.39
1981	5M-E	⑧	Not Recommended			90	11.5	3,500	NA	0.39
1982–83	5M-GE		Not Recommended			90	11.5	3,500	NA	0.551

NA—Not available
① 40 or 60 available as an option
② 60 available as an option
③ Models equipped with a direct drive starter
④ 60 for all models W/AC; 60 also available as an option
⑤ Models equipped with a reduction gear starter
⑥ Amps at 9.0 volts
⑦ 0.571 on 1982 models
⑧ Replace w/battery of at least same capacity; consult application chart at battery dealer

General Engine Specifications

Year	Engine Type	Engine Displacement Cu. in. (cc)	Carburetor Type	Horsepower (@ rpm) ▲	Torque @ rpm (ft. lbs.) ▲	Bore x Stroke (in.)	Compression Ratio	Oil Pressure @ rpm (psi)
1971	8R-C	113.4 (1858)	2-bbl	108 @ 5500	113 @ 3800	3.38 x 3.15	9.0 : 1	56.9 @ 2500
1972–74	18R-C	123.0 (1980)	2-bbl	97 @ 5500	106 @ 3600	3.48 x 3.15	8.5 : 1	54.0 @ 2500
1975–78	20R	133.6 (2189)	2-bbl	96 @ ① 4800	120 @ ② 2800	3.48 x 3.50	8.4 : 1	64.0 @ 2500
1979–80	20R	133.6 (2189)	2-bbl	90 @ 4800	122 @ 2400	3.48 x 3.50	8.4 : 1	64.0 @ 2500
1981–83	22R	144.4 (2367)	2-bbl	96 @ 4800	129 @ 2800	3.62 x 3.50	9.0 : 1	64.0 @ ③ 2500
1983	22R-E	144.4 (2367)	EFI	105 @ 4800	137 @ 2800	3.62 x 3.50	9.0 : 1	71.1 @ 3000
1979–80	4M-E	156.4 (2563)	EFI	110 @ 4800	136 @ 2400	3.15 x 3.35	8.5 : 1	71–85 @ 2500
1981	5M-E	168.4 (2759)	EFI	116 @ 4800	145 @ 3600	3.27 x 3.35	8.8 : 1	71–85 @ 2500
1982	5M-GE	168.4 (2759)	EFI	145 @ 5200	155 @ 4400	3.27 x 3.35	8.8 : 1	71.1 @ 3000
1983	5M-GE	168.4 (2759)	EFI	150 @ 5200	159 @ 4400	3.27 x 3.35	8.8 : 1	71.1 @ 3000

▲ Horsepower and torque rating given in SAE net figures
EFI—Electronic fuel injection
① 1978 California—90 @ 4800
② 1978— 122 @ 2400
③ 1982—71.1 @ 3000

E. A new inline six was made standard in the Supra for 1982, and continues for 1983. The 5M-GE retains the 5M-E's bore and stroke (for the same 2759cc displacement), and most of its predecessor's lower end, but the new motor has a double-overhead cam cylinder head for much better high-rpm potential. The camshafts are driven by a cogged rubber belt instead of the camchain on the 4M-E and 5M-E; the 5M-GE is also fuel injected.

Engine Removal and Installation

All Four Cylinder Engines Except 22R-E

1. Drain the radiator, cooling system, transmission, and engine oil.

2. Disconnect the battery-to-starter cable at the positive battery terminal, after first disconnecting the negative cable.

3. Scribe marks on the hood and its hinges to aid in alignment during installation.

4. Remove the hood supports from the body. Remove the hood.

NOTE: *Do not remove the supports from the hood.*

5. Remove the headlight bezel and the radiator grille.

6. Remove the radiator shroud, the hood lock base and the base support. Remove the coupling fan with the fan.

7. Detach both the upper and lower hoses from the radiator. On cars with automatic transmissions, disconnect and plug the lines from the oil cooler. Remove the radiator.

8. Unfasten the clamps and remove the heater and by-pass hoses from the engine. Remove the heater control cable from the water valve. If the car has power steering, remove the pump with bracket.

9. Remove the wiring from the coolant temperature and oil pressure sending units.

10. Remove the air cleaner from its bracket, complete with its attendant hoses.

11. Unfasten the accelerator torque rod from the carburetor. On models equipped with automatic transmissions, remove the transmission linkage as well.

12. Remove the emission control system hoses and wiring including the oxygen sensor wire (if equipped), as necessary. (Mark them to aid in installation.)

13. Remove the clutch hydraulic line support bracket.

14. Unfasten the high-tension and primary wires from the coil.

Valve Specifications

Year	Engine Type	Seat Angle (deg)	Face Angle (deg)	Spring Test Pressure (lbs.)		Spring Installed Height (in.)		Stem to Guide Clearance (in.) ▲		Stem Diameter (in.)	
				Inner	Outer	Inner	Outer	Intake	Exhaust	Intake	Exhaust
1971	8R-C	45	45	15.2	50.6	1.480	1.640	0.0010–0.0022	0.0014–0.0030	0.3140	0.3136
1972–74	18R-C	45	45	15.2	50.6	1.480	1.640	0.0010–0.0022	0.0014–0.0030	0.3140	0.3136
1975–77	20R	45	44.5	—	60.0	—	1.594	0.0006–0.0024	0.0012–0.0026	0.3141	0.3140
1978–80	20R	45	44.5	—	55.1	—	1.594	0.0008–0.0024	0.0012–0.0026	0.3138–0.3146	0.3136–0.3142
1981–83	22R 22R-E	45	44.5	—	55.1	—	1.594	0.0008–0.0024	0.0012–0.0028	0.3188–0.3145	0.3136–0.3142
1979–80	4M-E	45	44.5	15.6	41.6	1.492	1.630	0.0010–0.0024	0.0014–0.0028	0.3138–0.3144	0.3134–0.3140
1981	5M-E	45	44.5	14.1–17.2	37.3 41.4	1.492	1.630	0.0010–0.0024	0.0014–0.0028	0.3138–0.3144	0.3134–0.3140
1982–83	5M-GE	45	45.5	—	①	—	②	0.0010–0.0024	0.0012–0.0026	0.3138–0.3144	0.3136–0.3142

▲ Valve guides are removable
① Intake springs 76.5–84.4 lbs.; exhaust 73.4–80.9 lbs.
② Intake 1.575 in.; exhaust 1.693 in.

Crankshaft and Connecting Rod Specifications
(All measurements are given in inches)

Year	Engine Type	Crankshaft				Connecting Rod		
		Main Brg Journal Dia	Main Brg Oil Clearance	Shaft End-Play	Thrust on No.	Journal Diameter	Oil Clearance	Side Clearance
1971	8R-C	2.3613– 2.3622	0.0008– 0.0020	0.0020– 0.0100	3	2.0857– 2.0866	0.0008– 0.0020	0.0043– 0.0097
1972–74	18R-C	2.3613– 2.3622	0.0008– 0.0020	0.0008– 0.0080	3	2.0857– 2.0866	0.0010– 0.0021	0.0060– 0.0102
1975–80	20R	2.3614– 2.3622	0.0010– 0.0022	0.0008–① 0.0079	3	2.0862– 2.0866	0.0010– 0.0022	0.0063– 0.0100
1981–83	22R 22R-E	2.3614– 2.3622	0.0006– 0.0020	0.0008– 0.0087	3	2.0862– 2.0866	0.0010– 0.0022	0.0063– 0.0102
1979–80	4M-E	2.3617– 2.3627	0.0013– 0.0023	0.0020– 0.0098	4	2.0463– 2.0472	0.0008– 0.0021	0.0063– 0.0117
1981	5M-E	2.3617– 2.3627	0.0013– 0.0023	0.0020– 0.0098	4	2.0463– 2.0472	0.0008– 0.0021	0.0063– 0.0117
1982–83	5M-GE	2.3617– 2.3627	0.0013– 0.0023	0.0020– 0.0098	4	2.0463– 2.0472	0.0008– 0.0021	0.0063– 0.0117

① 1978–80—0.0010–0.0080

Piston and Ring Specifications
(All measurements in inches)

Year	Engine Type	Piston Clearance 68°F	Ring Gap			Ring Side Clearance		
			Top Compression	Bottom Compression	Oil Control	Top Compression	Bottom Compression	Oil Control
1971	8R-C	0.0010– 0.0020	0.004– 0.012	0.004– 0.012	0.004– 0.012	0.0012– 0.0028	0.0012– 0.0028	0.0008– 0.0028
1972–74	18R-C	0.0020– 0.0030	0.004– 0.012	0.004– 0.012	0.004– 0.012	0.0012– 0.0028	0.0012– 0.0028	0.008– 0.0028
1975–80	20R	0.0012– 0.0020	0.004– 0.012	0.004– 0.012	—	0.008	0.008	—
1981–83	22R	0.0020– 0.0028	0.0094– 0.0142	0.0071– 0.0154	—	0.008	0.008	—
1979–80	4M-E	0.0020– 0.0028	0.0039– 0.0110	0.0039– 0.0110	0.0079– 0.0200	0.0012– 0.0028	0.0008– 0.0024	—
1981	5M-E	0.0020– 0.0028	0.0039– 0.0110	0.0039– 0.0110	0.0079– 0.0200	0.0012– 0.0028	0.0008– 0.0024	—
1982–83	5M-GE	0.0020– 0.0028	0.0083– 0.0146	0.0067– 0.0209	0.0079– 0.0276	0.0012– 0.0028	0.0008– 0.0024	—

Camshaft Specifications
(All measurements in inches)

Year	Engine	Journal Diameter							Bearing Clearance	Lobe Lift		Camshaft End Play
		1	2	3	4	5	6	7		Intake	Exhaust	
1971	8R-C	1.3768–1.3778	1.3768–1.3778	1.3768–1.3778	1.3768–1.3778	—	—	—	0.001–0.002	0.4	0.4	0.0017–0.0066
1972–74	18R-C	1.3773–1.3782	1.3773–1.3782	1.3773–1.3782	1.3773–1.3782	—	—	—	0.00047–0.00142	0.3126–0.3205	0.3150–0.3228	0.0016–0.0067
1975–80	20R	1.2984–1.2992	1.2984–1.2992	1.2984–1.2992	1.2984–1.2992	—	—	—	0.0004–0.0020	—	—	0.0031–0.0071
1981–83	22R	1.2984–1.2992	1.2984–1.2982	1.2984–1.2992	1.2984–1.2992	—	—	—	0.0004–0.0020	—	—	0.0031–0.0071
1979–80	4M-E	1.3378–1.3384	1.3378–1.3384	1.3378–1.3384	1.3378–1.3384	1.3378–1.3384	1.3378–1.3384	1.3378–1.3384	0.0007–0.0022	—	—	0.003–0.007
1981	5M-E	1.3378–1.3384	1.3378–1.3384	1.3378–1.3384	1.3378–1.3384	1.3378–1.3384	1.3378–1.3384	1.3378–1.3384	0.0007–0.0022	—	—	0.0031–0.0071
1982–83	5M-GE	1.4944–1.4951	1.6913–1.6919	1.7110–1.7116	1.7307–1.7313	1.7504–1.7510	1.7700–1.7707	1.7897–1.7904	0.0010–0.0026	—	—	0.0020–0.0098

—Not Available

Torque Specifications
(All readings in ft. lbs.)

Year	Engine Type	Cylinder Head Bolts	Rod Bearing Bolts	Main Bearing Bolts	Crankshaft Pulley Bolt	Flywheel to Crankshaft Bolts	Manifold	
							Intake	Exhaust
1971	8R-C	75.0–85.0	42.0–48.0	72.0–80.0	43.0–51.0	42.0–58.0	20.0–25.0①	
1972–74	18R-C	72.0–82.0	39.0–48.0	69.0–83.0	43.0–51.0	51.0–58.0	30.0–35.0①	
1975–80	20R	52.0–64.0	39.0–48.0	69.0–83.0	80.0–② 94.0	62.0–③ 68.0	11.0–④ 15.0	29.0–36.0
1981–83	22R	53.0–63.0	40.0–47.0	69.0–83.0	102.0–130.0	73.0–86.0	13.0–19.0	29.0–36.0
1979–80	4M-E	55.0–61.0	31.0–34.0	72.0–78.0	98.0–119.0	51.0–57.0	10.0–15.0	13.0–16.0
1981	5M-E	55–61.0	31.0–34.0	72.0–78.0	98.0–119.0	51.0–57.0	10.0–15.0	13.0–16.0
1982–83	5M-GE	55–62.0	31.0–35.0	71.0–79.0	97.0–119.0	50.0–58.0	15.0–17.0	25.0–33.0

① Intake and exhaust manifolds are combined
② 1978–80— 102– 130
③ 1978–79—73–79; 1980—73–86
④ 1980—13–19

15. Mark the spark plug cables and remove them from the distributor.

16. Detach the right-hand front engine mount. Disconnect the engine shock absorber at its upper mounting.

17. Remove the fuel line at the pump (filter on 1975–76 models with electric pumps).

18. Detach the downpipe from the exhaust manifold.

19. Detach the left-hand front engine mount. Disconnect the engine shock absorber from its lower mounting.

20. Disconnect all of the wiring harness multiconnectors.

Perform the following steps on 1971–72 models with manual transmissions:

21. Remove the center console if so equipped.

22. Remove the shift lever boot(s).

23. Unfasten the four shift lever cap retaining screws. Remove the cap and withdraw the shift lever assembly.

Perform the following steps on models equipped with automatic transmissions:

24. Remove the transmission selector linkage; disconnect the control rod from transmission.

25. Disconnect the neutral safety switch wiring connector.

Perform the following steps on all models:

26. Raise the rear of the vehicle with jacks and support it on jackstands.

CAUTION: *Be sure that the vehicle is securely supported.*

27. Remove the retaining screws and re-move the parking brake equalizer support bracket. Disconnect the cable which runs between the lever and the equalizer.

28. Remove the speedometer cable from the transmission. Disconnect the back-up light wiring.

29. Detach the driveshaft from the rear of the transmission.

NOTE: *If oil runs out of the transmission, an old U-joint yoke sleeve makes an excellent plug. If a sleeve is not available, plug with a rag.*

30. Detach the clutch release cylinder assembly, complete with hydraulic lines. Do not disconnect the lines.

31. Unbolt the rear support member mounting insulators.

32. Support the transmission and detach the rear support member retaining bolts. With-draw the support member from under the car.

33. Install lifting hooks on the engine lifting brackets. Attach a suitable hoist to the engine.

34. Remove the jack from under the transmission.

35. Raise the engine and move it toward the front of the car. Use care to avoid damaging the components which remain on the car.

36. Support the engine on a workstand.

Installation of the engine is the reverse order of removal. Refer to the appropriate chapters for transmission and carburetor adjustments. Install the hood and adjust it as outlined in Chapter 10. Replenish the engine oil, coolant, and transmission oil to the proper levels, as outlined in Chapter 1.

22R-E Fuel Injected Four

1. Follow steps 1 through 10 of the above procedure for carbureted four cylinder engines.

2. Disconnect the automatic transmission actuator cable, accelerator cable and throttle cable from the bracket on the side of the EFI intake chamber.

3. Tag and disconnect the PCV hoses, the brake booster hose, the actuator hose (if equipped with cruise control), the air control valve hose and the air control valve.

4. Remove the EGR vacuum modulator and bracket after tagging and disconnecting the EGR modulator hoses.

5. Tag and disconnect the remaining emission control hoses as necessary, including the air valve hoses from the intake chamber and throttle body, the water by-pass hoses from the throttle body, the air control valve hose to the actuator and the pressure regulator hose from the intake chamber.

6. Tag and disconnect the cold start injector pipe and cold start injector.

7. Tag and disconnect the throttle position sensor wire and the air valve wire.

8. Remove the bolt holding the EGR valve to the intake chamber. Disconnect the chamber from the stay, then remove the chamber from the intake manifold with the throttle body attached.

9. Tag and disconnect the water temperature sender, overdrive (with A/T) thermo switch, start injection time, temperature sensor and injection wires.

10. Remove the two set bolts from the top and bottom of the steering universal, and remove the sliding yoke.

11. Disconnect the tie rod ends (see Chapter 8). Disconnect the pressure line mounting bolts from the front crossmember.

12. Without disconnecting the oil pipe, remove the mounting bolts to the rack-and-pinion assembly and carefully suspend it from the front crossmember without stretching the fluid hoses.

13. Follow steps 13 through 36 of the above procedure for carbureted four cylinder engines.

4M/E and 5M-E Six Cylinder Engines

1. Disconnect the battery cables and remove the battery.

2. Scribe aligning marks on the hood and hinges to aid in their assembly. Remove the hood.

3. Remove the fan shroud and drain the cooling system.

4. Disconnect both the upper and lower radiator hoses. Unfasten the oil lines from the oil cooler on cars with automatic transmissions.

5. Detach the hose which runs to the thermal expansion tank, at the tank. Remove the expansion tank from its mounting bracket.

6. Remove the radiator.

7. Disconnect the heater and by-pass hoses from the engine.

8. Disconnect the oil pressure light sender wiring, the alternator multiconnector, and the back-up light switch wiring.

9. Unfasten the power brake unit vacuum lines.

10. Disconnect the engine oil cooler hoses at the oil filter, if so equipped.

Power steering pump removal

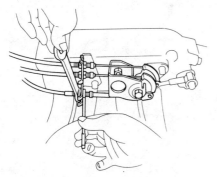

Disconnecting accelerator linkage on the fuel injected engines

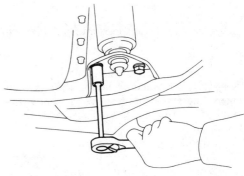

Disconnecting the engine shock absorber

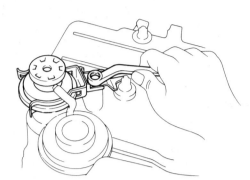

Removing the EGR vacuum module bracket

11. Disconnect the power steering fluid cooler hose, if so equipped.

12. Remove the air cleaner assembly from its bracket, complete with hoses.

13. Detach the emission control system wires and hoses, as required. Mark them first.

14. Unfasten the distributor primary wire and the high-tension wire from the coil.

15. Disconnect the wiring from the starter and temperature gauge sender.

16. Remove the fuel line from the fuel filter.

17. Disconnect the heater control cable from the water valve. Unfasten the heater control vacuum hose.

18. Tag and disconnect any remaining hoses, lines or wires which may still be attached to the engine.

19. Detach the clutch hydraulic line from its master cylinder connections (manual transmission only). Install a cap on the master cylinder fitting to keep the hydraulic fluid from running out.

20. Detach the pressure-feed lines from the steering gear housing on models equipped with power steering.

21. Raise both the front and the rear of the car with jacks. Support the car with jackstands.

CAUTION: *Be sure that the car is securely supported.*

22. Detach the exhaust pipe from the downpipe and remove the exhaust pipe hangers.

23. Disconnect the speedometer cable from the right-side of the transmission.

24. On models with a manual transmission:

a. Remove the center console securing screws, the gearshift knob, the gearshift boot, and then unfasten the console wiring multiconnector. Lift the console over the gearshift lever;

b. Remove the four screws which attach the shift lever retainer to the shift tower and withdraw the shift lever assembly.

25. On models equipped with an automatic

transmission, unfasten the connecting rod swivel nut and detach the control rod from the gear selector lever.

26. Disconnect the parking brake lever rod, return spring, intermediate rod, and the cable from the equalizer.

27. Disconnect the driveshaft from the end of the transmission.

NOTE: *If oil runs out of the transmission, an old U-joint yoke makes a good plug, or secure a plastic bag over the opening with rubber bands.*

28. Remove the left-hand gravel shield and then the front engine mounts.

29. Support the transmission with a jack.

30. Remove the rear engine mounts and the rear crossmember.

31. Attach a hoist to the engine and lift it up and forward, so that it clears the car.

Installation is in the reverse order of removal. Adjust the transmission and carburetor linkages, as detailed in the appropriate chapters. Bleed the clutch as outlined in Chapter 6. Install the hood and adjust it. (See Chapter 10.) Replenish the fluid levels as outlined in Chapter 1.

5M-GE Twin Cam Six

1. Follow steps 1 through 6 of the above procedure for the other two six cylinder engines.

2. Remove the air cleaner assembly, including the air flow meter and air intake connector pipe.

3. On cars equipped with automatic transmissions, remove the throttle cable bracket from the cylinder head. On all models, remove the accelerator and actuator cable bracket from the cylinder head.

4. Tag and disconnect the cylinder head ground cable, the oxygen sensor wire, oil pressure sending unit and alternator wires, the high tension coil wire, the water temperature sending unit and thermo switch (A/T) wires, and the starter wires.

5. Tag and disconnect the ECT connec-

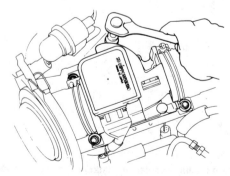

Removing the air flow meter

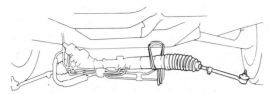

The steering rack assembly must be dropped on 1982 and later cars

tors and the solenoid resistor wire connector.

6. Tag and disconnect the brake booster vacuum hose from the air intake chamber, along with the EGR valve vacuum hose and the actuator vacuum hose from the air intake chamber (if equipped with cruise control).

7. Disconnect the heater and by-pass hoses from the engine.

8. Remove the glove box, and remove the ECU computer module. Disconnect the three connectors, and pull out the EFI (fuel injection) wiring harness from the engine compartment side of the firewall.

9. Remove the four shroud and four fluid coupling screws, and the shroud and coupling as a unit.

10. Remove the engine undercover protector.

11. Disconnect the coolant reservoir hose and remove the radiator. Remove the coolant expansion tank.

12. Remove the A/C compressor drive belt, and remove the compressor mounting bolts. Without disconnecting the refrigerant hoses, lay the compressor to one side and secure it.

CAUTION: *The A/C system is charged with the the refrigerant R-12, which is dangerous when released. DO NOT disconnect the A/C hoses when removing the engine; if the hoses have to be disconnected at any time, the work should be done by a trained air conditioning mechanic.*

13. Disconnect the power steering pump drive belt and remove the pump stay. Unbolt the pump and lay it aside without disconnecting the fluid hoses.

14. Remove the engine mounting bolts from each side of the engine. Remove the engine ground cable.

15. On manual transmission cars, remove the shift lever from inside the car.

16. Jack up the car and safely support it with jackstands. Drain the engine oil.

17. Disconnect the exhaust pipe from the exhaust manifold. Remove the exhaust pipe clamp from the transmission housing.

18. On manual transmission cars, remove the clutch slave cylinder.

19. Disconnect the speedometer cable at the transmission.

20. On automatic transmission cars, disconnect the shift linkage from the shift lever. On manual transmission cars, disconnect the wire from the back-up light switch.

21. Remove the stiffener plate from the ground cable.

22. Disconnect the fuel line from the fuel filter and the return hose from the fuel hose support. Be sure to catch any leaking fuel. Plug the fuel line.

23. Follow steps 10 through 12 of the 22R-E engine removal procedure.

24. Remove the intermediate shaft from the driveshaft.

25. Position a hydraulic jack under the transmission, with a wooden block between the two to prevent damage to the transmission case. Place a wooden block between the cowl panel and cylinder head rear end to prevent damage to the heater hoses.

26. Unbolt the engine rear support member from the frame, along with the ground cable.

27. Make sure all wiring is disconnected (and tagged for later assembly), all hoses disconnected, and everything clear of the engine and transmission. Attach an engine lift hoist chain to the lift brackets on the engine, and carefully lift the engine and transmission up and out of the car. *It is very helpful to have two or three helpers on this job.* Place the engine on a work stand, and remove the transmission at this time.

Installation is the reverse of removal.

Camshaft Cover
REMOVAL AND INSTALLATION
All Engines Except 5M-GE

1. Remove the air cleaner assembly. On the 4M-E/5M-E series, disconnect and remove the air intake hose.

2. Disconnect the PCV hose(s) from the cam cover.

3. Remove the acorn nuts and washers. Lift the cam cover off the cylinder head. Cover the oil return hole in the head to prevent dirt or objects from falling in. Remove the cam cover gasket.

4. To install, replace the valve cover gasket if it shows any signs of damage, breaks or cracking. Tighten the acorn nuts evenly, reconnect the PCV hose and install the air cleaner assembly.

5M-GE

1. Disconnect the air intake hose by loosening the clamps at either end. Remove the hose.

2. Tag and disconnect all PCV and other hoses which obstruct cam cover removal.

3. Remove the Phillips screws and lift off the cam covers and their gaskets.

4. Installation is the reverse of removal. Be sure to replace the cover gaskets if they are cracked or broken.

Valve Rocker Shafts

REMOVAL AND INSTALLATION

Valve rocker shaft removal and installation is given as part of the various "Cylinder Head Removal and Installation" procedures.

Perform only the steps of the appropriate "Cylinder Head Removal and Installation" procedures necessary to remove and install the rocker shafts. All rocker shaft assemblies may require a pry bar to remove them from the head.

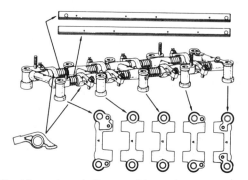

Double rocker shaft assembly; rocker arms must be assembled in their original positions

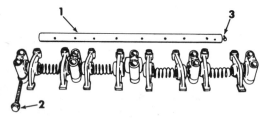

Single rocker shaft (8R-C, 18R) assembly. Note support attaching bolts (#2) and shaft retaining screw (#3)

Rocker Arms

REMOVAL AND INSTALLATION

All Engines Except 5M-GE

1. Remove the rocker shaft assemblies.

2. On the single rocker shaft engines (8R-C, 18R), remove the rocker shaft support attaching bolts (#2 in illustration)

8R-C and 18R-C rocker shaft bolt removal sequence

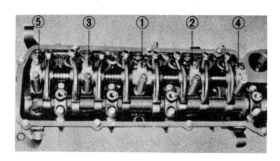

8R-C and 18R-C valve rocker support tightening sequence

rocker shaft retaining screw (#3 in illustration). Slide the tension springs, rocker arms and rocker supports off of the shafts. *Make sure you keep the parts in order as they were removed from the shaft—this is very important.*

3. On the double rocker shaft engines, remove the rocker shaft assemblies. Remove the three retaining screws and slide the rocker supports, springs and rocker arms off of the shafts. Keep all parts in order; *the shafts must be reassembled in the correct order.*

4. Assembly is in the opposite order of removal; make sure all components are reassembled into their original positions. Adjust the valves.

INSPECTION

The oil clearance between the rocker arm and shaft is measured in two steps. Measure the outside diameter of the rocker shaft with a micrometer. Measure the inside diameter of the rocker arms with a dial indicator. The difference between the rocker arm inner diameter and the shaft outer diameter is the oil clearance. Clearance specs are as follows:

- 8R-C—0.0012–0.015 in.
- 18R—0.00067–0.00201 in.
- 20R—0.0004–0.0020 in.
- 22R/22R-E—0.0004–0.0020 in.
- 4M-E/5M-E—0.0005–0.0013 in.

If specs are not within these ranges, replace

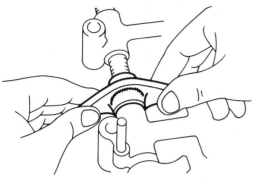

Check rocker arm-to-shaft wear by wiggling arm laterally on the shaft; little or no movement should be felt

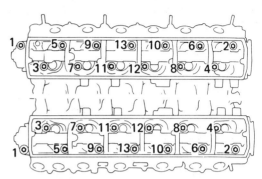

5M-GE camshaft housing bolt removal sequence. Loosen bolts gradually on three passes

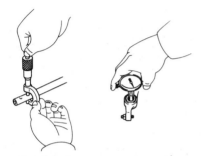

Mike up the shaft diameter and check rocker arm inner diameter; difference is the oil clearance

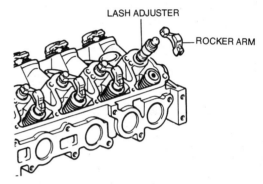

Removing lash adjuster and rocker arm, 5M-GE

Face of cam followers should be smooth and shiny

either the rocker shaft or rocker arm. Clearance can also be checked by moving the rocker arm laterally on the shaft when assembled. *There should be little or no movement.*

While disassembled, check the cam follower end (the flat end that contacts the camshaft) of the rocker arm for excess wear. The surface should be smooth and shiny. If excess wear is evident, check also the lobe of the camshaft—it may also be worn.

Reassemble the rocker shaft assemblies in the exact opposite order of removal. Accelerated camshaft wear and/or sloppy valve action will result if rocker arms are mixed and end up operating against the wrong cam lobes.

5M-GE Twin Cam Six

1. Remove the two camshaft covers.
2. Remove the timing gears and timing belt assembly.

3. Following the sequence shown, loosen the camshaft housing nuts and bolts in two passes. Remove the housings (with camshafts) from the cylinder head.

4. Remove the rocker arms, one at a time, from the head. As you remove each rocker, wipe it off and either tag it or mark it as to its proper location. *It is critical that each rocker be re-installed in its correct location.*

5. Remove each lash adjuster from the head (see "Lash Adjusters Inspection" below first), one at a time, and either *mark or tag each one* for correct installation later.

INSPECTION

Inspect the three contact areas of each rocker arm for pitting and/or extreme or unusual wear: the cup end, which works against the ball of the lash adjuster; the valve stem end; and the pad on top of the rocker which works against the lobe of the camshaft. Replace the rocker arm(s) if there is evidence of such wear.

Hydraulic Lash Adjusters
INSPECTION

The hydraulic valve lash adjusters used on the twin cam six must be bled and their leak down rate checked before they are reassembled into the motor. Both of these procedures require special service equipment and should be performed by a professional mechanic at a quality machine shop. If you have the head disassembled for a valve job, cam replacement, etc., you will probably be taking the head to a machine shop anyway; the adjusters can be left in their recesses, removed and checked while the head is in the shop.

INSTALLATION

1. Remove and inspect the oil pressure regulator before reassembly (see "Oil Pressure Regulator" below).

2. Make sure that the match hole on each No. 2 cam journal is aligned with the hole on the respective camshafts.

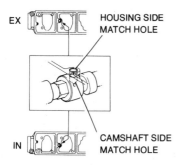

Before installing cam housings, align the match hole on each No. 2 cam journal with the hole in the housing

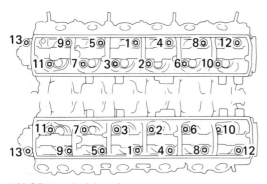

5M-GE camshaft housing torque sequence

3. Install the lash adjusters and rocker arms in their correct locations in the head.

4. Place new gaskets over the dowels on the head, and position the cam housings over the dowels on the head.

5. Install and tighten the housing nuts and bolts gradually in three passes in the sequence shown. On the final pass, torque the nuts and bolts to 15–17 ft. lbs.

6. Install the remaining components in the reverse order of removal, using new gaskets on the cam covers. Set the timing.

Oil Pressure Regulator

REMOVAL AND INSTALLATION

5M-GE Twin Cam Only

NOTE: *The oil pressure regulator should be removed and checked whenever the lash adjusters have been removed and bled.*

1. Remove the No. 3 timing belt cover (see "Timing Belt" in this chapter). Remove the timing belt cover stay.

2. Unbolt and remove the oil pressure regulator and gasket.

3. Installation is in the reverse order of removal.

INSPECTION

Unscrew the relief valve plug and remove the spring and valve. Wipe all parts clean with a rag, and flush out the regulator body with solvent. Blow the body out with compressed air or let air dry—do not wipe out with a rag, as it may leave lint particles. Check the relief valve for scoring or wear; replace if wear is evident.

Reassemble the regulator in the reverse order of disassembly. Using a new gasket, install the regulator on the cylinder head. Install the timing cover stay and timing belt cover. Check for leaks when the engine is first started.

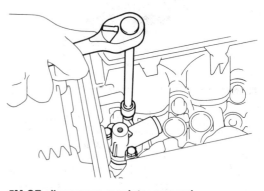

5M-GE oil pressure regulator removal

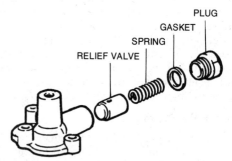

Oil pressure regulator, exploded view

Check condition of relief valve

Intake Manifold
REMOVAL AND INSTALLATION
20R and 22R Engines

1. Disconnect the battery.
2. Drain the cooling system.
3. Remove the air cleaner assembly, complete with hoses, from the carburetor.
4. Disconnect the vacuum lines from the EGR valve and carburetor. Mark them first to aid in the installation.
5. Remove the fuel lines, electrical leads, accelerator linkage, and water hose from the carburetor.
6. Remove the water by-pass hose from the manifold.

7. Unbolt and remove the intake manifold, complete with carburetor and EGR valve.
8. Cover the cylinder head ports with clean shop cloths to keep anything from falling into the cylinder head or block.

Installation is the reverse of removal. Replace the gasket with a new one. Torque the mounting bolts to the figure given in the "Torque Specifications" chart. Tighten the bolts in several stages working from the inside bolts outward. Remember to refill the cooling system.

22R-E Fuel Injected Four

1. Disconnect the battery.
2. Drain the cooling system.
3. Disconnect the air intake hose from both the air cleaner assembly on one end and the air intake chamber on the other.
4. Tag and disconnect all vacuum lines attached to the intake chamber and manifold.
5. Tag and disconnect the wires to the cold start injector, throttle position sensor, and the water hoses from the throttle body.
6. Remove the EGR valve from the intake chamber.
7. Tag and disconnect the actuator cable, accelerator cable and A/T throttle cable (if

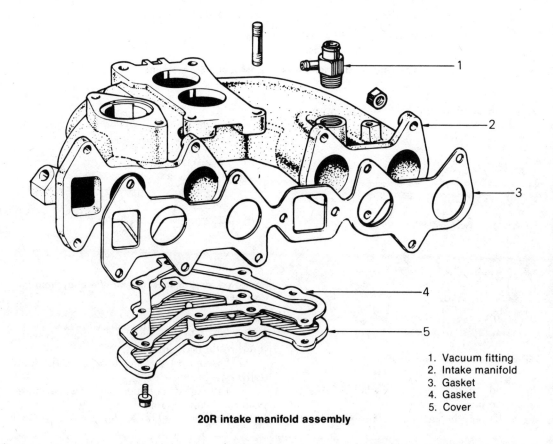

1. Vacuum fitting
2. Intake manifold
3. Gasket
4. Gasket
5. Cover

20R intake manifold assembly

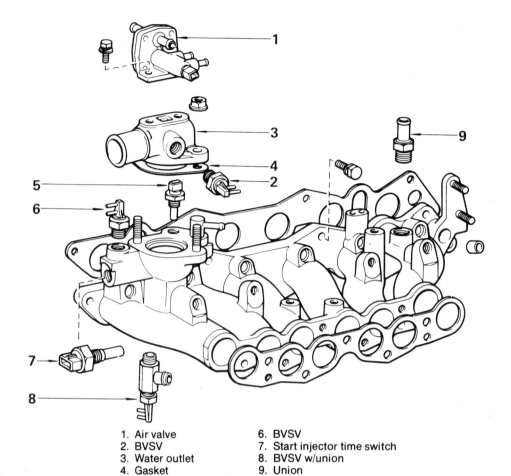

1. Air valve
2. BVSV
3. Water outlet
4. Gasket
5. Water thermo sensor
6. BVSV
7. Start injector time switch
8. BVSV w/union
9. Union

Intake manifold assembly on the 4M-E and 5M-E engines

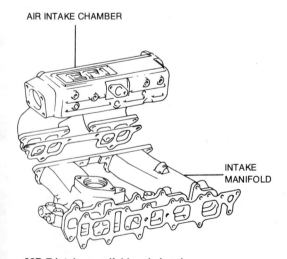

22R-E intake manifold and chamber

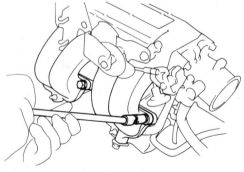

Removing air chamber and throttle body from intake manifold

equipped) from the cable bracket on the intake chamber.

8. Unbolt the air intake chamber from the intake manifold and remove the chamber with the throttle body attached.

9. Disconnect the fuel hose from the fuel delivery pipe.

10. Tag and disconnect the air valve hose from the intake manifold.

11. Make sure all hoses, lines and wires are

tagged for later installation and disconnected from the intake manifold. Unbolt the manifold from the cylinder head, removing the delivery pipe and injection nozzle in unit with the manifold.

4M-E and 5M-E Six Cylinder Engines

NOTE: *Removal of the intake manifolds on these engines is a complicated and tedious procedure. Make sure all wires, hoses and lines are tagged to simplify installation. It is advisable to have this work done by a professional familiar with the complex fuel injection systems of these engines.*

1. Follow steps 1 through 14 of the "4M-E and 5M-E Cylinder Head Removal" procedure, tagging all hoses, lines and wires for later assembly.

2. Installation is in the reverse order of removal.

5M-GE Twin Cam Six

1. Perform steps 1 through 13 of the "5M-GE Cylinder Head Removal" procedure, tag-

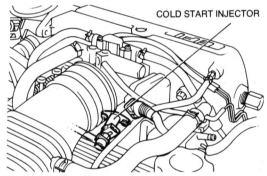

COLD START INJECTOR

Cold start injector location, 5M-GE

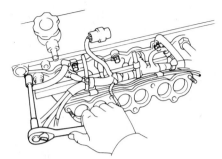

5M-GE intake manifold removal; when installing, torque to 15–17 ft. lbs

ging all hoses, lines and wires for later assembly.

2. Disconnect the three EFI (fuel injection) connectors and tag them for later assembly.

3. Perform steps 15 through 17 of the "5M-GE Cylinder Head Removal" procedure.

4. Installation is in the reverse order of removal.

Exhaust Manifold

REMOVAL AND INSTALLATON
20R and 22R/22R-E Engines

1. Remove the three exhaust pipe flange bolts and disconnect the exhaust pipe from the manifold.

2. Tag and disconnect the spark plug leads.

3. Position the spark plug wires out of the way. It may be best to tie them so they don't flop back in your way.

4. Remove the air cleaner tube from the heat stove on carbureted engines, and remove the outer part of the heat stove.

5. Use a 14 mm wrench to remove the manifold securing nuts.

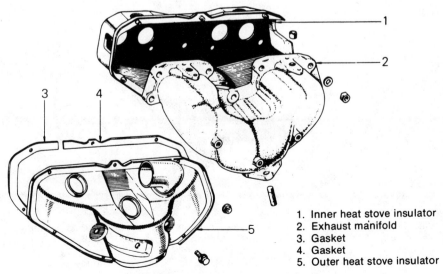

1. Inner heat stove insulator
2. Exhaust manifold
3. Gasket
4. Gasket
5. Outer heat stove insulator

20R exhaust manifold assembly

6. Remove the manifold, complete with air injection tubes and the inner portion of the heat stove.

7. Separate the inner portion of the heat stove from the manifold.

Installation is the reverse of removal. Tighten the retaining nuts to 29–36 ft. lbs., working from the inside out, and in several stages. Install the distributor and set the timing as previously outlined. Tighten the exhaust pipe flange nuts to 25–32 ft. lbs.

4M-E and 5M-E Engines

1. Raise the front and the rear of the car and support it with jackstands.

CAUTION: *Be sure that the car is securely supported.*

2. Remove the right-hand gravel shield from beneath the engine.

3. Remove the exhaust pipe support bracket.

4. Unfasten the bolts from the flange and detach the exhaust pipe from the manifold.

5. Disconnect the connector for the oxygen sensor.

6. In order to remove the manifold, unfasten the manifold retaining bolts.

CAUTION: *Remove and tighten the bolts in two or three stages, starting from the inside and working out.*

Installation is performed in the reverse order of removal. Always use a new gasket. Tighten the retaining bolts to the specifications given in two or three stages.

5M-GE T win Cam Six

NOTE: *The air intake hose may have to be removed to give access to all the manifold nuts.*

1. Jack up the front end of the car and safely support it with jackstands.

2. Remove the right-hand gravel shield from underneath the car.

3. Remove the exhaust pipe support stay.

4. Unbolt the exhaust pipe from the exhaust manifold flange.

5. Disconnect the oxygen sensor connector.

6. Remove the seven nuts and remove the exhaust manifold.

7. Installation is the reverse of removal. Use a new manifold gasket and torque all nuts evenly to 25–33 ft. lbs.

Combination Manifold
REMOVAL AND INSTALLATION

CAUTION: *Do not perform this prcedure on a warm engine. The exhaust and intake manifolds are connected and get very hot.*

8R-C and 18R-C Engines

1. Remove the air cleaner assembly, complete with hoses, from its mounting bracket.

2. Remove the fuel line, vacuum lines, automatic choke stove hoses, PCV hose, and accelerator linkage from the carburetor.

3. Unfasten the carburetor securing nuts. Remove the torque rod support, carburetor, and heat insulator.

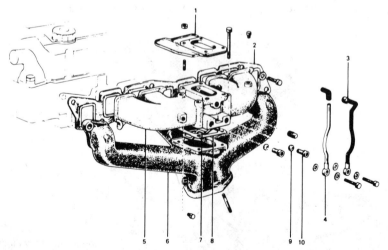

1. Heat insulator	4. Choke stove intake pipe	8. Manifold gasket (intake-to-
2. Manifold gasket (manifold-to-	5. Intake manifold	exhaust)
head)	6. Exhaust manifold	9. Sleeve
3. Choke stove outlet pipe	7. Choke stove pipe	10. Union

8R-C and 18R-C combination manifold assembly

ENGINE OVERHAUL

Most engine overhaul procedures are fairly standard. In addition to specific parts replacement procedures and complete specifications for your individual engine, this chapter also is a guide to accepted rebuilding procedures. Examples of standard rebuilding practice are shown and should be used along with specific details concerning your particular engine.

Competent and accurate machine shop services will ensure maximum performance, reliability and engine life. Procedures marked with the symbol shown above should be performed by a competent machine shop, and are provided so that you will be familiar with the procedures necessary to a successful overhaul.

In most instances it is more profitable for the do-it-yourself mechanic to remove, clean and inspect the component, buy the necessary parts and deliver these to a shop for actual machine work.

On the other hand, much of the rebuilding work (crankshaft, block, bearings, pistons, rods, and other components) is well within the scope of the do-it-yourself mechanic.

Tools

The tools required for an engine overhaul or parts replacement will depend on the depth of your involvement. With a few exceptions, they will be the tools found in a mechanic's tool kit (see Chapter 1). More in-depth work will require any or all of the following:
• a dial indicator (reading in thousandths) mounted on a universal base
• micrometers and telescope gauges
• jaw and screw-type pullers
• scraper
• valve spring compressor
• ring groove cleaner
• piston ring expander and compressor
• ridge reamer
• cylinder hone or glaze breaker

• Plastigage®
• engine stand

Use of most of these tools is illustrated in this chapter. Many can be rented for a one-time use from a local parts jobber or tool supply house specializing in automotive work.

Occasionally, the use of special tools is called for. See the information on Special Tools and the Safety Notice in the front of this book before substituting another tool.

Inspection Techniques

Procedures and specifications are given in this chapter for inspecting, cleaning and assessing the wear limits of most major components. Other procedures such as Magnaflux and Zyglo can be used to locate material flaws and stress cracks. Magnaflux is a magnetic process applicable only to ferrous materials. The Zyglo process coats the material with a flourescent dye penetrant and can be used on any material. Check for suspected surface cracks can be more readily made using spot check dye. The dye is sprayed onto the suspected area, wiped off and the area sprayed with a developer. Cracks will show up brightly.

Overhaul Tips

Aluminum has become extremely popular for use in engines, due to its low weight. Observe the following precautions when handling aluminum parts:
• Never hot tank aluminum parts (the caustic hot-tank solution will eat the aluminum)
• Remove all aluminum parts (identification tag, etc.) from engine parts prior to hot-tanking.
• Always coat threads lightly with engine oil or anti-seize compounds before installation, to prevent seizure.
• Never over-torque bolts or spark plugs, especially in aluminum threads.

Stripped threads in any component can be repaired using any of several commercial repair kits (Heli-Coil, Microdot, Keenserts, etc.)

When assembling the engine, any parts that will be in frictional contact must be pre-lubed to provide lubrication at initial start-up. Any product specifically formulated for this purpose can be used, but engine oil is not recommended as a pre-lube.

When semi-permanent (locked, but removable) installation of bolts or nuts is desired, threads should be cleaned and coated with Loctite® or other similar, commercial non-hardening sealant.

Repairing Damaged Threads

Several methods of repairing damaged threads are available. Heli-Coil® (shown here), Keenserts® and Microdot® are among the most widely used. All involve basically the same principle—drilling out stripped threads, tapping the hole and installing a prewound insert—making welding, plugging and oversize fasteners unnecessary.

Two types of thread repair inserts are usually supplied—a standard type for most Inch Coarse, Inch Fine, Metric Coarse and Metric Fine thread sizes and a spark plug type to fit most spark plug port sizes. Consult the individual manufacturer's catalog to determine exact applications. Typical thread repair kits will contain a selection of prewound threaded inserts, a tap (corresponding to the outside diameter threads of the insert) and an installation tool. Spark plug inserts usually differ because they require a tap equipped with pilot threads and a combined reamer/tap section. Most manufacturers also supply blister-packed thread repair inserts separately in addition to a master kit containing a variety of taps and inserts plus installation tools.

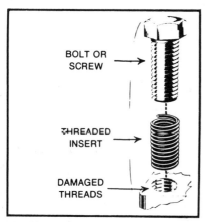

Damaged bolt holes can be repaired with thread repair inserts

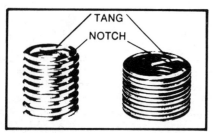

Standard thread repair insert (left) and spark plug thread insert (right)

Before effecting a repair to a threaded hole, remove any snapped, broken or damaged bolts or studs. Penetrating oil can be used to free frozen threads; the offending item can be removed with locking pliers or with a screw or stud extractor. After the hole is clear, the thread can be repaired, as follows:

Drill out the damaged threads with specified drill. Drill completely through the hole or to the bottom of a blind hole

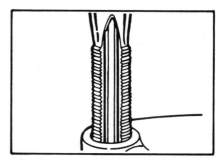

With the tap supplied, tap the hole to receive the thread insert. Keep the tap well oiled and back it out frequently to avoid clogging the threads

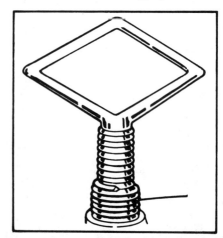

Screw the threaded insert onto the installation tool until the tang engages the slot. Screw the insert into the tapped hole until it is ¼–½ turn below the top surface, After installation break off the tang with a hammer and punch

Standard Torque Specifications and Fastener Markings

In the absence of specific torques, the following chart can be used as a guide to the maximum safe torque of a particular size/grade of fastener.

- There is no torque difference for fine or coarse threads.
- Torque values are based on clean, dry threads. Reduce the value by 10% if threads are oiled prior to assembly.
- The torque required for aluminum components or fasteners is considerably less.

U.S. Bolts

SAE Grade Number	1 or 2			5			6 or 7		
Number of lines always 2 less than the grade number.									
Bolt Size (Inches)—(Thread)	Maximum Torque			Maximum Torque			Maximum Torque		
	Ft./Lbs.	Kgm	Nm	Ft./Lbs.	Kgm	Nm	Ft./Lbs.	Kgm	Nm
¼ — 20	5	0.7	6.8	8	1.1	10.8	10	1.4	13.5
— 28	6	0.8	8.1	10	1.4	13.6			
5/16 — 18	11	1.5	14.9	17	2.3	23.0	19	2.6	25.8
— 24	13	1.8	17.6	19	2.6	25.7			
3/8 — 16	18	2.5	24.4	31	4.3	42.0	34	4.7	46.0
— 24	20	2.75	27.1	35	4.8	47.5			
7/16 — 14	28	3.8	37.0	49	6.8	66.4	55	7.6	74.5
— 20	30	4.2	40.7	55	7.6	74.5			
½ — 13	39	5.4	52.8	75	10.4	101.7	85	11.75	115.2
— 20	41	5.7	55.6	85	11.7	115.2			
9/16 — 12	51	7.0	69.2	110	15.2	149.1	120	16.6	162.7
— 18	55	7.6	74.5	120	16.6	162.7			
5/8 — 11	83	11.5	112.5	150	20.7	203.3	167	23.0	226.5
— 18	95	13.1	128.8	170	23.5	230.5			
¾ — 10	105	14.5	142.3	270	37.3	366.0	280	38.7	379.6
— 16	115	15.9	155.9	295	40.8	400.0			
7/8 — 9	160	22.1	216.9	395	54.6	535.5	440	60.9	596.5
— 14	175	24.2	237.2	435	60.1	589.7			
1 — 8	236	32.5	318.6	590	81.6	799.9	660	91.3	894.8
— 14	250	34.6	338.9	660	91.3	849.8			

Metric Bolts

Relative Strength Marking	4.6, 4.8			8.8		
Bolt Markings						
Bolt Size Thread Size x Pitch (mm)	Maximum Torque			Maximum Torque		
	Ft./Lbs.	Kgm	Nm	Ft./Lbs.	Kgm	Nm
6 x 1.0	2–3	.2–.4	3–4	3–6	.4–.8	5–8
8 x 1.25	6–8	.8–1	8–12	9–14	1.2–1.9	13–19
10 x 1.25	12–17	1.5–2.3	16–23	20–29	2.7–4.0	27–39
12 x 1.25	21–32	2.9–4.4	29–43	35–53	4.8–7.3	47–72
14 x 1.5	35–52	4.8–7.1	48–70	57–85	7.8–11.7	77–110
16 x 1.5	51–77	7.0–10.6	67–100	90–120	12.4–16.5	130–160
18 x 1.5	74–110	10.2–15.1	100–150	130–170	17.9–23.4	180–230
20 x 1.5	110–140	15.1–19.3	150–190	190–240	26.2–46.9	160–320
22 x 1.5	150–190	22.0–26.2	200–260	250–320	34.5–44.1	340–430
24 x 1.5	190–240	26.2–46.9	260–320	310–410	42.7–56.5	420–550

4. Use a jack to raise the front of the car. Support the car with jackstands.

CAUTION: *Be sure that the car is securely supported.*

5. Unfasten the bolts which attach the downpipe flange to the exhaust manifold.

6. In order to remove the manifold assembly, unfasten the manifold retaining bolts. On 1974 California engines, remove the EGR valve and tubes first.

CAUTION: *Remove and tighten the bolts in two or three stages, starting from the inside and working out.*

Installation is performed in the reverse order of removal. Always use *new* gaskets. Tighten the manifold securing bolts to the figure shown in the "Torque Specifications" chart, in the reverse sequence of removal.

Cylinder Head

REMOVAL AND INSTALLATION

8R-C and 18R-C Engine

CAUTION: *Do not perform this procedure on a warm engine.*

1. Disconnect the battery and drain the cooling system.

2. Remove the air cleaner assembly from its bracket, complete with its attendant hoses.

3. Detach the accelerator cable from its support on the cylinder head cover and also from the carburetor throttle arm.

4. Remove the choke cable and fuel lines from the carburetor.

5. Remove the water hose bracket from the cylinder head cover.

6. Unfasten the water hose clamps and remove the hoses from the water pump and the water valve. Detach the heater temperature control cable from the water valve.

7. Disconnect the PCV line from the cylinder head cover.

8. Remove the vacuum lines from the distributor vacuum unit. Remove the lines which run from the vacuum switching valve to the

various emission control system components on the cylinder head. Disconnect the EGR lines (1974 California only).

9. Remove the fuel and vacuum lines from the carburetor.

10. Remove the pipes from the automatic choke stove.

11. Tag and unfasten the wires from the spark plugs. Remove the spark plugs.

12. Remove the cylinder head cover retaining bolts and withdraw the cover.

NOTE: *Use a clean cloth, placed over the timing cover opening, to prevent anything from falling down into it.*

13. Remove the radiator upper hose from the cylinder head water outlet.

14. Remove the outlet elbow and thermostat.

15. Unfasten the downpipe clamp from the exhaust manifold. Remove the manifold from the head.

16. Remove the valve rocker assembly mounting bolts and the oil delivery pipes. Withdraw the valve rocker shaft assembly.

CAUTION: *When removing the rocker shaft securing bolts, loosen them in two or three stages and in the proper sequence. (See the illustration.)*

17. Remove the timing gear from the camshaft. *Support it so that the chain does not fall down into the cover.*

18. Remove the camshaft bearing caps and withdraw the camshaft. Remove the camshaft bearings.

NOTE: *Temporarily assemble the bearings and caps to keep them with their mates. Be sure to keep the bearings in proper order.*

19. Remove the gear from the timing chain. Support the timing chain so that it does not fall into the cover.

20. Loosen the head bolts in two or three stages; in the sequence illustrated. Lift the head assembly off the block.

CAUTION: *Do not try to slide the head off the block as it is held in place by dowels.*

Installation is performed in the following order:

1. Remove any water from the cylinder head bolt holes.

2. Clean the mating surfaces of the cylinder head and block. Use liquid sealer around the oil holes on the head and cylinder block. *Do not get sealer in the holes.*

3. Lower the cylinder head on to the block.

CAUTION: *Do not slide the head across the block, because of the dowels located on the block.*

4. Tighten the cylinder head bolts in the proper sequence (see the diagrams) and in three or four stages. Tighten them to the spec-

8R-C and 18R-C cylinder head bolt tightening sequence

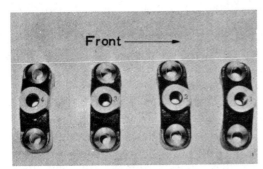

Installation direction of 8R-C and 18R-C cam bearing cap

ifications given in the "Torque Specifications" chart.

5. Install each lower bearing half into the seat from which it was removed.

6. Place the camshaft in the cylinder head.

7. Install each bearing into the cap from which it was removed.

8. Install the camshaft bearing caps on the head, in their numbered sequence, with the numbers facing forward. Tighten to 12–17 ft. lbs.

9. First, check the camshaft bearing clearance and end-play, using Plastigage®.

NOTE: *This is checked in the same manner that connecting rod and crankshaft bearings are checked. For the procedure see "Engine Rebuilding" at the end of the chapter.*

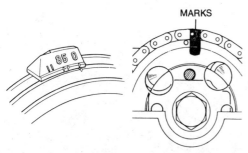

Matchmark the cam sprocket to the camchain; set No. 1 cylinder at TDC

The oil clearance should be 0.001–0.002 in.; the end-play should be 0.0017–0.0066 in.

10. Crank the engine so that the No. 1 piston is at TDC of its compression stroke.

11. Align the mark on the timing chain with the dowel hole on the camshaft timing gear and the stamped mark on the camshaft.

NOTE: *All three marks should be aligned so that they are facing upward.*

12. Install the valve rocker assembly. Tighten its securing bolts to 12–17 ft. lbs., in the sequence illustrated, and in two or three stages.

13. Attach the oil delivery pipe to the valve

rocker assembly and camshaft bearing caps. Tighten their securing bolts to 11–16 ft. lbs.

14. Adjust the valve clearance as outlined in Chapter 2, to the following *cold* specifications:

- Intake—0.007 in.
- Exhaust—0.013 in.

15. The rest of installation is performed in the reverse order of removal.

20R and 22R Engines

CAUTION: *Do not perform this operation on a warm engine.*

1. Disconnect the battery.

2. Remove the three exhaust pipe flange nuts and separate the pipe from the mainfold.

3. Drain the cooling system (both radiator and block). If the coolant is to be reused, place a large, clean container underneath the drains.

4. Remove the air cleaner assembly, complete with hoses, from the carburetor.

NOTE: *Cover the carburetor with a clean shop cloth so that nothing can fall into it.*

5. Mark all vacuum hoses to aid installation and disconnect them. Remove all linkages, fuel lines, etc., from the carburetor, cylinder head, and manifolds. Remove the wire supports.

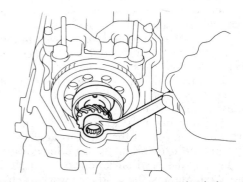

Use a 19mm wrench on the cam sprocket bolt

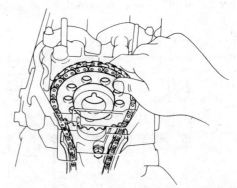

Do not allow the camchain to slip off the sprocket and fall into the lower end when removing the cam sprocket

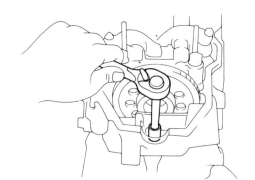

Before removing the head bolts, remove the cam chain cover bolt

6. Mark the spark plug leads and disconnect them from the plugs.

7. Matchmark the distributor housing and block. Disconnect the primary lead and remove the distributor. Installation will be easier if you leave the cap and leads in place.

8. Unfasten the four 14 mm nuts which secure the cam cover.

9. Remove the rubber camshaft seals. Turn the crankshaft until the No. 1 piston is at TDC on its compression stroke. Matchmark the timing sprocket to the cam chain, and remove the semi-circular plug. Using a 19mm wrench, remove the cam sprocket bolt. Slide the distributor drive gear and spacer off the cam and wire the cam sprocket in place.

10. Remove the timing chain cover 14 mm bolt at the front of the head. *This must be done before the head bolts are removed.*

11. Remove the cylinder head bolts in the order shown below. Improper removal could cause head damage.

12. Using pry bars applied evenly at the front and the rear of the valve rocker assembly, pry the assembly off its mounting dowels.

13. Lift the head off its dowels. Do NOT pry it off. Support the head on a workbench.

14. Drain the engine oil from the crankcase *after* the head has been removed, because the oil will become contaminated with coolant while the head is being removed.

Installation is performed in the following order:

1. Apply liquid sealer to the front corners of the block and install the head gasket.

2. Lower the head over the locating dowels. Do not attempt to slide it into place.

3. Rotate the camshaft so that the sprocket aligning pin is at the top. Remove the wire and hold the cam sprocket. Manually rotate the engine so that the sprocket hole is also at the top. Wire the sprocket in place again.

4. Install the rocker arm assembly over its positioning dowels.

5. Tighten the cylinder head bolts evenly, in three stages, and in the order shown, under "Torque Sequences," to a specified torque of 52–63 ft. lbs.

6. Install the timing chain cover bolt and tighten it to 7–11 ft. lbs.

7. Remove the wire and fit the sprocket over the camshaft dowel. If the chain won't allow the sprocket to reach, rotate the crankshaft back and forth, while lifting up on the chain and sprocket.

8. Install the distributor drive gear and tighten the crankshaft bolt to 51–65 ft. lbs.

9. Set the No. 1 piston at TDC of its compression stroke and adjust the valves as outlined in Chapter 2.

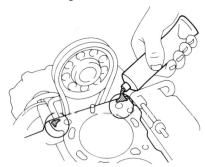

Apply liquid sealer to the front corners of the cylinder block

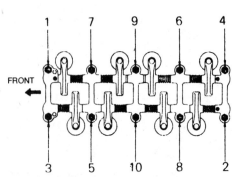

20R, 22R, 22R-E engine head bolt removal sequence

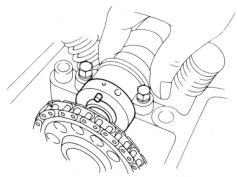

Rotate the 20R and 22R cam so that the pin is at the top

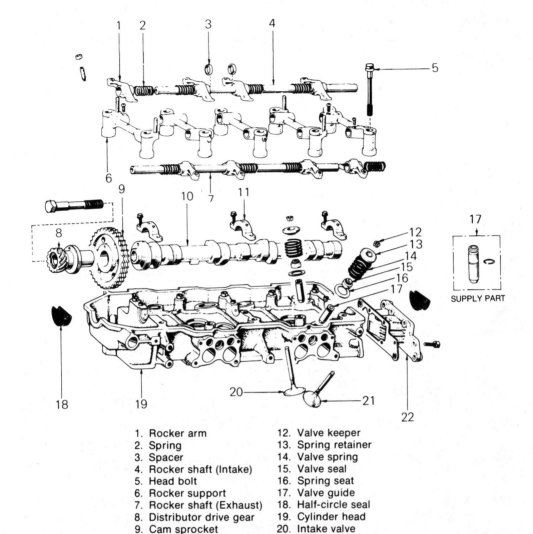

1. Rocker arm	12. Valve keeper
2. Spring	13. Spring retainer
3. Spacer	14. Valve spring
4. Rocker shaft (Intake)	15. Valve seal
5. Head bolt	16. Spring seat
6. Rocker support	17. Valve guide
7. Rocker shaft (Exhaust)	18. Half-circle seal
8. Distributor drive gear	19. Cylinder head
9. Cam sprocket	20. Intake valve
10. Camshaft	21. Exhaust valve
11. Camshaft bearing cap	22. Rear cover (EGR cooler)

20R, 22R series cylinder head components

10. After completing valve adjustment, rotate the crankshaft 352°, so that the 8° BTDC mark on the pulley aligns with the pointer.

11. Install the distributor, as outlined above.

12. Install the spark plugs and leads.

13. Make sure that the oil drain plug is installed. Fill the engine with oil after installing the rubber cam seals. Pour the oil over the distributor drive gear and the valve rockers.

14. Install the rocker cover and tighten the bolts to 8–11 ft. lbs.

15. Connect all the vacuum hoses and electrical leads which were removed during disassembly. Install the spark plug lead supports. Fill the cooling system. Install the air cleaner.

16. Tighten the exhaust pipe-to-manifold flange bolts to 25–33 ft. lbs.

17. Reconnect the battery. Start the engine and allow it to reach normal operating temperature. Check and adjust the timing and valve clearance. Adjust the idle speed and mixture. Road-test the vehicle.

4M-E and 5M-E Engines

NOTE: *Due to the complexity of the hose and line routing on the electronic fuel injection system, it is advisable to have this procedure performed by a professional mechanic.*

1. Disconnect the negative battery cable.

2. Drain the cooling system.

3. Remove the water hose bracket from the cylinder head cover.

4. Unfasten the hose clamps and remove the hoses from the water pump and the water valve.

5. Disconnect the heater temperature control cable from the water valve.

6. Disconnect the PCV hoses from the cylinder head cover and the intake air connector.

7. Disconnect the air valve and the air control valve hoses from the intake air connector.

8. Disconnect the intake air connector from the air intake chamber and the air flow meter and remove it.

9. Tag and disconnect all hoses, lines and wires leading from the air intake chamber and the throttle body (it is a good idea to follow the numerical removal sequence shown in the illustration).

10. Unscrew the seven mounting bolts and remove the air intake chamber and the throttle body as one unit.

11. Tag and disconnect the wiring connectors at the fuel injectors.

NOTE: *For further illustrations, refer to Chapter 4.*

12. Unscrew the four mounting bolts and remove the fuel delivery pipe with the injectors.

CAUTION: *When removing the injectors and the delivery pipe, be sure to have a container underneath, to catch the large quantity of fuel.*

13. Remove or disconnect the following parts as shown in the illustration.

14. Unscrew the eight mounting bolts and remove the intake manifold.

15. Remove the spark plug wires from the spark plugs and from their bracket on the cylinder head cover.

16. Remove the distributor.

17. Remove the exhaust manifold and the oil pressure sender unit.

18. Unscrew the retaining bolts and remove the cylinder head cover.

NOTE: *Place a clean cloth over the timing gear to prevent anything from falling into the timing gear cover.*

19. Remove the valve rocker shaft assem-

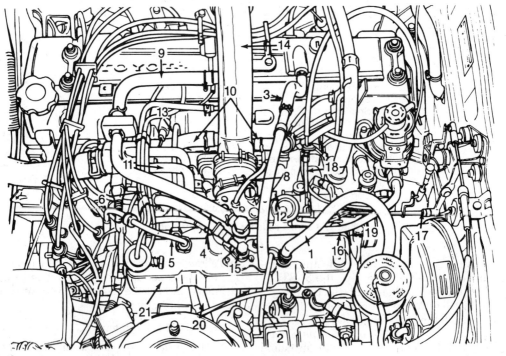

1. Hose	12. Water hose
2. Hose	13. Hose
3. Hose (for PCV)	14. Intake air connector
4. Hose	15. Cold start injector w/gasket
5. Hose	16. EGR pipe
6. Hose (for Idle-up)	17. Throttle link
7. Wiring	18. Throttle wire for A/T
8. Hose	19. Ground wire
9. Hose	20. Hose
10. Hose	21. Air intake chamber
11. Water hose	

Before removing the air intake chamber on the 4M-E and 5M-E, remove the hoses in this order

1. Pressure regulator
2. EGR valve
3. Heater hose
4. Radiator hose
5. Vacuum pipes and hoses
6. Distributor cap
7. Intake manifold and gasket

Remove or disconnect these components on the 4M-E and 5M-E in this order

Valve rocker shaft removal sequence for the 4M-E/5M-E six cylinder engine; first remove the oil union bolt (1) and then remove the union itself (2)

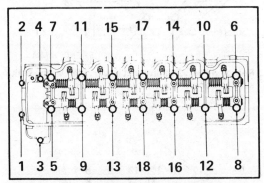

4M-E/5M-E engine head bolt removal sequence

bly retaining bolts in the sequence illustrated and then remove the rocker assembly.

20. Remove the timing chain tensioner.

21. Straighten out the lock-plate and unfas-

ten the timing gear retaining bolt (left hand thread). Withdraw the timing gear from the camshaft.

22. Remove the camshaft bearing caps and withdraw the camshaft. Remove the camshaft bearings.

NOTE: *Temporarily assemble the bearings and caps to keep them with their mates. Be sure to keep the bearings in proper order.*

23. Remove the gear from the timing chain. *Support the timing chain so that it does not fall into the cover.*

24. Loosen the head bolts in two or three stages; in the sequence illustrated. Lift the head assembly off the block.

CAUTION: *Do not try to slide the head off the block as it is held in place by dowels.*

Installation is performed in the following order:

1. Remove any water from the cylinder head bolt holes.

2. Clean the mating surfaces of the cylinder head and block. Use liquid sealer around the oil holes on the head and cylinder block. *Do not get sealer in the holes.*

3. Lower the cylinder head on to the block.

CAUTION: *Do not slide the head across the block, because of the dowels located on the block.*

4. Tighten the cylinder head bolts in the proper sequence (see the diagrams) and in three or four stages. Tighten them to the spec-

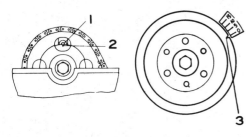

1. Valve timing mark (⁵/₃₂ in. hole)
2. V-notch—camshaft flange
3. V-notch—crankshaft pulley

Crankshaft and camshaft timing marks on the 4M-E/5M-E six cylinder engine

ifications given in the "Torque Specifications" chart.

5. Install each lower bearing half into the seat from which it was removed.

6. Place the camshaft in the cylinder head.

7. Install each bearing into the cap from which it was removed.

8. Install the camshaft bearing caps on the head, in their numbered sequence, with the numbers facing toward. Tighten to 12–17 ft. lbs.

9. First, check the camshaft bearing clearance and end-play, using Plastigage®.

NOTE: *This is checked in the same manner that connecting rod and crankshaft bearings are checked. For the procedure see "Engine Rebuilding" at the end of the chapter.*

The oil clearance should be 0.001–0.002 in.; the end-play should be 0.0017–0.0066 in.

10. Crank the engine so that the No. 1 piston is at TDC of its compression stroke.

11. Align the V-notch on the camshaft with the ⁵/₃₂ in. hole on the No. 1 camshaft bearing.

NOTE: *Be sure that the V-notch is also aligned with the mark on the timing chain cover.*

12. Install the camshaft timing gear, with the chain, on the end of the camshaft. Align the pin on the camshaft flange with the hole in the gear.

13. Install the timing gear bolt and lockplate. Fasten the bolt with the lockplate.

NOTE: *The bolt has a left-hand thread. Tighten it to 47–54 ft. lbs.*

14. Install the chain tensioner, complete with shim. Tighten it to 22–29 ft. lbs.

15. Turn the crankshaft two complete revolutions while checking to ensure that valve timing is correct. If, at the end of the two revolutions, the timing marks do not align, repeat Steps 11–13.

16. Apply pressure to the chain tensioner arm. If its movement is less than ³/₁₆ in., add additional shims.

17. Install the valve rocker assembly and tighten the bolts to 22–29 ft. lbs., in the sequence illustrated, and in three or four stages.

NOTE: *The stud bolt should only be tightened to 11–14 ft. lbs.*

18. Install the union on the No. 1 rocker support and the No. 1 camshaft bearing cap. Tighten the union bolts to 6–9 ft. lbs.

19. Adjust the valve clearance, as outlined in Chapter 2, to the following *cold* specifications:

- Intake—0.006 in.
- Exhaust—0.008 in.

20. Installation of the remaining components is in the reverse order of removal.

5M-GE Twin Cam Six

1. Disconnect the battery cables.

2. Drain the cooling system.

3. Disconnect the exhaust pipe from the exhaust manifold.

4. Remove the throttle cable bracket from the cylinder head if equipped with automatic transmission, and remove the accelerator and actuator cable bracket.

5. Tag and disconnect the ground cable, oxygen sensor wire, high tension coil wire, distributor connector, solenoid resistor wire connector and thermo switch wire (A/T).

6. Tag and disconnect the brake booster vacuum hose, EGR valve vacuum hose, fuel hose from the intake manifold and actuator vacuum hose (if equipped with cruise control).

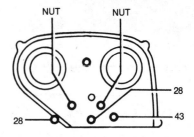

Removing No. 2 timing belt cover, 5M-GE six. Make sure fasteners are installed in correct order

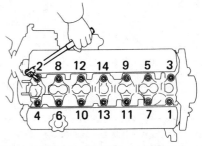

5M-GE cylinder headbolt removal sequence. Loosen bolts in two or three passes

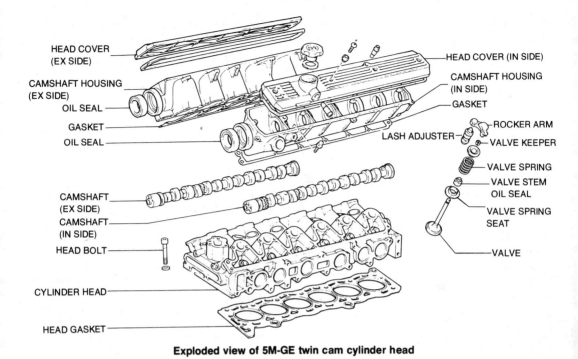

HEAD COVER
(EX SIDE)

HEAD COVER (IN SIDE)

CAMSHAFT HOUSING
(EX SIDE)

CAMSHAFT HOUSING
(IN SIDE)

OIL SEAL

GASKET

GASKET

ROCKER ARM

OIL SEAL

LASH ADJUSTER

VALVE KEEPER

VALVE SPRING

CAMSHAFT
(EX SIDE)

VALVE STEM
OIL SEAL

CAMSHAFT
(IN SIDE)

VALVE SPRING
SEAT

HEAD BOLT

VALVE

CYLINDER HEAD

HEAD GASKET

Exploded view of 5M-GE twin cam cylinder head

7. Disconnect the radiator upper hose from the thermostat housing, and disconnect the two heater hoses.

8. Disconnect the No. 1 air hose from the air intake connector. Remove the two clamp bolts, loosen the throttle body hose clamp and remove the air intake connector and the connector pipe.

9. Tag and disconnect all emission control hoses from the throttle body and air intake chamber, the two PCV hoses from the cam cover and the fuel hose from the fuel hose support.

10. Remove the air intake chamber stay and the vacuum pipe and ground cable.

11. Remove the bolt that attaches the spark plug wire clip, leaving the wires attached to the clip. Remove the distributor from the cylinder head with the cap and wires attached, by removing the distributor holding bolt.

12. Tag and disconnect the cold start injector wire and disconnect the cold start injector fuel hose from the delivery pipe.

13. Loosen the nut of the EGR pipe, remove the five bolts and two nuts and remove the air intake chamber and gasket.

14. Remove the glove box and remove the ECU module. Disconnect the three connectors and pull the EFI (fuel injection) wire harness out through the engine side of the firewall.

15. Remove the pulsation damper and the No. 1 fuel pipe.

16. Remove the water outlet housing by first loosening the clamp and disconnecting the water by-pass hose.

17. Remove the intake manifold.

18. Disconnect the power steering pump drive belt and remove the power steering pump without disconnecting the fluid hoses. Temporarily secure the pump out of the way.

19. Disconnect the oxygen sensor connector and remove the exhaust manifold.

20. Remove the timing belt and camshaft timing gears.

21. Remove the timing belt cover stay, and remove the oil pressure regulator and gasket.

22. Remove the No. 2 timing belt cover and gasket.

23. Tag and disconnect any other wires, linkage and/or hoses still attached to the cylinder head.

24. Using a long extension on your ratchet handle (thin enough to get inside the head bolt recesses), remove the fourteen head bolts gradually in two or three passes in the numerical order shown.

CAUTION: *Head warpage or cracking could result from removing the head bolts in incorrect order.*

25. Carefully lift the cylinder head from the dowels on the cylinder block, resting the mating surface on wooden blocks on the work bench. If the head is difficult to remove, tap around the mating surface gently with a rubber hammer. *Keep in mind the head is aluminum and is easily damaged.*

Installation is performed by first following

steps 1 through 4 of the 4M-E/5M-E cylinder head installation procedure, then reversing the above installation procedures. Use new gaskets everywhere. Fill the radiator with coolant and set the timing. Road test the car and check for leaks.

TORQUE SEQUENCES

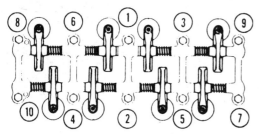

20R and 22R

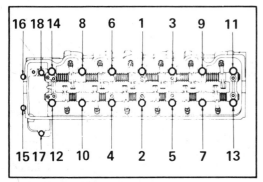

4M-E and 5M-E

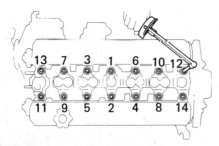

Head bolt torque sequence, 5M-GE

8R-C and 18R-C engines

CLEANING AND INSPECTION

When the rocker assembly and valve train have been removed from the cylinder head (see "Valves and Springs" below), set the head on two wooden blocks on the bench, combustion chamber side up. Using a scraper or putty knife, carefully scrape away any gasket material that may have stuck to the head-to-block mating surface when the head was removed. Make sure you DO NOT gouge the mating surface with the tool.

Using a wire brush chucked into your electric drill, remove the carbon in each combustion chamber. Make sure the brush is actually removing the carbon and not merely burnishing it.

Clean all the valve guides using a valve guide brush (available at most auto parts or auto tool shops) and solvent. A fine-bristled rifle bore cleaning brush also works here.

Inspect the threads of each spark plug hole by screwing a plug into each, making sure it screws down completely. Heli-coil® any plug hole that is damaged.

CAUTION: *DO NOT hot tank the cylinder head! The head material on most Celica engines is aluminum, which is ruined if subjected to the hot tank solution. Some of the early 8R-C and 18-R engines were equipped with cast iron heads, which can be hot-tanked (a service performed by most machine shops which immerses the head in a*

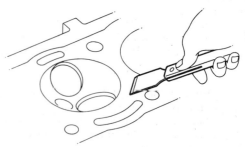

Do not scratch the head mating surface when removing old gasket material

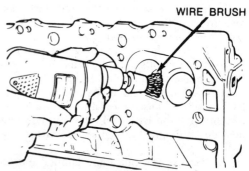

Removing combustion chamber carbon; make sure it is removed and not merely burnished

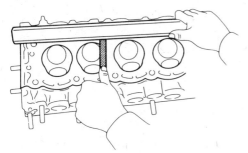

Check head mating surface straightness with a precision straight-edge and a feeler gauge

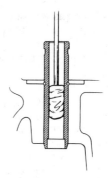

Cleaning the valve guides

hot, caustic solution for cleaning). To be sure your engine's cylinder head is aluminum, check around its perimeter with a magnet. Your engine has an iron head if the magnet sticks.

NOTE: *Before hot-tanking any overhead-cam head, check with the machine shop doing the work. Some cam bearings are easily damaged by the hot tank solution.*

Finally, go over the entire head with a clean shop rag soaked in solvent to remove any grit, old gasket particles, etc. Blow out the bolt holes, coolant galleys, intake and exhaust ports, valve guides and plug holes with compressed air.

RESURFACING

While the head is removed, check the head-to-block mating surface for straightness. If the engine has overheated and blown a head gasket, this must be done as a matter of course. A warped mating surface must be resurfaced (milled); this is done on a milling machine and is quite similar to planing a piece of wood.

Using a precision steel straight-edge and a blade-type feeler gauge, check the surface of the head across its length, width and diagonal length as shown in the illustrations. Also check the intake and exhaust manifold mating surfaces, and the camshaft housing (5M-GE) and cam cover (all) mating surfaces. If warpage ex-

ceeds .003 in. in a 6 in. span, or .006 in. over the total length, the head must be milled. If warpage is highly excessive, the head must be replaced. Again, consult the machine shop operator on head milling limitations.

CYLINDER BLOCK CLEANING

While the cylinder head is removed, the top of the cylinder block and pistons should also be cleaned. Before you begin, rotate the crankshaft until one or more pistons are flush with the top of the block (on the four cylinder engines, you will either have Nos. 1 and 4 "up," or Nos. 2 and 3 "up"). Carefully stuff clean rags into the cylinders in which the pistons are "down." This will help keep grit and carbon chips out during cleaning. Using care not to gouge or scratch the block-to-head mat-

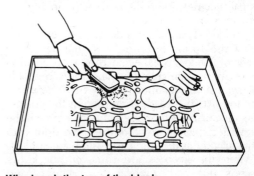

Wire brush the top of the block

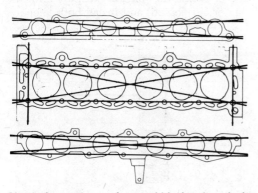

Check the mating surfaces widthwise, lengthwise and diagonally

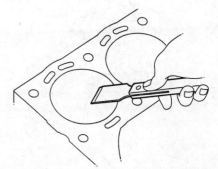

Removing carbon from the piston tops; do not scratch pistons

ing surface and the piston top(s), clean away any old gasket material with a wire brush and/or scraper. On the piston tops, make sure you are actually removing the carbon and not merely burnishing it.

Remove the rags from the "down" cylinders after you have wiped the top of the block with a solvent soaked rag. Rotate the crankshaft until the other pistons come up flush with the top of the block, and clean those pistons.

NOTE: *Because you have rotated the crankshaft, you will have to re-time the engine following the procedure listed under the "Timing Chain/Timing Belt" removal.*

Make sure you wipe out each cylinder thoroughly with a solvent-soaked rag, to remove all traces of grit, before the head is reassembled to the block.

Valves and Springs

ADJUSTMENT (AFTER ENGINE SERVICE)

The valves on all engines covered here, except the 5M-GE Twin Cam Six, must be adjusted following any valve train disassembly. Follow the procedure listed in Chapter 2 for valve adjustment.

REMOVAL AND INSTALLATION

A valve spring compressor is needed to remove the valves and springs; these are available at most auto parts and auto tool shops. A small magnet is very helpful for removing the keepers and spring seats.

Set the head on its side on the bench. Install the spring compressor so that the fixed side of the tool is flat against the valve head in the combustion chamber, and the screw side is against the retainer. Slowly turn the screw in towards the head, compressing the spring. As the spring compresses, the keepers will be revealed; pick them off of the valve stem with the magnet as they are easily fumbled and lost. When the keepers are removed, back the screw out and remove the retainers and

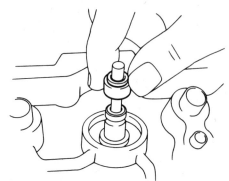

Always install new valve stem seals

springs. Remove the compressor and pull the valves out of the head from the other side. Remove the valve seals by hand and remove the spring seats with the magnet.

Since it is very important that each valve and its spring, retainer, spring seat and keepers is reassembled in its original location, you must keep these parts in order. The best way to do this is to cut either eight (four cylinder) or twelve (six cylinder) holes in a piece of heavy cardboard or wood. Label each hole with the cylinder number and either "IN" or "EX", corresponding to the location of each valve in the head. As you remove each valve, insert it into the holder, and assemble the seats, springs, keepers and retainers to the stem on the labeled side of the holder. This way each valve and its attending parts are kept together, and can be put back into the head in their proper locations.

After lapping each valve into its seat (see "Valve Lapping" below), oil each valve stem, and install each valve into the head in the reverse order of removal, so that all parts except the keepers are assembled on the stem. *Always use new valve stem seals.* Install the spring compressor, and compress the retainer and spring until the keeper groove on the valve stem is fully revealed. Coat the groove with a wipe of grease (to hold the keepers until the retainer is released) and install both keepers,

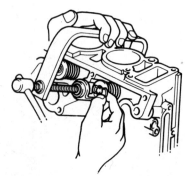

After compressing the valve spring, be careful removing the keepers—they are easily fumbled

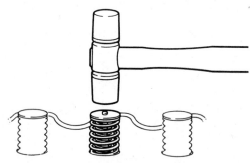

Lightly tap each assembled valve stem to ensure correct fit of the keepers, retainers and seals

wide end up. Slowly back the screw of the compressor out until the spring retainer covers the keepers. Remove the tool. Lightly tap the end of each valve stem with a rubber hammer to ensure proper fit of the retainers and keepers.

INSPECTION

Before the valves can be properly inspected, the stem, lower end of the stem and the entire valve face and head must be cleaned. An old valve works well for chipping carbon from the valve head, and a wire brush, gasket scraper or putty knife can be used for cleaning the valve face and the area between the face and lower stem. Do not scratch the valve face during cleaning. Clean the entire stem with a rag soaked in thinners to remove all varnish and gum.

Thorough inspection of the valves requires the use of a micrometer, and a dial indicator is needed to measure the inside diameter of the valve guides. If these instruments are not available to you, the valves and head can be taken to a reputable machine shop for inspection. Refer to the "Valve Specifications" chart for valve stem and stem-to-guide specifications.

If the above instruments are at your disposal, measure the diameter of each valve stem at the locations illustrated. Jot these measurements down. Using the dial indicator, mea-

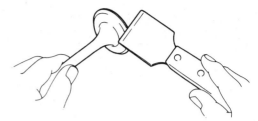
Carefully scrape carbon from the valve head

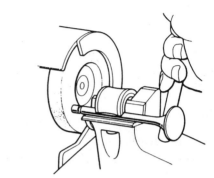
Grinding the valve stem tip

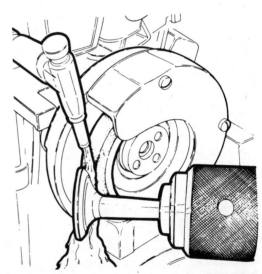
Valve refacing should be handled by a reputable machine shop

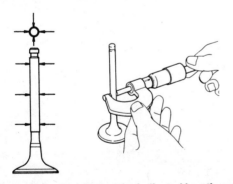
Mike up the valve stem at the indicated locations

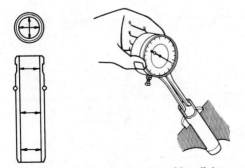
Check valve guide inside diameter with a dial gauge

sure the inside diameter of the valve guides at their bottom, top and midpoint 90° apart. Jot these measurements down also. Subtract the valve stem measurement from the valve guide inside measurement; if the clearance exceeds that listed in the specifications chart under "Stem-to-Guide Clearance", replace the valve(s). Stem-to-guide clearance can also be checked at a machine shop, where a dial indicator would be used.

Check the top of each valve stem for pitting and unusual wear due to improper rocker adjustment, etc. The stem tip can be ground flat if it is worn, but no more than 0.020 in. can be removed; if this limit must be exceeded to make the tip flat and square, then the valve must be replaced. If the valve stem tips are ground, make sure you fix the valve securely into a jig designed for this purpose, so the tip contacts the grinding wheel squarely at exactly 90°. Most machine shops that handle automotive work are equipped for this job.

REFACING

Valve refacing should only be handled by a reputable machine shop, as the experience and equipment needed to do the job are beyond that of the average owner/mechanic. During the course of a normal valve job, refacing is necessary when simply lapping the valves into their seats will not correct the seat and face wear. When the valves are reground (resurfaced), the valve seats must also be recut, again requiring special equipment and experience.

VALVE LAPPING

The valves must be lapped into their seats after resurfacing, to ensure proper sealing. Even if the valves have not been refaced, they should be lapped into the head before reassembly.

Set the cylinder head on the workbench, combustion chamber side up. Rest the head on wooden blocks on either end, so there are two or three inches between the tops of the valve guides and the bench.

1. Lightly lube the valve stem with clean engine oil. Coat the valve seat completely with valve grinding compound. Use just enough compound that the full width and circumference of the seat are covered.

2. Install the valve in its proper location in the head. Attach the suction cup end of the valve lapping tool to the valve head. It usually helps to put a small amount of saliva into the suction cup to aid it sticking to the valve.

3. Rotate the tool between the palms, changing position and lifting the tool often to prevent grooving. Lap the valve in until a smooth, evenly polished seat and valve face are evident.

4. Remove the valve from the head. Wipe away all traces of grinding compound from the valve face and seat. Wipe out the port with a solvent soaked rag, and swab out the valve guide with a piece of solvent soaked rag to make sure there are no traces of compound grit inside the guide. *This cleaning is important.*

5. Proceed through the remaining valves, one at a time. Make sure the valve faces, seats, cylinder ports and valve guides are clean before reassembling the valve train.

Valve Springs
INSPECTION

Valve spring squareness, length and tension should be checked while the valve train is disassembled. Place each valve spring on a flat surface next to a steel square. Measure the length of the spring, and rotate it against the edge of the square to measure distortion. If spring length varies (by comparison) by more than $1/16$ in. or if distortion exceeds $1/16$ in., replace the spring.

Spring tension must be checked on a spring

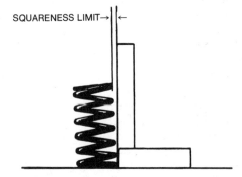

Check spring length and squareness with a steel square

Lapping a valve in by hand

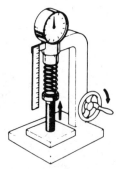

Have spring tension checked at a machine shop

tester. Springs used on the Celica engines should be within one pound of each other when tested at their specified installed heights.

Valve Seats

The valve seats in the engines covered in this guide are all non-replaceable, and must be recut when service is required. Seat recutting requires a special tool and experience, and should be handled at a reputable machine shop. Seat concentricity should also be checked by a machinist.

Valve Guides

INSPECTION

Valve guides should be cleaned as outlined earlier, and checked when valve stem diameter and stem-to-guide clearance is checked. Generally, if the engine is using oil through the guides (assuming the valve seals are OK) and the valve stem diameter is within specification, it is the guides that are worn and need replacing.

Valve guides which are not excessively worn or distorted may, in some cases, be knurled rather than replaced. Knurling is a process in which metal inside the valve guide bore is displaced and raised (forming a very fine cross-hatch pattern), thereby reducing clearance. Knurling also provides for excellent oil control. The possibility of knurling rather than replacing the guides should be discussed with a machinist.

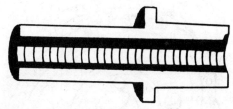

Cross-section of a knurled valve guide

REMOVAL AND INSTALLATION

Valve guide replacement on all Celica engines requires breaking off the top end of the guides, heating the cylinder head to almost 200°F, then driving the rest of the guide out of the head with a hammer and drift. Unless you and your family don't mind baking an oily cylinder head in the oven (and probably smelling it in the house for months), take the head to a machine shop and have a machinist replace the guides.

Timing Chain/Timing Belt Cover
REMOVAL AND INSTALLATION
All Engines Except 5M-GE Twin Cam

1. Perform the "Cylinder Head Removal" procedure as detailed in the appropriate previous sections.
2. Remove the radiator (see "Engine Cooling").
3. Remove the alternator (see "Alternator").
4. On engines equipped with air pumps, unfasten the adjusting link bolts and the drive belt. Remove the hoses from the pump; remove the pump and bracket from the engine.
    NOTE: *If the car is equipped with power steering, see Chapter 8 for its pump removal procedure.*
5. Remove the fan and water pump as a complete assembly.
    CAUTION: *To prevent the fluid from running out of the fan coupling, do not tip the assembly over on its side.*
6. Unfasten the crankshaft pulley securing bolt and remove the pulley with a gear puller.
    CAUTION: *Do not remove the 10 mm bolt from its hole, if installed, as it is used for balancing.*
7. Loosen the bolts securing the front of the oil pan, after draining the engine oil. Lower the front of the oil pan.

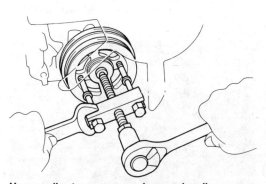

Use a puller to remove engine crank pulley

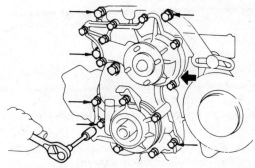

22R front cover removal

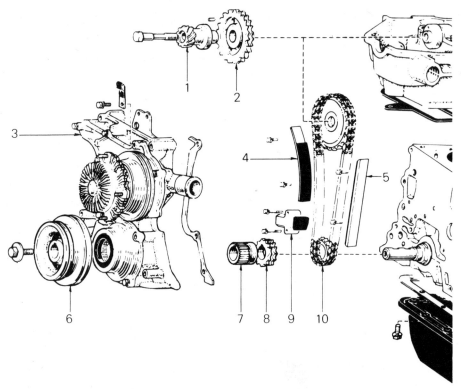

1. Distributor drive gear
2. Camshaft sprocket
3. Chain cover
4. Chain damper No. 2
5. Chain damper No. 1
6. Crankshaft pulley
7. Pump drive spline
8. Crankshaft sprocket
9. Chain tensioner
10. Chain

Front cover and timing chain components—20R, 22R series

1. Timing chain tensioner gear
2. Timing chain tensioner arm
3. Damper guide
4. Vibration damper
5. Vibration damper
6. Crankshaft oil slinger

Removing the 4M-E timing chain (engine inverted)

8. Remove the bolts securing the timing chain cover. Withdraw the cover.

9. Installation is performed in the reverse

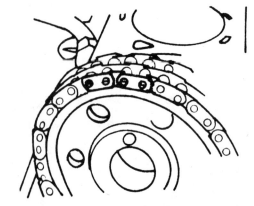

Timing mark alignment—20R, 22R series

order of removal. Apply sealer to the gaskets for both the timing chain cover and the oil pan.

NOTE: *The 4M-E and 5M-E engines use two gaskets on the timing chain cover.*

Tighten the crankshaft pulley bolt to specification listed under the "Torque Specifications" chart, and tighten all chain cover bolts until snug.

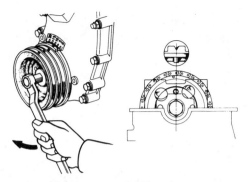

Timing mark alignment; 4M-E engine

5M-GE Twin Cam Six

NOTE: *Please refer to the timing belt assembly exploded view when timing belt covers 1, 2, and 3 are mentioned.*

1. Disconnect the negative battery cable.
2. Drain the cooling system.
3. Remove the air cleaner case by disconnecting it from the intake hose.
4. Remove the upper radiator hose.
5. Remove the fan shroud, and remove the fan and fluid coupling.
6. Loosen and remove the drive belts.
7. Remove the air intake connector.
8. Set No. 1 cylinder to TDC on its compression stroke, by aligning the notch on the crankshaft pulley with the "0" mark on the front cover, while feeling the piston come up with your thumb over the No. 1 spark plug hole.

9. Remove the five bolts and remove the No. 3 timing cover and gasket.
10. Remove the crankshaft pulley set bolt. Using a pulley extractor or gear puller, remove the pulley.
11. Remove the screws and remove the No. 1 timing belt cover.
12. Installation of the covers is in the reverse order of removal. Torque the crankshaft pulley bolt to 97–119 ft. lbs. Tighten the belt cover bolts until snug.

TIMING CHAIN COVER OIL SEAL REPLACEMENT

All Engines Except 5M-GE and 20R, 22R

NOTE: *The 5M-GE timing belt case oil seal replacement is covered following the "Timing Belt" removal procedure for that engine.*

1. Remove the timing chain cover, as previously detailed in the appropriate section.
2. Inspect the oil seal for signs of wear, leakage, or damage.
3. If worn, pry the old oil seal out, using a large flat-bladed screwdriver. Remove it toward the *front* of the cover.

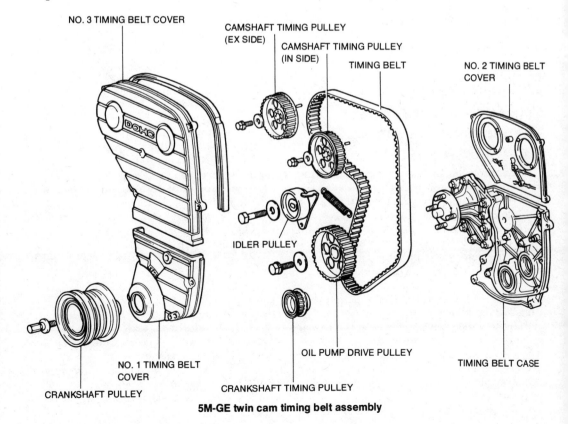

NO. 3 TIMING BELT COVER

CAMSHAFT TIMING PULLEY (EX SIDE)

CAMSHAFT TIMING PULLEY (IN SIDE)

TIMING BELT

NO. 2 TIMING BELT COVER

IDLER PULLEY

NO. 1 TIMING BELT COVER

OIL PUMP DRIVE PULLEY

TIMING BELT CASE

CRANKSHAFT PULLEY

CRANKSHAFT TIMING PULLEY

5M-GE twin cam timing belt assembly

Carefully pry seals from the cover; tap in new seals with an old socket

NOTE: *Once the oil seal has been removed, it must be replaced with a new one.*

4. Use a socket, pipe, or block of wood and a hammer to drift the oil seal into place. Work from the *front* of the cover.

CAUTION: *Be extremely careful not to damage the seal or else it will leak.*

5. Install the timing chain cover as previously outlined.

20R and 22R

NOTE: *When repairing the oil pump, the oil pan and strainer should be removed and cleaned.*

1. Remove the fan shroud and fan assembly.
2. Remove all drive belts.
3. Remove the crankshaft pulley.
4. Unbolt the oil pump from the front cover and remove.
5. Using a flat-bladed screwdriver, remove the old oil seal from the pump.
6. Lightly oil the new seal, and using an old socket or block of wood and hammer, carefully drive the new seal into place, working from the front of the pump.
7. Installation is the reverse of removal.

Timing Chain and Tensioner
REMOVAL AND INSTALLATION
8R-C and 18R-C Engines

1. Remove the cylinder head and timing chain cover as previously detailed.
2. Remove the timing chain (front) together with the camshaft drive sprocket.
3. Remove the crankshaft sprocket and oil pump jack shaft, complete with the pump jack shaft, complete with the pump drive chain (rear). Remove the chain vibration damper.

CAUTION: *Both timing chains are identical; tag them for proper identification during installation.*

4. Inspect the chains and sprockets for wear or damage. Clean the chains with solvent.
5. Use a vernier caliper to measure the amount of stretch of both chains. Measure any 17 links while pulling the chain which is being measured taut.
6. Repeat Step 5 at two other places on each

| 1. Camshaft timing chain | 3. Chain tensioner |
| 2. Camshaft drive gear | 4. Chain tensioner |

8R-C and 18R-C camshaft timing chain removal (engine inverted)

chain. Replace either of the chains if any of the 17 link measurements exceed 5.792 in. or if the difference between the minimum and maximum readings is more than 0.0078 in., on any one chain.

7. Remove the plunger and spring from one of the chain tensioners. Inspect all of the parts of the tensioner for wear or damage. Fill it with oil and assemble it if it is not defective.
8. Repeat Step 7 for the other tensioner.

CAUTION: *Do not mix the parts of the two chain tensioners together.*

Installation is performed in the following manner:

1. Position the No. 1 piston at TDC by having the crankshaft keyway point straight up (perpendicular to) toward the cylinder head.
2. Align the oil pump jack shaft, with its keyway pointing straight up as well.
3. Align the marks on the timing sprocket and the oil pump drive sprocket with each of the marks on the chain.
4. Install the chain and sprocket assembly over the keyways, while retaining alignment of the chain/sprocket timing marks.

CAUTION: *Use care not to disengage the welch plug at the rear of the oil pump driveshaft by forcing the sprocket over its keyway.*

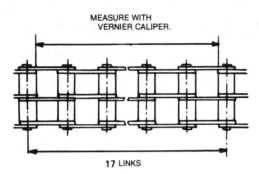

MEASURE WITH
VERNIER CALIPER.

17 LINKS

Timing chain stretch measurement—8R-C and 18R-C

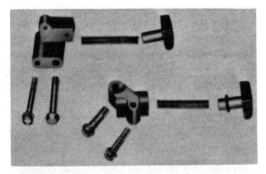

8R-C and 18R-C chain tensioner assemblies

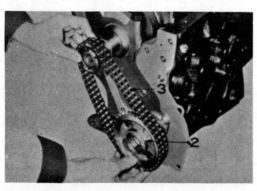

1. Crankshaft timing gear mark
2. Oil pump driveshaft mark
3. Oil pump chain timing mark

Aligning the timing marks on the oil pump drive chain (engine inverted)

5. Install the oil pump drive chain vibration damper.

6. Install the gasket for the timing chain cover.

NOTE: *Use liquid sealer on the gasket before installation.*

7. Install both of the chain tensioners in their respective places, being careful not to mix them up. Tighten their securing bolts to 12–17 ft. lbs.

CAUTION: *Use care when installing the*

chain tensioner bolts; they have oil holes tapped in them.

8. Fit the camshaft drive sprocket over the keyway on the oil pump driveshaft. Tighten its securing nut to 58–72 ft. lbs.

9. Install the camshaft drive chain over the camshaft drive sprocket. Align the mating marks on the chain and sprocket.

10. Apply tension to the chain by tying it to the chain tensioner. This will prevent it from falling back into the timing chain cover once it is installed.

11. Install the timing chain cover and cylinder head as previously outlined.

20R and 22R/RE Engines

1. Remove the cylinder head and timing chain cover as previously outlined.

2. Separate the chain from the damper, and remove the chain, complete with the camshaft sprocket.

3. Remove the crankshaft sprocket and the oil pump drive with a puller.

4. Inspect the chain for wear or damage. Replace it if necessary.

5. Inspect the chain tensioner for wear. If it measures less than 0.43 in., replace it.

6. Check the dampers for wear. If their measurements are below the following specifications, replace them:
 • Upper damper—0.20 in.
 • Lower damper—0.18 in.

Installation is performed in the following order:

1. Rotate the crankshaft until its key is at TDC. Slide the sprocket in place over the key.

2. Place the chain over the sprocket so that its *single* bright link aligns with the mark on the camshaft sprocket.

3. Install the cam sprocket so that the timing mark falls between the *two* bright links on the chain.

4. Fit the oil pump drive spline over the crankshaft key.

5. Install the timing cover gasket on the front of the block.

6. Rotate the camshaft sprocket counterclockwise to remove the slack from the chain.

7. Install the timing chain cover and cylinder head as previously outlined.

4M-E and 5M-E Engines

1. Remove the cylinder head and timing chain cover as previously outlined.

2. Remove the chain tensioner assembly (arm and gear).

3. Unfasten the bolts retaining the chain damper and damper guide and withdraw the damper and guide.

4. Remove the oil slinger from the crank-shaft.

5. Withdraw the timing chain.

6. Inspect the chain for wear or damage. Replace it if necessary.

Installation is performed in the following manner:

1. Position the No. 1 cylinder at TDC.

2. Position the crankshaft sprocket "O" mark downward, facing the oil pan.

3. Align the "Toyota" trademarks on the sprockets as illustrated.

4. Fit the tensioner gear assembly on the block.

NOTE: *Its dowel pin should be positioned 1.5 in. from the surface of the block.*

5. Install the chain over the two gears while maintaining tension.

6. Install both of the vibration dampers and the damper guide.

7. Fit the oil slinger to the crankshaft.

8. Tie the chain to the upper vibration damper, to keep it from falling into the chain cover, once the cover is installed.

9. Install the timing chain cover as previously detailed.

10. Perform the cylinder head installation procedure as detailed previously.

NOTE: *If proper valve timing cannot be obtained, it is possible to adjust it by placing the camshaft slotted pin in the second or third hole on the camshaft timing gear, as required. If the timing is out by more than 15°, replace the chain and both of the sprockets.*

Timing Belt and Idler Pulley
REMOVAL AND INSTALLATION
5M-GE Twin Cam Six

1. Follow steps 1 through 9 of the "Timing Belt Cover" removal procedure. *Do not rotate the crankshaft or camshafts during this procedure. If shafts are turned, see procedure below.*

2. Loosen the idler pulley set bolt a bit and shift the pulley over to the alternator side with a small pry bar and wrench.

3. Finger tighten the set bolt, then relieve the tension on the timing belt.

4. Mark an arrow on the timing belt showing direction of belt rotation. *This is important if the same belt is to be reinstalled.* Slide the belt off the camshaft timing pulleys, and remove the belt from the engine. Remove the idler pulley and spring.

5. Inspect the belt and idler pulley assembly for damage and/or unusual wear as described below.

6. To install the belt, first install the idler

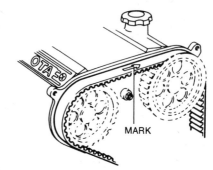

Mark the rotation direction on the timing belt with an arrow before removal

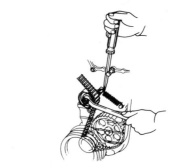

Loosen the idler pulley and push it out of the way

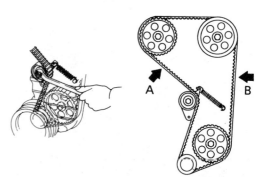

Timing belt tension should be equal at these two points following adjustment

pulley and spring. Push the pulley toward the alternator as far as it will go and tighten it temporarily. Install the timing belt in the proper direction of rotation by checking the arrow on the belt. Loosen the idler pulley set bolt until the pulley swings over and tightens the belt.

7. Temporarily snug the pulley set bolt, and turn the crankshaft clockwise for two full rotations. Check timing belt tension in the center between the two camshaft sprockets. Belt deflection should measure between 0.16–0.24 in. (4–6 mm) with the engine cold. If not within this limit, or too tight, adjust belt tension by loosening the idler pulley nut and moving the pulley accordingly. Make sure timing belt tension is equal at points A and B as shown in the illustration. When properly

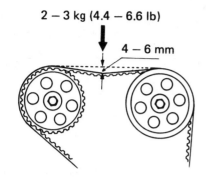

Check belt deflection here

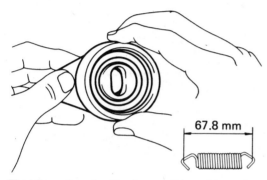

The idler pulley should spin smoothly and its spring should measure the correct length

adjusted, torque the idler pulley set bolt to 32–40 ft. lbs.

INSPECTION

The timing belt and idler tensioning system should be inspected after removal. Belt teeth should be checked along their bases for any signs of cracking and the belt replaced if cracks exist. Check the face of the belt; if cracks or wear are in evidence, examine the idler pulley lock for nicks and replace the pulley if necessary. If damage or wear exists on one edge of the belt only, check the belt guide and pulley alignment. Finally, if the teeth are unusually worn, check the timing belt cover gasket for damage or improper installation.

Inspect the idler pulley by spinning it; it should spin smoothly and freely. Check the outer surface of the pulley for nicks or wear which might cause the belt to wear quickly. The pulley spring should measure 2.67 in. (67.8 mm); install a new spring if it is not of this length or has been bent.

TIMING BELT CASE—OIL SEAL REPLACEMENT

NOTE: *The following procedure covers front oil seal and oil pump seal removal with the front timing belt case removed from the block. It is possible to remove the seal with* the case installed, but a special service tool is required.

1. Remove the timing belt covers, timing belt assembly and lower timing pulleys from the engine.

2. Remove the timing belt case (the rear section of the timing belt cover) from the cylinder block.

3. Using a small pry bar, remove the front oil seal and the pump drive oil seal. *Do not gouge the case.*

4. Apply a multipurpose grease to the lips of the new oil seals. Carefully install the new seals using an old socket or oil seal tool.

5. Reinstall all parts in the reverse order of removal.

VALVE TIMING—ENGINE DISTURBED

5M-GE Twin Cam Six

If the camshafts and/or crankshaft are turned while the timing belt is removed, the valve timing must be reset before the engine can be started. The following procedure sets the engine up so the belt can be reinstalled.

1. Turn the crankshaft clockwise and set the No. 1 cylinder to TDC.

2. Check that the matchmarks of the camshaft timing pulleys are aligned with the marks on the rear half (No. 2 in the timing belt illustration) of the timing belt cover. If the matchmarks are not aligned, (if there is more than one tooth of the timing pulley between the matchmarks) rotate the camshaft timing pulley with the proper spanner until the matchmarks are aligned.

3. Install the timing belt and let the idler pulley take up any slack. Loosen the pulley set bolt and turn the crankshaft clockwise about 10°. Tighten the idler pulley set bolt, and check belt tension—it should be equal on both sides.

4. Turn the crankshaft clockwise, using a socket wrench, two full turns and set the No. 1 cylinder to TDC on the compression stroke. Recheck the cam pulley timing marks.

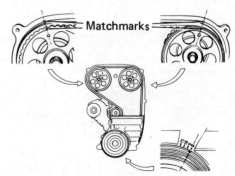

Set the crankshaft pulley to TDC on compression and align the cam pulley matchmarks

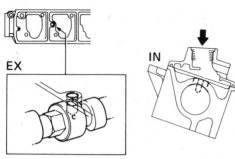

Align the camshaft and cam housing match holes; crank pulley timing mark should be plus or minus 5°TDC.

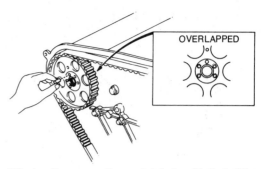

Aligning the cam pulley match hole with that of the camshaft

5. Make sure the camshaft match holes are clean; if not, blow them out with compressed air. Align the match hole in the camshaft with that of the camshaft housing by rotating the crankshaft pulley. Match hole alignment should be done separately for both the intake and exhaust camshafts. Check the crankshaft pulley timing mark in relation to the degree marks on the timing belt cover; if the pulley is within plus or minus 5° of TDC, the engine is properly timed and all there is left to do is check timing belt tension. If the mark on the pulley exceeds plus or minus 5° from TDC, proceed to step 6.

6. Hold the camshaft pulley with the spanner (available at auto tool shops or Toyota dealers) and remove the pulley set bolt. *DO NOT hold the pulley by holding the timing belt.*

7. Check to make sure that the camshaft housing match hole is aligned with that of the camshaft. Using a magnet, remove the match pin from the pin hole of the camshaft timing pulley. Set the No. 1 cylinder to TDC on the compression stroke.

8. Select the one hole in the timing pulley that is overlapped, and insert the match pin into it. If there is no overlapped hole, find one that nearly is and rotate the crankshaft *slightly* until the hole is overlapped. Insert the pin. Note that when you change the pin hole, you

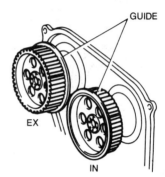

5M-GE cam pulley installation. Note guide position difference

change the degree angle on the crankshaft pulley.

9. Hold the timing pulley with the spanner, and install the pulley set bolt. Torque the bolt to 48—55 ft. lbs.

10. Turn the crankshaft clockwise two full turns and set the No. cylinder to TDC on compression. Recheck the crankshaft pulley degree angle, and check timing belt tension. Reassemble the belt cover and other components in the reverse order of removal.

Timing Gears/Pulleys
REMOVAL AND INSTALLATION

All of the camshaft drive sprockets and pulleys are retained on their respective shafts by bolts. The engines with chain-driven camshafts (all except the 5M-GE Six) have their sprockets keyed onto the cam in addition to the bolt; the 5M-GE does not have a keyway. To remove the sprockets or pulleys on all engines, first follow the timing chain or belt removal procedures, then follow below.

1. Remove the retaining bolt(s) for the drive sprocket you wish to remove. D not use the timing chain or belt as a means of holding the sprocket—use a spanner that is made for the job.

2. Gently pry the sprocket or pulley off the

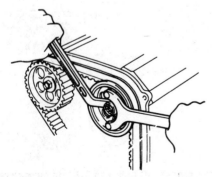

Removing the cam pulley set bolt

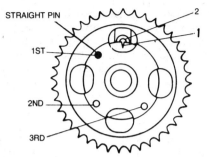

4M-E/5M-E camshaft sprocket—normal valve timing

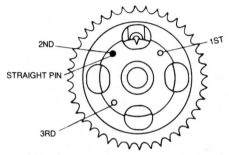

Camshaft sprocket—valve timing retarded 3 to 9°, 4M-E/5M-E

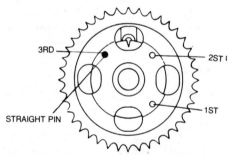

Camshaft sprocket—valve timing retarded 9 to 12°, 4M-E/5M-E

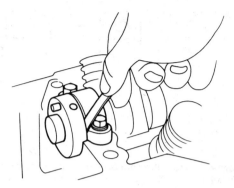

Use a flat feeler gauge to measure the camshaft end-play

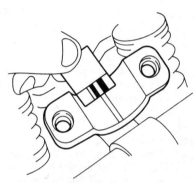

Use a piece of Plastigage® to measure the camshaft bearing oil clearance

shaft. If the sprocket or pulley is stubborn, use a gear puller. *Never* hammer on the sprocket or the camshaft!

3. Remove the sprocket or pulley and be careful not to lose the key if equipped.

4. Installation is the reverse of removal. On the engines with timing positioning pins, make sure the pins are properly aligned. On the 5M-GE Six, install the exhaust-side pulley with the belt guide facing the rear of the engine, and install the intake-side pulley with the guide facing the front of the engine.

Camshaft and Bearings

REMOVAL AND INSTALLATION

All Engines Except 5M-GE

1. Perform the "Cylinder Head Removal" procedure (for your engine) far enough to gain access to the camshaft bearing cap bolts. If you are going to remove the head anyway, remove the cam after removing the cylinder head.

2. Prior to removing the camshaft, measure its end-play with a feeler gauge. The end-play limit is 0.0098 in. for the 8R-C, 18R-C, 20R and 22R engines; 0.01 for the 4M-E and 5M-E engines. If the end-play is beyond this, replace the head.

3. Use a 12 mm wrench to remove the bearing cap bolts. Remove the caps. Keep them in order, or mark them.

4. Measure the bearing oil clearance by placing a piece of Plastigage® on each journal. Replace the caps and tighten their bolts to 13–16 ft. lbs.

5. Remove the caps and measure each piece of Plastigage®. If the clearance is greater than 0.004 in., replace the head and cam.

6. Lift the camshaft out of the head.

Camshaft installation is performed in the following order:

1. Coat all of the camshaft bearing journals with engine oil.

2. Lay the camshaft in the head.

3. Install the bearing caps in numerical order with their arrows pointing forward (toward the front of the engine).

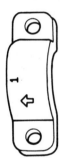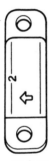

Number or mark the cam bearing caps for later installation

4. Install the cap bolts and tighten them to 13–16 ft. lbs.

5. Complete the cylinder head installation procedure as previously outlined.

5M-GE

1. Follow steps 1 through 3 of the "5M-GE Rocker Arm Removal" procedure, removing the camshaft housings (with cams) from the cylinder head.

2. Before removing the camshafts, check camshaft end-play using a dial indicator set on the bench at one the front end of the camshaft. If this instrument is not available to you, take the housings to a reputable machine shop. Standard clearance is 0.0020–0.0098 in. If clearance is greater than this specification, the camshaft and/or cam housing must be replaced.

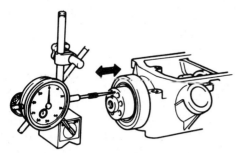

Measure 5M-GE camshaft end play with a dial indicator

3. Remove the camshaft housing rear covers. Squirt clean oil down around the cam journals in the housing, to lubricate the lobes, oil seals and bearings as the cam is removed. Begin to pull the camshaft out of the back of the housing slowly, turning it as you pull. Remove the cam completely.

4. To install, lubricate the entire camshaft with clean oil. Insert the cam into the housing from the back, and slowly turn it as you push it into the housing. Install new O-rings and the housing end covers.

CAMSHAFT INSPECTION

A dial indicator, micrometer and inside micrometer are all needed to properly measure the camshaft and camshaft housing. If these instruments are available to you, proceed; if they are not available, have the parts checked at a reputable machine shop. Camshaft specifications are included in a table in this chapter.

1. Using the micrometer, measure the height of each cam lobe. If a lobe height is less than the minimum specified, the lobe is worn and the cam must be replaced. Minimum intake and exhaust lobe heights are as follows:

- 8R-C   1.721 in. Intake
           1.724 in. Exhaust
- 18R   1.7206 in. Intake
           1.7245 in. Exhaust
- 20R   1.6783 to 1.6819 in. Intake
           1.6806 to 1.6841 in. Exhaust

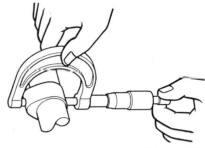

Measure lobe height (shown) and journal diameter with a micrometer

Slowly turn the cam as you remove it from the back of the housing

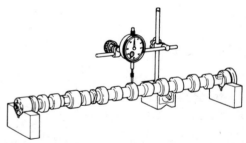

Camshaft run-out must be measured with a dial indicator

Use an inside micrometer to measure camshaft housing bore diameter

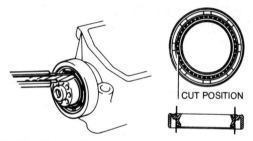

Cutting the seal lip

- 22R   1.6783 to 1.6819 in. Intake
             1.6807 to 1.6842 in. Exhaust
- 4M-E   1.6797 to 1.6822 in. Intake
             1.664 to 1.666 in. Exhaust
- 5M-E   1.6961 in. Intake
             1.6988 in. Exhaust
- 5M-GE   1.3963 in. Intake
             1.3963 in. Exhaust

2. Place the cam in V-blocks and measure its run-out at the center journal with a dial indicator. If run-out exceeds 0.008 in. (0.002 on 4M-E and 5M-E engines, and 0.0016 in. on 5M-GE) replace the cam.

3. Using the micrometer, measure journal diameter, jot down the readings, and compare the readings with those listed in the "Camshaft Specifications" chart. Measure the housing bore inside diameter with the inside micrometer, and jot the measurements down. Subtract the journal diameter measurement from the housing bore measurement—if the clearance is greater than the maximum listed under "Bearing Clearance" in the chart, replace the camshaft and/or the housing.

Camshaft Housing Oil Seal

REMOVAL AND INSTALLATION

5M-GE Six

NOTE: *The camshaft housing oil seals can be removed with the camshaft either installed or removed. Both methods are covered below.*

CAMSHAFT REMOVED

1. Using a small pry bar, carefully pry out the oil seals.

2. Coat the new oil seals with multipurpose grease. Using an old socket or oil seal tool, gently tap the new seals into place.

CAMSHAFT AND HOUSING INSTALLED.

1. Carefully cut the oil seal lip off of each seal using a utility knife. The lip is the inner diameter portion of the seal, closest to the camshaft.

2. Tape the blade end of a small pry bar so

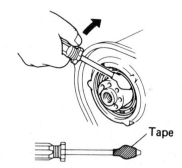

Pry the seal from the housing; do not scratch the cam

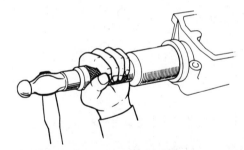

Installing an oil seal using an oil seal tool—an old socket also works

as not to damage the camshaft. Pry out the remaining part of the oil seals.

3. Coat the new seals with multipurpose grease. Using an old socket or oil seal tool, gently tap the new seals into place.

Oil Pump Drive Shaft

REMOVAL AND INSTALLATION

All Engines Except 20R and 22R/R-E

1. Remove the timing covers and the timing chains or belt assemblies, depending on engine. Remove the pump shaft drive sprocket or pulley with a gear puller.

2. Remove the bolt holding the shaft thrust plate to the front of the block.

3. Slowly pull the shaft out of the block, turning it as you pull. Use care as not to damage the shaft bearing.

4. To install, lubricate the shaft with clean engine oil. Turn the shaft slowly as you insert

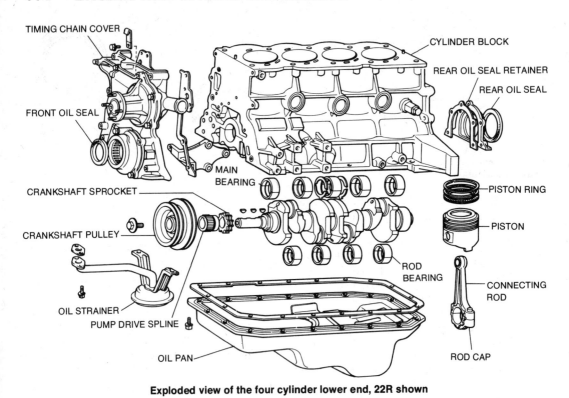

Exploded view of the four cylinder lower end, 22R shown

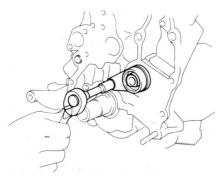

Removing the oil pump shaft thrust plate

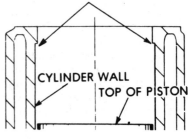

Ridge caused by cylinder wear

it into the block. Bolt the thrust plate to the block, and install the timing chain or belt assemblies and timing covers.

Pistons and Connecting Rods
REMOVAL AND INSTALLATION

All Engines

NOTE: *Before removing the piston assemblies, connecting rod bearing clearance and side clearance should be checked. Refer to the "Connecting Rod Inspection" procedure in this chapter.*

1. Remove the cylinder head as outlined in the appropriate preceding section.

2. Remove the oil pan and pump; see "Engine Lubrication."

Removing the ridge with a ridge reamer

3. Position a cylinder ridge reamer into the top of the cylinder bore. Keeping the tool square, ream the ridges from the top of the bore. Clean out the ridge material with a sol-

Cover the rod bolts with rubber tubing (arrow) before removing piston and rod assemblies

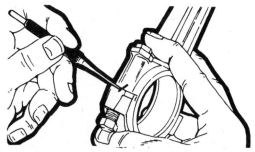

Matchmark each rod cap to its connecting rod

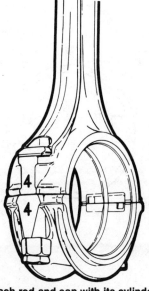

Number each rod and cap with its cylinder number for correct assembly

vent-soaked rag, or blow it out with compressed air.

4. Remove the oil strainer if it is in the way. Unbolt the connecting rod caps, after matchmarking each cap to its connecting rod.

5. Place pieces of rubber hose over the rod

bolts, to protect the cylinder walls and crank journals from scratches. Push the connecting rod and piston up and out of the cylinder from the bottom, using a wooden hammer handle.

CAUTION: *Use care not to scratch the crank journals or the cylinder walls.*

6. Mark each connecting rod with the number of the cylinder from which it was removed. Number stamps are available at most hardware or auto supply stores.

Installation is performed in the following order:

1. Apply a light coating of engine oil to the pistons, rings, and outer ends of the wrist pins.

2. Examine the piston to ensure that it has been assembled with its parts positioned correctly. (See the illustrations.) Be sure that the ring gaps are not pointed toward the thrust face of the piston and that they do not overlap.

3. Place pieces of rubber hose over the connecting rod bolts, to keep the threads from damaging the crank journal and cylinder bore. Install the pistons, using a ring compressor, into the cylinder bore. Be sure that the appropriate marks on the piston are facing the front of the cylinder.

NOTE: *It is important that the pistons, rods, bearings, etc., be returned to the same cylinder bore from which they were removed.*

4. Install the connecting rod bearing caps and tighten them to the torque figures given in the "Torque Specifications" chart.

NOTE: *Be sure that the mating marks on the connecting rods and rod bearing caps are aligned.*

5. The rest of the removal procedure is performed in the reverse order of installation.

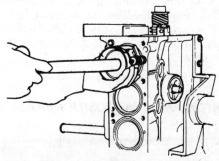

Install the piston and connecting rod into the cylinder with a ring compressor

PISTON AND CONNECTING ROD IDENTIFICATION

The pistons are marked with a notch in the piston head. When installed in the engine, the notch markings must be facing towards the front of the engine.

The connecting rods should be installed in

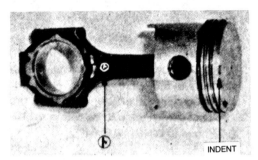

8R-C. 18R-C. 20R and 22R engines

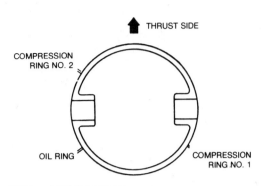

4M-E and 5M-E engines

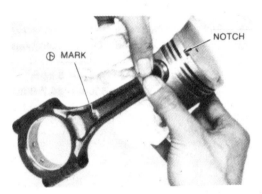

4M-E, 5M-E, 5M-GE engines

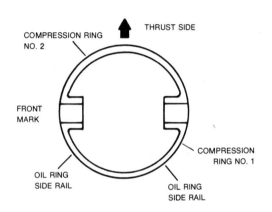

4M-E engine

the engine with the forged marks on the bearing caps and on the bottom of the rod facing toward the front of the engine also.

NOTE: *It is advisable to number the pistons, connecting rods and bearing caps in some manner so that they can be reinstalled in the same cylinder, facing the same direction, from which they were removed.*

The piston rings must be installed with their gaps in the same position as shown in the illustrations.

PISTON AND RING POSITIONING

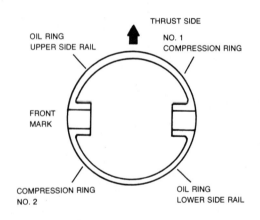

5M-E engine

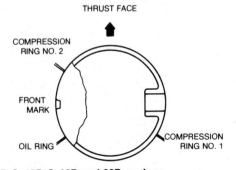

8R-C, 18R-C, 20R and 22R engines

PISTON RING REPLACEMENT

NOTE: *The cylinder walls must be de-glazed (honed) when the piston rings are replaced. De-glazing ensures proper ring seating and oil retention.*

Using a piston ring expander, remove the rings one by one. Always remove and replace the rings of each piston before going on to the

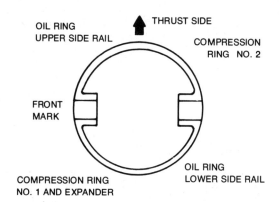

OIL RING
UPPER SIDE RAIL

THRUST SIDE

COMPRESSION
RING   NO. 2

FRONT
MARK

COMPRESSION RING
NO. 1 AND EXPANDER

OIL RING
LOWER SIDE RAIL

5M-GE engine

Use needle-nose or snap-ring pliers to remove the piston pin snap-rings

next—this helps avoid mixing up the rings. When the rings have been removed from each piston, perform the end gap and piston inspection and cleaning procedure below. The rings are marked on one side, the mark denoting the "up" side for installation.

Install the rings using the ring expander, starting with the top compression ring and working down. *Make sure the marks are facing up on each ring.* Position the rings so that the ring and gaps are set as in the illustrations. Never align the end gaps!

Rock the piston at a right angle to the wrist pin to check pin and small-end bushing wear

When fully heated, the wrist pin should be able to be pushed into place by hand

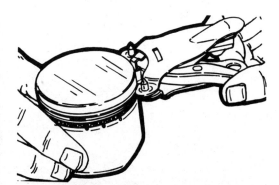

Remove and install the rings with a ring expander

WRIST PIN REMOVAL AND INSTALLATION

Wrist pin and/or connecting rod small-end bushing wear can be checked by rocking the piston at a right angle to the wrist pin by hand. If more than *very slight* movement is felt, the pin and/or rod bushing must be replaced.

The pistons on the engines covered here must be heated in hot water to expand them before the wrist pins can be removed and installed. The four cylinder pistons must be heated to 176°F (80°C), and all six cylinder

pistons must be heated to 140°F (60°F). This job can be performed at a machine shop if the idea of boiling pistons in the kitchen doesn't appeal to you. If you decide to do it, however, remember that each piston, pin and connecting rod assembly is a matched set and must be kept together until reassembly.

1. Using needle-nose or snap-ring pliers, remove the snap rings from the piston.

2. Heat the piston(s) in hot water (as noted above depending on engine).

3. Using a plastic-faced hammer and driver, lightly tap the wrist pin out of the piston. Remove the piston from the connecting rod.

4. Assembly is in the opposite order of disassembly. The piston must again be heated to install the wrist pin and rod; it should be able to be pushed into place with your thumb when heated. *When assembling, make sure the marks*

on the piston and connecting rod are aligned on the same side as shown.

CLEANING AND INSPECTION

Clean the piston after removing the rings, by first scraping any carbon from the piston top. *Do not scratch the piston in any way during cleaning.* Use a broken piston ring or ring cleaning tool to clean out the ring grooves. Clean the entire piston with solvent and a brush (NOT a wire brush).

Once the piston is thoroughly cleaned, insert the side of a good piston ring (both No. 1 and No. 2 compression on each piston) into its respective groove. Using a feeler gauge, measure the clearance between the ring and its groove. If clearance is greater than the maximum listed under "Ring Side Clearance" in

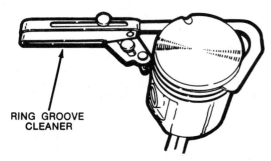

RING GROOVE
CLEANER

Clean the ring grooves with this tool or the edge of an old ring

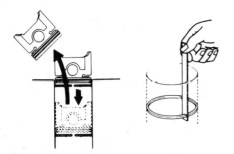

To check ring end gap, push the ring to the bottom of its travel; check gap with feeler gauge

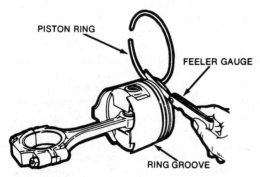

PISTON RING

FEELER GAUGE

RING GROOVE

Checking ring side clearance

the "Piston and Ring" chart, replace the ring(s) and if necessary, the piston.

To check ring end-gap, insert a compression ring into the cylinder. Lightly oil the cylinder bore and push the ring down into the cylinder with a piston, to the bottom of its travel. Measure the ring end-gap with a feeler gauge. If the gap is not within specification, replace the ring; DO NOT file the ring ends.

CYLINDER BORE INSPECTION

Place a rag over the crankshaft journals. Wipe out each cylinder with a clean, solvent-soaked rag. Visually inspect the cylinder bores for roughness, scoring or scuffing; also check the bores by feel. Measure the cylinder bore diameter with an inside micrometer, or a telescope gauge and micrometer. Measure the bore at points parallel and perpendicular to the engine centerline at the top (below the ridge) and bottom of the bore. Subtract the bottom measurements from the top to determine cylinder taper.

Measure the piston diameter with a micrometer; since this micrometer may not be part of your tool kit as it is necessarily large, you may have to have the pistons miked at a machine shop. Take the measurements at right angles to the wrist pin center line, about an inch down the piston skirt from the top. Compare this measurement to the bore diameter

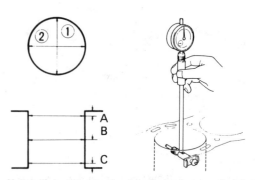

Use a dial gauge to check cylinder bore and piston clearance

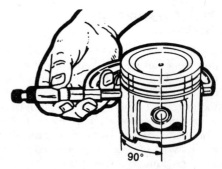

90°

Check piston diameter at these points

of each cylinder—the difference is the piston clearance. If the clearance is greater than that specified in the "Piston and Ring Specifications" chart, have the cylinders honed or rebored and replace the pistons with an oversize set. Piston clearance can also be checked by inverting a piston into an oiled cylinder, and sliding in a feeler gauge between the two.

CONNECTING ROD INSPECTION AND BEARING REPLACEMENT

Connecting rod side clearance and big-end bearing inspection and replacement should be performed while the rods are still installed in the engine. Determine the clearance between the connecting rod sides and the crankshaft using a feeler gauge. If clearance is below the minimum tolerance, check with a machinist about machining the rod to provide adequate clearance. If clearance is excessive, substitute an unworn rod and recheck; if clearance is still outside specifications, the crankshaft must be welded and reground, or replaced.

To check connecting rod big-end bearing clearances, remove the rod bearing caps one at a time. Using a clean, dry shop rag, thoroughly clean all oil from the crank journal and bearing insert in the cap.

NOTE: *The Plastigage® gaging material you will be using to check clearances with is soluble in oil; therefore any oil on the journal or bearing could result in an incorrect reading.*

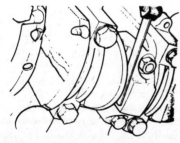

Checking connecting rod side clearance. Make sure feeler gauge is between shoulder of crank journal and side of rod

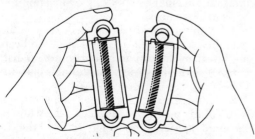

Inspect the rod bearings for scuffing and other wear; also check the crankshaft journal

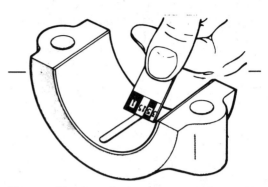

Measure Plastigage® width by using the scale on the envelope

Lay a strip of Plastigage® along the full length of the bearing insert (along the crank journal if the engine is out of the car and inverted). Reinstall the cap and torque to specifications listed in the "Torque Specifications" chart.

3. Remove the rod cap and determine bearing clearance by comparing the width of the now flattened Plastigage® to the scale on the Plastigage® envelope. Journal taper is determined by comparing the width of the Plastigage® strip near its ends. Rotate the crankshaft 90° and retest, to determine journal eccentricity.

NOTE: *Do not rotate the crankshaft with the Plastigage® installed.*

If the bearing insert and crank journal appear intact and are within tolerances, no further service is required and the bearing caps can be reinstalled (remove Plastigage® before installation). If clearances are not within tolerances, the bearing inserts in both the connecting rod and rod cap must be replaced with undersize inserts, and/or the crankshaft must be reground. To install the bearing insert halves, press them into the bearing caps and connecting rods. Make sure the tab in each insert fits into the notch in each rod and cap. Lube the face of each insert with engine oil prior to installing each rod into the engine.

The connecting rods can be further inspected when they are removed from the engine and separated from their pistons. Rod alignment (straightness and squareness) must be checked by a machinist, as the rod must be set in a special fixture. Many machine shops also perform a Magnafluxing service, which is a process that shows up any tiny cracks that you may be unable to see.

Crankshaft and Main Bearings
REMOVAL AND INSTALLATION

NOTE: *Before removing the crankshaft, check main bearing clearances as described under "Main Bearing Clearance Check" below.*

1. Remove the piston and connecting rod assemblies following the procedure in this chapter.

2. Check crankshaft thrust clearance (end play) before removing the crank from the block. Using a pry bar, pry the crankshaft the extent of its travel forward, and measure thrust clearance at the center main bearing (No. 4 bearing on 6-cylinder engines, No. 3 on 4-cylinder engines) with a feeler gauge. Pry the crankshaft the extent of its rearward travel, and measure the other side of the bearing. If clearance is greater than that specified, the thrust

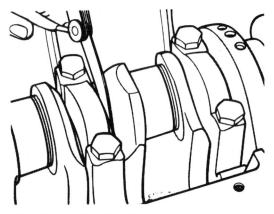

Checking crankshaft end play

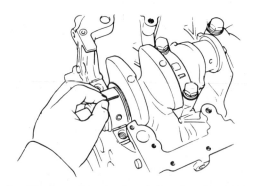

Use Plastigage® to check main bearing clearance

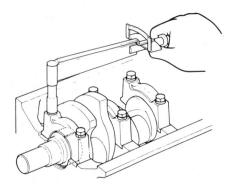

Torque all main bearing caps to specifications

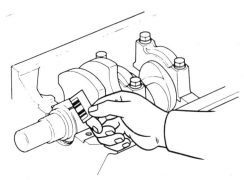

Compare width of now-flattened Plastigage® with scale on Plastigage® envelope

washers must be replaced (see main bearing installation, below).

3. Using a punch, mark the corresponding main bearing caps and saddles according to position—one punch on the front main cap and saddle, two on the second, three on the third, etc. This ensures correct reassembly.

4. Remove the main bearing caps after they have been marked.

5. Remove the crankshaft from the block.

6. Follow the crankshaft inspection, main bearing clearance checking and replacement procedures below before reinstalling the crankshaft.

INSPECTION

Crankshaft inspection and servicing should be handled exclusively by a reputable machinist, as most of the necessary procedures require a dial indicator and fixing jig, a large micrometer, and machine tools such as a crankshaft grinder. While at the machine shop, the crankshaft should be thoroughly cleaned (especially the oil passages), Magnafluxed (to check for minute cracks) and the following checks made: Main journal diameter, crank pin (connecting rod journal) diameter, taper and out-of-round, and run-out. Wear, beyond specification limits, in any of these areas means the crankshaft must be reground or replaced.

MAIN BEARING CLEARANCE CHECK

Checking main bearing clearances is done in the same manner as checking connecting rod big-end clearances.

1. With the crankshaft installed, remove the main bearing cap. Clean all oil from the bearing insert in the cap and from the crankshaft journal, as the Plastigage® material is oil-soluble.

2. Lay a strip of Plastigage® along the full width of the bearing cap (or along the width of the crank journal if the engine is out of the car and inverted).

3. Install the bearing cap and torque to specification.

NOTE: *Do not rotate the crankshaft with the Plastigage® installed.*

4. Remove the bearing cap and determine bearing clearance by comparing the width of the now-flattened Plastigage® with the scale on the Plastigage® envelope. Journal taper is determined by comparing the width of the Plastigage® strip near its ends. Rotate the crankshaft 90° and retest, to determine journal eccentricity.

5. Repeat the above for the remaining bearings. If the bearing journal and insert appear in good shape (with no unusual wear visible) and are within tolerances, no further main bearing service is required. If unusual wear is evident and/or the clearances are outside specifications, the bearings must be replaced and the cause of their wear found.

MAIN BEARING REPLACEMENT

Main bearings can be replaced with the crankshaft both in the engine (with the engine still in the car) and out of the engine (with the engine on a workstand or bench). Both procedures are covered here. The main bearings *must* be replaced if the crankshaft has been reground; the replacement bearings being available in various undersize increments from most auto parts jobbers or your local Toyota dealer.

Engine Out of Car

1. Remove the crankshaft from the engine block.

2. Remove the main bearing inserts from the bearing caps and from the main bearing saddles. Remove the thrust washers from the No. 3 (4-cylinder) or No. 4 (6-cylinder) crank journal.

3. Thoroughly clean the saddles, bearing caps, and crankshaft.

4. *Make sure the crankshaft has been fully checked and is ready for reassembly.* Place the upper main bearings in the block saddles so that the oil grooves and/or oil holes are correctly aligned with their corresponding grooves or holes in the saddles.

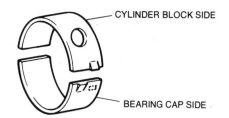

Bearing insert halves must be installed with oil notches and holes properly positioned

5. Install the thrust washers on the center main bearing, with the oil grooves facing out.

6. Lubricate the faces of all bearings with clean engine oil, and place the crankshaft in the block.

7. Install the main bearing caps in numbered order with the arrows or any other orientation marks facing forward. Torque all bolts except the center cap bolts in sequence in two or three passes to the specified torque. Rotate the crankshaft after each pass to ensure even tightness.

8. Align the thrust bearing by prying the crankshaft the extent of its axial travel several times with a pry bar. On last movement hold the crankshaft toward the front of the engine and torque the thrust bearing cap to specifications. Measure the crankshaft thrust clearance (end play) as previously described in this chapter. If clearance is outside specifications (too sloppy), install a new set of oversize thrust washers and check clearance again.

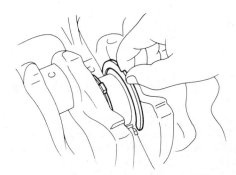

Install thrust washers with oil grooves facing out

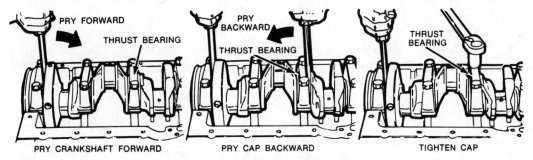

Aligning the crankshaft thrust bearing

Engine and Crankshaft Installed

1. Remove the main bearing caps and keep them in order.

2. Make a bearing roll-out pin from a cotter pin as shown.

3. Carefully roll out the old inserts from the upper side of the crankshaft journal, noting the positions of the oil grooves and/or oil

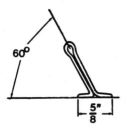

Home-made bearing roll-out pin

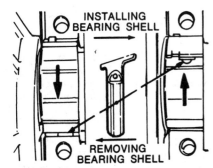

Upper bearing insert installation and removal

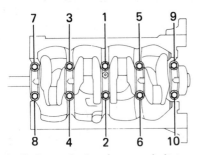

Four cylinder main bearing cap bolt torque sequence

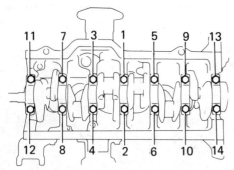

Six cylinder main bearing cap bolt torque sequence

holes so the new inserts can be correctly installed.

4. Roll each new insert into its saddle after lightly oiling the crankshaft-side face of each. Make sure the notches and/or oil holes are correctly positioned.

5. Replace the bearing inserts in the caps with new inserts. Oil the face of each, and install the caps in numbered order with the arrows or other orientation marks facing forward. Torque the bolts to the specified torque in two or three passes in the sequence shown.

Cylinder Block

Most inspection and service work on the cylinder block should be handled by a machinist or professional engine rebuilding shop. Included in this work are bearing alignment checks, line boring, deck resurfacing, hot-tanking and cylinder honing or boring. A block that has been checked and properly serviced will last much longer than one which has not had the proper attention when the opportunity was there for it.

Cylinder de-glazing (honing) can, however, be performed by the owner/mechanic who is careful and takes his or her time. The cylinder bores become "glazed" during normal operation as the rings continually ride up and down against them. This shiny glaze must be removed in order for a new set of piston rings to be able to properly seat themselves.

Cylinder hones are available at most auto tool stores and parts jobbers. With the piston and rod assemblies removed from the block, cover the crankshaft completely with a rag or cover to keep grit from the hone and cylinder

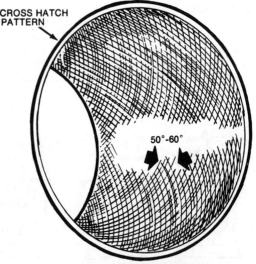

Cylinders should be honed to look like this

material off of it. Chuck a hone into a variable-speed power drill (preferable here to a constant-speed drill), and insert it into the cylinder.

NOTE: *Make sure the drill and hone are kept square to the cylinder bore throughout the entire honing operation.*

Start the hone and move it up and down in the cylinder at a rate which will produce approximately a 60° crosshatch pattern. DO NOT extend the hone below the cylinder bore! After developing the pattern, remove the hone and recheck piston fit. Wash the cylinders with a detergent and water solution to remove the hone and cylinder grit. Wipe the bores out several times with a clean rag soaked in clean engine oil. Remove the cover from the crankshaft, and check closely to see that no grit has found its way onto the crankshaft.

Oil Pan

REMOVAL AND INSTALLATION

All Engines

1. Drain the oil.
2. Raise the front end of the car with jacks and support it with jackstands.

CAUTION: *Be sure that the car is supported securely. Remember, you will be working underneath it.*

3. Detach the steering relay rod and the tie rods from the idler arm, pitman arm, and steering knuckles, as detailed in Chapter 8.
4. Remove the engine stiffening plates.
5. Remove the splash shields from underneath the engine. Remove the fan shroud and fluid coupling on the 5M-GE.
6. Support the front of the engine with a jack and remove the front engine mount attaching bolts.
7. Remove the engine shock absorber if equipped.
8. Raise the front of the engine *slightly* with the jack.

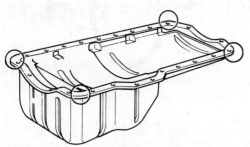

Apply sealer to the corners of the 20R oil pan gaskets

CAUTION: *Be sure that the hood is open before raising the front of the engine.*

9. Unbolt and withdraw the oil pan.
10. Installation is performed in the reverse order of removal. Apply liquid sealer to the four corners of the oil pan gasket used on 20R, 22R and R-E, and 5M-GE engines. Torque the oil pan securing bolts to the following specifications:

- 8R-C and 18R-C engines:
  3.0–5.0 ft. lbs.
- 20R and 22R engine:
  3.0–6.0 ft. lbs.
- 4M-E and 5M-E engines:
  3.0–5.0 ft. lbs.
- 5M-GE engine:
  5.5–7.0 ft. lbs.

Oil Pump

REMOVAL AND INSTALLATION

All Engines—Except 20R, 22R/E

1. Remove the oil pan, as outlined above.
2. On the 5M-GE six, remove the oil pump outlet pipe.
3. Unbolt the oil pump securing bolts and remove it as an assembly.
4. Installation is the reverse of removal. Fill the pump with oil to prevent it from cavitating (sucking air) on initial start-up.

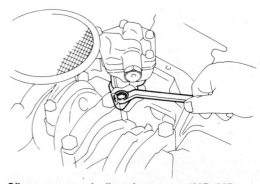

Oil pump removal, all engines except 20R, 22R

20R, 22R and 22R-Engine

1. Remove the oil pan as previously outlined.
2. Unfasten the three bolts which secure the oil strainer.
3. Remove the drive belts, the pulley bolt, and the crankshaft pulley.
4. Unfasten the bolts which secure the oil pump housing to the timing chain cover, and remove the pump assembly.
5. Remove the oil pump drive spline and the rubber O-ring.
6. Installation is performed in the reverse

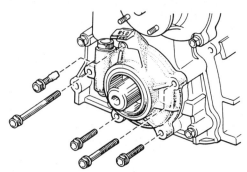

20R and 22R series oil pump removal

order of removal. Apply sealer to the top oil pump housing bolt. Use a new oil strainer gasket. Fill the pump with oil to prevent it from cavitating (sucking air) on initial start-up.

OVERHAUL

The Celica engines utilize three types of oil pumps. The 4M-E, 5M-E and 5M-GE engines use a geared impeller-type pump. The 20R and 22R series use an automatic transmission-type gear pump. The 8R-C and 18R use a trochoid rotary-type pump. In both gear types, there is a drive gear and a driven gear; pump inspection procedures are very similar on both types. Inspection of the trochoid pumps is similar to the gear types.

20R, 22R Type

1. Remove the oil pump.
2. Disassemble the pump by unscrewing the relief valve plug and removing the spring and relief valve piston. Remove the drive and driven gears, and clean all parts in solvent. Inspect all parts for unusual wear and replace if necessary.
3. Assemble the gears into the pump body. Using a feeler gauge, measure the clearance between the driven gear and the pump body. If clearance exceeds 0.008 in., replace the gear and/or body.
4. Measure the clearance between both gear

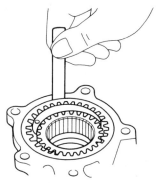

Checking driven gear-to-body clearance on 20R type pump

1. Relief valve spring
2. Relief valve
3. Oil pump housing
4. Drive gear
5. Driven gear
6. O-ring
7. Drive spline

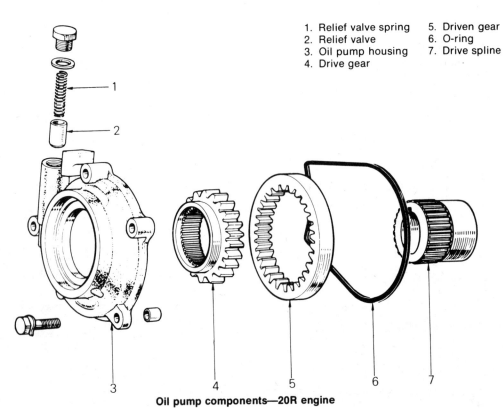

Oil pump components—20R engine

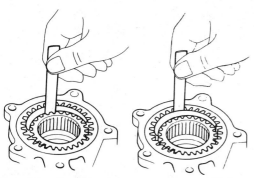

Measuring gear tip-to-crescent clearance

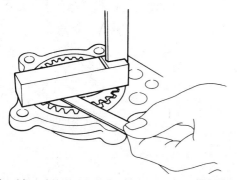

Checking side clearance, 20R type pump. Checking is similar on other two pump types

tips and the crescent with a feeler gauge. If clearance exceeds 0.012 in., replace the gears and/or body.

5. Using a feeler gauge and steel square or flat steel block, measure the gear side clearance as shown. If the clearance is greater than 0.15 in., replace the gears and/or body.

6. Assemble the pump in the reverse order of disassembly.

4M-E, 5M-E and 5M-GE Type

1. Remove the oil pump.

2. Disassemble the pump by removing the relief valve plug, spring and relief valve. Remove the pump cover and driven gear. Using needle-nose pliers, remove the snap ring and remove the spacer, drive shaft gear, key and shaft subassembly.

3. Clean all parts in solvent, and inspect for scoring or other unusual wear. Replace any part that looks worn or damaged.

4. Measure driven gear-to-body clearance with a feeler gauge; if clearance exceeds 0.008 in., replace the gear and/or body.

5. Insert a feeler gauge between the meshing faces of the two gears (gear backlash measurement). If the backlash is greater than 0.035, replace the shaft subassembly and/or driven gear.

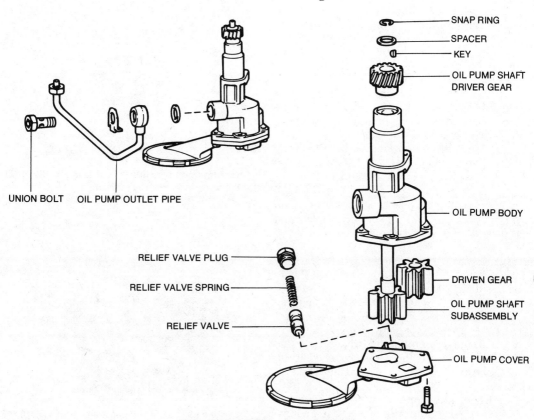

4M-E, 5M-E, 5M-GE gear type oil pump

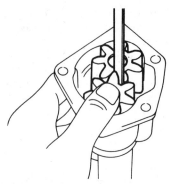

Measuring gear blacklash on six-cylinder type pump

6. Using a feeler gauge and steel square or flat steel block, measure the side clearance. If clearance is greater than 0.0059 in., replace the gears and/or pump body.

7. Reassemble the pump in the reverse order of disassembly. Check pump operation by immersing the suction end of the pump in clean engine oil and turning the shaft counterclockwise by hand. Oil should come out of the discharge hole. Close the discharge hole with your thumb, and turn the shaft. The shaft should be difficult to turn.

8R-C, 18R Type

1. Remove the oil pump.

2. Disassemble the pump by removing the oil strainer, relief valve plug, gasket, spring, and relief valve from the pump cover. Remove the cover, drive shaft and driven rotor from the pump body.

3. Clean all parts in solvent and inspect for unusual wear and/or damage. Replace any parts if necessary. Pay special attention to the pump shaft, drive and driven rotors.

4. Check drive-to-driven rotor tip clearance, using a feeler gauge. If clearance exceeds 0.008 in., replace the rotors as a set.

5. Using the feeler gauge and a steel square or steel block, check side clearance between the rotor and pump cover surface. Replace the rotor and/or body if clearance exceeds 0.006 in.

6. Measure the clearance between the driven rotor and pump body; clearance should be less than 0.008 in. Replace the body and/or rotors as a set if clearance exceeds this figure.

7. Reassemble the pump in the reverse order of disassembly. Stamped marks are provided on the drive rotor and driven rotor, and should face toward the pump cover side (toward the underneath of the engine when installed).

8. Check pump operation by following step 7 of the 4M-E pump procedure. Use a screwdriver to rotate the rotor shaft.

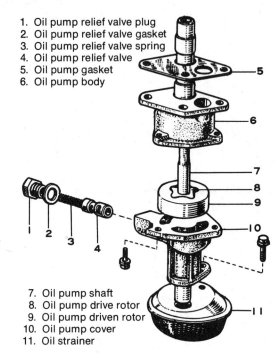

1. Oil pump relief valve plug
2. Oil pump relief valve gasket
3. Oil pump relief valve spring
4. Oil pump relief valve
5. Oil pump gasket
6. Oil pump body

7. Oil pump shaft
8. Oil pump drive rotor
9. Oil pump driven rotor
10. Oil pump cover
11. Oil strainer

Trochoidal oil pump, 8R-C, 18R engines

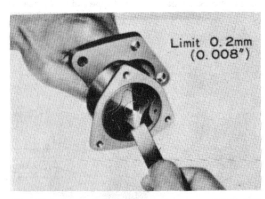

Checking trochoidal pump tip clearance, 8R-C, 18R pumps

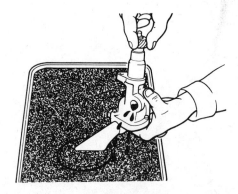

Checking oil pump operation, all models except 20R, 22R

Rear Main Oil Seal

REPLACEMENT

All Engines

NOTE: *This procedure applies only to those models with manual transmissions. If your car has an automatic transmission, leave removal of the oil seal to a professional mechanic.*

1. Remove the transmission as detailed in Chapter 6.

2. Remove the clutch cover assembly and flywheel. See Chapter 6 also.

3. Remove the oil seal retaining plate, complete with the oil seal.

4. Use a screwdriver to pry the old seal from the retaining plate. Be careful not to damage the plate.

5. Install the new seal, carefully, by using a block of wood to drift it into place.

CAUTION: *Do not damage the seal; a leak will result.*

6. Lubricate the lips of the seal with multipurpose grease.

7. Installation is performed in the reverse order from removal.

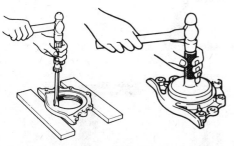

Rear oil seal removal and installation, all engines

Flywheel and Ring Gear

REMOVAL AND INSTALLATION

All Engines

1. Remove the transmission, if the engine is installed in the car.

2. Remove the clutch assembly, if equipped.

3. Remove the flywheel.

4. To install, use new flywheel bolts. Torque the bolts in a criss-cross pattern to the torque specified in the chart in this chapter.

Water Pump

REMOVAL AND INSTALLATION

All Engines

1. Drain the cooling system.

2. Remove the air cleaner casing on the 5M-GE engine.

3. Unfasten the fan shroud securing bolts and remove the fan shroud, if so equipped.

4. Loosen the alternator adjusting link bolt and remove the drive belt.

5. Repeat Step 3 for the air and/or power steering pump drive belt, if so equipped.

6. Detach the by-pass hose from the water pump.

7. Unfasten the water pump retaining bolts and remove the water pump and fan assembly, using care not to damage the radiator with the fan.

CAUTION: *If the fan is equipped with a fluid coupling, do not tip the fan/pump assembly on its side, as the fluid will run out.*

8. Installation is performed in the reverse order of removal. Always use a new gasket between the pump body and its mounting. Remember to check for leaks after installation is completed.

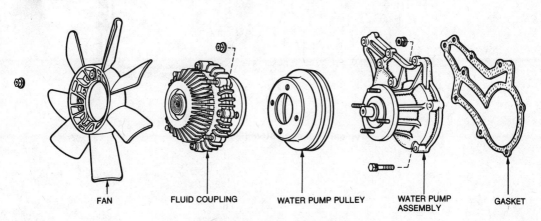

FAN   FLUID COUPLING   WATER PUMP PULLEY   WATER PUMP ASSEMBLY   GASKET

Typical water pump assembly

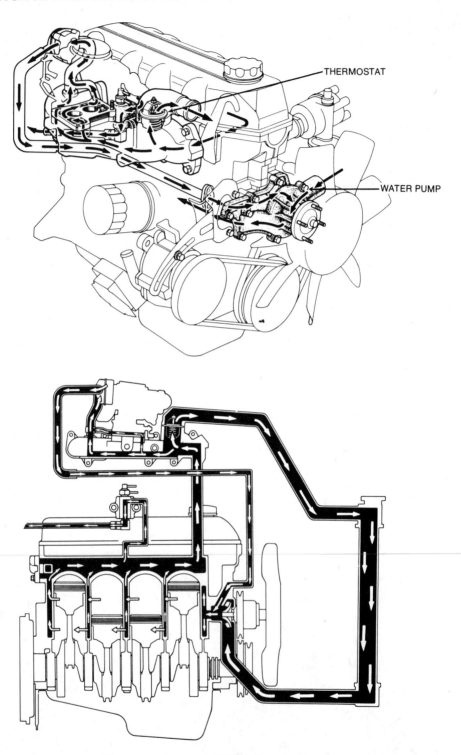

THERMOSTAT

WATER PUMP

Typical cooling system (20R shown)

Thermostat

REMOVAL AND INSTALLATION

All Engines

1. Drain the cooling system.
2. Unfasten the clamp and remove the upper radiator hose from the water outlet elbow.
3. Unbolt and remove the water outlet (thermostat housing).
4. Withdraw the thermostat.
5. Installation is performed in the reverse order of the removal procedure. Use a new gasket on the water outlet.

CAUTION: *Be sure that the thermostat is installed with the spring pointing down.*

Radiator

REMOVAL AND INSTALLATION

All Models

1. Drain the cooling system.
2. Unfasten the clamps and remove the radiator upper and lower hoses. If equipped with an automatic transmission, remove the oil cooler lines.
3. Detach the hood lock cable and remove the hood lock from the radiator upper support.

NOTE: *It may be necessary to remove the grille in order to gain access to the hood lock/radiator support assembly.*

4. Remove the fan shroud, if so equipped.
5. On models equipped with a coolant recovery system, disconnect the hose from the thermal expansion tank and remove the tank from its bracket.
6. Unbolt and remove the radiator upper support.
7. Unfasten the bolts and remove the radiator.

CAUTION: *Use care not to damage the radiator fins or the cooling fan.*

8. Installation is performed in the reverse order of removal. Remember to check the transmission fluid level on cars with automatic transmissions. (See Chapter 1.)

Fill the radiator to the specified level, as detailed under "Fluid Level Checks," in Chapter 1.

Emission Controls and Fuel System

EMISSION CONTROLS

There are three sources of automotive pollutants; crankcase fumes, exhaust gases, and gasoline evaporation. The pollutants formed from these substances fall into three categories: unburnt hydrocarbons (HC), carbon monoxide (CO), and oxides of nitrogen (NOx). The equipment used to limit these pollutants is called emission control equipment.

Due to varying state, federal, and provincial regulations, specific emission control equipment have been devised for each. The U.S. emission equipment is divided into two categories: California and 49 State. In this section, the term "California" applies only to cars originally built to be sold in California. California emissions equipment is generally not shared with equipment installed on cars built to be sold in the other 49 States. Models built to be sold in Canada also have specific emissions equipment, although in most years 49 State and Canadian equipment is the same.

The following abbreviations are used in this section:
- AAP—Auxiliary Acceleration Pump
- ABV—Air By-Pass Valve
- AI—Air Injection
- ASV—Air Switching Valve
- BVSV—Bi-Metal Vacuum Switching Valve
- C—Carbon
- CB—Choke Breaker
- CCo—Catalytic Converter
- CO—Carbon Monoxide
- CO_2—Carbon Dioxide
- EACV—Electronic Air Control Valve
- EGR—Exhaust Gas Recirculation
- H—Hydrogen
- HAC—High Altitude Compensation
- HAI—Hot Air Intake
- HC—Hydrocarbon
- HIC—Hot Idle Compensation
- H_2O—Water
- MC—Mixture Control
- N—Nitrogen
- NOx—Nitrogen Oxides
- PCV—Positive Crankcase Ventilation
- SC—Spark Control
- TP—Throttle Positioner
- TVSV—Thermostatic Vacuum Switching Valve
- TVTV—Thermostatic Vacuum Transmitting Valve
- VCV—Vacuum Control Valve
- VSV—Vacuum Switching Valve
- VTV—Vacuum Transmitting Valve

Positive Crankcase Ventilation (PCV) System

A closed, positive crankcase ventilation system is employed on all Celicas and Supras. This system cycles incompletely burned fuel which works its way past the piston rings back into the intake manifold for reburning with the fuel/air mixture. The oil filler cap is sealed and the air is drawn from the top of the crankcase

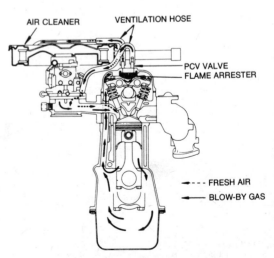

Typical carbureted four cylinder PCV flow

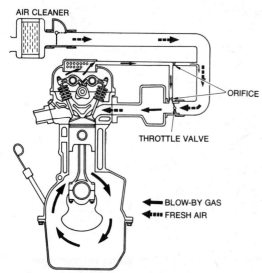

Positive crankcase ventilation system on the 4M-E engine (5M-E similar)

into the intake manifold through a valve with a variable orifice (the 4M-E, 5M-E and 5M-GE engines have no valve, only an orifice).

This valve (commonly known as the PCV valve) regulates the flow of air into the manifold according to the amount of manifold vacuum. When the throttle plates are open fairly wide, the valve opens to maximize the flow. However, at idle speed, when manifold vacuum is at a maximum, the PCV valve throttles the flow in order not to unnecessarily affect the small volume of mixture passing into the engine.

During most driving conditions, manifold vacuum is high and all of the vapor from the crankcase, plus a small amount of excess air, is drawn into the manifold via the PCV valve. However, at full throttle, the increase in the volume of blow-by and the decrease in manifold vacuum make the flow via the PCV valve inadequate. Under these conditions, excess vapors are drawn into the air cleaner and pass into the engine.

REMOVAL AND INSTALLATION

Remove the PCV valve from the cylinder head cover on all but the 4M-E, 5M-E and 5M-GE engines. Remove the hose from the valve.

On the remainder of the engines, remove the valve from the manifold-to-crankcase hose.

Installation is the reverse of removal.

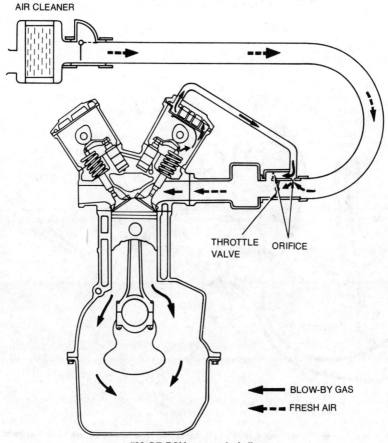

5M-GE PCV gas and air flow

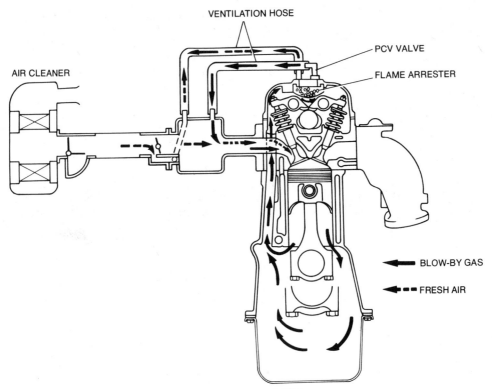

1983 and later 22R-E PCV flow

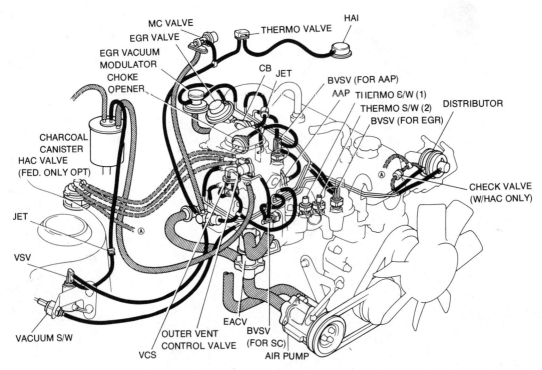

Emission control components and hoses, 1983 22R. Location and applications vary between engines and years

TESTING

Check the PCV system hoses and connections, to ensure that there are no leaks; then replace or tighten, as necessary.

To check the valve, remove it and blow through both of its ends. When blowing from the side which goes toward the intake manifold, very little air should pass through it. When blowing from the crankcase (valve cover) side, air should pass through freely.

Replace the valve with a new one, if the valve fails to function as outlined.

NOTE: *Do not attempt to clean or adjust the valve; replace it with a new one.*

Evaporative Emissions Control System

In order to prevent HC emissions from entering the atmosphere, all Celicas and Supras utilize an evaporation control system. This system employs:

1. A sealed fuel filler cap with a safety valve.
2. An activated charcoal canister with check valves.
3. A vacuum control valve (VCV)—Supra to 1982 only.
4. A vacuum switching valve (VSV)—Celica and 5M-GE Supra only.

5. A thermostatic vacuum switching valve (TVSV)—1980–82 Celica only.
6. A bi-metal vacuum switching valve (BVSV)—Supra and 1982 and later Celica.
7. An outer vent control valve—California Celicas only.

CHECKING THE FILLER CAP

Check that the filler cap seals effectively. Remove the filler cap and pull the safety valve outward to check for smooth operation. Replace the filler cap if the seal is defective or if it is not operating properly.

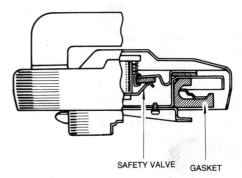

SAFETY VALVE   GASKET

The fuel filler cap with a safety valve

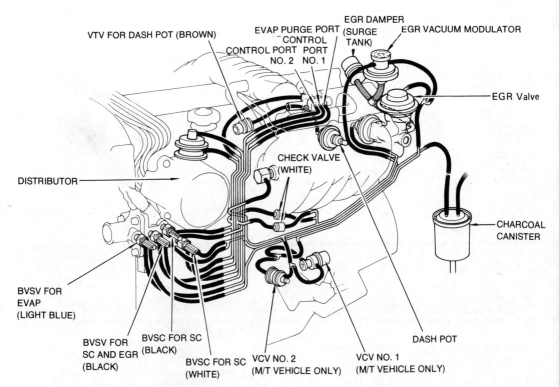

1982 5M-GE emission components. 1983 and later models have only one BVSV (for EVAP), no VCV or check valves

CHECKING THE CHARCOAL CANISTER AND CHECK VALVES

Remove the charcoal canister from the engine compartment and visually inspect it for cracks or other damage.

Check for stuck check valves. All models from 1971–78 have one check valve in the line between the fuel tank and the charcoal canister. It is located in the trunk. To check:

1. Remove the check valve from the line. NOTE: *Mark which end goes toward the fuel tank and which end goes toward the charcoal canister.*

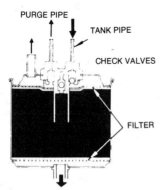

Testing the charcoal canister check valves

2. Blow into the fuel tank end. A slight resistance should be felt at first.

3. Blow through the other end. No resistance should be felt at all.

4. If your results differ from those above, the check valve will require replacement. 1979 to 1982 models have two check valves, both are located in the charcoal canister. 1983 and later fuel injected models have three check valves in the canister. To check:

1. Using low pressure compressed air, blow into the tank pipe. The air should flow from the other pipes without resistance.

2. If the air flow is incorrect, the check valve will require replacement.

Before installing the canister, clean the filter. Blow compressed air into the purge pipe while keeping the other blocked with your fingers.

NOTE: *Do not attempt to wash the charcoal canister. While cleaning the canister, under no circumstances should any activated charcoal be removed.*

CHECKING THE VCV—SUPRA ONLY

1. Locate the VCV by the intake air chamber and remove all the vacuum lines.

2. Apply vacuum to pipe S, blow into Y and check that the valve is open.

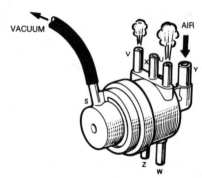

When applying vacuum to the VCV, the valve should be open

3. Stop the vacuum and blow into Y again and check that the valve is closed.

4. If the valve is not operating properly, it will require replacement.

CHECKING THE VSV—CELICA AND 5M-GE SUPRA ONLY

1. Disconnect the VSV electrical connector.

2. Connect the VSV terminals to the battery terminals.

3. Blow into the pipe and check that the valve is open.

4. Disconnect the positive battery terminal.

5. Blow into the pipe and check that the valve is closed.

6. If the valve is not operating properly it will require replacement.

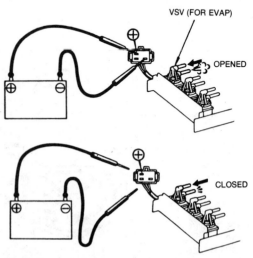

Checking the VSV

CHECKING THE TVSV—1980–82 CELICAS ONLY

1. Locate the TVSV on the intake manifold and remove all vacuum lines.

Checking the TVSV with the engine cold

Checking the TVSV with the engine warm

2. Blow into the middle pipe and check that the air comes out of the top pipe.

3. Warm up the engine until it reaches normal operating temperature and then blow into the middle pipe again. The air should come out of the bottom pipe.

4. If the valve is not operating properly it will require replacement.

CHECKING THE BVSV—SUPRA AND 1982 AND LATER CELICA ONLY

1. Drain the engine coolant and remove the BVSV from the water outlet on the engine block.

2. Place the end of the BVSV in cool water and blow into the top connection. The valve should be closed.

3. Heat the water to a temperature above

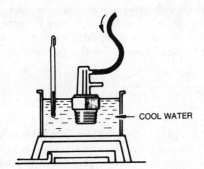

When cold, the BVSV should be closed

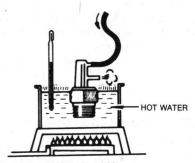

When hot, the BVSV should be open

129°F (54°C) and again blow into the top connection. This time, the valve should be open.

4. If the valve is not operating properly it will require replacement.

5. Apply liquid sealer to the threads and reinstall the BVSV.

6. Refill the engine with coolant.

CHECKING THE OUTER VENT CONTROL VALVE—CALIFORNIA CELICAS ONLY

1. Remove the vacuum lines from the valve.

2. With the ignition switch "OFF," blow into the top pipe on the valve. The valve should be open.

3. With the ignition switch "ON," blow into the top pipe again, the valve should now be closed.

4. If the valve is not working properly, first check the fuse and all the wiring connections. If they are all correct, the valve will require replacement.

Dual-Diaphragm Distributor

Some models are equipped with a dual-diaphragm distributor unit. This distributor has a retard diaphragm, as well as a diaphragm for advance.

Retarding the timing helps to reduce exhaust emissions, as well as making up for the lack of engine braking on models equipped with a throttle positioner.

TESTING

1. Connect a timing light to the engine. Check the ignition timing.

NOTE: *Before proceeding with the tests, disconnect any spark control devices, distributor vacuum valves, etc. If these are left connected, inaccurate results may be obtained.*

2. Remove the retard hose from the distributor and plug it. Increase the engine speed. The timing should advance. If it fails to do so, then the vacuum unit is faulty and must be replaced.

3. Check the timing with the engine at nor-

mal idle speed. Unplug the retard hose and connect it to the vacuum unit. The timing should instantly be retarded from 4 to 10 degrees. If this does not occur, the retard diaphragm has a leak and the vacuum unit must be replaced.

Engine Modifications System

Toyota uses an assortment of engine modifications to regulate exhaust emissions. Most of these devices fall into the category of engine vacuum controls. There are three principal components used on the engine modifications system, as well as a number of smaller parts. The three major components are: a speed sensor; a computer (speed marker); and a vacuum switching valve.

The vacuum switching valve and computer circuit operates most of the emission control components. Depending upon year and engine usage, the vacuum switching valve and computer may operate the pure control for the evaporative emission control system; the transmission controlled spark (TCS) or speed controlled spark (SCS); the dual-diaphragm distributor, the throttle positioner systems, the EGR system, the catalyst protection system, etc.

The functions of the evaporative emission control system, the throttle positioner, and the dual-diaphragm distributor are described in detail in the preceding sections. However, a word is necessary about the functions of the TCS and SCS systems before discussing the operation of the vacuum switching valve/computer circuit.

The major difference between the transmission controlled spark and speed controlled spark systems is the manner in which system operation is determined. Toyota TCS systems use a mechanical switch to determine which gear is selected; SCS systems use a speed sensor built into the speedometer cable.

Below a predetermined speed, or any gear other than Fourth, the vacuum advance unit on the distributor is rendered inoperative or the timing retarded. By changing the distributor advance curve in this manner, it is possible to reduce emissions of oxides of nitrogen (NO_x).

NOTE: *Some engines are equipped with a thermo-sensor so that the TCS or SCS system only operates when the coolant temperature is 140°–212°F.*

Aside from determining the preceding conditions, the vacuum switching valve computer circuit operates other devices in the emission control system (EGR, catalytic converter, etc.).

The computer acts as a speed marker; at

certain speeds it sends a signal to the vacuum switching valve which acts as a gate, opening and closing the emission control system vacuum circuits.

The vacuum switching valve on some 1971 engines is a simple affair; a single solenoid operates a valve which uncovers certain vacuum ports at the same time others are covered.

The valve used on all 1972 and later and some 1971 engines contains several solenoid and valve assemblies so that different combinations of opened and closed vacuum ports are possible. This allows greater flexibility of operation for the emission control system.

SYSTEM CHECKS

Due to the complexity of the components involved, about the only engine modification system checks which can be made, are the following:

1. Examine the vacuum lines to ensure that they are not clogged, pinched, or loose.

2. Check the electrical connections for tightness and corrosion.

3. Be sure that the vacuum sources for the vacuum switching valve are not plugged.

4. On models equipped with speed controlled spark, a broken speedometer cable could also render the system inoperative.

Beyond these checks, servicing the engine modifications system is best left to an authorized service facility.

NOTE: *A faulty vacuum switching valve or computer could cause more than one of the emission control systems to fail. Therefore, if several systems are out, these two units (and the speedometer cable) would be the first things to check.*

Throttle Positioner

On carbureted Toyotas with an engine modification system, a throttle positioner is included to reduce exhaust emissions during deceleration. The positioner prevents the throttle from closing completely. Vacuum is reduced under the throttle valve which, in turn, acts on the retard chamber of the distributor vacuum unit. This compensates for the loss of engine braking caused by the partially opened throttle.

NOTE: *For a description of the operation of the dual-diaphragm distributor, see "Dual-Diaphragm Distributor."*

Once the vehicle drops below a predetermined speed, the vacuum switching valve provides vacuum to the throttle positioner diaphragm; the throttle positioner retracts allowing the throttle valve to close completely.

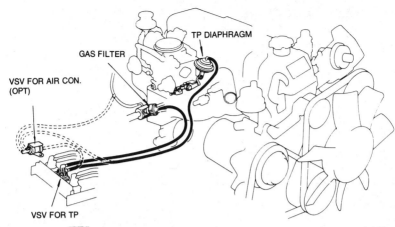

Throttle positioner vacuum hose routing (gas filter refers to crankcase gases) 22R shown

The distributor also is returned to normal operation.

ADJUSTMENT

1. Start the engine and allow it to reach normal operating temperature.

2. Adjust the idle speed as detailed in Chapter 1.

NOTE: *Leave the tachometer connected after completing the idle adjustments, as it will be needed in Step 5.*

3. Detach the vacuum line from the positioner diaphragm unit and plug the line up.

4. Accelerate the engine slightly to set the throttle positioner in place.

5. Check the engine speed with a tachometer when the throttle positioner is set.

6. If necessary, adjust the engine speed, with the throttle positioner adjusting screw, to the specifications given in the "Throttle Positioner Settings" chart at the end of this section.

7. Connect the vacuum hose to the positioner diaphragm.

8. The throttle lever should be freed from the positioner as soon as the vacuum hose is connected. Engine idle should return to normal.

9. If the throttle positioner fails to function properly, check its linkage, and vacuum diaphragm. If there are no defects in either of these, the fault probably lies in the vacuum switching valve or the speed marker unit.

NOTE: *Due to the complexity of these two components, and also because they require special test equipment, their service is best left to an authorized facility.*

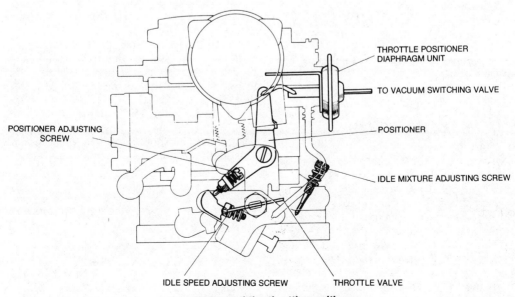

Components of the throttle positioner

Throttle Positioner Settings
(rpm)

Year	Engine	Engine rpm (positioner set)
1971	8R-C	1400
1972–74	18R-C	1400
1975–77	20R	1400 MT 1050 AT
1978–80	20R	1050
1981	22R	1050

MT—Manual Transmission
AT—Automatic Transmission

Mixture Control System (MC)— 1980–81 Celica With Manual Transmission Only

The mixture control system is used on late model Celicas with manual transmissions in order to reduce HC and CO emissions under sudden deceleration. When the throttle is suddenly closed, the vacuum created opens the valve and allows fresh air to pass into the intake manifold.

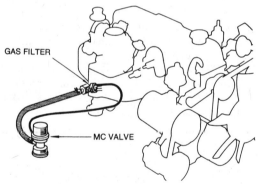

GAS FILTER

MC VALVE

Mixture control system layout (gas filter refers to crankcase gases)

CHECKING THE MC SYSTEM

1. Start the engine.
2. Disconnect the vacuum sensing hose (top) from the MC valve.
3. Place your hand over the air inlet of the valve and check that no suction can be felt.
4. Reconnect the vacuum sensing hose. Suction should be felt momentarily.
   NOTE: *At this time the engine will idle roughly or stall out altogether. This is normal.*
5. If the valve is not operating properly it will require replacement.

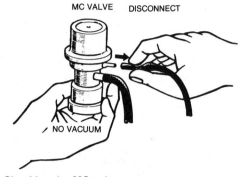

MC VALVE   DISCONNECT

NO VACUUM

Checking the MC valve

Spark Control System (SC)

The spark control system is used to reduce the NO_x and HC emissions. The system serves to delay the vacuum advance for a given time, while also lowering the maximum combustion temperature.

CHECKING THE SC SYSTEM

1979 Celica—Federal

1. Connect a vacuum gauge to the line leading from the distributor advance diaphragm.
2. Start the engine.
3. Check that the vacuum reading changes quickly when the throttle valve is opened and closed. If it does not change, check the TVTV.
4. Run the engine until it reaches normal operating temperature and then pinch the line between the TVTV and the advance port.
5. Rev the engine to 2000 rpm and release the hose.
6. The reading on the vacuum gauge should be at least 4 in. Hg within 2–4 seconds after releasing the hose.
7. With the engine speed maintained at 2000 rpm, check to see that the vacuum gauge indicates zero vacuum when the hose is disconnected from the advancer port. If it does not, check the TVTV.
8. Remove the TVTV and place its end in cool water. When blowing into one pipe, a large flow of air should be felt at the other one. Test both pipes in the same manner.

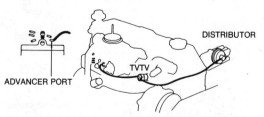

DISTRIBUTOR

TVTV

ADVANCER PORT

Spark control system; 1979 Celica (Federal)

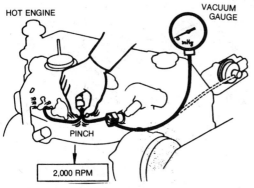

Checking the SC system

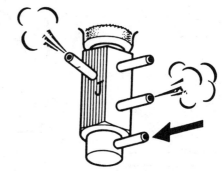

Checking the TVSV with the engine cold

9. Heat the water to a temperature above 129°F (54°C). Blow into the vertical pipe. Air flow from the horizontal pipe should be good.

10. Blow into the horizontal pipe. Air flow from the vertical pipe should be minimal.

11. If the valve is not operating properly it will require replacement.

1979 Celica—California

1. Perform Steps 1–3 of the "1979 Celica-Federal" procedure.

2. Run the engine until it reaches normal operating temperature and then pinch the line between the TVSV and the spark control port.

3. Maintain the engine speed at 2000 rpm; the vacuum gauge should indicate at least 4 in. Hg within 2–4 seconds.

4. Release the hose. The gauge should indicate less than 4 in. Hg. If the preceding tests were positive, the procedure is finished. If not, inspect the TVSV and the VTV.

5. With the engine cold, blow into the pipe on the outside end of the TVSV. The air should come out of the middle pipe and the one on the side. No air should be felt coming out of the pipe on the inside end of the valve.

6. Run the engine until it reaches normal operating temperature and then blow into the middle pipe. The air should come out of the pipe on the side and the one on the inside end. No air should be felt coming from the pipe on the outside end of the valve. Replace the valve if it is not operating properly.

7. Remove the VTV and blow into the light colored side. The air should flow freely out of the other side.

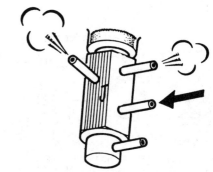

Checking the TVSV with the engine hot

Checking the VTV

8. Blow into the dark side of the valve. The flow of air coming out of the other side should be minimal. Replace the valve if it is not operating properly.

1980 and Later Celica

1. Perform Steps 1–7 of the "1979 Celica-Federal" procedure.

NOTE: *When performing Steps 1–7, remember that on 1980–81 Celicas there is no TVTV, only a VTV. 1982 and later Celicas use a BVSV in place of the VTV. Substitute VTV and BVSV for TVTV whenever necessary.*

2. Remove the VTV and blow into each side. Air should flow without resistance from the dark side to the light side with WITH resistance from the light side to the dark side.

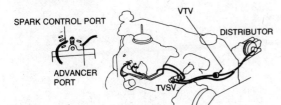

Spark control system; 1979 Celica (Calif.)

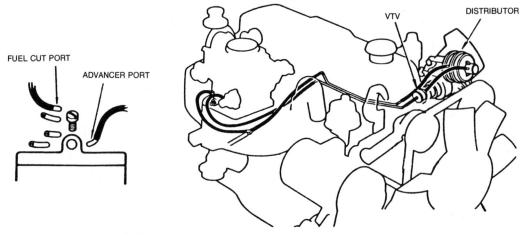

Spark control system; 1980–81 Celica (Federal)

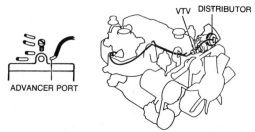

Spark control system; 1980–81 Celica (Calif.)

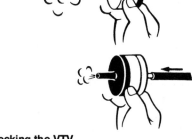

1979½–81 Supra

1. Start the engine and connect a vacuum gauge to the hose leading from the inside half of the distributor diaphragm. The vacuum gauge should indicate high vacuum.

2. Run the engine until it reaches normal operating temperature. The gauge should indicate low vacuum. If the preceding tests

Checking the VTV

were positive, the procedure is finished. If not, inspect the check valve and the BVSV.

3. Remove the check valve. When air is blown into the white pipe, the valve should be open. When air is blown into the black pipe, the valve should be closed.

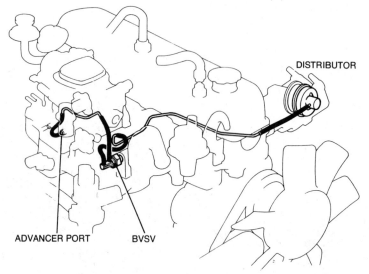

1982 and later Spark Control System, Celica with carburetor

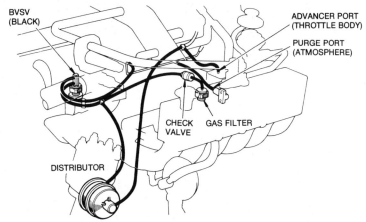

Spark control system, 4M-E and 5M-E engine Supra (gas filter is for crankcase gases)

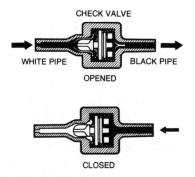

Checking the check valve

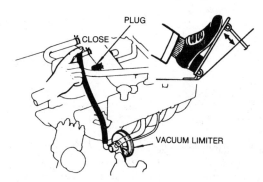

Checking the vacuum limiter

4. Check the BVSV as detailed earlier in the "Evaporative Emissions Control" section.

Vacuum Limiter System—Supra to 1981

The vacuum limiter system is much like the mixture control system discussed earlier. It allows fresh air to enter the air intake chamber of the intake manifold when the car is suddenly decelerated. Under sudden deceleration, the increased vacuum which is created forces open the vacuum limiter valve and allows air from the air cleaner to enter directly into the air intake chamber.

CHECKING THE VACUUM LIMITER

1. Disconnect the air inlet hose of the vacuum limiter from the air intake connector and plug the air intake port.
2. Start the engine.
3. Put your finger over the open end of the air inlet hose and have a friend step on the gas pedal a few times. Each time the gas pedal is released, you should momentarily feel a suction on your finger.
4. If no suction is felt, the vacuum limiter will probably require replacement.

Exhaust Gas Recirculation (EGR)

Starting with 1974 models, exhaust gas recirculation (EGR) is used in all California Celicas. All 1975 and later engines use EGR.

In all cases, the EGR valve is controlled by the same computer and vacuum switching valve which is used to operate other emission control system components.

On 18R-C and 20R engines, the EGR valve is operated by vacuum supplied from a port above the throttle blades and fed through the vacuum switching valve.

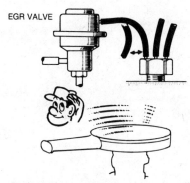

Checking the EGR valve; 1974–78

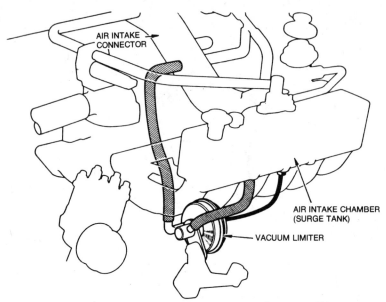

Components of the vacuum limiter system, Supra to 1981

On all engines there are several conditions, determined by the computer which permit exhaust gas recirculation to take place:

1. Vehicle speed.
2. Engine coolant temperature.
3. EGR valve temperature.
4. Carburetor flange temperature.

On 18R-C and 20R engines equipped with EGR, the exhaust gases are carried from the exhaust manifold to the EGR valve and from the EGR valve to the carburetor, via external tubing. The 20R engine has an exhaust gas cooler mounted on the back of the cylinder head.

EGR VALVE CHECK—1974–78

1. Allow the engine to warm up and remove the top from the air cleaner.

NOTE: *Do not remove the entire air cleaner assembly.*

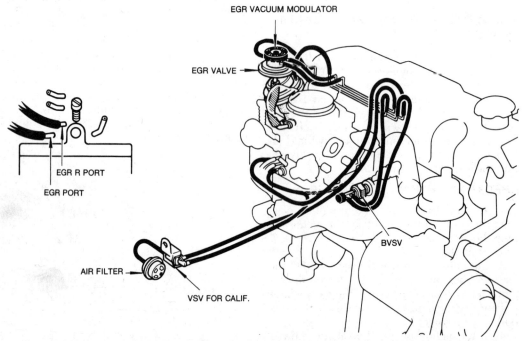

Components of the EGR system on the 1980 Celica (other years with carburetors similar)

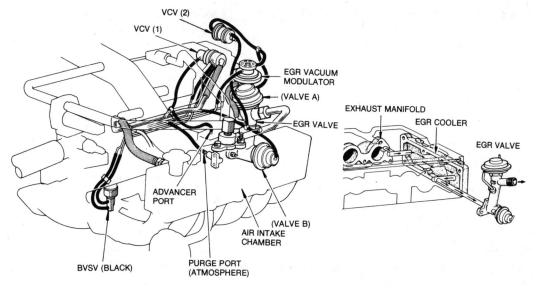

Components of the EGR system on the 1981 and earlier Supra

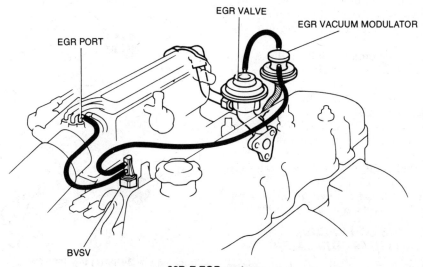

22R-E EGR system

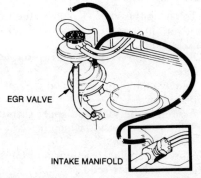

When applying vacuum directly to the EGR valve, the engine should stall

2. Disconnect the hose (white tape coded), which runs from the vacuum switching valve to the EGR valve, at its EGR valve end.

3. Remove the intake manifold hose (red coded) from the vacuum switching valve and connect it to the EGR valve. When the engine is at idle, a "hollow" sound should be heard coming from the air cleaner.

4. Disconnect the hose from the EGR valve; the hollow sound should disappear.

5. If the sound doesn't vary, the EGR valve is defective and must be replaced.

6. Reconnect the vacuum hoses as they were originally found. Install the top of the air cleaner.

EGR VALVE CHECK—1979–AND LATER

1. Start the engine.
2. Disconnect the vacuum hose leading from the EGR valve.
3. Disconnect the hose coming from the intake manifold and connect it to the empty pipe on the EGR valve.
4. When applying vacuum directly to the EGR valve, the engine should stall, if not, the EGR valve will probably require replacement.

EGR VALVE THERMO-SENSOR—18 R-C, 20R, 5M-GE

1. Disconnect the electrical lead which runs to the EGR valve thermo-sensor.
2. Remove the thermo-sensor from the side of the EGR valve.
3. Heat the thermo-sensor in a pan of water to the following temperature:
   • 260°F—18R-C and 20R
   • 248°F—5M-GE
4. Connect an ohmmeter, in series with a 10 ohm resistor, between the thermo-sensor terminal and case (between both terminals on 5M-GE).
5. With the ohmmeter set on the k-ohm scale, the following reading should be obtained:
   2.55 k-ohms—18R-C and 20R
   0.1 k-ohm—5M-GE
6. Replace the thermo-sensor if the ohmmeter readings vary considerably from those specified.
7. To install the thermo-sensor on the EGR valve, tighten it to 15–21 ft. lbs.
   CAUTION: *Do not tighten the thermo-sensor with an impact wrench.*

CHECKING THE EGR VACUUM MODULATOR—1979–AND LATER

1. Tag and disconnect all hoses leading from the vacuum modulator.
2. Remove the vacuum modulator.
3. Unscrew the vented top plate and remove the filter.
4. Check the filter for any contamination or other damage.

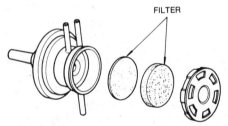

FILTER

Unscrew the end cap to remove the vacuum modulator filter

5. Clean the filter using compressed air.
6. Installation is in the reverse order of removal.

CHECKING THE BVSV

NOTE: *To check the BVSV on Supras, refer to the "Evaporative Emissions Control" section.*

1. With the engine cold, blow into the inside pipe on the BVSV. The air should come out of the air filter on the end and not from the other pipe.
2. Start the engine and run it until it reaches normal operating temperature.
3. Blow air into the inside pipe again. This time the air should come out of the other pipe and not from the air filter on the end.
4. If the valve is not operating properly, it will probably require replacement.

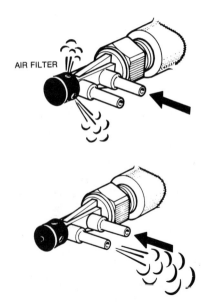

AIR FILTER

Checking the BVSV on the 1980 Celica

CHECKING THE VCV—SUPRA

1. To check the VCV (1), follow the procedure given in the "Evaporative Emissions Control" section.
2. Remove the VCV (2) and unscrew the end plate.
3. Remove the filter inside and clean it with compressed air.
4. Assemble the VCV and apply vacuum to the small pipe on the side which has two. The valve should be open.
5. Stop the applied vacuum and check to see that the valve is closed.
6. If the valve is not operating properly it will require replacement.

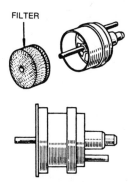

FILTER

Clean the filter on the VCV (2)

CHECKING THE VSV—CELICA TO 1982

1. Disconnect the electrical plug to the EGR VSV.

2. Connect the VSV terminals to the battery terminals.

3. Blow air into pipe 'E' and check that it comes out of pipe 'F'.

4. Disconnect the battery and then blow air into pipe 'E' again. This time the air should come out of the air filter which is attached to the valve.

5. If the valve is not operating properly it will probably require replacement.

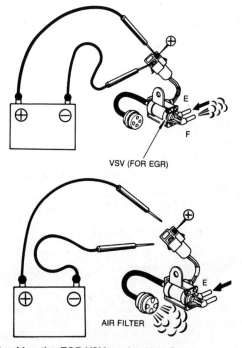

E

F

VSV (FOR EGR)

E

AIR FILTER

Checking the EGR VSV on the 1980 Celica

SYSTEM CHECKS

If, after having completed the above tests, the EGR system still doesn't work right but every-

thing else checks out, the fault probably lies in the computer. If this is the case, it is best to have the car checked out by test facility which has the necessary Toyota emission system test equipment.

NOTE: *A good indication that the fault doesn't lie in the EGR system, but rather in the vacuum supply system, would be if several emission control systems were not working properly.*

Air Injection System—1975 and Later

On 1975 through 1981 engines, a belt-drive air pump supplies air to an injection manifold which has nozzles in each exhaust port. Injection of air at this point causes combustion of unburned hydrocarbons in the exhaust manifold rather than allowing them to escape into the atmosphere. An antibackfire valve controls the flow of air from the pump to prevent backfiring which results from an overly rich mixture under closed throttle conditions. There are two types of antibackfire valve used on Celicas: 1971 models use "gulp" valves; 1972 and later models "air by-pass" valves.

A check valve prevents hot exhaust gas backflow into the pump and hoses, in case of a pump failure, or when the antibackfire valve is not working.

In addition all 1975–82 engines (except for the 4M-E and 5M-E) have an air switching valve (ASV). On engines without catalytic converters, the ASV is used to stop air injection under a constant heavy engine load condition.

On 1975–81 engines with catalytic converters, the ASV is also used to protect the catalyst from overheating, by blocking the injected air necessary for the operation of the converter.

On all 1975–82 engines, the pump relief valve is built into the ASV.

On 1982 and later carbureted 22R engines, the air injection system incorporates a "feedback" loop. An oxygen sensor threaded into the exhaust manifold monitors the oxygen concentration in the exhaust gas, and indirectly signals the air pump to divert compressed air to either the exhaust ports or the air cleaner, depending on the oxygen levels in the exhaust (see "Oxygen Sensor System" in this chapter). On 1983 and later engines, an EACV (electronic air control valve) serves as gate keeper for the air flow according to engine temperature. The EACV takes the place of the ASV on earlier engines. Thus, the feedback system constantly readjusts itself in order to reduce hydrocarbon, carbon monoxide and nitrogen oxides in the exhaust. If the catalytic converter overheats during operation, a con-

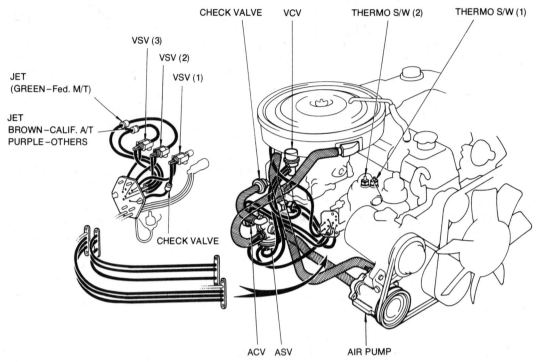

1982 22R air injection component locations. The EACV replaces VSVs, ACV and ASV and their hoses on 1983 engines

verter-mounted sensor will temporarily shut the air injection system off.

REMOVAL AND INSTALLATION

Air Pump

1. Disconnect the air hoses from the pump.
2. Loosen the bolt on the adjusting link and remove the drive belt.
3. Remove the mounting bolts and withdraw the pump.

CAUTION: *Do not pry on the pump housing; it may be distorted.*

Installation is in the reverse order of removal. Adjust the drive belt tension after installation. Belt deflection should be ½–¾ in. with 22 lbs. pressure.

Air Injection Manifold

1. Remove the check valve, as previously outlined.
2. Loosen the air injection manifold attachment nuts and withdraw the manifold.

NOTE: *On 20R engines, it will first be necessary to remove the exhaust manifold.*

Installation is in the reverse order of removal.

Air Injection Nozzles

1. Remove the air injection manifold as previously outlined.

2. Remove the cylinder head, as detailed in Chapter 3.
3. Place a new nozzle on the cylinder head.
4. Install the air injection manifold over it.
5. Install the cylinder head on the engine block.

TESTING

Air Pump

CAUTION: *Do not hammer, pry, or bend the pump housing while tightening the drive belt or testing the pump.*

BELT TENSION AND AIR LEAKS

1. Before proceeding with the tests, check the pump drive belt tension to ensure that it is within specifications.
2. Turn the pump by hand. If it has seized, the belt will slip, making a noise. Disregard any chirping, squealing, or rolling sounds from inside the pump; these are normal when it is turned by hand.
3. Check the hoses and connections for leaks. Hissing or a blast of air is indicative of a leak. Soapy water, applied lightly around the area in question, is a good method for detecting leaks.

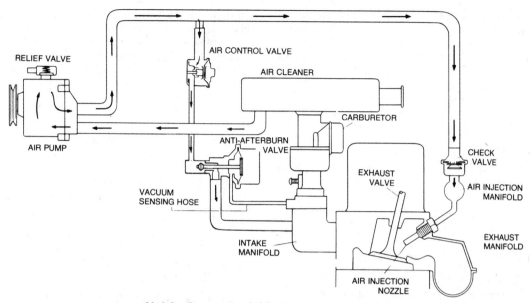

Air injection system (without catalytic converter)

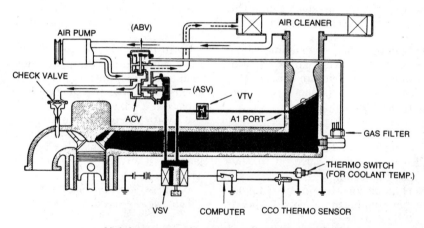

Air injection system (with catalytic converter)

AIR OUTPUT

1. Disconnect the air supply hose at the antibackfire valve.

2. Connect a vacuum gauge, using a suitable adaptor, to the air supply hose.

NOTE: *If there are two hoses, plug the second one.*

3. With the engine at normal operating temperature, increase the idle speed and watch the vacuum gauge.

4. The airflow from the pump should be steady and fall between 2 and 6 psi. If it is unsteady or falls below this, the pump is defective and must be replaced.

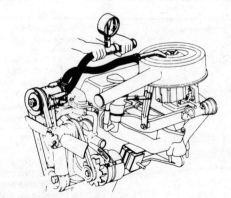

Checking the air pump output

PUMP NOISE DIAGNOSIS

The air pump is normally noisy; as engine speed increases, the noise of the pump will rise in pitch. The rolling sound the pump bearings make is normal. But if this sound becomes objectionable at certain speeds, the pump is defective and will have to be replaced.

A continual hissing sound from the air pump pressure relief valve at idle, indicates a defective valve. Replace the relief valve.

If the pump rear bearing fails, a continual knocking sound will be heard. Since the rear bearing is not separately replaceable, the pump will have to be replaced as an assembly.

Antibackfire Valve Tests

There are two different types of antibackfire valve used with air injection systems. A by-pass valve is used in 1972–81 engines, while 1971 engines use a gulp type of antibackfire valve. Test procedures for both types are given below.

GULP VALVE

1. Detach the air supply hose which runs between the pump and the gulp valve.
2. Connect a tachometer and run the engine to 1,500–2,000 rpm.
3. Allow the throttle to snap shut. This should produce a loud sucking sound from the gulp valve.
4. Repeat this operation several times. If no sound is present, the valve is not working or else the vacuum connections are loose.
5. Check the vacuum connections. If they are secure, replace the gulp valve.

BY-PASS VALVE

1. Detach the hose, which runs from the by-pass valve to the check valve, at the by-pass valve hose connection.
2. Connect a tachometer to the engine. With the engine running at normal idle speed, check to see that air is flowing from the by-pass valve hose connection.
3. Speed up the engine so that it is running at 1,500–2,000 rpm. Allow the throttle to snap shut. The flow of air from the by-pass valve at the check valve hose connection should stop momentarily and air should then flow from the exhaust port on the valve body or the silencer assembly.
4. Repeat Step 3 several times. If the flow of air is not diverted into the atmosphere from the valve exhaust port or if it fails to stop flowing from the hose connection, check the vacuum lines and connections. If these are tight, the valve is defective and requires replacement.
5. A leaking diaphragm will cause the air to flow out both the hose connection and the exhaust port at the same time. If this happens, replace the valve.

Check Valve Test—1975–78

1. Before starting the test, check all of the hoses and connections for leaks.
2. Detach the air supply hose from the check valve.
3. Insert a suitable probe into the check valve and depress the plate. Release it; the plate should return to its original position against the valve seat. If binding is evident, replace the valve.
4. With the engine running at normal operating temperature, gradually increase its speed to 1,500 rpm. Check for exhaust gas leakage. If any is present, replace the valve assembly.

NOTE: *Vibration and flutter of the check valve at idle speed is a normal condition and*

Air Injection System Diagnosis Chart

Problem	Cause	Cure
1. Noisy drive belt	1a Loose belt 1b Seized pump	1a Tighten belt 1b Replace
2. Noisy pump	2a Leaking hose 2b Loose hose 2c Hose contacting other parts 2d Diverter or check valve failure 2e Pump mounting loose 2g Defective pump	2a Trace and fix leak 2b Tighten hose clamp 2c Reposition hose 2d Replace 2e Tighten securing bolts 2g Replace
3. No air supply	3a Loose belt 3b Leak in hose or at fitting 3c Defective antibackfire valve 3d Defective check valve 3e Defective pump 3f Defective ASV	3a Tighten belt 3b Trace and fix leak 3c Replace 3d Replace 3e Replace 3f Replace
4. Exhaust backfire	4a Vacuum or air leaks 4b Defective antibackfire valve 4c Sticking choke 4d Choke setting rich	4a Trace and fix leak 4b Replace 4c Service choke 4d Adjust choke

does not mean that the valve should be replaced.

Check Valve Test—1979–81

1. Remove the check valve from the air injection manifold.

2. Blow into the manifold side (large side) and check that the valve is closed.

3. Blow into the ASV side (small side) and check that the valve is open.

4. If the valve is not operating properly it will probably require replacement.

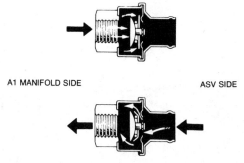

A1 MANIFOLD SIDE   ASV SIDE

Testing the 1979–81 check valve

Air Switching Valve (ASV) Tests

1. Start the engine and allow it to reach normal operating temperature and speed.

2. At curb idle, the air from the by-pass valve should be discharged through the hose which runs to the ASV.

3. When the vacuum line to the ASV is disconnected, the air from the by-pass valve should be diverted out through the ASV-to-air cleaner hose. Reconnect the vacuum line.

4. Disconnect the ASV-to-check valve hose and connect a pressure gauge to it.

5. Increase the engine speed. The relief valve should open when the pressure gauge registers 2.7–6.5 psi.

6. If the ASV fails any of the above tests, replace it. Reconnect all hoses.

Vacuum Delay Valve Test

The vacuum delay valve is located in the line which runs from the intake manifold to the vacuum surge tank. To check it, proceed as follows:

1. Remove the vacuum delay valve from the vacuum line. Be sure to note which end points toward the intake manifold.

2. When air is blown in from the ASV (surge tank) side, it should pass through the valve freely.

3. When air is blown in from the intake manifold side, a resistance should be felt.

4. Replace the valve if it fails either of the above tests.

5. Install the valve in the vacuum line, being careful not to install it backward.

EACV TEST—1983 AND LATER

The EACV should be checked with the engine in three stages: cold, idling warm, and running at 2,000 rpm at normal operating temperature.

1. Start the engine from cold and check that air is discharged from the air by-pass hose.

2. Warm the engine up to between 64°F and 109°F (after about two minutes worth of running). Idle the engine, and check that air is not discharging from the by-pass hose.

3. Run the engine up to 2,000 rpm after the thermostat has opened fully (normal operating temperature). Check that air is being discharged intermittently (in staggered impulses) from the hose.

Catalytic Converter

The catalytic converter is a muffler-like container built into the exhaust system to aid in the reduction of exhaust emissions. The catalyst element consists of individual pellets coated with a noble metal such as platinum, palladium, rhodium or a combination. When the exhaust gases come into contact with the

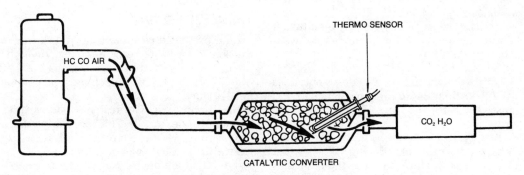

THERMO SENSOR

HC CO AIR

CO_2 H_2O

CATALYTIC CONVERTER

Oxidizing catalytic converter system

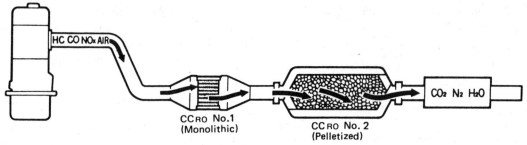

Three-way catalytic converter system

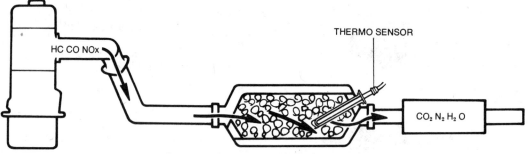

3-way catalyst system, '83 Celica shown

catalyst, a chemical reaction occurs which will reduce the pollutants into harmless substances like water and carbon dioxide.

There are essentially two types of catalytic converters: an oxidizing type and a three-way type. Both are used on the late-model Celicas. The oxidizing catalyst requires the addition of oxygen to spur the catalyst into reducing the engine's HC and CO emissions into H_2O and CO_2.

An air injection system is used to supply air to the exhaust system to aid in the reaction. A thermosensor, inserted into the converter, shuts off the air supply if the temperature of the catalyst becomes excessive.

The same sensor circuit will also cause an instrument panel warning light labeled "EXH TEMP" to come on when the catalyst temperature gets too high.

NOTE: *It is normal for the light to come on temporarily if the car is being driven downhill for long periods of time (such as descending a mountain).*

The light will come on and stay on if the air injection system is malfunctioning or if the engine is misfiring.

The oxidizing catalytic converter, while effectively reducing HC and CO emissions, does little, if anything, in the way of reducing NO_x emissions. Thus, the three-way catalytic converter.

The three-way converter, unlike the oxidizing type, is capable of reducing HC, CO and NO_x emissions; all at the same time. In theory, it seems impossible to reduce all three

pollutants in one system since the reduction of HC and CO requires the addition of oxygen, while the reduction of NO_x calls for the removal of oxygen. In actuality, the three-way system really can reduce all three pollutants, but only if the amount of oxygen in the exhaust system is precisely controlled. Due to this precise oxygen control requirement, the three-way converter system is used only in later cars equipped with an oxygen sensing system.

PRECAUTIONS

1. Use only unleaded fuel.
2. Avoid prolonged idling; the engine should run no longer than 20 min. at curb idle and no longer than 10 min. at fast idle.
3. Don't disconnect any of the spark plug leads while the engine is running.
4. Make engine compression checks as quickly as possible.

CATALYST TESTING

At the present time there is no known way to reliably test catalytic converter operation in the field. The only reliable test is a 12 hour and 40 min. "soak" test (CVS) which must be done in a laboratory.

An infrared HC/CO tester is not sensitive enough to measure the higher tailpipe emissions from a failing converter. Thus, a bad converter may allow enough emissions to escape so that the the car is no longer in compliance with Federal or state standards, but will still not cause the needle on a tester to move off zero.

The chemical reactions which occur inside a catalytic converter generate a great deal of heat. Most converter problems can be traced to fuel or ignition system problems which cause unusually high emissions. As a result of the increased intensity of the chemical reactions, the converter literally burns itself up.

A completely failed converter might cause a tester to show a slight reading. As a result, it is occasionally possible to detect one of these.

As long as you avoid severe overheating and the use of leaded fuels it is reasonably safe to assume that the converter is working properly. If you are in doubt, take the car to a diagnostic center that has a tester.

WATER THERMO SENSOR TESTING

The procedure for testing the water thermo sensor is included in the Fuel Injection section of this chapter. When checking resistance with the ohmmeter, consult the chart and remember that sensor resistance varies with coolant temperature as shown.

Oxygen Sensor System

The three way catalytic converter, which is capable of reducing HC, CO and NO_x into CO_2, H_2O, O_2 and N_2, can only function as long as the fuel/air mixture is kept within a critically precise range. The oxygen sensor system is what keeps the oxygen range in control.

Basically, the oxygen sensor system works like this: As soon as the engine warms up, the EFI computer begins to work. The oxygen sensor, located in the exhaust manifold, senses the oxygen content of the exhaust gases. The amount of oxygen in the exhaust varies according to the fuel/air mixture. The O_2 sensor produces a small voltage that varies depending on the amount of oxygen in the exhaust at the time. This voltage is picked up by the EFI computer. The EFI computer works together with the fuel distributor and together they will vary the amount of fuel which is delivered to the engine at any given time.

If the amount of oxygen in the exhaust system is low, which indicates a rich mixture, the sensor voltage will be high. The higher the voltage signal sent to the EFI computer, the more it will reduce the amount of fuel supplied to the engine. The amount of fuel is reduced until the amount of oxygen in the exhaust system increases, indicating a lean mixture. When the mixture is lean, the sensor will send a low voltage signal to the EFI computer. The computer will then increase the quantity of fuel until the sensor voltage in-

creases again and then the cycle will start all over.

OXYGEN SENSOR REPLACEMENT

1. Disconnect the negative battery cable.
2. Unplug the wiring connector leading from the O_2 sensor.

NOTE: *Be careful not to bend the waterproof hose as the oxygen sensor will not function properly if the air passage is blocked.*

3. Unscrew the two nuts and carefully pull out the sensor.
4. Installation is in the reverse order of removal. Please note the following:
- Always use a new gasket.
- Tighten the nuts to 13–16 ft. lbs.

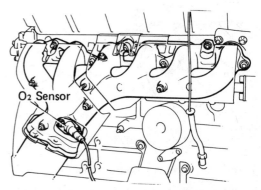

Remove the oxygen sensor carefully through the heat shield

OXYGEN SENSOR WARNING LIGHT

All Supras and 1982 and later Celicas are equipped with an oxygen sensor warning light on the instrument panel. The light may go on when the car is started, then it should go out. If the light stays on, check your odometer. The light is hooked up to an elapsed mileage counter which goes off every 30,000 miles. This is your signal that it is time to replace the oxygen sensor and have the entire system checked out. After replacement of the sensor,

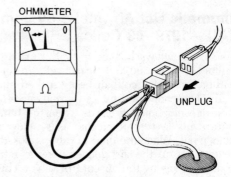

Checking thermosensor resistance

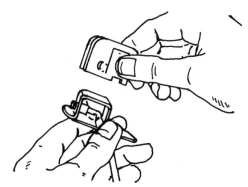

In order to reset the counter, you must first remove the cover

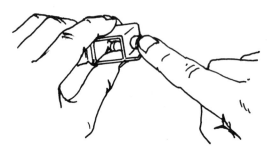

To reset the counter, push the switch

the elapsed mileage counter must be reset. To reset:

1. Locate the counter. It can be found under the left side of the instrument panel, on the brake pedal bracket.

2. Unscrew the mounting bolt, disconnect the wiring connector and remove the counter.

3. Remove the bolt on top of the counter.

4. Lift off the counter cover and push the reset switch.

NOTE: *The warning light on the instrument panel must go out at this time.*

5. Installation is in the reverse order of removal.

Automatic Hot Air Intake System (HAI)—1979–83 Celica

This system allows hot air from the exhaust manifold to be routed to the carburetor in cold weather. Instead of cold air being sucked into the air cleaner all the time, a thermo valve in the air cleaner housing closes when the temperature inside the air cleaner falls below a certain point. When the thermo valve is closed, a diaphragm on the air cleaner neck is activated and it opens the air control valve. This prevents cold outside air from entering the air

cleaner, but allows the hotter air from around the exhaust manifold to flow in. Not only does this system improve driveability, but it prevents carburetor icing in extremely cold weather.

CHECKING THE HAI SYSTEM

1. Visually inspect all hoses and connections for cracks, leaks or other damage.

2. Remove the air cleaner top.

3. Cool the thermo valve by blowing compressed air on it.

4. With the engine idling and the thermo valve closed (cool), check to see if the air control valve in the neck of the air cleaner is open and allowing hot air to enter the air cleaner.

5. Install the top of the air cleaner and run the engine until it reaches normal operating temperature.

6. Check that the air control valve is now closed and only cool air is being allowed to enter the air cleaner.

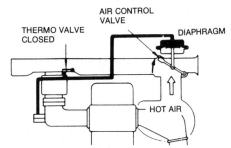

When the air control valve is open, it allows hot air to enter the air cleaner

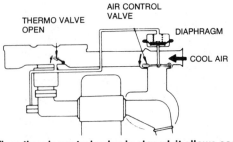

When the air control valve is closed, it allows cool air to enter the air cleaner

Automatic Choke System

The purpose of the automatic choke is to temporarily richen the fuel/air mixture to the engine by closing the choke valve when the engine is cold. By shutting the choke valve you are effectively 'choking' the engine by reducing the amount of air which is allowed to enter the carburetor. This then enables the fuel/air mixture to be ignited sooner (faster).

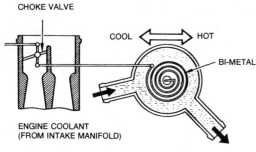

CHOKE VALVE

COOL ⟷ HOT

BI-METAL

ENGINE COOLANT
(FROM INTAKE MANIFOLD)

(TO WATER BYPASS PIPE)

When the engine coolant is cold, the spring expands and closes the choke valve. When it gets hot, the spring tightens and opens the choke

CHECKING THE AUTOMATIC CHOKE SYSTEM

1. Check the choke housing and its hoses for any leaks, cracks or other damage.

2. Check that the middle mark on the thermostatic case is aligned with the mark on the coil housing.

NOTE: *Loosen only the three screws around the outside edge of the case. Do not loosen the bolt at the center of the case because it will allow coolant to come out.*

3. Remove the top of the air cleaner.

4. With the engine cold and turned off, press down on the gas pedal and release it. The small valve in the center of the carburetor bore should be almost completely closed.

5. Run the engine until it reaches normal operating temperature and then check that the choke valve has opened up.

6. Reinstall the top of the air cleaner.

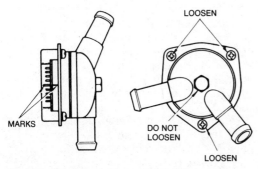

LOOSEN

MARKS

DO NOT
LOOSEN

LOOSEN

A close-up view of the choke housing

Choke Breaker System (CB)— Canada

The choke breaker system is used to monitor the automatic choke system. To prevent too rich a mixture when the choke is closed, the choke breaker forces the choke valve open slightly.

CHECKING THE CB SYSTEM

1. Start the engine.

2. Disconnect the hose from the choke breaker diaphragm and check that the choke linkage returns to its previous position.

3. Reconnect the hose to the diaphragm and check that the choke linkage is pulled back by the diaphragm.

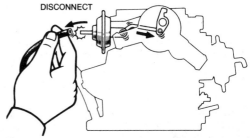

DISCONNECT

When the vacuum hose is pulled from the diaphragm on the Canadian car, the choke linkage should move

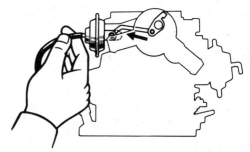

When the hose is reconnected, the linkage should return to its original position

Choke Breaker System (CB)— USA

This system performs the same function that the previous one does except that it goes one step further and forces the choke valve to open up even further after the engine has warmed up.

CHECKING THE CB SYSTEM

1. Carefully note the position of the choke breaker linkage rod.

2. Disconnect the vacuum hose between the choke breaker diaphragm and the 3-way connector at the diaphragm side.

3. Start the engine and check that the choke breaker linkage moves from its former position.

4. Reconnect the vacuum hose to the diaphragm. The linkage should move even further than it was.

5. Check the VSV and the TVSV as de-

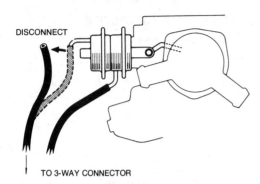

When checking the choke breaker (USA), remove the vacuum hose coming from the 3-way connection

tailed in the "Evaporative Emission Control" section.

Fast Idle Cam Breaker System (FICB)—Celica with Carburetor

After the engine has warmed up, this vacuum operated system forces the fast idle cam to move to the third step, which in turn lowers the engine speed.

CHECKING THE FICB SYSTEM

1. Disconnect the vacuum hose from the fast idle cam breaker diaphragm.
2. While holding the throttle valve slightly open, pull up the fast idle cam linkage and then release the throttle. This will set the fast idle cam.
3. Start the engine but do not touch the gas pedal.
4. Reconnect the hose. The fast idle cam should be released to the third step and the engine speed should thereby be lowered.
5. Apply vacuum to the FICB diaphragm and check that the linkage moves. If it does not, replace the diaphragm.
6. Check the VSV and the TVSV as detailed earlier in the "Evaporative Emission Control" section.

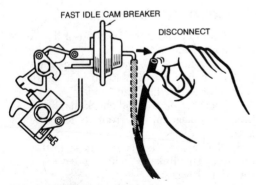

Disconnect the vacuum hose

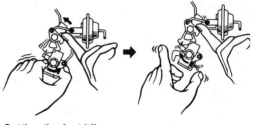

Setting the fast idle cam

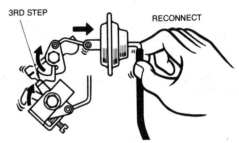

When the vacuum hose is reconnected, the fast idle cam should move to the 3rd step

Auxiliary Enrichment System 1974–83

An auxiliary enrichment system, which Toyota calls an "Auxiliary Accelerator Pump (AAP) System," is used on all carbureted models, starting in 1975.

When the engine is cold, an auxiliary enrichment circuit in the carburetor is operated to squirt extra fuel into the accelerator circuit in order to prevent the mixture from becoming too lean.

A thermostatic vacuum sensing valve (TVSV), which is threaded into the intake manifold, controls the operation of the enrichment circuit. Below a specified temperature, the valve is opened and manifold vacuum is allowed to act on a diaphragm in the carburetor. The vacuum pulls the diaphragm down, allowing fuel to flow into a special chamber above it.

Under sudden acceleration manifold vacuum drops momentarily, allowing the diaphragm to be pushed up by spring tension. This in turn forces the fuel from the chamber through a passage and out the accelerator pump jet.

When the coolant temperature goes above specification, the thermostatic vacuum valve closes, preventing the vacuum from reaching the diaphragm which makes the enrichment system inoperative.

TESTS

1. Check the clogged, pinched, disconnected, or misrouted vacuum lines.

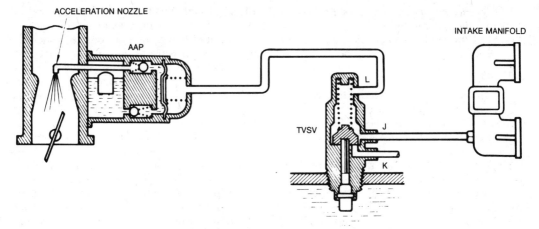

Components of the auxiliary enrichment system

2. With the engine cold (below 75°F), remove the top of the air cleaner, and allow the engine to idle.

3. Disconnect the vacuum line from the carburetor AAP unit. Gasoline should squirt out of the accelerator pump jet.

4. If gas doesn't squirt out of the jet, check for vacuum at the AAP vacuum line with the engine idling. If there is no vacuum and the hoses are in good shape, the thermostatic vacuum valve is defective and must be replaced.

5. If the gas doesn't squirt out and vacuum is present at the vacuum line in Step 4, the AAP unit is defective and must be replaced.

6. Repeat Step 3 with the engine at normal operating temperature. If gasoline squirts out of the pump jet, the thermostatic vacuum valve is defective and must be replaced.

7. Reconnect all of the vacuum lines and install the top of the air cleaner.

FUEL SYSTEM

Understanding the Fuel System

An automotive fuel system consists of everything between the fuel tank and the carburetor or fuel injection unit. This includes the tank itself, all the lines, one or more fuel filters, a fuel pump (mechanical or electric), and the carburetor or fuel injection unit.

With the exception of the carburetor or fuel injection unit, the fuel system is quite simple in operation. Fuel is drawn from the tank through the fuel line by the fuel pump, which forces it to the fuel filter, and from there to the carburetor where it is distributed to the cylinders.

Mechanical Fuel Pump

All 1971–74 and 1980–83 Celicas are equipped with a mechanically operated fuel pump of

diaphragm construction (1980–83 cars use two different types of pump). A separate fuel filter is incorporated into the fuel line (see Chapter 1 for its required service). On 1971–74 models, the fuel pump is located on the right side of the engine block. On 1980–83 models, it is located on the right side of the cylinder head.

REMOVAL AND INSTALLATION

1971–74

1. Disconnect the negative battery cable.

2. Disconnect and plug both of the fuel lines from the fuel pump.

3. Unscrew and remove the two fuel pump mounting bolts.

4. Withdraw the fuel pump assembly from the engine block.

5. Installation is in the reverse order of removal.

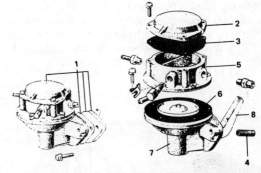

1. Fuel pump assembly
2. Fuel pump cover
3. Fuel pump cover gasket
4. Rocker arm spring
5. Fuel pump upper body
6. Diaphragm
7. Fuel pump lower body
8. Rocker arm

Mechanical fuel pump; 1971–74

NOTE: *Always use a new gasket when installing the fuel pump.*

6. Start the engine and check the pump for any leaks.

1980–83

1. Disconnect the negative battery cable.
2. Drain the radiator coolant.

NOTE: *When draining the radiator, use a clean container so that the coolant may be reused.*

3. Disconnect the upper radiator hose and wire it out of the way.
4. Disconnect and plug the three fuel lines from the fuel pump.
5. Unscrew the two fuel pump retaining bolts and remove the fuel pump and gasket.
6. Installation is in the reverse order of removal.

NOTE: *Always use a new gasket when installing the fuel pump.*

7. Start the engine and check for any leaks.

TESTING

Fuel pumps should always be tested on the vehicle. The larger line between the pump and tank is the suction side of the system and the smaller line, between the pump and carburetor or fuel injection pump is the pressure side. A leak in the pressure side would be apparent because of dripping fuel. A leak in the suction side is usually only apparent because of a reduced volume of fuel delivered to the pressure side.

1. Tighten any loose line connections and look for any kinks or restrictions.
2. Disconnect the fuel line at the carburetor or fuel injection pump. Disconnect the distributor-to-coil primary wire (gasoline engines). Place a container at the end of the fuel line and crank the engine a few revolutions. If little or no fuel flows from the line, either the fuel pump is inoperative or the line is plugged.

Blow through the lines with compressed air and try the test again. Reconnect the line.

3. If fuel flows in good volume, check the fuel pump pressure to be sure (pressure tests are possible only on gasoline engines).
4. Attach a pressure gauge to the pressure side of the fuel line. On cars equipped with a vapor return system, squeeze off the return hose.
5. Run the engine at idle and note the reading on the gauge. Stop the engine and compare the reading with the specifications listed in the "Tune-Up Specifications" chart. If the pump is operating properly, the pressure will be as specified and will be constant at idle speed. If pressure varies sporadically or is too high or low, the pump should be replaced.
6. Remove the pressure gauge.

The following flow test can also be performed:

1. Disconnect the fuel line from the carburetor or the fuel injection pump. Run the fuel line into a suitable measuring container.
2. Run the engine at idle until there is one pint of fuel in the container. One pint should be pumped in 30 seconds or less.
3. If the flow is below minimum, check for a restriction in the line.

The only way to check fuel pump pressure is by connecting an accurate pressure gauge to the fuel line at the carburetor level. Never replace a fuel pump without performing this simple test. If the engine seems to be starving out, check the ignition system first. Also check for a plugged fuel filter or a restricted fuel line before replacing the pump.

Electric Fuel Pump

All 1975 through 1979 Celicas and all Supras are equipped with an electric fuel pump. The pump on the Celica is located inside the fuel

TYPE I

TYPE II

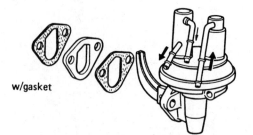

w/gasket

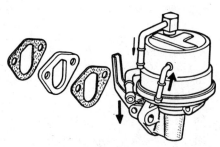

The two types of mechanical fuel pumps used on the 1980–81 Celica

55 WAYS TO IMPROVE FUEL ECONOMY

CHILTON'S
FUEL ECONOMY
& TUNE-UP TIPS

Tune-up • Spark Plug Diagnosis • Emission Controls

Fuel System • Cooling System • Tires and Wheels

General Maintenance

CHILTON'S FUEL ECONOMY & TUNE-UP TIPS

Fuel economy is important to everyone, no matter what kind of vehicle you drive. The maintenance-minded motorist can save both money and fuel using these tips and the periodic maintenance and tune-up procedures in this Repair and Tune-Up Guide.

There are more than 130,000,000 cars and trucks registered for private use in the United States. Each travels an average of 10-12,000 miles per year, and, and in total they consume close to 70 billion gallons of fuel each year. This represents nearly ⅔ of the oil imported by the United States each year. The Federal government's goal is to reduce consumption 10% by 1985. A variety of methods are either already in use or under serious consideration, and they all affect you driving and the cars you will drive. In addition to "down-sizing", the auto industry is using or investigating the use of electronic fuel delivery, electronic engine controls and alternative engines for use in smaller and lighter vehicles, among other alternatives to meet the federally mandated Corporate Average Fuel Economy (CAFE) of 27.5 mpg by 1985. The government, for its part, is considering rationing, mandatory driving curtailments and tax increases on motor vehicle fuel in an effort to reduce consumption. The government's goal of a 10% reduction could be realized — and further government regulation avoided — if every private vehicle could use just 1 less gallon of fuel per week.

How Much Can You Save?

Tests have proven that almost anyone can make at least a 10% reduction in fuel consumption through regular maintenance and tune-ups. When a major manufacturer of spark plugs sur-

TUNE-UP

1. Check the cylinder compression to be sure the engine will really benefit from a tune-up and that it is capable of producing good fuel economy. A tune-up will be wasted on an engine in poor mechanical condition.

2. Replace spark plugs regularly. New spark plugs alone can increase fuel economy 3%.

3. Be sure the spark plugs are the correct type (heat range) for your vehicle. See the Tune-Up Specifications.

Heat range refers to the spark plug's ability to conduct heat away from the firing end. It must conduct the heat away in an even pattern to avoid becoming a source of pre-ignition, yet it must also operate hot enough to burn off conductive deposits that could cause misfiring.

The heat range is usually indicated by a number on the spark plug, part of the manufacturer's designation for each individual spark plug. The numbers in bold-face indicate the heat range in each manufacturer's identification system.

Manufacturer	Typical Designation
AC	R **45** TS
Bosch (old)	WA **145** T30
Bosch (new)	HR **8** Y
Champion	RBL **15** Y
Fram/Autolite	**4**15
Mopar	P-**62** PR
Motorcraft	BRF-**42**
NGK	BP **5** ES-15
Nippondenso	W **16** EP
Prestolite	14GR **5** 2A

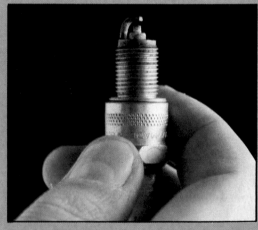

Periodically, check the spark plugs to be sure they are firing efficiently. They are excellent indicators of the internal condition of your engine.

On AC, Bosch (new), Champion, Fram/Autolite, Mopar, Motorcraft and Prestolite, a higher number indicates a hotter plug. On Bosch (old), NGK and Nippondenso, a higher number indicates a colder plug.

4. Make sure the spark plugs are properly gapped. See the Tune-Up Specifications in this book.

5. Be sure the spark plugs are firing efficiently. The illustrations on the next 2 pages show you how to "read" the firing end of the spark plug.

6. Check the ignition timing and set it to specifications. Tests show that almost all cars have incorrect ignition timing by more than 2°.

veyed over 6,000 cars nationwide, they found that a tune-up, on cars that needed one, increased fuel economy over 11%. Replacing worn plugs alone, accounted for a 3% increase. The same test also revealed that 8 out of every 10 vehicles will have some maintenance deficiency that will directly affect fuel economy, emissions or performance. Most of this mileage-robbing neglect could be prevented with regular maintenance.

Modern engines require that all of the functioning systems operate properly for maximum efficiency. A malfunction anywhere wastes fuel. You can keep your vehicle running as efficiently and economically as possible, by being aware of your vehicle's operating and performance characteristics. If your vehicle suddenly develops performance or fuel economy problems it could be due to one or more of the following:

PROBLEM	POSSIBLE CAUSE
Engine Idles Rough	Ignition timing, idle mixture, vacuum leak or something amiss in the emission control system.
Hesitates on Acceleration	Dirty carburetor or fuel filter, improper accelerator pump setting, ignition timing or fouled spark plugs.
Starts Hard or Fails to Start	Worn spark plugs, improperly set automatic choke, ice (or water) in fuel system.
Stalls Frequently	Automatic choke improperly adjusted and possible dirty air filter or fuel filter.
Performs Sluggishly	Worn spark plugs, dirty fuel or air filter, ignition timing or automatic choke out of adjustment.

Check spark plug wires on conventional point type ignition for cracks by bending them in a loop around your finger.

Be sure that spark plug wires leading to adjacent cylinders do not run too close together. (Photo courtesy Champion Spark Plug Co.)

7. If your vehicle does not have electronic ignition, check the points, rotor and cap as specified.

8. Check the spark plug wires (used with conventional point-type ignitions) for cracks and burned or broken insulation by bending them in a loop around your finger. Cracked wires decrease fuel efficiency by failing to deliver full voltage to the spark plugs. One misfiring spark plug can cost you as much as 2 mpg.

9. Check the routing of the plug wires. Misfiring can be the result of spark plug leads to adjacent cylinders running parallel to each other and too close together. One wire tends to pick up voltage from the other causing it to fire "out of time".

10. Check all electrical and ignition circuits for voltage drop and resistance.

11. Check the distributor mechanical and/or vacuum advance mechanisms for proper functioning. The vacuum advance can be checked by twisting the distributor plate in the opposite direction of rotation. It should spring back when released.

12. Check and adjust the valve clearance on engines with mechanical lifters. The clearance should be slightly loose rather than too tight.

SPARK PLUG DIAGNOSIS

Normal

APPEARANCE: This plug is typical of one operating normally. The insulator nose varies from a light tan to grayish color with slight electrode wear. The presence of slight deposits is normal on used plugs and will have no adverse effect on engine performance. The spark plug heat range is correct for the engine and the engine is running normally.

CAUSE: Properly running engine.

RECOMMENDATION: Before reinstalling this plug, the electrodes should be cleaned and filed square. Set the gap to specifications. If the plug has been in service for more than 10-12,000 miles, the entire set should probably be replaced with a fresh set of the same heat range.

Oil Deposits

APPEARANCE: The firing end of the plug is covered with a wet, oily coating.

CAUSE: The problem is poor oil control. On high mileage engines, oil is leaking past the rings or valve guides into the combustion chamber. A common cause is also a plugged PCV valve, and a ruptured fuel pump diaphragm can also cause this condition. Oil fouled plugs such as these are often found in new or recently overhauled engines, before normal oil control is achieved, and can be cleaned and reinstalled.

RECOMMENDATION: A hotter spark plug may temporarily relieve the problem, but the engine is probably in need of work.

Incorrect Heat Range

APPEARANCE: The effects of high temperature on a spark plug are indicated by clean white, often blistered insulator. This can also be accompanied by excessive wear of the electrode, and the absence of deposits.

CAUSE: Check for the correct spark plug heat range. A plug which is too hot for the engine can result in overheating. A car operated mostly at high speeds can require a colder plug. Also check ignition timing, cooling system level, fuel mixture and leaking intake manifold.

RECOMMENDATION: If all ignition and engine adjustments are known to be correct, and no other malfunction exists, install spark plugs one heat range colder.

Photos Courtesy Fram Corporation

Carbon Deposits

APPEARANCE: Carbon fouling is easily identified by the presence of dry, soft, black, sooty deposits.

CAUSE: Changing the heat range can often lead to carbon fouling, as can prolonged slow, stop-and-start driving. If the heat range is correct, carbon fouling can be attributed to a rich fuel mixture, sticking choke, clogged air cleaner, worn breaker points, retarded timing or low compression. If only one or two plugs are carbon fouled, check for corroded or cracked wires on the affected plugs. Also look for cracks in the distributor cap between the towers of affected cylinders.

RECOMMENDATION: After the problem is corrected, these plugs can be cleaned and reinstalled if not worn severely.

MMT Fouled

APPEARANCE: Spark plugs fouled by MMT (Methycyclopentadienyl Maganese Tricarbonyl) have reddish, rusty appearance on the insulator and side electrode.

CAUSE: MMT is an anti-knock additive in gasoline used to replace lead. During the combustion process, the MMT leaves a reddish deposit on the insulator and side electrode.

RECOMMENDATION: No engine malfunction is indicated and the deposits will not affect plug performance any more than lead deposits (see Ash Deposits). MMT fouled plugs can be cleaned, regapped and reinstalled.

High Speed Glazing

APPEARANCE: Glazing appears as shiny coating on the plug, either yellow or tan in color.

CAUSE: During hard, fast acceleration, plug temperatures rise suddenly. Deposits from normal combustion have no chance to fluff-off; instead, they melt on the insulator forming an electrically conductive coating which causes misfiring.

RECOMMENDATION: Glazed plugs are not easily cleaned. They should be replaced with a fresh set of plugs of the correct heat range. If the condition recurs, using plugs with a heat range one step colder may cure the problem.

Ash (Lead) Deposits

APPEARANCE: Ash deposits are characterized by light brown or white colored deposits crusted on the side or center electrodes. In some cases it may give the plug a rusty appearance.

CAUSE: Ash deposits are normally derived from oil or fuel additives burned during normal combustion. Normally they are harmless, though excessive amounts can cause misfiring. If deposits are excessive in short mileage, the valve guides may be worn.

RECOMMENDATION: Ash-fouled plugs can be cleaned, gapped and reinstalled.

Detonation

APPEARANCE: Detonation is usually characterized by a broken plug insulator.

CAUSE: A portion of the fuel charge will begin to burn spontaneously, from the increased heat following ignition. The explosion that results applies extreme pressure to engine components, frequently damaging spark plugs and pistons.

Detonation can result by over-advanced ignition timing, inferior gasoline (low octane) lean air/fuel mixture, poor carburetion, engine lugging or an increase in compression ratio due to combustion chamber deposits or engine modification.

RECOMMENDATION: Replace the plugs after correcting the problem.

Photos Courtesy Champion Spark Plug Co.

EMISSION CONTROLS

13. Be aware of the general condition of the emission control system. It contributes to reduced pollution and should be serviced regularly to maintain efficient engine operation.

14. Check all vacuum lines for dried, cracked or brittle conditions. Something as simple as a leaking vacuum hose can cause poor performance and loss of economy.

15. Avoid tampering with the emission control system. Attempting to improve fuel econ-

FUEL SYSTEM

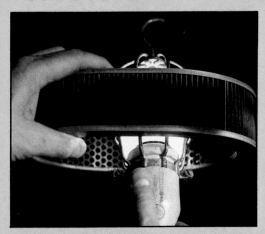

Check the air filter with a light behind it. If you can see light through the filter it can be reused.

Extremely clogged filters should be discarded and replaced with a new one.

18. Replace the air filter regularly. A dirty air filter richens the air/fuel mixture and can increase fuel consumption as much as 10%. Tests show that ⅓ of all vehicles have air filters in need of replacement.

19. Replace the fuel filter at least as often as recommended.

20. Set the idle speed and carburetor mixture to specifications.

21. Check the automatic choke. A sticking or malfunctioning choke wastes gas.

22. During the summer months, adjust the automatic choke for a leaner mixture which will produce faster engine warm-ups.

COOLING SYSTEM

29. Be sure all accessory drive belts are in good condition. Check for cracks or wear.

30. Adjust all accessory drive belts to proper tension.

31. Check all hoses for swollen areas, worn spots, or loose clamps.

32. Check coolant level in the radiator or expansion tank.

33. Be sure the thermostat is operating properly. A stuck thermostat delays engine warm-up and a cold engine uses nearly twice as much fuel as a warm engine.

34. Drain and replace the engine coolant at least as often as recommended. Rust and scale

TIRES & WHEELS

38. Check the tire pressure often with a pencil type gauge. Tests by a major tire manufacturer show that 90% of all vehicles have at least 1 tire improperly inflated. Better mileage can be achieved by over-inflating tires, but never exceed the maximum inflation pressure on the side of the tire.

39. If possible, install radial tires. Radial tires deliver as much as ½ mpg more than bias belted tires.

40. Avoid installing super-wide tires. They only create extra rolling resistance and decrease fuel mileage. Stick to the manufacturer's recommendations.

41. Have the wheels properly balanced.

omy by tampering with emission controls is more likely to worsen fuel economy than improve it. Emission control changes on modern engines are not readily reversible.

16. Clean (or replace) the EGR valve and lines as recommended.

17. Be sure that all vacuum lines and hoses are reconnected properly after working under the hood. An unconnected or misrouted vacuum line can wreak havoc with engine performance.

23. Check for fuel leaks at the carburetor, fuel pump, fuel lines and fuel tank. Be sure all lines and connections are tight.

24. Periodically check the tightness of the carburetor and intake manifold attaching nuts and bolts. These are a common place for vacuum leaks to occur.

25. Clean the carburetor periodically and lubricate the linkage.

26. The condition of the tailpipe can be an excellent indicator of proper engine combustion. After a long drive at highway speeds, the inside of the tailpipe should be a light grey in color. Black or soot on the insides indicates an overly rich mixture.

27. Check the fuel pump pressure. The fuel pump may be supplying more fuel than the engine needs.

28. Use the proper grade of gasoline for your engine. Don't try to compensate for knocking or "pinging" by advancing the ignition timing. This practice will only increase plug temperature and the chances of detonation or pre-ignition with relatively little performance gain.

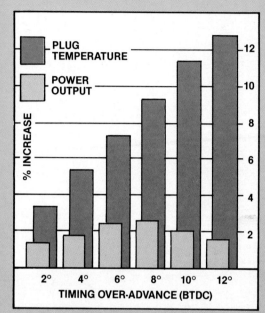

Increasing ignition timing past the specified setting results in a drastic increase in spark plug temperature with increased chance of detonation or preignition. Performance increase is considerably less. (Photo courtesy Champion Spark Plug Co.)

that form in the engine should be flushed out to allow the engine to operate at peak efficiency.

35. Clean the radiator of debris that can decrease cooling efficiency.

36. Install a flex-type or electric cooling fan, if you don't have a clutch type fan. Flex fans use curved plastic blades to push more air at low speeds when more cooling is needed; at high speeds the blades flatten out for less resistance. Electric fans only run when the engine temperature reaches a predetermined level.

37. Check the radiator cap for a worn or cracked gasket. If the cap does not seal properly, the cooling system will not function properly.

42. Be sure the front end is correctly aligned. A misaligned front end actually has wheels going in differed directions. The increased drag can reduce fuel economy by .3 mpg.

43. Correctly adjust the wheel bearings. Wheel bearings that are adjusted too tight increase rolling resistance.

Check tire pressures regularly with a reliable pocket type gauge. Be sure to check the pressure on a cold tire.

GENERAL MAINTENANCE

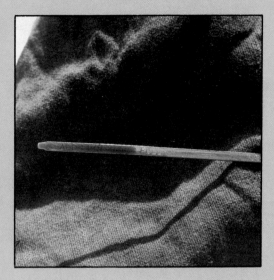

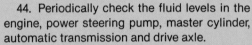

Check the fluid levels (particularly engine oil) on a regular basis. Be sure to check the oil for grit, water or other contamination.

A vacuum gauge is another excellent indicator of internal engine condition and can also be installed in the dash as a mileage indicator.

44. Periodically check the fluid levels in the engine, power steering pump, master cylinder, automatic transmission and drive axle.

45. Change the oil at the recommended interval and change the filter at every oil change. Dirty oil is thick and causes extra friction between moving parts, cutting efficiency and increasing wear. A worn engine requires more frequent tune-ups and gets progressively worse fuel economy. In general, use the lightest viscosity oil for the driving conditions you will encounter.

46. Use the recommended viscosity fluids in the transmission and axle.

47. Be sure the battery is fully charged for fast starts. A slow starting engine wastes fuel.

48. Be sure battery terminals are clean and tight.

49. Check the battery electrolyte level and add distilled water if necessary.

50. Check the exhaust system for crushed pipes, blockages and leaks.

51. Adjust the brakes. Dragging brakes or brakes that are not releasing create increased drag on the engine.

52. Install a vacuum gauge or miles-per-gallon gauge. These gauges visually indicate engine vacuum in the intake manifold. High vacuum = good mileage and low vacuum = poorer mileage. The gauge can also be an excellent indicator of internal engine conditions.

53. Be sure the clutch is properly adjusted. A slipping clutch wastes fuel.

54. Check and periodically lubricate the heat control valve in the exhaust manifold. A sticking or inoperative valve prevents engine warm-up and wastes gas.

55. Keep accurate records to check fuel economy over a period of time. A sudden drop in fuel economy may signal a need for tune-up or other maintenance.

© 1980 Chilton Book Company, Radnor, PA 19089

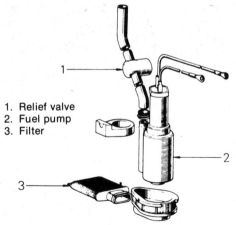

1. Relief valve
2. Fuel pump
3. Filter

Components of the electric fuel pump

tank, while the one on the Supra is attached to the front side of the tank.

REMOVAL AND INSTALLATION

1975–79 Celica

1. Disconnect the negative battery cable.
2. Remove the trim panel from inside the trunk.
3. Remove the screws which secure the pump access plate to the fuel tank.
4. Withdraw the plate, gasket and pump assembly as one unit.
5. Disconnect all leads and hoses from the fuel pump.
6. Installation is in the reverse order of removal.
   NOTE: *Always use a new gasket when installing the fuel pump.*
7. Start the engine and check for any leaks.

1979½–83 Supra

1. Disconnect the negative battery cable.
2. Unplug the fuel pump wiring connector inside the trunk.
3. Unscrew the four bolts and remove the service hole cover.

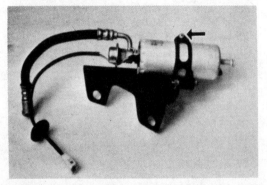

On the Supra, the electric fuel pump is located on the outside of the fuel tank

After removing the fuel pipe bracket (left), disconnect the outlet hose (right).

4. Disconnect and plug the fuel pump inlet hose.
5. Remove the bolt at the fuel pump bracket.
6. Raise the rear of the car and support it with jack stands.
7. Remove the fuel pipe bracket. Slowly loosen and then disconnect the fuel pump outlet hose.
8. Unscrew the two remaining fuel pump bracket bolts and then remove the pump.
9. Installation is in the reverse order of removal.
10. Start the engine and check for any leaks.

TESTING

1975–79 Celica

CAUTION: *Do not operate the fuel pump unless it is immersed in gasoline and connected to its resistor.*

1. Disconnect the lead from the oil pressure warning light sender.
2. Unfasten the line from the outlet side of the fuel filter.
3. Connect a pressure gauge to the filter outlet with a length of rubber hose.
4. Turn the ignition switch on the "ON" position, but do not start the engine.

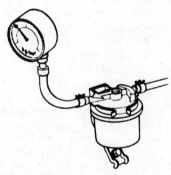

Testing electric fuel pump discharge pressure

5. Check the pressure gauge reading against the figure given in the "Tune-Up Specifications" chart in Chapter 2.

6. Check for a clogged filter or pinched lines if the pressure is not up to specification.

7. If there is nothing wrong with the filter or lines, replace the fuel pump.

8. Turn the ignition off and reconnect the fuel line to the filter. Connect the lead to the oil pressure sender also.

Supra

1. Turn the ignition switch to the "ON" position, but don't start the engine.

2. Remove the rubber cap from the fuel pump check connector and short both terminals.

3. Check that there is pressure in the hose to the cold start injector.

NOTE: *At this time you should be able to hear the fuel return noise from the pressure regulator.*

4. If no pressure can be felt in the line, check the fuses and all other related electrical connections. If everything is alright, the fuel pump will probably require replacement.

5. Remove the service wire, reinstall the rubber cap and turn off the ignition switch.

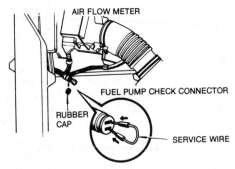

Shorting the fuel pump check connection

Carburetor

The carburetor is the most complex part of the entire fuel system. Carburetors vary greatly in construction, but they all operate basically the same way; their job is to supply the correct mixture of fuel and air to the engine in response to varying conditions.

Despite their complexity in operation, carburetors function because of a simple physical principle (the venturi principle). Air is drawn into the engine by the pumping action of the pistons. As the air enters the top of the carburetor, it passes through a venturi, which is nothing more than a restriction in the throttle bore. The air speeds up as it passes through the venturi, causing a slight drop in pressure.

This pressure drop pulls fuel from the float bowl through a nozzle into the throttle bore, where it mixes with the air and forms a fine mist, which is distributed to the cylinders through the intake manifold.

There are six different systems (fuel/air circuits) in a carburetor that make it work; the Float system, Main Metering system, Idle and Low-Speed system, Accelerator Pump system, Power system, and the Choke system. The way these systems are arranged in the carburetor determines the carburetor's size and shape.

It's hard to believe that the two-barrel carburetor used on 4 cylinder engines have all the same basic systems as the enormous 4-barrels used on V8 engines. Of course, the 4-barrels have more throttle bores ("barrels") and a lot of other hardware you won't find on the little two-barrels. But basically, all carburetors are similar, and if you understand a simple two-barrel, you can use that knowledge to understand a 4-barrel. If you'll study the explanations of the various systems on this stage, you'll discover that carburetors aren't as tricky as you thought they were. In fact, they're fairly simple, considering the job they have to do.

It's important to remember that carburetors seldom give trouble during normal operation. Other than changing the fuel and air filters and making sure the idle speed and mixture are OK at every tune-up, there's not much maintenance you can perform on the average carburetor.

The carburetors used on Toyota models are conventional two-barrel, down-draft types similar to domestic carburetors. The main circuits are: *primary,* for normal operational requirements; *secondary,* to supply high-speed fuel needs; *float,* to supply fuel to the primary and secondary circuits; *accelerator,* to supply fuel for quick and safe acceleration; *choke,* for reliable starting in cold weather; and *power valve,* for fuel economy. Although slight differences in appearance may be noted, these carburetors are basically alike. Of course, different jets and settings are demanded by the different engines to which they are fitted.

REMOVAL AND INSTALLATION

1. Disconnect the negative battery cable.

2. Loosen the radiator drain plug and drain the coolant into a suitable container.

3. Unscrew the mounting screws and remove the air filter housing. Disconnect all hoses and lines leading from the air cleaner.

4. Tag and disconnect all fuel, vacuum, coolant and electrical lines or hoses leading from the carburetor.

5. Disconnect the accelerator linkage from

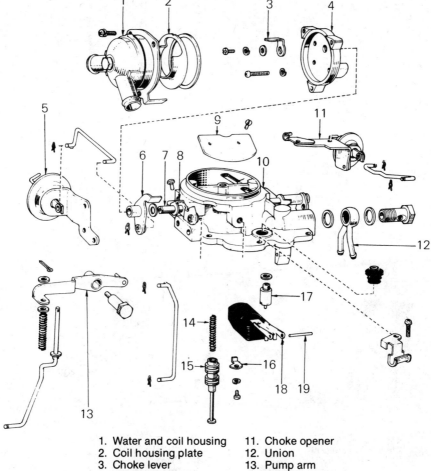

1. Water and coil housing
2. Coil housing plate
3. Choke lever
4. Coil housing body
5. Choke breaker
6. Relief lever
7. Choke shaft
8. Connecting lever
9. Choke valve
10. Air horn
11. Choke opener
12. Union
13. Pump arm
14. Spring
15. Power piston
16. Piston retainer
17. Needle valve set
18. Float
19. Float pivot pin

Air horn assembly; 1979 20R (others similar)

the carburetor. On cars equipped with an automatic transmission, disconnect the throttle cable linkage running from the transmission.

6. Remove the four carburetor mounting bolts and lift off the carburetor and its gasket.

NOTE: *Cover the manifold opening with a clean rag to prevent anything from falling into the engine.*

7. Installation is in the reverse order of removal.

8. Start the engine and check for any leaks. Check the float level.

FLOAT LEVEL ADJUSTMENT

Float level adjustments are unnecessary on models equipped with a carburetor sight glass,

if the fuel level falls within the lines when the engine is running.

There are two float level adjustments which may be made on Toyota carburetors. One is with the air horn inverted, so that the float is in a fully *raised* position; the other is with the air horn in an upright position, so that the float falls to the bottom of its travel.

The float level is either measured with a special carburetor float level gauge, which comes with a rebuilding kit, or with a standard wire gauge.

1. Turn the air horn upside down and let the float hang down by its own weight.

2. Using a special float gauge (available at your local dealer), check the clearance be-

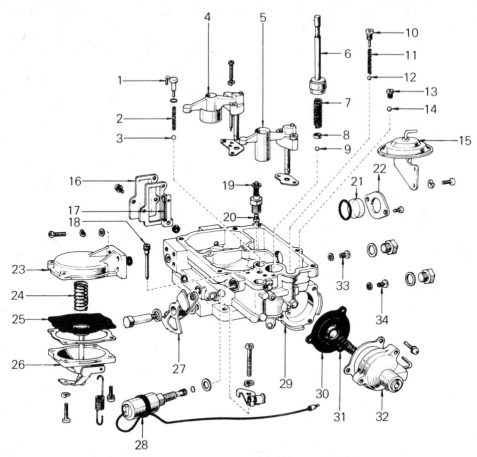

1. Pump jet	18. Primary slow jet
2. Spring	19. Power valve
3. Outlet check ball	20. Power jet
4. Secondary small venturi	21. Sight glass
5. Primary small venturi	22. Glass retainer
6. Pump plunger	23. Diaphragm housing cap
7. Spring	24. Spring
8. Ball retainer	25. Diaphragm
9. Inlet check ball	26. Housing
10. Plug	27. Fast idle cam
11. Spring	28. Solenoid valve
12. AAP outlet check ball	29. Carburetor body
13. Plug	30. Diaphragm
14. AAP inlet check ball	31. Spring
15. Throttle positioner	32. AAP housing
16. Thermostatic valve cover	33. Secondary main jet
17. Thermostatic valve	34. Primary main jet

Main body assembly; 1979 20R (others similar)

tween the tip of the float and the flat surface of the air horn. The clearance should be:

8R-C—0.370 in.

18R-C—0.200 in.

20R—0.197 in., 1975–77; 0.276 in., 1978–80

22R—0.413 in., 1982; 0.386 in., 1981 and 1983

NOTE: *This measurement should be made without the gasket on the air horn.*

3. If the float clearance is not within speci-

fications, adjust it by bending the upper (center) float tab.

4. Lift up the float and check the clearance between the needle valve plunger and the float lip. Clearance on the 8R-C and 18R-C engines may be checked with a special float gauge or with a standard wire feeler gauge. 20R and 22R engines must only use the special float gauge. The clearance should be 0.039 in. on all engines.

5. If the clearance is not within specifica-

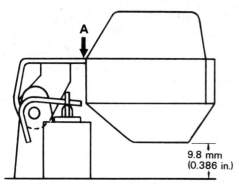

Adjust float in raised position by bending tab at point A. Measurement shown for 1983 22R

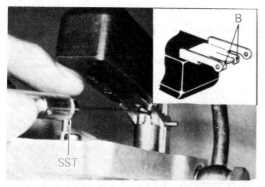

To adjust the float in the lowered position, bend the outer tabs (b)

tions, adjust it by bending the lower float tabs (2).

FAST IDLE ADJUSTMENT

Off-Vehicle

The fast idle adjustment is performed with the choke valve fully *closed*.

Adjust the gap between the throttle valve edge and bore to the specifications, where given, in the "Fast Idle Adjustment" chart. Use a wire gauge to determine the gap.

The chart also gives the proper primary throttle valve opening angle, where necessary, and the proper means of fast idle adjustment.

NOTE: *The throttle valve opening angle is measured with a gauge supplied in the car-*

Fast idle adjustment, carburetor off vehicle

buretor rebuilding kit. It is also possible to make one out of cardboard by using a protractor to obtain the correct angle.

UNLOADER ADJUSTMENT

The unloader adjustment is made with the primary throttle valve fully open. With the valve open, check the choke valve angle with a special gauge supplied in the rebuilding kit or with a gauge of the proper angle fabricated out of cardboard. The angle of the choke valve opening should be;

- 8R-C—51°
- 18R-C—47°
- 20R—50°
- 22R—45° (50° 1983)

All angles should be measured from the horizontal plane created by a closed choke valve.

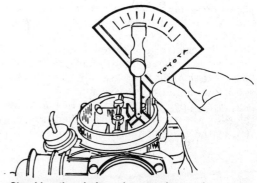

Checking the choke valve opening angle

Fast Idle Adjustment

Engine	Throttle Valve to Bore Clearance (in.)	Primary Throttle Angle (deg)	To Adjust Fast Idle:
8R-C	0.029	11—from closed	Turn the fast idle adjusting screw
18R-C	0.041	13—from closed	Turn the fast idle adjusting screw
20R	0.047	—	Turn the fast idle screw

To adjust the angle, bend the fast idle lever until the proper measurement is achieved.

On Vehicle—1975 and Later

NOTE: *Disconnect the EGR valve vacuum line on 20R engines.*

1. Perform the idle speed/mixture adjustments as outlined in Chapter 2. Leave the tachometer connected.
2. Remove the top of the air cleaner.
3. Open the throttle valve slightly and close the choke valve. Next, hold the choke valve with your finger and close the throttle valve. The choke valve is now fully closed.
4. Without depressing the accelerator pedal, start the engine.
5. Check to see that the engine fast idle speed is 2400 rpm.
6. If the reading on the tachometer is not within specifications, adjust the fast idle speed by turning the fast idle screw.
7. Disconnect the tachometer, install the air cleaner cover, and connect the EGR valve vacuum line if it was disconnected.

RELOADER ADJUSTMENT

A reloader is used on the 8R-C engine to prevent the throttle valve from opening during automatic choke operation.

1. When the choke valve is opened 45° from the closed position, the reloader lever should disengage from its stop.

NOTE: *Angle, "A," in the illustration, should be 20° when measured with a gauge.*

2. To adjust, bend the portion of the linkage where angle "A" was measured.
3. When the primary throttle valve is full opened, with the reloader in operating position, the clearance between the secondary throttle valve edge and bore should be 0.014 0.030. Measure the clearance with a wire gauge and bend the reloader tab to adjust it.
4. Fully open the choke valve by hand; the reloader lever should be disengaged from its stop by the weight on its link.

CHOKE BREAKER ADJUSTMENT

1975–79

1. Push the rod which comes out of the upper (choke breaker) diaphragm so that the choke valve opens.
2. Measure the choke valve opening angle. It should be 40°.
3. Adjust the angle, if necessary, by bending the relief lever link.

1980–83

1. Apply vacuum to the larger of the two diaphragms.
2. Check that the angle of the choke plate is 38°, measured from the horizontal plane. Angle on 1983 and later 22R engines is 42°.
3. If the angle is incorrect, adjust it by bending the choke breaker link.
4. Apply vacuum to both of the diaphragms and check the choke plate angle again. It should be approximately 60° (measured from the horizontal plane as before).
5. If the angle is not within specifications, the choke breaker will require replacement.

INITIAL IDLE MIXTURE SCREW ADJUSTMENT

When assembling the carburetor, turn the idle mixture screw the number of turns specified below. After the carburetor is installed, perform the appropriate idle speed/mixture adjustment as detailed in Chapter 2.

- 8R-C—2 turns from seating.
- 18R-C—2½ turns from fully closed.
- 20R—1¾ turns from fully closed, 1975–79; 2½ turns from fully closed, 1980 Federal; 1⅓ turns from fully closed, 1980 California.
- 22R—2½ turns from fully closed, 1982; 4 turns from fully closed, 1983.

NOTE: *Idle mixture on the 1981 Celicas is preset at the factory and not adjustable.*

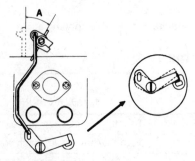

Measure the angle at "A" (20°)

Idle mixture and adjustment screw (1)

KICK-UP ADJUSTMENT

1972 and Later

1. Open the primary throttle valve. On 18R-C engines, the valve should be open 64° from bore; on 20R engines, the valve should be open all the way.

2. The secondary throttle valve-to-bore clearance should be 0.008 in. If not, adjust the clearance by bending the secondary throttle lever.

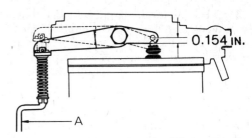

To adjust the pump stroke, bend the connecting link (A)

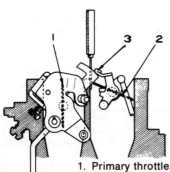

1.	Primary throttle valve
2.	Secondary throttle valve
3.	Secondary throttle lever

Kick-up adjustment

THROTTLE POSITIONER ADJUSTMENT

1. Apply vacuum to the throttle positioner diaphragm.

2. The throttle valve opening angle should be 16.5° from the horizontal plane. If not, adjust it by turning the adjusting screw.

Throttle positioner adjustment; adjusting screw (1), throttle lever tab (2)

PUMP STROKE ADJUSTMENT

Check that the length of the pump stroke (length that the pump lever travels) is 0.154 in. If it is not, it can be adjusted by bending the connecting link.

OVERHAUL

Efficient carburetion depends greatly on careful cleaning and inspection during overhaul, since dirt, gum, water, or varnish in or on the carburetor parts are often responsible for poor performance.

Overhaul your carburetor in a clean, dust-free area. Carefully disassemble the carburetor, referring often to the exploded views. Keep all similar and look-alike parts segregated during disassembly and cleaning to avoid accidental interchange during assembly. Make a note of all jet sizes.

When the carburetor is disassembled, wash all parts (except diaphragms, electric choke units, pump plunger, and any other plastic, leather, fiber, or rubber parts) in clean carburetor solvent. Do not leave parts in the solvent any longer than is necessary to sufficiently loosen the deposits. Excessive cleaning may remove the special finish from the float bowl and choke valve bodies, leaving these parts unfit for service. Rinse all parts in clean solvent and blow them dry with compressed air to allow them to air dry. Wipe clean all cork, plastic, leather, and fiber parts with a clean, lint-free cloth.

NOTE: *Carburetor solvent is available in various-sized solvent cans, which are designed with a removable small parts basket in the top. The carburetor choke chamber and body, and all small parts can be soaked in this can until clean. These solvent cans are available at most auto parts stores, and are quite handy for soaking other small engine parts.*

Blow out all passages and jets with compressed air and be sure that there are no restrictions or blockages. Never use wire or similar tools to clean jets, fuel passages, or air bleeds. Clean all jets and valves separately to avoid accidental interchange.

Check all parts for wear or damage. If wear or damage is found, replace the defective parts. Especially check the following:

1. Check the float needle and seat for wear. If wear is found, replace the complete assembly.

2. Check the float hinge pin for wear and the float(s) for dents or distortion. Replace the float if fuel has leaked into it.

3. Check the throttle and choke shaft bores for wear or an out-of-round condition. Damage or wear to the throttle arm, shaft, or shaft bore will often require replacement of the throttle body. These parts require a close tolerance of fit; wear may allow air leakage, which could affect starting and idling.

NOTE: *Throttle shafts and bushings are not included in overhaul kits. They can be purchased separately.*

4. Inspect the idle mixture adjusting needles for burrs or grooves. Any such condition requires replacement of the needle, since you will not be able to obtain a satisfactory idle.

5. Test the accelerator pump check valves. They should pass air one way but not the other. Test for proper seating by blowing and sucking on the valve. Replace the valve if necessary. If the valve is satisfactory, wash the valve again to remove breath moisture.

6. Check the bowl cover for warped surfaces with a straightedge.

7. Closely inspect the valves and seats for wear and damage, replacing as necessary.

8. After the carburetor is assembled, check the choke valve for freedom of operation.

Carburetor overhaul kits are recommended for each overhaul. These kits contain all gaskets and new parts to replace those that deteriorate most rapidly. Failure to replace all parts supplied with the kit (especially gaskets) can result in poor performance and a leaky carburetor later.

Most carburetor manufacturers supply overhaul kits in at least one of three basic types: minor repair; major repair; and gasket kits. Basically, they contain the following, and are available at most auto parts jobbers and Toyota dealers:

- Minor Repair Kits:
    All gaskets
    Float needle valve
    Volume control screw
    All diaphragms
    Spring for the pump diaphragm
- Major Repair Kits:
    All jets and gaskets
    All diaphragms
    Float needle valve
    Volume control screw
    Pump ball valve
    Main jet carrier
    Float
- Gasket Kits:
    All gaskets

After cleaning and checking all components, reassemble the carburetor, using new parts and referring to the exploded view. When reassembling, make sure that all screws and jets are tight in their seats, but do not over-

tighten as the tips will be distorted. Tighten all screws gradually in rotation. Do not tighten needle valves into their seats; uneven jetting will result. Always use new gaskets. Be sure to adjust the float level when reassembling.

Fuel Injection

The fuel injection system used on the Toyota Supra and 1983 and later 22R-E Celica is known as the EFI (electronic fuel injection) system. The EFI on the Supra can be broken down into three basic systems; the fuel system, the air induction system, and the electronic control system.

The main components of the fuel system are the fuel tank, the fuel pump and the fuel injectors. The electric fuel pump supplies sufficient fuel from the fuel tank, under a constant pressure, to the EFI fuel injectors. These injectors in turn inject a metered quantity of fuel into the intake manifold in accordance with signals given by the EFI computer. Each injector injects, at the same time, one half of the fuel required for ideal combustion with each engine revolution.

The air induction system consists of the air cleaner, an air flow meter, an air valve and an air intake chamber. All of these components contribute to the supply of the proper amount of air to the intake manifold as controlled by the EFI computer.

The main component of the electronic control system is the EFI computer. The computer receives signals from various sensors indicating changing engine operating conditions such as:

- Intake air volume
- Intake air temperature
- Coolant temperature
- Engine load
- Acceleration/deceleration
- Exhaust oxygen content, etc.

These signals are utilized by the computer to determine the injection duration necessary for an optimum air/fuel ratio.

TROUBLESHOOTING

Engine troubles are not usually caused by the EFI system. When troubleshooting, always check first the condition of all other related systems.

Many times the most frequent cause of problems is a bad contact in a wiring connector, so always make sure that the connections are secure. When inspecting the connector, pay particular attention to the following points:

1. Check to see that the terminals are not bent.

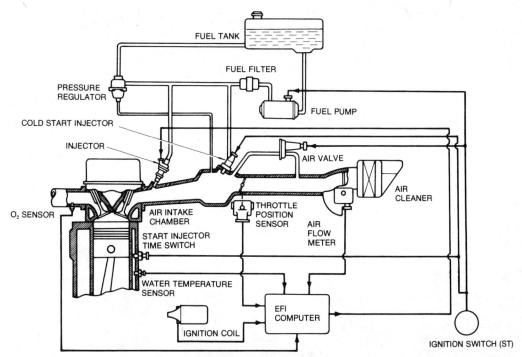

Main components of the Supra 4M-E and 5M-E EFI system, 1981 and earlier

2. Check to see that the connector is pushed in all the way and locked.

3. Check that there is no change in signal when the connector is tapped or wiggled.

Actual troubleshooting of the EFI system and the EFI computer is a complex process which requires the use of a few expensive and hard to find tools. Other than checking the operation of the main components individually, we suggest that you leave any further troubleshooting to an authorized service facility.

NOTE: *The worst enemy of any fuel injection system is water or moisture. The best (i.e., cheapest and simplest) insurance for your car's injection system is to change the fuel filter as frequently as the maintenance schedule recommends. When you follow the filter change interval strictly, many possible expensive injection system problems are eliminated.*

Cold Start Injector

During cold engine starting, the cold start injector is used to supply additional fuel to the intake manifold to aid in initial start-up. The opening and closing of the injector is determined by the Start Injector Time Switch. When the engine coolant temperature falls below a certain point, the switch is tripped and then opens the cold start injector. As the en-

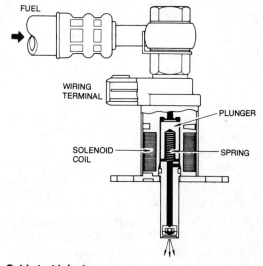

Cold start injector

gine coolant warms up, the switch will eventually close the injector.

REMOVAL AND INSTALLATION

All Engines Except 5M-GE

1. Disconnect the negative battery cable.

2. Remove the cold start injector union bolt on the delivery pipe.

NOTE: *Before removing the union bolt, place a suitable container under it to catch any escaping fuel.*

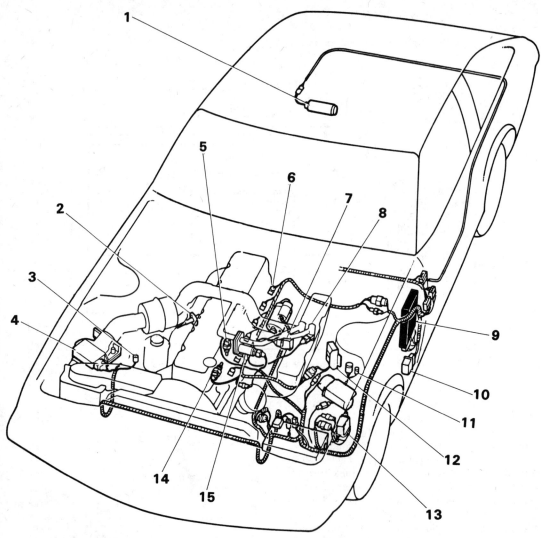

1. Fuel pump
2. Oxygen sensor
3. Fuel pump check connector
4. Air flow meter
5. Water thermo sensor
6. Injector
7. Throttle position sensor
8. Cold start injector
9. Computer
10. Circuit opering relay
11. Service connector
12. Resistor
13. Main relay
14. Cold start injector time switch
15. Air valve

1981 Celica Liftback 5M-E EFI and emission components

3. Disconnect the wiring connector at the injector.

4. Unscrew the two mounting bolts and then remove the cold start injector from the air intake chamber.

5. Installation is in the reverse order of removal.

NOTE: *Always use new gaskets when reinstalling the injector.*

6. Start the engine and check for any leaks.

5M-GE Twin Cam

NOTE: *Refer to "Cylinder Head Removal" for more illustrations.*

1. Drain the cooling system.

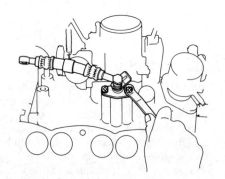

Removing cold start injector, 5M-GE

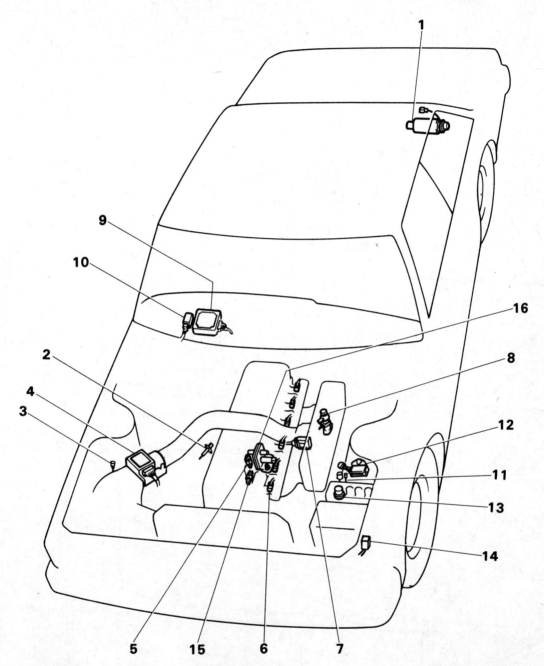

1. Fuel pump
2. Oxygen sensor
3. Fuel pump check connector
4. Air flow meter
5. Water thermo sensor
6. Injector
7. Throttle position sensor
8. Cold start injector
9. Computer
10. Circuit opening relay
11. Service connector
12. Resistor
13. No. 1 main relay
14. No. 2 main relay
15. Cold start injector time switch
16. Air valve

1981 Celica coupe 5M-E EFI and emission components

2. Remove the air intake connector at the throttle body.

3. Tag and disconnect all hoses from the air intake chamber, and all hoses from the throttle body which may interfere in intake chamber removal.

4. Tag and disconnect the accelerator linkage and cable from the throttle body.

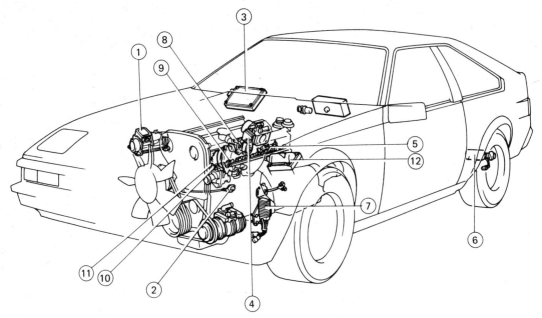

1. Air flow meter
2. Oxygen sensor
3. ECU
4. Throttle position sensor
5. Cold start injector
6. Fuel pump
7. Resistor
8. ISC valve
9. Injector
10. Water thermo sensor
11. Cold start injector time switch
12. Igniter w/ignition coil

1982 and later Supra EFI and emission control components

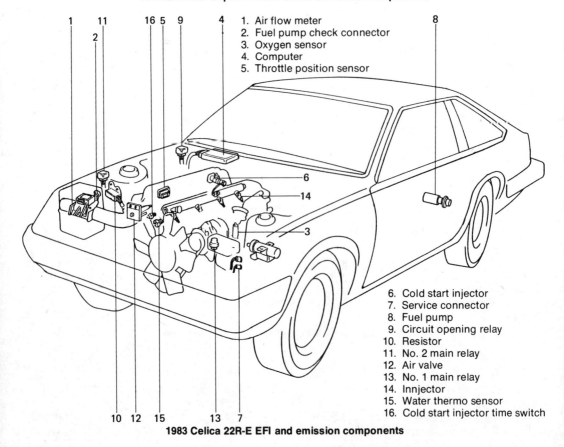

1. Air flow meter
2. Fuel pump check connector
3. Oxygen sensor
4. Computer
5. Throttle position sensor
6. Cold start injector
7. Service connector
8. Fuel pump
9. Circuit opening relay
10. Resistor
11. No. 2 main relay
12. Air valve
13. No. 1 main relay
14. Innjector
15. Water thermo sensor
16. Cold start injector time switch

1983 Celica 22R-E EFI and emission components

5. Tag and disconnect the cold start injector wire, throttle position sensor wire, and the two wiring connectors near the distributor.

6. Remove the air intake chamber stay and the vacuum pipe subassembly.

7. Loosen the EGR pipe connecting nut. Disconnect the cold start fuel hose from the delivery pipe.

8. Remove the air intake chamber from the cylinder head, and remove the cold start injector from the intake chamber.

9. Installation is in the reverse order of removal. *Always use new gaskets under the cold start injector.*

10. Start the engine and check for leaks.

CHECKING

1. Unplug the wiring connector and remove the cold start injector from the air intake chamber.

NOTE: *Do not disconnect the fuel line.*

2. Using Special Tool 09843-30011, connect one end to the injector and the other to the battery.

3. Remove the rubber cap from the Fuel Pump Check terminal and short both terminals with a wire.

4. Hold the injector over a suitable container and then turn the ignition switch to the 'ON' position. *Do not start the engine.*

5. Check that the fuel splash pattern is even and V-shaped.

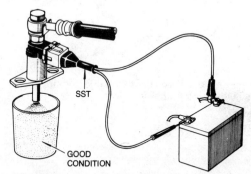

The fuel spray pattern should be an even, V-shaped one

6. Disconnect the test probes from the battery and check that the fuel does not leak from the injector tip any more than one drop per minute.

7. Remove the Special Tool and reinstall the cold start injector.

8. Check the resistance of the injector. It should be 3–4 ohms.

9. If the cold start injector did not operate properly in any of these tests, it will require replacement.

Pressure Regulator

The pressure regulator maintains correct fuel pressure throughout the system. The regulator is vacuum controlled to provide a relatively constant pressure differential.

The regulator is open during most engine operating conditions. This provides for better recirculation of the fuel to lower the temperature of the fuel supply.

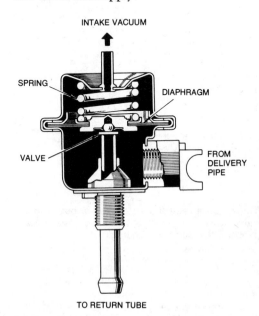

Pressure regulator

CHECKING

1. Disconnect the negative battery cable.

2. Unplug the wiring connector from the cold start injector.

3. Place a suitable container under the front end of the delivery pipe and slowly remove the union bolt for the cold start injector. Drain all of the fuel in the delivery pipe.

4. Install a fuel pressure gauge in the union bolt's place, connect the battery cable and start the engine.

5. Disconnect the vacuum sensing hose from the pressure regulator and block it off.

6. Measure the fuel pressure at idle. It should be 33–38 psi. If the pressure is high, replace the regulator.

7. Installation is in the reverse order of removal.

REMOVAL AND INSTALLATION

1. Remove the throttle body as detailed later in this Chapter.

2. Disconnect the negative battery cable.

3. Place a suitable container under the union and pipe support.

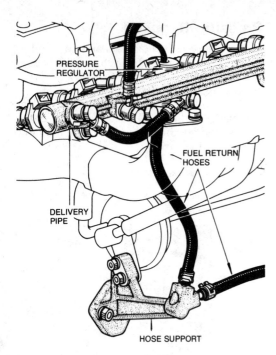

The pressure regulator is located in between the fuel delivery pipe and the cylinder head—5M-E shown, 22R-E and 5M-GE similar

4. Disconnect the vacuum sensing hose from the top of the regulator.

5. Disconnect the fuel return hose and plug the pipe of the hose support.

6. Remove the union bolt from the regulator.

7. Unscrew the two regulator mounting bolts and lift out the regulator.

8. Installation is in the reverse order of removal.

9. Start the engine and check for any leaks.

Fuel Injectors

There is one fuel injector for each cylinder. They spray fuel into the intake port, in front of the intake valve. When the injector is energized, the coil pulls the plunger up, opening the needle valve and allowing the fuel to pass through the injector. Opening of the injectors is controlled by the EFI computer. The injectors operate at low pressure and are open for only a fraction of a second at a time.

REMOVAL AND INSTALLATION

1. Disconnect the negative battery cable.

2. Place a suitable container under the intake manifold to catch any dripping fuel.

3. Remove the air intake chamber as detailed in "Cylinder Head Removal and Installation" section. Throttle body also removed on 22R-E.

4. On 5M-GE, remove the distributor. On all engines, tag and disconnect all hoses and wires which interfere with injector removal.

5. Unplug the wiring connectors from the tops of the fuel injectors and remove the two

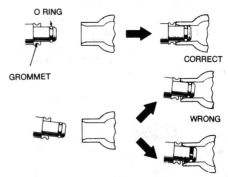

Make sure that you insert the injector into the fuel delivery pipe properly

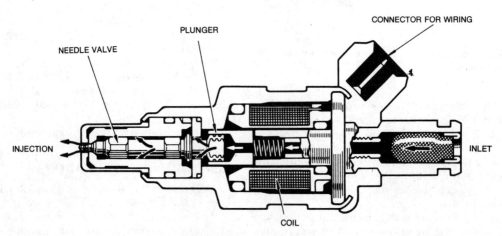

Cut-away view of a fuel injector

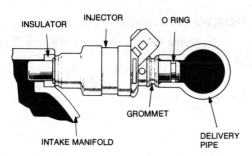

A cut-away view of how it should look upon reinstallation

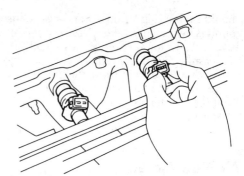

When installing, make sure injectors rotate smoothly; if not, check O-rings

plastic clamps that hold the wiring harness to the fuel delivery pipe.

6. Unscrew the four mounting bolts and remove the delivery pipe with the injectors attached. *Do not remove the injector cover.*

7. Pull the injectors out of the delivery pipe. To install:

8. Insert six new insulators into the injector holes on the intake manifold.

9. Install the grommet and a new O-ring to the delivery pipe end of each injector.

10. Apply a thin coat of gasoline to the O-ring on each injector and then press them into the delivery pipe.

11. Install the injectors together with the delivery pipe in the intake manifold. Tighten the mounting bolts to 11–15 ft. lbs.

12. Installation of the remaining components is in the reverse order of removal. On the 5M-GE, time the engine.

13. Start the engine and check for any fuel leaks.

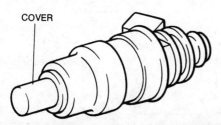

Do not remove the cover after each injector is removed

CHECKING

We recommend that any checking or testing of the injectors, other than that included below, be left to an authorized service facility.

Injector operation can be checked with the injectors installed in the engine. A sound scope is needed here (a stethescope-like device you can usually rent from tool rental shops; they are also available new from most auto tool and parts jobbers).

With the engine running or cranking, check each injector for normal operating noise (a buzzing or humming), which changes in proportion to engine rpm. If a sound scope is not available to you, check injector operation by touching each injector with your finger—it

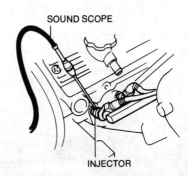

Injectors should emit a buzzing sound

Installing injectors with delivery pipe

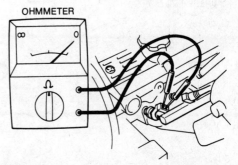

Measuring injector resistance across both terminals

should be buzzing. If no sound or an unusual sound is heard, check the wiring connector, or have the injector checked professionally.

Measure injector resistance by unplugging the wiring connector from the injector, and connecting an ohmmeter. Check the continuity at both terminals; resistance should be 1.5–3.0 ohms.

Air Flow Meter

Air is drawn in through the air filter to the air flow meter. The volume of air being drawn in depends on the throttle plate opening as controlled by the accelerator pedal. The volume of air and the temperature of the air is measured by the air flow meter which then converts the measurement to a voltage signal that is sent to the EFI computer.

REMOVAL AND INSTALLATION

1. Unscrew the mounting bolts and remove the air cleaner inlet.
2. Remove the air cleaner element.
3. Unplug the electrical connector from the top of the meter and remove the oxygen sensor wire from the clamp on the side of the meter.
4. Loosen the hose clamp and pull off the intake air connector.

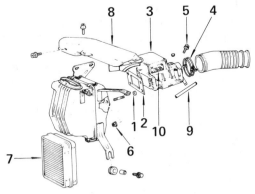

1. Spacers
2. Gasket
3. Air flow meter
4. Hose clamp
5. Bracket bolts
6. Nuts
7. Air cleaner element
8. Air cleaner inlet
9. Oxygen sensor wire
10. Air flow meter wire

Air flow meter and associated components

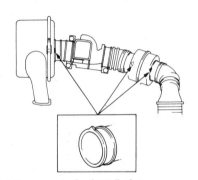

Align air hose marks for installation

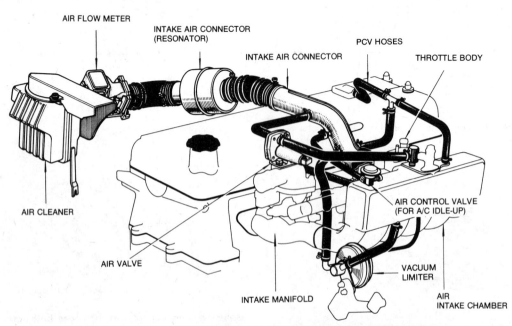

Air intake system, 4M-E/5M-E shown. Other fuel injected models similar

5. Unscrew the meter support bracket bolt.

6. Unscrew the four air flow meter mounting bolts from inside the air cleaner housing and remove the meter.

7. Installation is in the reverse order of removal. On the 5M-GE, align the marks on the air cleaner case and the No. 3 air cleaner hose. Tighten the clamp. Align the marks on the air connector pipe and the No. 2 air cleaner hose. Tighten the hose.

CHECKING

NOTE: *Check the air flow meter with the unit out of the car.*

1. Using an ohmmeter, check the resistance between each terminal of the electrical connector by moving the measuring plate.

NOTE: *Resistance between E_2 and Vs will be changed in accordance with the measuring plate opening.*

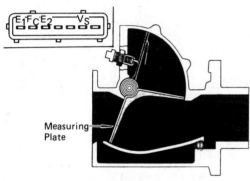

Checking the air flow meter

Air Valve

4M-E, 5M-E, 22R-E Engines

During cold engine operation, the air valve is open, providing a bypass circuit past the throttle plate opening. This causes the volume of air being drawn in to increase, the increased volume is sensed by the air flow meter which in turn signals the EFI computer to increase the fuel flow. This provides a higher idle speed during cold engine operation. As the valve gradually closes, the air volume is reduced, thereby reducing the fuel flow.

CHECKING

1. Start the engine and pinch the hose between the air valve and the intake air chamber. The engine rpm should drop noticeably.

2. Run the engine until it reaches normal operating temperature and pinch the hose again. This time the engine speed should not drop more than 150 rpm.

3. After the engine has cooled off, restart it and remove the above hose from the air valve.

Resistance

Terminal	Resistance (Ω)	Measuring Plate Opening
E_1–FC	∞ (Infinity)	fully closed
	Zero	other than closed position
E_2–Vs	20–100	fully closed
	20–1,000	fully closed to fully open position

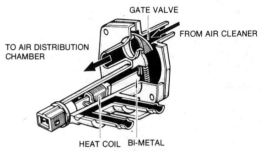

Cut-away view of the air valve

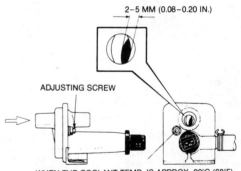

WHEN THE COOLANT TEMP. IS APPROX. 20°C (68°F).

Adjusting the air valve

You should be able to see that the valve is slightly open. If it is not, turn the adjusting screw until it is open slightly.

4. Check the heat coil resistance by removing the electrical connector and measuring across the two terminals with an ohmmeter. The resistance should be 40–60 ohms.

REMOVAL AND INSTALLATION

1. Drain the engine coolant.

2. Squeeze the hose clamps and remove the two air hoses from the valve.

3. Unplug the electrical connector.

4. Unscrew the hose clamps and remove the two water hoses from the valve.

5. Unscrew the mounting bolts and remove the air valve.

6. Installation is in the reverse order of removal.

Throttle Body
CHECKING
All Engines

1. Check that the throttle linkage moves smoothly.
2. Start the engine and remove the hose from the vacuum port.
3. With your finger, check that there is no vacuum at idle and that there IS vacuum at anything other than idle.
4. Unplug the electrical connector from the throttle position sensor.
5. Insert a flat feeler gauge between the throttle stop screw and the stop lever.
6. Using an ohmmeter, check the continuity between each terminal on the sensor.
7. Check the dash pot as detailed in Chapter 2.

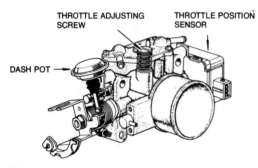

THROTTLE ADJUSTING SCREW — THROTTLE POSITION SENSOR — DASH POT

Throttle body

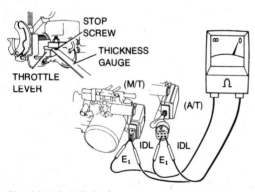

STOP SCREW — THICKNESS GAUGE — THROTTLE LEVER — (M/T) — (A/T) — IDL — IDL — E₁ — E₁

Checking throttle body

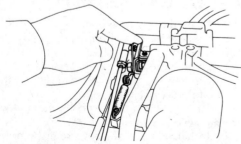

Check throttle linkage for smooth movement

REMOVAL AND INSTALLATION

1. Drain the engine coolant.
2. Tag and disconnect all lines, hoses or wires that lead from the throttle body. Position them out of the way. Remove the air intake connector.
3. Unscrew the mounting bolts and remove the throttle body and gasket.
4. Installation is in the reverse order of removal.

Start Injector Time Switch
CHECKING

1. Locate the switch on the front left side of the engine block on the 4M-E and 5M-E engines, and on the right side of the block on the 22R-E and 5M-GE engines. Unplug the electrical connector.
2. Using an ohmmeter, measure the resistance between terminals STA—STJ on all engines, and between terminals STA—Ground on all engines except 22R-E. Resistance should be:

- STA—STJ, 4M-E/5M-E: 20–40 ohms with coolant temperature below 95°F; 40–60 ohms with coolant temperature above 95°F.
- STA—STJ, 5M-GE: 30–50 ohms with coolant below 72°F; 70–90 ohms with coolant above 72°F.
- STA—STJ, 22R-E: 25–35 ohms with coolant below 72°F; 64–76 ohms with coolant above 72°F.
- STA—Ground, 4M-E/5M-E: 20–80 ohms.
- STA—Ground, 5M-GE, 30–90 ohms

REMOVAL AND INSTALLATION

1. Drain the engine coolant.
2. Unplug the electrical connector.
3. Unscrew and remove the switch.
4. Installation is in the reverse order of removal.

Water Thermo Sensor
CHECKING

1. Unplug the electrical connector.
2. Using an ohmmeter, measure the resistance between the terminals on the switch. See the chart for the proper resistance.

Clearance between Lever and Stop Screw	Continuity of Terminal		
	IDL–TL	PSW–TL	IDL–PSW
0.44 mm (0.017 in.)	Continuity	No continuity	No continuity
0.66 mm (0.026 in.)	No continuity	No continuity	No continuity
	No continuity	Continuity	No continuity

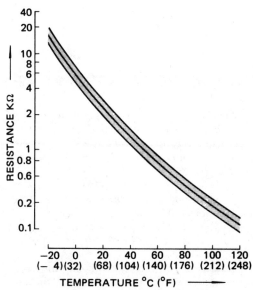

When checking the water thermo sensor, use this chart

REMOVAL AND INSTALLATION

1. Drain the engine coolant.
2. Unplug the electrical connector.
3. Remove the water outlet.
4. Unscrew and remove the thermo sensor.
5. Installation is in the reverse order of removal.

EFI Computer

The EFI computer is located below the instrument panel in the left kick panel on 1979–81 Liftbacks, and underneath the glove box area on other fuel injected Celicas and Supras. Removal and/or inspection of this unit should be left to an authorized service facility.

Chassis Electrical

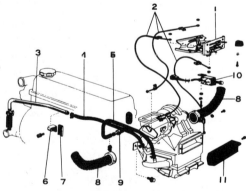

HEATER

NOTE: *On some models with air conditioning, the air conditioner is integral with the heater, and therefore, heater removal procedures may differ from those which are detailed below.*

Heater Housing

REMOVAL AND INSTALLATION

1971–74

1. Drain the engine coolant.
2. Unscrew and remove the gear shift knob.
3. Unscrew the mounting bolts and lift the console box up and over the shift lever.
4. Unscrew the mounting bolts and remove the center console

1. Heater controls
2. Heater cables
3. Water pipe
4. Water hose
5. Water hose
6. Retainer, water hose
7. Bracket, water hose
8. Defroster hoses
9. Joint
10. Blower switch
11. Ventilation louver

Heater housing assembly; 1971–74

NOTE: *If your car is equipped with a clock, unplug the electrical connector before removing the center console.*

5. Disconnect the accelerator pedal from its linkage.
6. Disconnect the two defroster hoses.
7. Disconnect the two water hoses from the left side of the housing.
8. Tag and disconnect all wires and cables that are attached to the heater and position them out of the way.
9. Unscrew the heater housing mounting screws and remove the unit toward the passenger's side of the car.
10. Installation is in the reverse order of removal.

1975 and Later

1. Perform Steps 1–3 of the previous procedure.
2. Unscrew the mounting bolts and remove the center console (1975–77).
NOTE: *Unplug any electrical connections leading from the center console before removing it.*
3. Disconnect the accelerator pedal from its linkage.
4. Remove the heater rear duct (if so equipped).
5. Remove the vacuum hose for the sub-damper valve (if installed).
6. Unscrew the mounting screws and remove the under tray from the right side of the car.
7. Release the two clamps and remove the blower duct from the right side of the heater housing.
8. Remove the two remaining air ducts.
9. Disconnect the two water hoses from the rear of the housing.
10. Tag and disconnect all wires and cables leading from the housing and position them out of the way.
11. Unscrew the three mounting bolts and

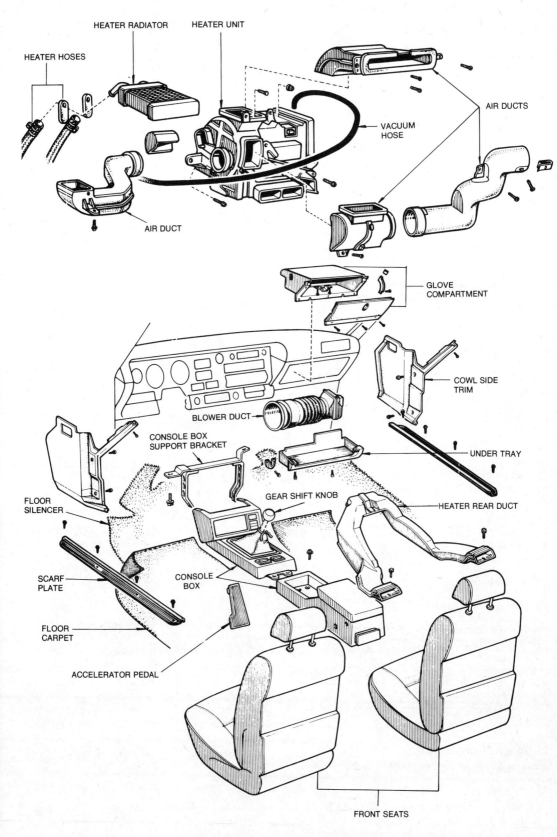

Heater housing assembly; 1975 and later

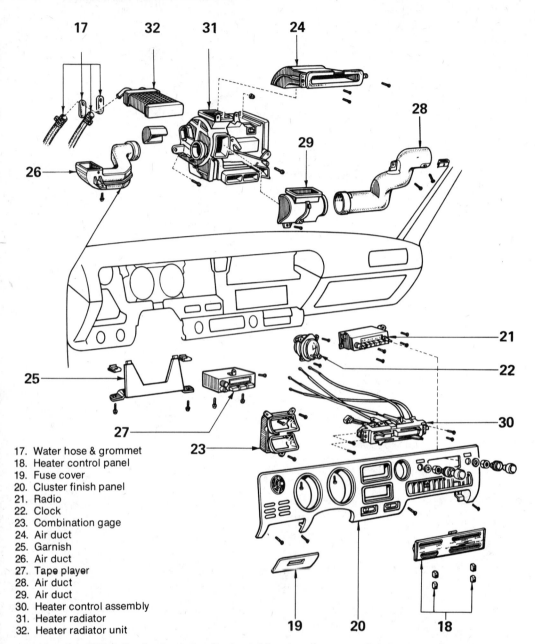

17. Water hose & grommet
18. Heater control panel
19. Fuse cover
20. Cluster finish panel
21. Radio
22. Clock
23. Combination gage
24. Air duct
25. Garnish
26. Air duct
27. Tape player
28. Air duct
29. Air duct
30. Heater control assembly
31. Heater radiator
32. Heater radiator unit

1981 Celica heater and radio assemblies; locations vary slightly among years

remove the heater housing toward the passenger's side of the car.

12. Installation is in the reverse order of removal.

Blower Motor

REMOVAL AND INSTALLATION

1971–74

1. Remove the heater housing assembly as previously detailed.

2. Locate the blower motor on the right side of the heater housing. Unscrew the three mounting screws and remove the motor and fan together.

3. Unscrew the nut on the blower motor shaft and slide the fan off. Make sure you don't lose any of the washers or spacers.

4. Installation is in the reverse order of removal.

1975 and Later

1. Underneath the right side of the instrument panel is the under tray. Unscrew the mounting bolts and remove it.

2. Release the two clamps holding the

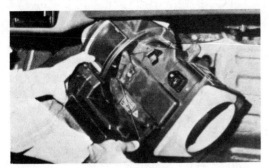

Remove the heater housing toward the passenger side

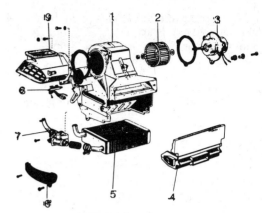

blower duct to the blower motor and disconnect the blower duct.

3. Disconnect the control cable from the blower motor and position it out of the way.

4. Disconnect the vacuum hose from the subdamper valve (if installed).

5. Unplug the electrical connection from the blower motor.

6. Unscrew the mounting bolts and remove the blower motor assembly.

1. Heater housing
2. Fan
3. Blower motor
4. Heater cover
5. Heater core
6. Water valve cover
7. Water valve
8. Blower register
9. Air damper assembly

Components of the 1971–74 heater housing

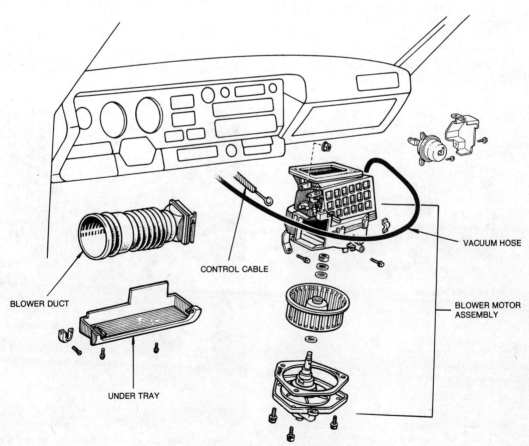

VACUUM HOSE

CONTROL CABLE

BLOWER DUCT

BLOWER MOTOR ASSEMBLY

UNDER TRAY

Typical blower motor system, 1975–81

7. Unscrew the three bolts at the bottom of the blower motor assembly and remove the blower motor and the fan as one unit.

8. Unscrew the nut on the blower motor shaft and slide off the fan. Do not lose any of the washers or spacers.

9. Installation is in the reverse order of removal.

Heater Core
REMOVAL AND INSTALLATION
1971–74

1. Perform Steps 1–7 of the "1971–74 Heater Housing Removal and Installation" procedure.

2. Unscrew the mounting bolts for the bottom cover/intake assembly and remove the assembly.

3. Unscrew the two mounting bolts and remove the cover for the water valve.

4. Remove the water valve.

5. Withdraw the heater core.

6. Installation is in the reverse order of removal.

1975 and Later

1. Remove the heater housing assembly as previously detailed.

2. Grasp the heater core by the end plate and carefully pull it out of the heater housing.

3. Installation is in the reverse order of removal.

Removing the heater core; 1975 and later

RADIO

CAUTION: *Never operate the radio without a speaker; severe damage to the output transistors will result. If the speaker must be replaced, use a speaker of the correct impedance (ohms) or else the output transistors will be damaged and require replacement.*

REMOVAL AND INSTALLATION

1. Remove the knobs from the radio.

2. Remove the nuts from the radio control shafts.

3. Detach the antenna lead from the jack on the radio case.

4. Remove the cowl air intake duct.

5. Detach the power and speaker leads.

6. Remove the radio support nuts and bolts.

7. Withdraw the radio from beneath the dashboard.

8. Installation is in the reverse order of removal.

WINDSHIELD WIPER

Blade and Arm
REPLACEMENT
Celica

NOTE: *Wiper blade element replacement is covered in Chapter 1.*

1. To remove the wiper blades, lift up on the spring release tab on the wiper blade-to-wiper arm connector.

2. Pull the blade assembly off the wiper arm.

3. There are two types of replacements for Toyotas:

a. Pre-1973—replace the entire wiper blade as an assembly. Simply snap the replacement into place on the arm.

On some models you must lift the cover to expose the acorn nut

b. Post-1973—press the old wiper blade insert down, away from the blade assembly, to free it from the retaining clips on the blade ends. Slide the insert out of the blade. Slide the new insert into the blade assembly and bend the insert upward slightly to engage the retaining clips.

4. To replace a wiper arm, unscrew the acorn nut which secures it to the pivot and carefully pull the arm upward and off the pivot. Install the arm by reversing this procedure.

NOTE: *Later models are equipped with a cover over the acorn nut. To expose the nut, lift the wiper arm and the cover at the same time; this will afford access to the nut.*

Supra

NOTE: *The Supra and later Celicas utilize the rise-up type front windshield wiper. Unless it is installed properly, the wiper will not operate correctly.*

NOTE: *Wiper blade element replacement is covered in Chapter 1.*

1. Using a phillips screwdriver, install the sub-arm on the wiper pivot.

2. Using a piece of wood, fabricate a block (0.8–1.0 in. wide) to aid in the positioning of the wiper arm.

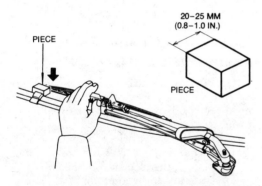

Positioning the wiper arm on the Supra

3. Place the block of wood at the bottom lip of the windshield and move the wiper arm so that the blade tip is resting against the block.

4. Place the main arm in position and lightly press down on the head.

5. Turn the ignition to the 'ON' position. Operate the wiper motor at low speed and then turn it off. This will set the "hide-down" position.

6. Make sure that the blade tip is still resting against the wooden block and then secure the main arm.

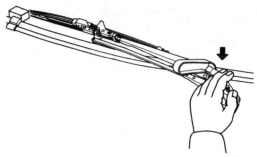

After positioning the wiper arm, press down lightly on the head

Motor and Linkage (Front)
REMOVAL AND INSTALLATION

1. Remove the wiper arms and blades.

2. Remove the access hole covers and the ventilator louver (1975 and later only).

3. Insert a screwdriver between the linkage and the wiper motor crank arm and pry the link from the arm.

4. Unplug the electrical connector from the wiper motor.

5. Unscrew the mounting bolts and remove the wiper motor.

6. Insert a screwdriver between the link and the pivot arm and pry the link from the arm.

7. Remove the screws holding the pivot arms and then remove the wiper linkage.

To install:

8. Install the wiper linkage and connect the link to the pivot arm.

9. Plug the electrical connector into the wiper motor.

10. Turn the ignition switch to the 'ON' position. Turn the wiper motor on 'HI' for a minute and then turn everything off. Make sure that the wiper motor crank arm is in the position shown in the illustrations.

11. Install the wiper motor.

12. Press the link on to the wiper motor crank arm.

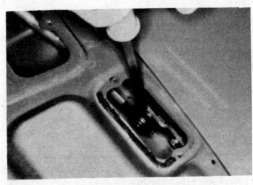

Use a screwdriver to remove the wiper links

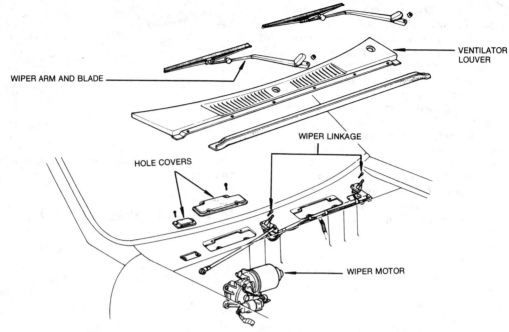

Wiper motor and linkage assembly; 1980 Celica (others similar)

13. Installation of the remaining components is in the reverse order of removal.

Motor and Linkage (Rear)
REMOVAL AND INSTALLATION

1. Remove the wiper arm and blade.
2. Unscrew the mounting screws on the inside of the rear door and remove the trim panel.
3. Insert a screwdriver between the link and the wiper motor crank arm and pry it off.
4. Unplug the electrical connector.
5. Unscrew the mounting bolts and remove the wiper motor.
6. Remove the link and support.

To install:

7. Install the support and the link.
8. Plug the electrical connector into the wiper motor.
9. Turn the ignition switch to the 'ON' position. Pull the rear wiper switch out, then push it in. Make sure that the wiper motor crank arm is in the position shown in the illustration.
10. Install the wiper motor.
11. Grease the end of the wiper link and then connect it to the crank arm.
12. Installation of the remaining components is in the reverse order of removal.

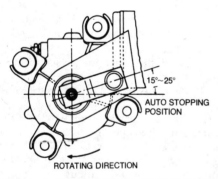

Install the wiper motor with the crank in this position; 1971–77

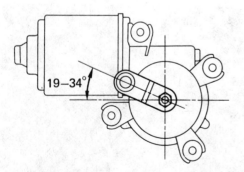

Install the wiper motor with the crank in this position; 1978–81

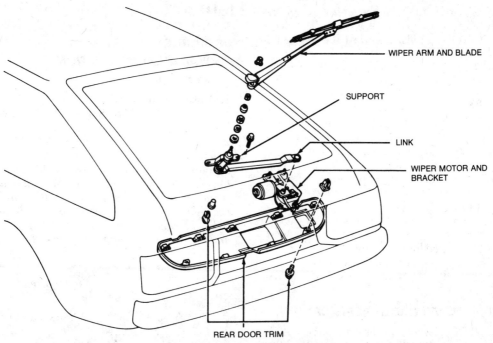

WIPER ARM AND BLADE

SUPPORT

LINK

WIPER MOTOR AND BRACKET

REAR DOOR TRIM

Rear windshield wiper assembly

INSTRUMENT CLUSTER

REMOVAL AND INSTALLATION

1971–77

1. Disconnect the battery.
2. Detach the heater control cables at the heater box.
3. Loosen the steering column clamping nuts and lower the column.
4. Loosen the instrument panel screws and tilt the panel forward.
5. Detach the speedometer cable and wir-

Removing the instrument cluster from the Celica

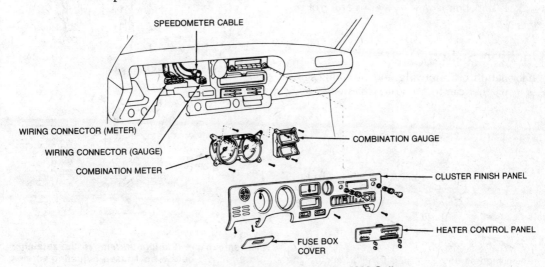

SPEEDOMETER CABLE

WIRING CONNECTOR (METER)

WIRING CONNECTOR (GAUGE)

COMBINATION METER

COMBINATION GAUGE

CLUSTER FINISH PANEL

HEATER CONTROL PANEL

FUSE BOX COVER

Removing the instrument cluster on the 1980 Celica

ing connectors. Remove the entire panel assembly.

6. Remove the instruments from the panel as required.

Installation is performed in the reverse order of removal.

1978–83

1. Disconnect the negative battery cable.

2. Remove the fuse box cover from under the left side of the instrument panel.

3. Remove the heater control knobs.

4. Using a screwdriver, pry off the heater control panel.

5. Unscrew the cluster finish panel retaining screws and pull out the bottom of the panel.

6. Unplug the two electrical connectors and unhook the speedometer cable.

7. Remove the instrument cluster.

8. Installation is in the reverse order of removal.

SPEEDOMETER CABLE REPLACEMENT

NOTE: *Depending on the particular model, there are two types of methods for attaching the cable to the speedometer. One is the conventional screw-in type, while the other employs a locking lever to secure the cable.*

1. Remove the instrument cluster and disconnect the cable from the speedometer.

NOTE: *On some models, cable disconnection can be accomplished by simply reaching under the dash. If possible, this method is much easier than removing the entire instrument cluster.*

2. Feed the cable through its hole in the firewall and then trace it down to where it connects to the transmission.

3. Unscrew the cable from the transmission end.

4. Installation is in the reverse order of removal.

Ignition Switch

Information on removing and installing ignition switches can be found in Chapter 8.

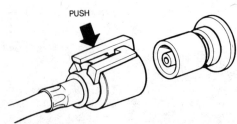

Some models use a locking lever to secure the speedometer cable

LIGHTING

Headlights
REMOVAL AND INSTALLATION
1971–81 Models

1. Unscrew the headlight bezel (1971–77) or headlight grille (1978–81) retaining screws. Remove the bezel or grille.

2. Loosen, but do not remove, the three headlight retaining ring screws and rotate the ring counterclockwise to remove it (1971–79).

CAUTION: *Do not mistake the adjusting screws for the retaining ring screws. There are only two adjusting screws for each headlight. They are located right next to the top and the side retaining ring screws. Turning*

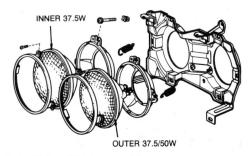

1971–79 headlight assembly

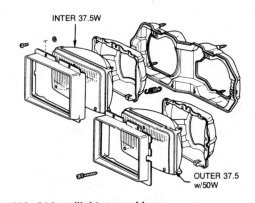

1980–81 headlight assembly

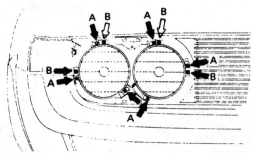

To remove the headlights, remove the retaining screws "A"; but do not loosen adjusting screws "B"

these screws will result in improper headlight adjustment.

3. On models with square headlights (1980–81), remove the four headlight retaining ring screws and then remove the ring.

4. Pull the headlight away from its positioning ring slightly and unplug the electrical connection at its rear.

5. Remove the headlight.

6. Installation is in the reverse order of removal.

CAUTION: *Do not interchange the inner and outer headlights.*

1982 and Later Celica and Supra

NOTE: *See "Caution" above under 1971–81 removal.*

1. Raise the headlight by twisting the headlight switch in the first click stop.

2. Disconnect the fusible link at the battery.

CAUTION: *Unless power is disconnected, the headlights could suddenly retract and cause personal injury.*

3. Remove the ornament and the beam unit retaining screws, ring and partially remove the sealed beam unit.

4. Compress the lock releases and disconnect the wire connector behind the beam unit. Remove the beam unit completely.

NOTE: *If the wire connector is tight, wiggle*

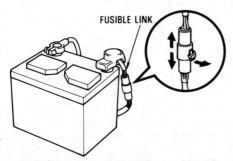

On 1982 and later models, disconnect fusible link before working on headlights

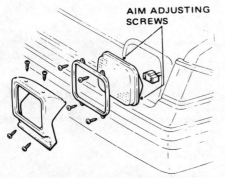

Pop-up headlight assembly 1982 and later Celica. Supra similar

it while holding in the lock releases and pulling out.

5. Installation is in the reverse order of removal. Install the beam unit with the single protrusion on the glass face-up. Use only a beam unit with the same number and wattage—regular sealed beam units are 65/55 watt, and halogen units are either 65/55 or 65/35 watt. Reconnect the fusible link, and check headlight aim.

Retractable Headlights—Manual Operation

1982 and Later Models

The retractable headlights on 1982 and later Celicas and Supras can be manually operated if their electrical mechanism fails. To raise or lower the lights, remove the rubber cover from the manual operation knob (under the hood next to the headlight unit) and turn the knob clockwise. Manual operation should only be used if the system has failed; be sure to check the electrical operation of the lights as soon as possible.

Fog Lights (Includes Parking Light)

REMOVAL AND INSTALLATION

1982 and Later Supra

1. Remove the grille by removing the central screw and releasing the tabs as shown.

2. Remove the turn signal light next to whichever fog light you intend to remove by removing the screw and pulling the turn signal light housing toward you. The other side of the turn signal light is self-attaching and is simply pulled out. At this point the turn signal bulb can be replaced if necessary.

3. Remove the retaining ring and partially remove the light housing. Disconnect the wire connector for the fog light and the bulb socket for the parking light. Remove the light housing completely.

4. Installation is in the reverse order of re-

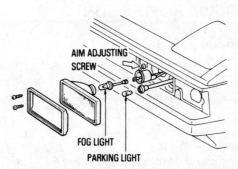

Fog/parking light assembly, 1982 and later Supra

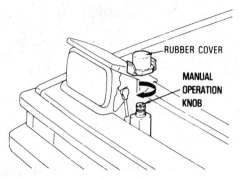

1982 and later emergency headlight operation

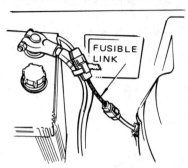

Fusible links can be found by the positive battery terminal

moval. Replace bulbs with the same number and wattage (55W, fog light; 3.8W, parking light). Make sure the wiring waterproof rubber cover fits snugly on the fog light housing.

HEADLIGHT ADJUSTMENT

1. Remove the headlight bezel or grille.
2. On 1971–79 models there are two adjusting screws for each headlight. The vertical adjustment screw is located at the top of the headlight, next to the retaining ring screw. The horizontal adjustment screw is located on the side of the headlight, also next to the retaining ring screw.
3. On 1980–81 models, the two adjusting screws are found on the top and on the side of the headlight. They can each be found in a recess in the retaining ring. As with the earlier models, the top screw is for the vertical adjustments and the side screw is for the horizontal adjustment.
4. On 1982 and later models, the two adjusting screws are found on the bottom and on the side of the headlight. The bottom screw is for vertical adjustments and the side screw is for horizontal adjustment.

NOTE: *Headlight adjusting heights and angles may differ from state to state so check with a local service facility for proper specifications.*

CIRCUIT PROTECTION

Fusible Links

Fusible links are protective devices used in the electrical circuits. When current increases beyond the amperage the link is designed to withstand, the fusible metal of the link melts, breaking the circuit and preventing further damage to other components and wiring. Whenever a fusible link has melted because of a short circuit, correct the cause before installing a new link.

CAUTION: *Always use replacements of the same electrical capacity as the original, available from your dealer. Replacements of a different electrical value will not provide adequate system protection.*

All 1971–77 models have only one fusible link which is located in-line at the positive battery terminal. Main circuit protection is for the ignition system.

All 1978 and later models have three fusible links, all of which are located in-line at the battery. Circuits protected include the ignition circuit, the headlight circuit and the heater circuit.

Circuit Breakers

On 1980–81 models, a circuit breaker is used in place of a fuse for the rear window defogger. It is located under the left side of the instrument panel, behind the kick panel. Circuit breakers are also used for air conditioning, power windows, magnetic door locks and power sun roof on 1982 and later models. If the circuit breaker cuts off:

1. Remove the left kick panel.
2. Unplug the wiring connector from the circuit breaker and then remove the circuit breaker assembly.

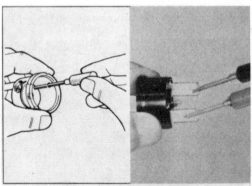

Resetting the circuit breaker (L) and checking it for continuity (R)

3. Unlock the stopper and pull out the circuit breaker.

4. To reset the circuit breaker, insert a needle into the reset hole and push it.

5. Using an ohmmeter, check for continuity between the two circuit breaker terminals. If there isn't any, the circuit breaker will require replacement.

6. Installation is in the reverse order of removal.

NOTE: *If the circuit breaker continues to cut off, a short circuit is indicated; have the system checked out by an authorized service facility.*

Fuses and Flashers

The fuse block on all 1971–77 Celicas is located under the left side of the instrument panel, near the hood release lever.

The fuse block is by the hood on 1971–77 models

The fuse block on 1978–79 models is located behind a panel on the far left side of the instrument panel. The cover panel is next to the steering column and below the warning light display.

The fuse block on 1978 –81 cars is located behind a cover in the front of the dash

All 1980 and later models have two fuse blocks, one is behind a panel in the dash (same

1980–81 models have a second fuse block located on the left front fender apron

as 1978–79), while the other can be found on the left front fender apron.

All 1982 and later models also have two fuse blocks, one being inside the driver's kick panel and the other being under the hood between the battery and ignition coil. There is also a small, two-fuse box on the passenger side kick panel of these models.

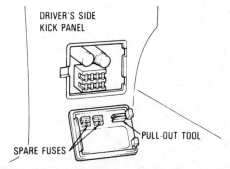

1982 and later fusebox; others are on passenger kickpanel and under hood

If a blown fuse is suspected, turn off the ignition switch. Open the fuse box lid, and pull the suspected fuse straight out with the pull-out tool. Look carefully at the fuse; if the thin wire is broken, the fuse is blown. If you are not sure, try replacing it with a fuse you know to be good.

CAUTION: *Always install a fuse with the same amperage rating as the one removed; NEVER use a higher-amperage fuse.*

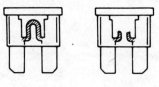

Always replace a bad fuse with one of equal amperage

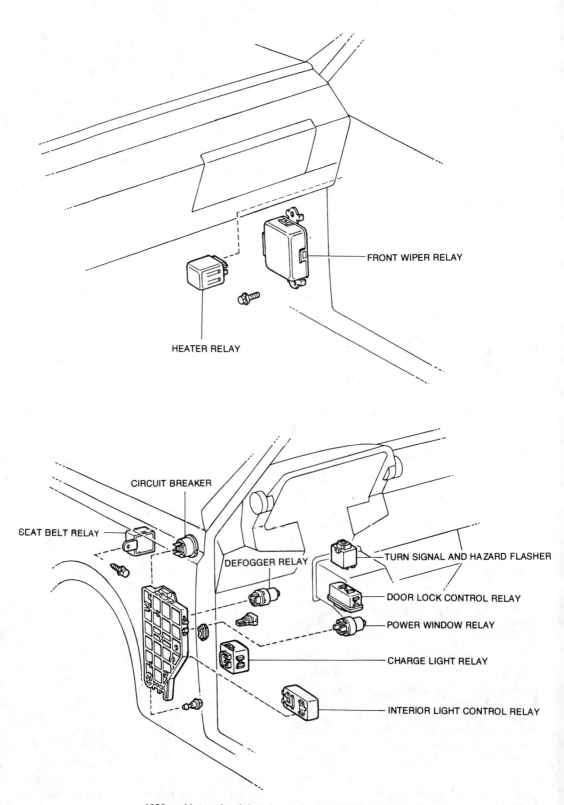

FRONT WIPER RELAY

HEATER RELAY

CIRCUIT BREAKER

SEAT BELT RELAY

DEFOGGER RELAY

TURN SIGNAL AND HAZARD FLASHER

DOOR LOCK CONTROL RELAY

POWER WINDOW RELAY

CHARGE LIGHT RELAY

INTERIOR LIGHT CONTROL RELAY

1982 and later circuit breaker, relay and flasher location

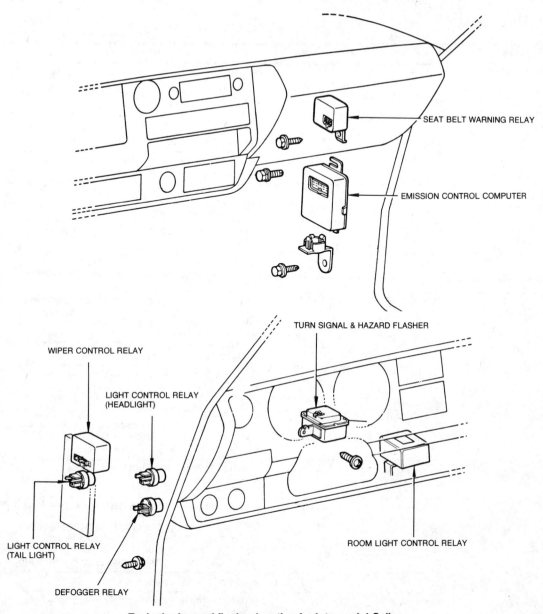

Typical relay and flasher location for late model Celicas

If the new fuse blows out, there is a problem with the electrical system. Always carry a set of spare fuses.

All Celicas have the turn signals and hazard warning flashers combined as one unit. The flasher unit on 1971–77 models is located underneath the left side of the instrument panel, next to the fuse block.

NOTE: *It may be necessary to remove the fuse block support bracket in order to gain access to the flasher.*

The flasher unit on all 1978 and later models is located underneath and behind the center of the driver's side of the instrument panel.

Fuse Specifications

Year	Fuse Holder	Amperage	Circuits Controlled
1971–73	Main R	10	Headlight high beam—right; High beam indicator light
	Main L	10	Headlight high beam—left
	Dim R	10	Headlight low beam—right
	Dim L	10	Headlight low beam—left
	Tail	10	Parking light; Tail light; License plate light; Meter pilot light; Heater control light
	Horn	20	Horn; Brake Warning light; Hazard warning light
	Lighter	20	Cigarette lighter; Clock; Interior light
	Heater	20	Gauges; Back-Up light; Parking brake warning light; Heater
	Wiper	15	Windshield wiper motor; Windshield washer motor
	Turn	15	Turn signal light
1974–77	Tail Meter PL	15	Instrument panel lights; Switch knob illumination lights; Glove box light; Parking lights; Side marker lights; Tail lights; License plate lights
	Horn Stop	20	Key warning buzzer; Stop lights; Horns; Hazard warning lights
	Lighter Room	20	Cigarette lighter; Clock; Air conditioner; Interior light; Courtesy lights
	Radio	15	Radio; Stereo tape player
	Heater Gauge	20	Back-Up lights; Brake warning lights; Heater (Air conditioner) blower; Rear window defogger; Gauges
	Turn Gen	15	Alternator; Regulator; Turn signal lights
	IG Coil	15	Ignition coil positive terminal
	Wiper	15	Windshield wiper motor; Windshield washer motor
1978–79	Tail	15	Tail light; License plate light; Clearance light; Side marker lights; Glove box light; Cigarette lighter light; Transmission indicator light; Combination meter; Clock and Heater control illumination lights
	Stop	15	Stop light; Hazard warning light
	Lighter	15	Cigarette lighter; Dome light; Door courtesy lights; Clock
	Defogger	20	Rear window defogger
	Gauge	15	Back-Up light; Fuel gauge; Fuel warning light; Water temp. gauge; Charge warning light; Oil pressure gauge; Low oil pressure warning light; Brake warning light; Rear window defogger switch; Heater relay
	Turn	15	Windshield wiper motor; Windshield washer motor; Turn signal lights; Headlight cleaner; Rear wiper
	Engine	15	Voltage regulator; Fuel pump relay; Emission control computer
	Radio	5	Radio; Stereo tape player
1980–81			In Passenger Compartment
	Dome	5	Dome light; Door courtesy lights; Clock
	Tail	15	Tail lights; License plate lights; Clearance lights; Side marker lights; Glove box light; Cigarette

Fuse Specifications (cont.)

Year	Fuse Holder	Amperage	Circuits Controlled
1980–81			lighter light; Transmission indicator light; Combination meter, Clock and Heater control panel illumination lights
	Gauges	15	Back-Up lights; Fuel gauge; Fuel warning light; Water temp. gauge; Charge warning light; Oil pressure gauge; Low oil pressure warning light; Brake warning light; Rear window defogger switch; Heater relay; Seat belt relay; Tachometer
	Turn	15	Windshield wiper motor; Windshield washer motor; Turn signal lights; Rear wiper
	Engine	15	IC regulator; Emission control computer; Discharge warning light relay
	Radio	7.5	Radio; Stereo tape player
	Cig L	15	Cigarette lighter
	In Engine Compartment		
	Heater	20	Heater; Air conditioner
	Stop	15	Horn; Stop light; Hazard light
	Head RH	15	Headlight (RH)
	Head LH	15	Headlight (LH)

WIRING DIAGRAMS

Wiring diagrams have been left out of this book. As cars have become more complex, and available with longer and longer option lists, wiring diagrams have grown in size and complexity also. It has become virtually impossible to provide a readable reproduction in a reasonable number of pages. Information on ordering wiring diagrams from the vehicle manufacturer can be found in the owner's manual.

Clutch and Transmission

6

MANUAL TRANSMISSION

ADJUSTMENTS

All Toyota Celicas sold in the U.S. utilize a floor-mounted shifter and an internally-mounted shift linkage. On some older models, the linkage is contained in a side cover which is bolted on to the transmission case, but the majority of all Celicas have the linkage mounted inside the top of the transmission case itself.

No external adjustments are either necessary or possible.

REMOVAL AND INSTALLATION

1971–81

1. Place the gear shift in Neutral. Loosen the retaining screws and remove the center console.
2. Remove the trim boot at the base of the shift lever and then the boot underneath it on the shift tower.
3. Unscrew the four shift lever plate retaining screws. Remove the shift lever assembly and the gasket.

NOTE: *Cover the hole with a clean cloth to prevent anything from falling into the transmission case.*

4. Disconnect the negative battery cable.
5. Remove the air cleaner with all its hoses.
6. Unfasten the accelerator torque rod at the carburetor.
7. Unbolt the clutch hydraulic line support bracket from the firewall.
8. Tag and disconnect all wires leading from the starter and then remove the starter.
9. Remove the upper transmission-to-engine mounting bolts.
10. Raise the car and support it with jackstands.
11. Drain the transmission oil.
12. Detach the exhaust pipe from the manifold and then remove the exhaust pipe support bracket.
13. Disconnect the driveshaft from the end of the transmission (see Chapter 7).

NOTE: *It will be necessary to plug the end of the transmission to avoid spilling oil. Use an old yoke, or, if one is not available, cover it with a plastic bag secured by a rubber band.*

14. Remove both stiffener plates from the transmission housing.
15. Disconnect the back-up light switch from the bottom, left side of the transmission.
16. Disconnect the speedometer cable from the right side of the transmission.
17. Disconnect the clutch return spring, loosen the two mounting bolts and remove the clutch release (slave) cylinder. Position it out of the way.
18. Jack up the transmission slightly to remove the weight from the rear support.
19. Remove the ground strap and the rubber exhaust hanger from the rear support member.
20. Loosen the eight mounting bolts and then remove the rear support.
21. Remove the remaining transmission-to-engine bolts and remove the transmission down and toward the rear.
22. Installation is in the reverse order of removal. When installing, please note the following:

—apply a light coating of multi-purpose grease to the input shaft end, the input shaft splines, the clutch release bearing and the driveshaft end.

—use a clutch guide tool to align the clutch disc with the transmission input shaft spline.

—be sure that the clutch release cylinder push rod is properly aligned with the clutch fork.

—be sure that the felt dust protector and the washer are on the end of the speedometer cable before tightening it.

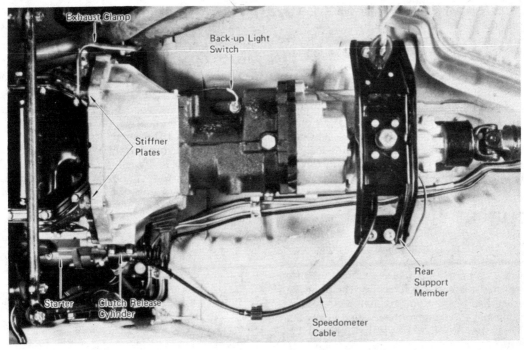

Transmission detachment points, all similar

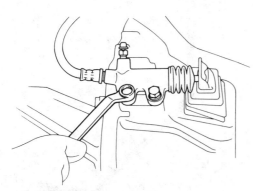

Removing the clutch slave cylinder

—be sure to refill the transmission housing with the specified amount of gear lubricant.

1982 and Later

1. Follow steps 1 through 4 of the preceding procedure.

2. Drain the coolant from the upper tank, and remove the upper coolant hose.

3. Jack up the car and safely support it with jackstands. Drain the transmission oil.

4. Unbolt the steering gear (rack) housing, and disconnect the housing from the steering linkage and steering column assembly. *Leave the steering fluid lines* connected, and suspend the housing from the front of the car as shown.

5. Have a rag handy before disconnecting the driveshaft from the transmission. Remove

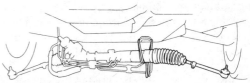

Suspend the steering rack housing; do not disconnect the fluid lines

the driveshaft (see Chapter 7) and immediately plug the transmission extension housing with the rag.

6. Remove the exhaust pipe clamp bolt.

7. Disconnect the speedometer cable and the back-up light switch connector from the transmission housing.

8. Remove the clutch slave cylinder.

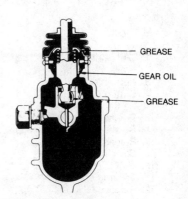

Floorshift lever lubrication points

9. Tag and disconnect all wires leading from the starter and remove the starter.

10. Jack up the transmission enough to take weight off of the transmission rear support.

11. Remove the transmission support, and unbolt the bell housing from the engine.

12. Using a hydraulic floor jack as an aid, ease the transmission down while pulling it towards the rear of the car.

13. Installation is in the reverse order of removal. Follow the installation notes included in the preceding procedure. Torque the bell housing-to-engine bolts to 37–57 ft. lbs.

CLUTCH

The clutch is a single-plate, dry disc type. Some early models use a coil-spring pressure plate. Later models use a diaphragm-spring pressure plate. Clutch release bearings are sealed ball bearing units which need no lubrication and should never be washed in any kind of solvent. All clutches are hydraulically operated.

PEDAL HEIGHT ADJUSTMENT

Pedal height is the distance between the floor of the car and the top of the clutch pedal pad. It should be between 6.3 and 6.6 in. To adjust it, loosen the lock nut on the stopper at the top of the clutch pedal and then turn the adjusting nut until the pedal height is within

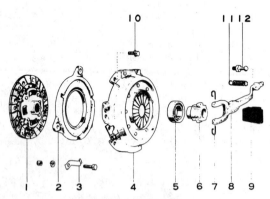

1. Clutch disc
2. Pressure plate
3. Retracting spring
4. Clutch cover
5. Radial ball bearing
6. Release bearing hub
7. Release bearing hub clip
8. Release fork
9. Clutch housing cover
10. Bolt
11. Tension spring
12. Release fork ball

Clutch assembly

specifications. After adjusting the height, always tighten the lock nut again.

CLUTCH PEDAL FREEPLAY ADJUSTMENT

Clutch pedal free play is the distance that the pedal travels from the rest position until the beginning of clutch resistance can just be felt. It should be 1.00–1.75 in. on 1971–77 models, 0.2–0.6 in. on 1978–79 models, 0.51–0.91 in. on 1980–81 models and 0.20–0.59 in. on 1982 and later models. To adjust, loosen the lock nut on the master cylinder push rod and turn the adjusting nut until the proper free play is achieved. Don't forget to retighten the lock nut.

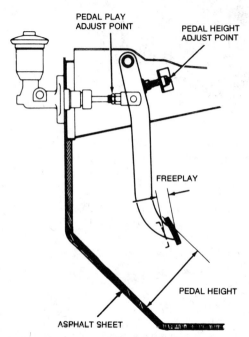

Clutch pedal adjustment points

BLEEDING

CAUTION: *Do not spill brake fluid on the painted surfaces of the vehicle.*

1. Fill the master cylinder reservoir with brake fluid.

2. Remove the cap and loosen the bleeder plug. Block the outlet hole with your finger.

3. Pump the clutch pedal several times, then take your finger from the hole while depressing the clutch pedal. Allow the air to flow out. Place your finger back over the hole and release the pedal.

4. After fluid pressure can be felt (with your finger), tighten the bleeder plug.

5. Fit a bleeder tube over the plug and place the other end into a clean jar half-filled with brake fluid.

Bleeding the clutch hydraulic system

6. Depress the clutch pedal, loosen the bleeder plug with a wrench, and allow the fluid to flow into the jar.

7. Tighten the plug and then release the clutch pedal.

8. Repeat Steps 6–7 until no air bubbles are visible in the bleeder tube.

9. When there are no more air bubbles, tighten the plug while keeping the clutch pedal fully depressed. Replace the cap.

10. Fill the master cylinder to the specified level. (See Chapter 1.)

11. Check the system for leaks.

REMOVAL AND INSTALLATION

CAUTION: *Do not drain the transmission oil and do not allow grease or oil to get on any part of the clutch disc, pressure plate or flywheel surfaces.*

1. Remove the transmission from the car as previously detailed.

2. Loosen the set bolts one turn at a time until the spring tension is relieved.

3. Remove the set bolts and then pull off the clutch assembly.

4. Unfasten the release fork bearing clips. Withdraw the release bearing hub, complete with the release bearing.

5. Remove the tension spring from the clutch linkage.

6. Remove the release fork and support.

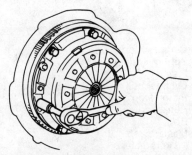

Loosen the set bolts on the clutch cover one turn at a time until the spring tension is relieved

Remove the clip to remove the release bearing and its hub

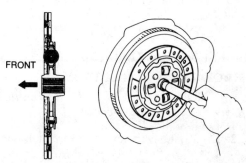

Use a clutch pilot tool to center the clutch disc on the flywheel

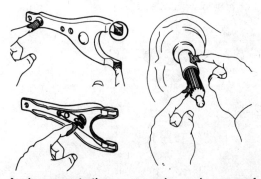

Apply grease to these areas; also pack groove of clutch hub with grease

7. Punch matchmarks on the clutch cover and the pressure plate so that the pressure plate can be returned to its original position during installation.

8. Slowly unfasten the screws which attach the retracting springs.

NOTE: *If the screws are released too fast, the clutch assembly will fly apart, causing possible injury or loss of parts.*

9. Separate the pressure plate from the clutch cover/spring assembly.

Inspect the parts for wear or deterioration. Replace parts as required.

Installation is performed in the reverse order of removal. Several points should be noted, however.

1. Be sure to align the matchmarks on the clutch cover and pressure plate which were made during disassembly.

2. Apply a thin coating of multipurpose grease to the release bearing hub and release fork contact points. Also, pack the groove inside the clutch hub with multipurpose grease.

3. Center the clutch disc by using a clutch pilot tool or an old input shaft. Insert the pilot into the end of the input shaft front bearing and bolt the clutch to the flywheel.

NOTE: *Bolt the clutch assembly to the flywheel in two or three stages, evenly and to the torque specified in the chart below.*

4. Adjust the clutch as outlined below.

Clutch Master Cylinder
REMOVAL AND INSTALLATION

CAUTION: *Do not spill brake fluid on the painted surfaces of the vehicle.*

1. Remove the clevis pin.
2. Detach the hydraulic line from the tube.
3. Unfasten the bolts which secure the master cylinder to the firewall. Withdraw the assembly.

Installation is performed in the reverse order of removal. Bleed the system as detailed

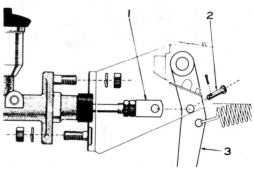

To unhook the master cylinder pushrod (1) from the clutch pedal (3), remove the clevis pin

following. Adjust the clutch pedal height and free-play as previously detailed.

OVERHAUL

NOTE: *Overhaul and assemble the master cylinder only in a clean working area.*

1. Clamp the master cylinder body in a vise with soft jaws.
2. Separate the reservoir assembly from the master cylinder.
3. Remove the snap-ring and remove the pushrod/piston assembly.
4. Inspect all of the parts and replace any which are worn or defective.

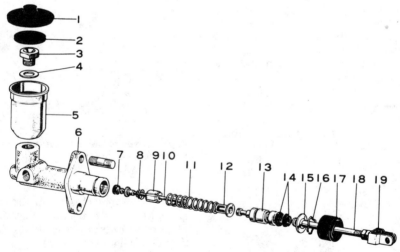

1. Reservoir filler cap	11. Compression spring
2. Reservoir float	12. Spring retainer
3. Bolt	13. Piston
4. Washer	14. Cylinder cup
5. Master cylinder reservoir	15. Piston stop plate
6. Master cylinder body	16. Hole snap ring
7. Inlet valve	17. Boot
8. Conical spring	18. Master push rod
9. Inlet valve case	19. Push rod clevis
10. Inlet valve connecting rod	

An exploded view of the clutch master cylinder

Removing the snap-ring on the clutch master cylinder

Assembly is performed in the following order:

1. Coat all parts with clean brake fluid, prior to assembly.
2. Install the piston assembly in the cylinder bore.
3. Fit the pushrod over the washer and secure them with the snap-ring.
4. Install the reservoir.

Clutch Slave Cylinder

REMOVAL AND INSTALLATION

CAUTION: *Do not spill brake fluid on the painted surface of the vehicle.*

1. Raise the front of the car and support it with jackstands. Be sure that it is supported *securely.*
2. If necessary, remove the rear gravel shield to gain access to the release cylinder.
3. Remove the clutch fork return spring.
4. Unfasten the hydraulic line from the release cylinder by removing its retaining nut.
5. Screw the threaded end of the pushrod in.
6. Remove the release cylinder retaining nuts and remove the cylinder.

Installation is performed in the reverse order of removal. Adjust the pushrod free-play and bleed the hydraulic system.

OVERHAUL

NOTE: *Overhaul the slave cylinder only in a clean working area.*

1. Remove the pushrod assembly and the rubber boot.
2. Withdraw the piston, complete with its cup; don't remove the cup unless it is being replaced.
3. Wash all the parts in brake fluid.
4. Replace any worn or damaged parts.
5. Replace the cylinder assembly if the piston-to-bore clearance is greater than 0.006 in.
6. Assembly is the reverse of disassembly. Coat all parts in clean brake fluid or rubber grease, prior to assembly.

AUTOMATIC TRANSMISSION

NOTE: *All automatic transmission repair should be referred to a competent automatic transmission mechanic and/or repair shop.*

PAN AND FILTER REMOVAL AND INSTALLATION

1. Clean the exterior of the transmission around the pan.
2. Remove the drain plug and drain the fluid into a suitable container.
3. Unscrew all the pan retaining bolts and carefully remove the pan assembly. Discard the gasket.

CAUTION: *There will still be some fluid in the oil pan. Be careful not to damage the filler tube or the O-ring.*

4. Remove the small magnet from the bottom of the oil pan and clean it thoroughly.
5. Clean the pan with a suitable solvent and allow it to air dry.
6. Remove the five retaining bolts and then remove the oil strainer. Be careful not to puncture the strainer upon removal.
7. Carefully clean the oil strainer with compressed air or a suitable solvent.

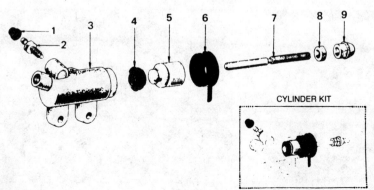

CYLINDER KIT

1. Cap
2. Bleeder plug
3. Release cylinder body
4. Cylinder cup
5. Piston
6. Boot
7. Pushrod
8. Nut
9. Nut

An exploded view of the clutch slave cylinder

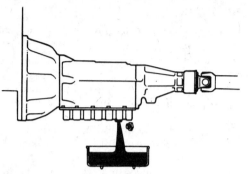

Remove the drain plug and drain the transmission fluid

Install the new pan gasket without sealer

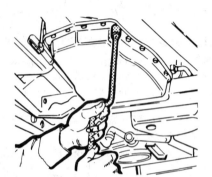

Removing the pan retaining bolts

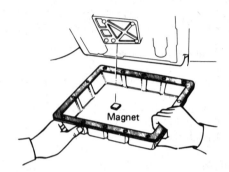

Position the magnet so that it is directly beneath the oil strainer

8. Installation is in the reverse order of removal. Please note the following:

—always use a new pan gasket, but never use gasket sealer

—before installing the pan, place a clean magnet on the bottom so that it will be positioned directly beneath the oil strainer.

—tighten the oil strainer retaining bolts to 44–52 in. lbs. (approximately 4 ft. lbs.)

—tighten the pan retaining bolts to 33–43 in. lbs. (approximately 3.25 ft. lbs.)

FRONT BAND ADJUSTMENT—1973 ONLY

1. Remove the oil pan as previously outlined.

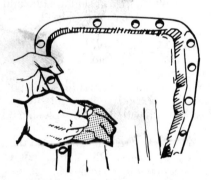

Clean the pan thoroughly and then allow it to air dry

Remove the oil strainer retaining bolts

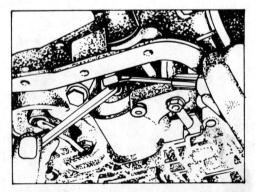

Adjusting the front band on the 1973 Celica

2. Pry the band engagement lever toward band with a screwdriver.

3. The gap between end of the piston rod and the engagement bolt should be 0.138 in.

4. If the gap does not meet the specification, adjust it by turning the engagement bolt.

5. Install the oil pan and refill the transmission as previously outlined.

REAR BAND ADJUSTMENT—1973 ONLY

The rear band adjusting bolt is located on the outside of the case, so it is not necessary to remove the oil pan in order to adjust the band.

1. Loosen the adjusting bolt locknut and fully screw in the adjusting bolt.

2. Loosen the adjusting bolt one turn.

3. Tighten the locknut while holding the bolt so that it cannot turn.

BAND ADJUSTMENTS—1974 AND LATER

1974 and later Toyota transmissions do not use bands, therefore, band adjustments are neither necessary or possible.

NEUTRAL SAFETY SWITCH ADJUSTMENT

If the engine will start with the selector in any range other than 'N' or 'P,' the neutral safety switch will require adjustment.

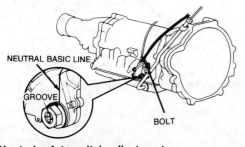

Neutral safety switch adjustment

1. Locate the neutral safety switch on the right side of the transmission and loosen the switch bolt.

2. Move the gear selector to the 'N' position.

3. Align the groove on the safety switch shaft with the basic line which is scribed on the housing.

4. With the groove and the line aligned, tighten the switch bolt.

5. Using an ohmmeter, check for continuity between the switch terminals as shown in the illustration. If a problem is found, replace the switch.

		B	N	RB	RL
P		O—	—O		
R				O—	—O
'N		O—	—O		

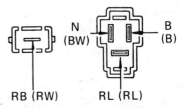

Check the neutral safety switch for continuity

SHIFT LINKAGE ADJUSTMENT

1973 Only

The transmission should be engaged, in the gear selected as indicated on the shift quadrant. If it is not, then adjust the linkage as follows:

1. Check all of the shift linkage bushings for wear. Replace any worn bushings.

2. Loosen the connecting rod swivel locknut.

3. Move the selector lever and check movement of the pointer in the shift quadrant.

4. When the control shaft is set in the neutral position the quadrant pointer should indicate "N" as well.

Steps 5–7 apply only to cars equipped with column-mounted gear selectors.

5. If the pointer does not indicate Neutral (N), then check the drive cord adjustment.

6. Remove the steering column shroud.

7. Turn the drive cord adjuster with a phillips screwdriver until the pointer indicates Neutral (N).

Steps 8–10 apply to both column-mounted and floor-mounted selectors:

8. Position the manual valve lever on the transmission so that it is in the Neutral position.

9. Lock the connecting rod swivel with the locknut so that the pointer, selector, and manual valve lever are all positioned in Neutral.

10. Check the operation of the gear selector by moving it through all ranges.

1974 and Later

1. Loosen the adjusting nut on the linkage and check the linkage for freedom of movement.

2. Push the manual valve lever toward the front of the car, as far as it will go.

3. Bring the lever back to its third notch (Neutral).

4. Have an assistant hold the shift lever in

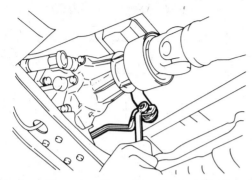

Loosen the nut on the connecting rod (1974 and later)

Neutral, while you tighten the linkage adjusting nut so that it can't slip.

THROTTLE LINKAGE ADJUSTMENT
1973 Only

1. Loosen the locknut at each end of the linkage adjusting turnbuckle.
2. Detach the throttle linkage connecting rod from the carburetor.
3. Align the pointer on the throttle valve lever with the mark stamped on the transmission case.
4. Rotate the turnbuckle so that the end of the throttle linkage rod and the carburetor throttle lever are aligned.
NOTE: *The carburetor throttle valve must be fully opened during this adjustment.*
5. Tighten the turnbuckle locknuts and reconnect the throttle rod to the carburetor.

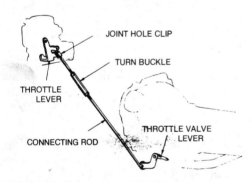

1973 throttle linkage components

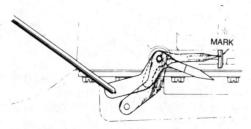

1973 throttle linkage alignment marks

6. Open the throttle valve and check the pointer alignment with the mark on the transmission case.
7. Road-test the car. If the transmission "hunts," i.e., keeps shifting rapidly back and forth between gears at certain speeds or if it fails to downshift properly when going up hills, repeat the throttle linkage adjustment.

1974 and Later

1. Remove the air cleaner.
2. Confirm that the accelerator linkage opens the throttle fully. Adjust the linkage as necessary.
3. Peel the rubber dust boot back from the throttle cable.
4. Loosen the adjustment nuts on the throttle cable bracket (rocker cover) just enough to allow cable housing movement.
5. Have an assistant depress the accelerator pedal fully.
6. Adjust the cable housing so that the distance between its end and the cable stop collar is 2.05 in. (.04 in. 1980 and later).

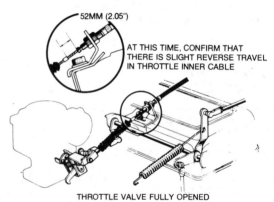

Throttle linkage adjustment; 1974–79

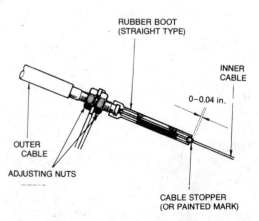

Throttle linkage adjustment; 1980 and later

7. Tighten the adjustment nuts. Make sure that the adjustment hasn't changed. Install the dust boot and the air cleaner.

Transmission Case
REMOVAL AND INSTALLATION

1. Disconnect the negative battery cable.

2. Drain the radiator coolant into a suitable container. If clean, the coolant can be reused.

3. Disconnect the upper radiator hose.

4. Remove the air cleaner assembly on carbureted cars; disconnect the air intake connector on fuel injected cars.

5. Disconnect the transmission throttle cable by loosening the adjusting nuts, disconnecting the cable housing from the bracket, removing the clip from the pin and disconnecting the cable from the linkage.

6. Jack up the car and safely support it with jackstands. Drain the transmission.

7. Disconnect the three connectors to the neutral start and back-up light switches near the starter.

8. Disconnect the intermediate driveshaft, as detailed in Chapter 7. Remove the driveshaft center bearing.

9. Disconnect the exhaust pipe from the tail pipe at the rear side of the catalytic converter. Remove the two rubber hangers, and remove the pipe clamp from the transmission case.

10. Remove the oil cooler pipe clamp from the transmission case, and disconnect the two oil cooler pipes from the transmission.

11. Disconnect the shift linkage at the rear connection.

12. Disconnect the speedometer cable.

13. Remove the exhaust pipe bracket, catalytic converter cover and both stiffener plates (if equipped) from the bellhousing and rear of cylinder block.

14. On 1982 and later cars with rack and pinion steering, remove the steering rack housing by following step 4 under "1982 and Later Manual Transmission Removal."

15. Jack the transmission up just enough to remove the weight from the rear transmission support member.

16. Remove the transmission ground cable. Place a wooden block between the cowl panel and the rear of the cylinder head to prevent damaging the heater hoses. Remove the transmission rear support member.

17. Remove the bottom engine cover.

18. Remove the six torque converter mounting bolts by turning the crankshaft to gain access to each bolt.

19. Make a guide pin by cutting the head off of a bolt that will screw into one of the torque converter bolt holes. Install the guide pin into one of the holes.

20. Remove the starter.

21. Remove the transmission bellhousing-to-engine block mounting bolts.

22. Using a pry bar, pry on the end of the guide pin to begin moving the transmission and converter assembly towards the rear of the car. The guide pin helps keep the converter with the transmission.

23. Using a hydraulic floor jack as an aid, pull out the transmission by drawing it down and towards the rear of the car.

CUATION: *Be careful not to catch the throttle cable or neutral start switch cable. Keep the oil pan positioned downward.*

24. Transmission installation is in the reverse order of removal. Torque the converter bolts evenly to 11–15 ft. lbs., and the transmission housing mounting bolts to 37–57 ft. lbs.

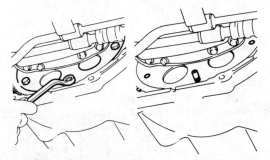

Remove the torque converter bolts and install a guide pin into one of the holes

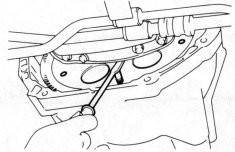

Use the guide pin as a fulcrum to pry the assembly back

Drive Train

7

DRIVELINE

Driveshaft and U-Joints
REMOVAL AND INSTALLATION

1. Raise the rear of the car and support the rear axle housing with jackstands.

CAUTION: *Be sure that the car is securely supported. Remember, you will be working underneath it.*

2. Scribe alignment marks on the two rear flanges (one comes out of the differential and one is attached to the propeller shaft, they are both attached to each other).

3. Loosen the four attaching bolts and remove the U-joint flange from the differential flange.

4. Remove the two bolts which hold the center support bearing to the body.

5. Pull on the driveshaft assembly so as to remove the yoke from the transmission.

NOTE: *Quickly insert a transmission plug or an old rag into the transmission to prevent fluid leakage.*

6. Scribe alignment marks across the two forward flanges of the propeller (rear) shaft.

7. Unscrew the four bolts and remove the propeller shaft from the intermediate (front) shaft.

8. Put alignment marks on the flange (attached to the center support bearing) and the intermediate shaft and then unscrew the retaining nut.

9. Slide the flange and the center support bearing off the intermediate shaft.

To install:

1. Coat the splines on the rear of the intermediate shaft with multi-purpose grease.

2. Slide the bearing and the flange onto the shaft and align the marks.

3. Place the flange in a soft-jawed vise and install a new nut to press the bearing into position. Tighten the nut to 123–144 ft. lbs. Loosen the nut and then tighten it again, this time to 19–25 ft. lbs.

4. Using a hammer and a punch, stake the nut.

5. Align the marks on the bearing flange and the propeller shaft flange and insert the bolts. Tighten the bolts to 15–28 ft. lbs.

6. Insert the yoke on the intermediate shaft into the transmission.

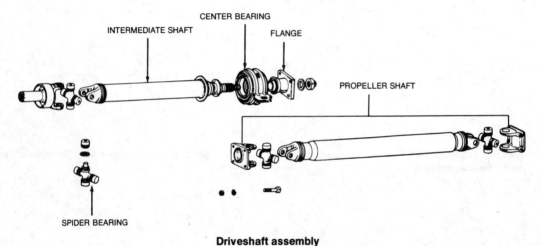

CENTER BEARING

INTERMEDIATE SHAFT

FLANGE

PROPELLER SHAFT

SPIDER BEARING

Driveshaft assembly

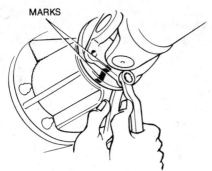

Scribe alignment marks on the two rear flanges before removal

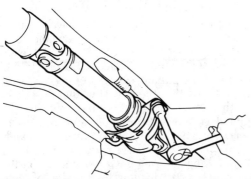

Removing the center support bearing mounting bolts

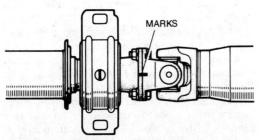

Removing the propeller shaft from the intermediate; the arrow indicates the matchmarks

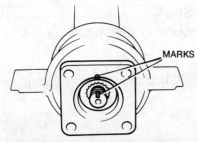

After removing the retaining nut, slide the center support bearing and the flange off the intermediate shaft (note matchmarks)

7. Align the marks on the propeller shaft flange and the differential flange and insert the bolts. Tighten the bolts to 15–28 ft. lbs.

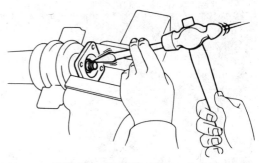

Once installed, use a hammer and a punch to stake the center support bearing retaining nut

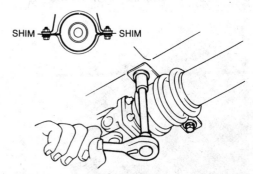

Attaching the center support bearing to the body of the car

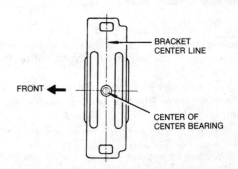

Positioning of the center support bearing is crucial

8. Place a height spacer between the body and the center support bearing and install the two mounting bolts finger tight.

9. Check that the bearing bracket is at right angles to the propeller shaft. Adjust if necessary.

10. Check that the center line of the bearing is set to the center line of the bracket when the car is in the no-load condition. Adjust if necessary.

11. Tighten the bearing mounting bolts to 22–32 ft. lbs.

U-JOINT OVERHAUL

1. Matchmark the yoke and the driveshaft.
2. Remove the snaprings from the bearings.

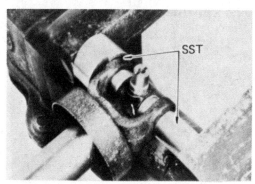

Use a vise to remove and install the bearings

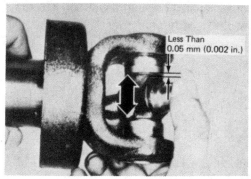

Checking the bearing axial play

3. Position the yoke on vise jaws. Using a bearing remover and a hammer, gently tap the remover until the bearing is driven out of the yoke about ½ in.

4. Place the tool in the vise and drive the yoke away from the tool until the bearing is removed.

5. Repeat Steps 3 and 4 for the other bearings.

6. Check for worn or damaged parts. Inspect the bearing journal surfaces for wear.

U-joint assembly is performed in the following order:

1. Install the bearing cups, seals, and O-rings in the spider.

2. Grease the spider and the bearings.

3. Position the spider in the yoke.

Thickness of snap ring		mm (in.)
Part No.	Thickness	Color code
90521–29070	2.375–2.425 (0.0935–0.0955)	None
90521–29071	2.425–2.475 (0.0955–0.0974)	Brown
90521–29072	2.475–2.525 (0.0974–0.0994)	Blue
90521–29073	2.525–2.575 (0.0994–0.1014)	None

4. Start the bearings in the yoke and then press them into place, using a vise.

5. Repeat Step 4 for the other bearings.

6. If the axial-play of the spider is greater than 0.002 in., select snaprings which will provide the correct play. Be sure that the snaprings are the same size on both sides or driveshaft noise and vibration will result.

7. Check the U-joint assembly for smooth operation.

REAR AXLE

Determining Axle Ratio

The drive axle of a car is said to have a certain axle ratio. This number (usually a whole number and a decimal fraction) is actually a comparison of the number of gear teeth on the ring gear and the pinion gear. For example, a 4.11 rear means that theoretically, there are 4.11 teeth on the ring gear and one tooth on the pinion gear or, put another way, the driveshaft must turn 4.11 times to turn the wheels once. Actually, on a 4.11 rear, there might be 37 teeth on the ring gear and 9 teeth on the pinion gear. By dividing the number of teeth on the ring gear, the numerical axle ratio (4.11) is obtained. This also provides a good method of ascertaining exactly which axle ratio one is dealing with.

Another method of determining gear ratio is to jack up and support the car so that both rear wheels are off the ground. Make a chalk mark on the rear wheel and the drive shaft. Put the transmission in neutral. Turn the rear wheel one complete turn and count the number of turns that the driveshaft makes. The number of turns that the driveshaft makes in one complete revolution of the rear wheel is an approximation of the rear axle ratio.

Axle Shaft

REMOVAL AND INSTALLATION

All Models Except 1982 and Later Supra; 1983 and Later GT-S

1. Raise the rear of the car and support it securely by using jackstands.

CAUTION: *Be sure that the vehicle is securely supported. Remember, you will be working underneath it.*

2. Drain the oil from the axle housing.

3. Remove the wheel cover (if equipped), unfasten the lug nuts, and remove the wheel.

4. Punch matchmarks on the brake drum and the axle shaft to maintain rotational balance.

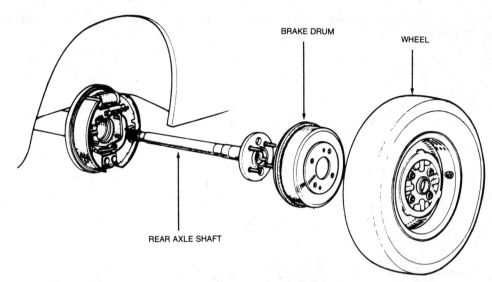

BRAKE DRUM

WHEEL

REAR AXLE SHAFT

Before removing the axle shaft, the wheel and the brake drum must be removed

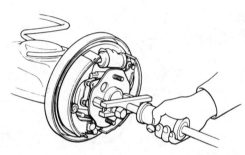

Using a slide hammer to remove the axle shaft

5. Remove the brake drum and related components, as detailed in Chapter 9.

6. Remove the backing plate attachment nuts through the access holes in the rear axle shaftflange.

7. Use a slide hammer with a suitable adapter to withdraw the axle shaft from its housing.

CAUTION: *Use care not to damage the oil seal when removing the axle shaft.*

8. Repeat the procedure for the axle shaft on the opposite side. *Be careful not to mix the components of the two sides.*

9. Installation is performed in the reverse order of removal. Coat the lips of the rear housing oil seal with multipurpose grease prior to installation of the rear axle shaft.

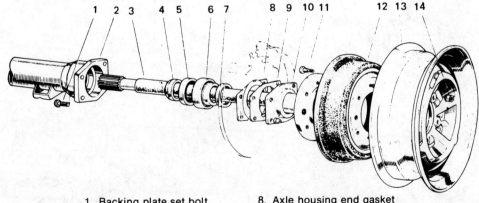

1 2 3   4 5   6 7   8 9 10 11   12 13 14

1. Backing plate set bolt
2. Rear axle housing
3. Rear axle shaft
4. Axle bearing inner retainer
5. Oil seal
6. Bearing
7. Spacer

8. Axle housing end gasket
9. Bearing retainer gasket
10. Axle bearing inner retainer
11. Hub bolt
12. Brake drum assembly
13. Wheel
14. Hub nut

Rear axle shaft and related components

**1982 and Later Supra; 1983 and Later
Celica GT-S**

These cars are equipped with a fully independent rear suspension system (IRS). The rear
axle assembly is comprised of right and left
swing axles, attached to the center differential
housing by constant-velocity joints which permit the axles to move up and down while they
turn.

Since five different special service tools (SST)
are required for axle shaft, bearing, and oil seal
removal and installation on the IRS axles, the
work is best performed by a reputable independent mechanic or an authorized Toyota
service facility.

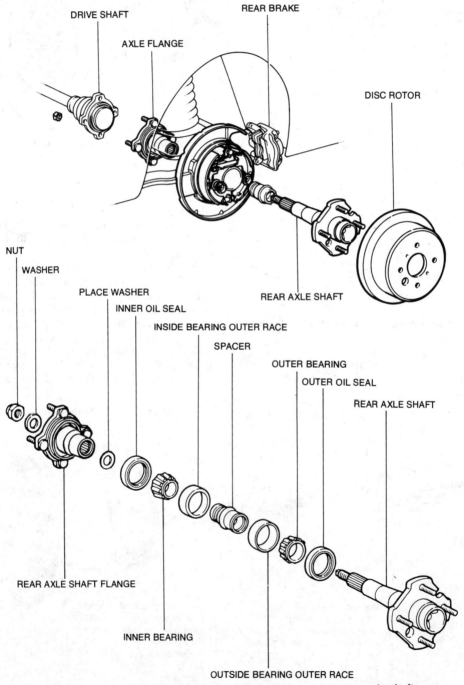

1982 and later Supra and 1983 and later Celica independent rear axle shaft

Suspension and Steering

8

FRONT SUSPENSION

The front suspension system is of the Mac-Pherson strut design. The struts used on either side are a combination spring and shock absorber with the outer casing of the shock actually supporting the spring at the bottom and thus forming a major structural component of the suspension. The wheel hub is attached to the bottom of the strut. A strut mounting bearing at the top and a ball joint at the bottom allow the entire strut to rotate in cornering maneuvers. The strut assembly, steering arm and the steering knuckle are all combined in one assembly; there is no upper control arm. A rubber-bushed transverse link (control arm) connects the lower portion of the strut to the front crossmember via the ball joint; the link thus allows for vertical movement.

NOTE: *Exercise extreme caution when working with the front suspension. Coil spring and other suspension components are under extreme tension and result in severe injury if released unexpectedly.*

Springs and Shock Absorbers
TESTING

The function of the shock absorber is to dampen harsh spring movement and provide a means of controlling the motion of the wheels so that the bumps encountered by the wheels are not totally transmitted to the body of the car and, therefore, to you and your passengers. As the wheel moves up and down, the shock absorber shortens and lengthens, thereby imposing a restraint on excessive movement by its hydraulic action.

A good way to see if your shock absorbers are working properly is to push on one corner of the car until it is moving up and down for almost the full suspension travel, then release it and watch its recovery. If the car bounces slightly about one more time and then comes to a rest, you can be fairly certain that the shock is OK. If the car continues to bounce excessively, the shocks will probably require replacement.

MacPherson Struts

The struts retain the springs under tremendous pressure, even when removed from the car. For this reason, several expensive special tools and substantial specialized knowledge are required to safely and effectively work on these components. If spring and shock absorber work is required, it is a good idea to remove the strut involved yourself and then take it to a repair facility which is fully equipped and familiar with MacPherson struts.

REMOVAL AND INSTALLATION

1. Remove the hubcap and loosen the lug nuts.
2. Raise the front of the car and support it with jackstands.
3. Remove the wheel.
4. Disconnect the brake line where the flexible hose attaches to the main line or unclip the line from the strut, remove the caliper assembly (as detailed in Chapter 9) and position it out of the way.
5. Raise the hood and remove the three strut mounting bolts on the fender apron.
6. Back underneath the car again, remove the two bolts that attach the steering knuckle arm to the bottom of the strut assembly.
7. Pry the lower control arm down and remove the strut assembly.

NOTE: *The steering knuckle bolt holes have collars that extend about 0.20 in. (5 mm). Be careful to clear them when separating the steering knuckle from the strut assembly.*

8. Installation is in the reverse order of removal. Please note the following:

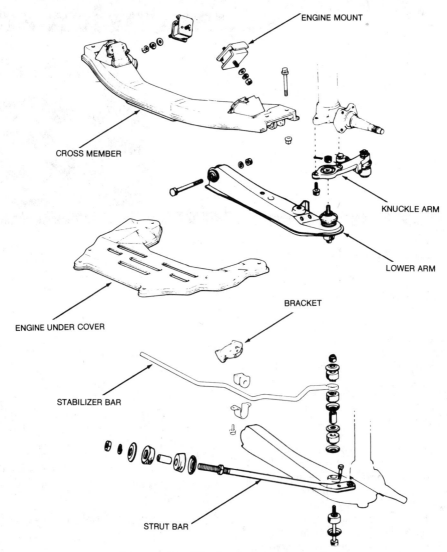

Components of the front suspension system

- tighten the steering knuckle-to-strut assembly bolts to 58–86 ft. lbs.
- tighten the three upper strut retaining nuts to 22–32 ft. lbs.

- bleed the brakes if the brake line was disconnected in Step 4
- check the front end alignment (see "Front End Alignment" later in this chapter)

Coil Springs
REMOVAL AND INSTALLATION

WARNING: *The coil springs are retained under considerable pressure. They can exert enough force when released to cause serious injury. Exercise extreme caution when disassembling the strut for coil spring removal.*

This procedure requires the use of a spring compressor; *it cannot be performed without one. If you do not have access to this special tool, do not attempt to disassemble the strut.*

1. Remove the strut assembly as previously detailed.

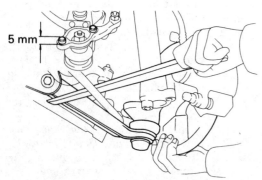

Make sure you clear the knuckle collars when prying down the control arm

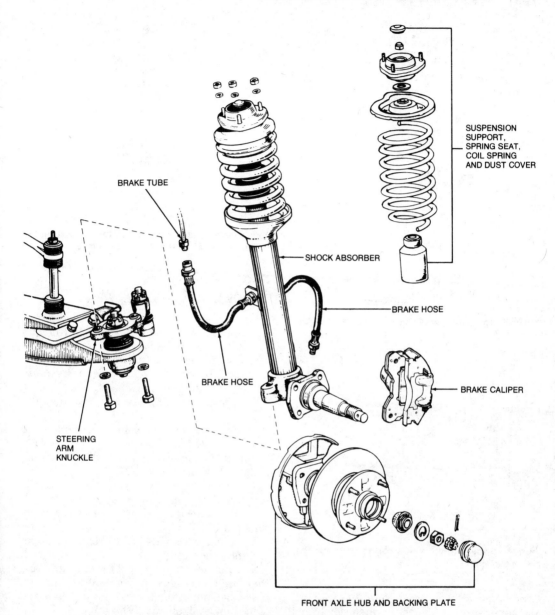

BRAKE TUBE

SUSPENSION
SUPPORT,
SPRING SEAT,
COIL SPRING
AND DUST COVER

SHOCK ABSORBER

BRAKE HOSE

BRAKE HOSE

BRAKE CALIPER

STEERING
ARM
KNUCKLE

FRONT AXLE HUB AND BACKING PLATE

Components of the MacPherson strut

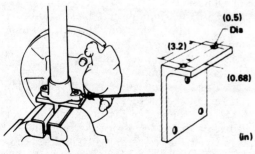

(0.5)
Dia
(3.2)
(0.68)

(in)

**Fabricate a shock absorber stand (arrow) and mount
it with the shock in the vise as shown**

2. Fabricate a strut assembly mounting
stand as illustrated. Bolt the assembly to the
stand and then mount the stand in a vise.

CAUTION: *Do not attempt to clamp the
strut assembly in a vise without the mounting stand as this will result in damage to the
strut tube.*

3. Attach a spring compressor and compress the spring until the upper spring retainer is free of any spring tension.

4. Use a spring seat holder to hold the support and then remove the nut on the strut
bearing plate.

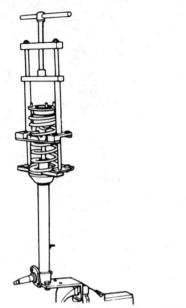

Spring compressor installed on the coil spring for removal

Hold the upper mount with a rod to unscrew the piston rod nut

5. Remove the bearing plate, the support, the upper spring retainer and then slowly and cautiously unscrew the spring compressor until all spring tension is relieved. Remove the spring and the dust cover.

NOTE: *Do not allow the piston rod to retract into the shock absorber. If it falls, screw a nut onto the rod and pull the rod out by the nut. Do not use pliers or the like to grip the rod as they will damage its surface, resulting in leaks, uneven operation or seal damage. Be extremely careful not to stress or contact the rod.*

6. Installation is in the reverse order of removal. Please note the following:

—pack the bearing in the suspension support with multi-purpose grease

—use a new retaining nut and tighten it to 29–39 ft. lbs.

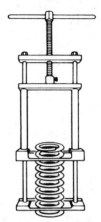

Spring compressor installed on the coil spring for installation—leave the upper coils free

Shock Absorbers

REMOVAL AND INSTALLATION

CAUTION: *Disassemble the shock absorber in a clean place. Do not allow dust or dirt to get on the disassembled parts. The piston rod is high precision finished, even a slight scratch can cause fluid leakage so be careful when handling the piston rod.*

1. Remove the strut assembly and then the coil spring.

2. Remove the wheel hub and the brake disc as detailed in Chapter 9.

3. Attach the strut tube to the mounting plate and clamp it in a vise.

4. Use a ring nut wrench and remove the ring nut at the top of the strut tube.

5. Use a needle and pick the gasket out of the strut tube.

6. Remove the guide, the rebound stopper and the piston rod.

7. Pull the cylinder out of the strut tube and then use a long blunt instrument to drive the base valve out of the bottom of the cylinder.

8. Empty all oil out of the tube.

NOTE: *Rebuilding kits are available through your local Toyota dealer.*

To install:

1. Press the base valve into the bottom of the cylinder.

2. Slide the cylinder into the strut tube.

3. Slide the piston rod and the rebound stopper into the cylinder.

4. Fill the cylinder with 325cc of NEW shock absorber fluid.

5. Press the rod guide and its gasket into the top of the strut tube.

6. Tape the end of the piston rod to avoid damaging the oil seal inside the ring nut.

7. Coat the oil seal with multi-purpose grease and then install the ring nut on the piston rod.

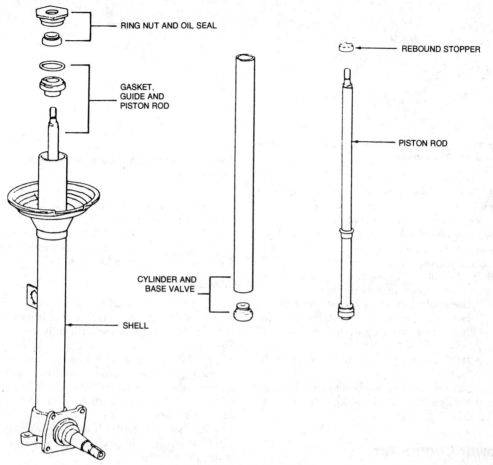

RING NUT AND OIL SEAL

GASKET,
GUIDE AND
PISTON ROD

REBOUND STOPPER

PISTON ROD

CYLINDER AND
BASE VALVE

SHELL

Front shock absorber assembly

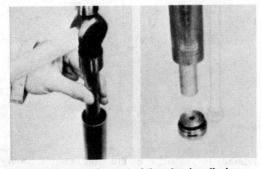

Drive the base valve out of the shock cylinder

8. Using a ring nut wrench, tighten the ring nut until the top of the piston rod is 3.15–3.54 in. above the top of the strut tube. Torque the nut to 73–108 ft. lbs.

9. Installation of the remaining components is in the reverse order of removal.

Ball Joints
INSPECTION

1. Raise the car so that all the weight has been removed from the front wheels.

2. Apply upward and downward pressure to the outer end of the lower control arm. Be careful to avoid any compression of the coil spring.

3. There should be no noticeable play between the bottom of the strut assembly and the ball joint. If play exists, the ball joint will require replacement.

NOTE: *The ball joint on all Toyotas is permanently connected to the lower control arm. If either of them go bad, they must be replaced as a unit.*

REMOVAL AND INSTALLATION

1. Remove the two bolts holding the steering knuckle to the bottom of the struct tube. Pull the lower control arm down and disconnect the strut from the steering knuckle arm.

2. Pull out the cotter pin and then remove the nut holding the steering knuckle arm to the ball joint (to the tie rod on 1982 and later).

3. Use a two-armed gear puller and pull the arm off of the ball joint (tie rod on 1982 and later).

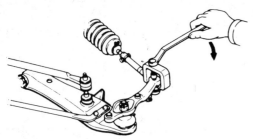

Use the tie rod tool to pull the knuckle arm from the tie rod on 1982 and later cars

4. Remove the nuts holding the stabilizer bar and the strut bar to the lower control arm and position them both out of the way.

5. Unscrew the bolt that attaches the control arm to the front crossmember and remove the control arm.

6. Installation is in the reverse order of removal. Please note the following:
- the control arm-to-crossmember bolt is not tightened until last. After all other bolts have been tightened, tighten the bolt to 51–65 ft. lbs.
- tighten the stabilizer bar bolt to 11–15 ft. lbs.
- tighten the strut bar bolt to 29–39 ft. lbs.
- tighten the steering knuckle bolt to 51–65 ft. lbs.

Lower Control Arm

Control arm removal and installation procedures are the same as those for the ball joint.

Front End Alignment

Alignment should only be performed after it has been verified that all parts of the steering and suspension systems are in good operating condition. The car must be empty. The tires must be cold and inflated to the correct pressure and the test surface must be level and horizontal.

Because special, elaborate equipment is required for proper front end alignment, it is recommended that the car be taken to a reputable alignment shop or Toyota service center.

CASTER

Caster is the tilt of the front steering axis either forward or backward away from the front of the vehicle.

If the caster is found to be out of tolerance with the specifications, it may be adjusted by turning the nuts on the rear end of the strut bar (where it attaches to the body). The caster is decreased by lengthening the strut bar and

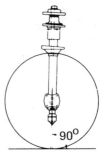

Caster is the forward or backward tilt of the steering axis

increased by shortening it. One turn of the adjusting nut is equal to 9′ (^{3}/$_{20}$ of 1°) of tilt.

NOTE: *If the caster still cannot be adjusted within the limits, inspect or replace any damaged or worn suspension parts.*

CAMBER

Camber is the slope of the front wheels from the vertical when viewed from the front of the vehicle. When the wheels tilt outward at the top, the camber is positive (+). When the wheels tilt inward at the top, the camber is negative (−). The amount of positive and negative camber is measured in degrees from the vertical and the measurement is called camber angle. Camber is preset at the factory, therefore it is not adjustable. If the camber angle is out of tolerance, inspect or replace worn or damaged suspension parts.

Camber is the slope of the front wheels when viewed from the front of the car

TOE

Toe is the amount, measured in a fraction of an inch, that the front wheels are closer together at one end than the other. Toe-in means that the front wheels are closer together at the front of the tire than at the rear; toe-out means that the rear of the tires are closer together than the front.

Although it is recommended that this adjustment be made by your dealer or a qualified shop, you can make it yourself if you make

Front Wheel Alignment Specifications

Year	Model	Caster			Camber			Toe-in (in.)	Steering Axis Inclination (deg)
		Range (deg)	Preferred Setting (deg)		Range (deg)	Preferred Setting (deg)			
1971–75	All	30'P–1°30'P	1'P		30'P–1°30'P	1°P		0.20–0.28	7P–8P
1976	ST	30'P–1°30'P	1°P		30'P–1°30'P	1°P		0.04–0.12	7P–8P
	GT	1°15'P–2°15'P	1°45'P		15°P–1°15'P	45'P		0.04–0.12	7P–8P
1977	①	1°15'P–2°45'P	1°45'P		30'P–1°30'P	1°P		0–0.08	7°15'P–8°15'P
1978	All	1°20'P–2°20'P	1°50'P		25'P–1°25'P	55'P		0–0.08②	7°30'P
1979	Celica	1°15'P–2°15'P	1°45'P		35'P–1°35'P	1°5'P		0–0.08	6°55'P–7°55'P
1980–81	Celica	1°10'P–2°10'P	1°40'P		25'P–1°25'P	55'P		0–0.08②	6°55'P–7°55'P
1979–81	Supra	1°15'P–2°15'P	1°45'P		20'P–1°20'P	50'P		0.04N–0.04P	7°10'P–8°10'P
1982–83	Celcia	2°75'P–3°65'P	3°20'P		10'P–1°40'P	55'P		0.12P–0.20P ③	8°50'P–9°40'P
1982–83	Supra	3°65'P–4°55'P	4°10'P		5'P–1°15'P	50'P		0.04N–0.028P	9°50'–10°40'P

① Figures are for ST, GT same as 1976
② W/power steering: 0.12–0.20
③ W/power steering: 0.16P–0.24P

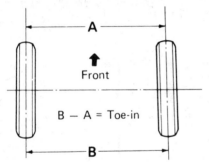

When the front of the tires are closer together than the rear, you have toe-in

very careful measurements. The wheels must be dead straight ahead. The car must have a full tank of gas, all fluids must be at their proper levels, all other suspension and steering adjustments must be correct and the tires must be properly inflated to their cold specification.

1. Toe can be determined by measuring the distance between the centers of the tire treads, at the front of the tire and the rear. If the tread pattern of your car's tires makes this impossible, you can measure between the edges of the wheel rims, but be sure to move the car and measure in a few places to avoid errors caused by bent rims or wheel run-out.

2. If the measurement is not within specifications on 1981 and earlier cars, loosen the four retaining clamp locknuts on the adjustable tie rods.

3. On 1982 and later cars (rack and pinion steering), remove the rack bolt clips and loosen the clamp bolts.

4. Turn the left and right tie rods EQUAL amounts until the measurements are within specifications.

5. Tighten the lock bolts and then recheck the measurements. Check to see that the steering wheel is still in the proper position. If not, remove it and reposition it as detailed later in this chapter.

REAR SUSPENSION

Shock Absorbers

TESTING

Shock absorbers require replacement if the car fails to recover quickly after hitting a large bump or if it sways excessively following a directional change.

A good way to test the shock absorbers is to intermittenly apply downward pressure to the side of the car until it is moving up and down for almost its full suspension travel. Release it and observe its recovery. If the car bounces

once or twice after having been released and then comes to a rest, the shocks are alright. If the car continues to bounce, the shocks will probably require replacement.

REMOVAL AND INSTALLATION

1971–81 All Models

1. Raise the rear of the car and support the rear axle with jackstands.

2. Unfasten the upper shock absorber retaining nuts. Use a screwdriver to keep the shaft from spinning.

NOTE: *Always remove and install the shock absorbers one at a time. Do not allow the rear axle to hang in place as this may cause undue damage.*

3. Remove the lower shock retaining nut where it attaches to the rear axle housing.

4. Remove the shock absorber.

5. Inspect the shock for wear, leaks or other signs of damage.

6. Installation is in the reverse order of removal. Please note the following:
- tighten the upper retaining nuts to 16–24 ft. lbs.
- tighten the lower retaining nuts to 22–32 ft. lbs. (1977—28.9–39.8 ft. lbs.)

1982 and Later Supra, 1983 and Later Celica GT-S

1. Jack up the rear end of the car, keeping the pad of the hydraulic floor jack underneath the differential housing. Support the suspension control arms with safety stands.

2. Remove the brake hose clips. Disconnect the stabilizer bar end.

3. Disconnect the drive halfshaft at the CV joint on the wheel side.

4. With a jackstand underneath the suspension control arm, unbolt the shock absorber at its lower end. Using a screwdriver to keep the shaft from turning, remove the nut holding the shock absorber to its upper mounting. Remove the shock.

5. Installation is in the reverse order of removal. Torque the halfshaft nuts to 44–57 ft. lbs.; torque the upper shock mounting nut to 14–22 ft. lbs., and the lower shock mounting nut to 22–32 ft. lbs.

INDEPENDENT REAR SUSPENSION

ADJUSTMENTS

Rear wheel alignment on independent rear suspension cars should be performed at a reputable wheel alignment shop or authorized

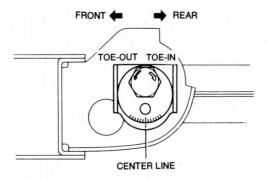

FRONT ⬅   ➡ REAR

TOE-OUT   TOE-IN

CENTER LINE

Toe adjustment, 1982 and later cars

Toyota service facility. Before proper alignment can be performed, check the tires for unusual wear and correct inflation. Check the rear wheel bearings for looseness, and give the rear shocks the standard bounce test.

Toe-in and camber can be adjusted on the IRS. Toe is adjusted at the rear suspension arm mounting bolt. Check camber with a wheel alignment tester; if camber is out of tolerance, inspect the rear wheel bearings, constant velocity joints and wheel runout. Replace any worn parts. Toe-in and camber specifications are as noted in chart on page 217.

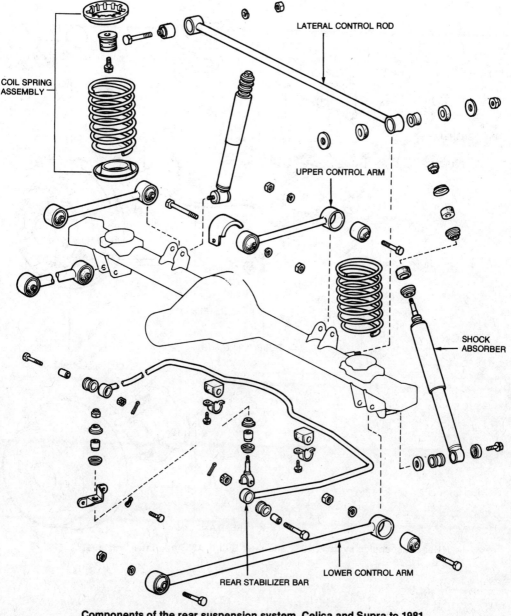

COIL SPRING ASSEMBLY

LATERAL CONTROL ROD

UPPER CONTROL ARM

SHOCK ABSORBER

REAR STABILIZER BAR

LOWER CONTROL ARM

Components of the rear suspension system, Celica and Supra to 1981

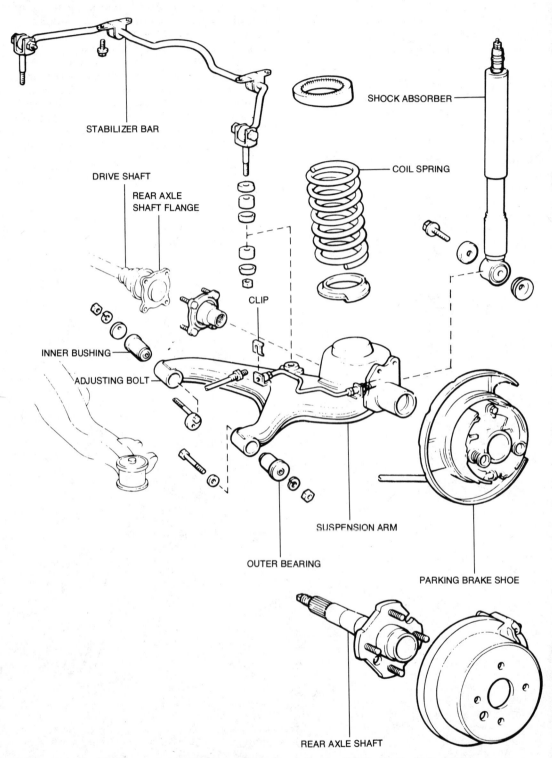

STABILIZER BAR

DRIVE SHAFT

REAR AXLE
SHAFT FLANGE

SHOCK ABSORBER

COIL SPRING

CLIP

INNER BUSHING

ADJUSTING BOLT

SUSPENSION ARM

OUTER BEARING

PARKING BRAKE SHOE

REAR AXLE SHAFT

Rear suspension system, 1982 and later Supra, 1983 and later Celica GT-S

IRS Rear Wheel Alignments

	Year/Model	Inspection Standard	Adjustment Standard	Left-right Error
Toe-in	1982–83 Supra 1983 Celica GT-S	0 ± 0.16 in.	0 ± 0.08 in.	
Camber	1982 Supra	6′ ± 45′	6′ ± 30′	30′
	1983 Supra	30′ ± 45′	30′ ± 30′	20′
	1983 Celica GT-S	6′ ± 45′	6′ ± 45′	30′

Coil Springs

REMOVAL AND INSTALLATION

WARNING: *The coil springs are retained under extreme pressure. They can extract enough force to cause serious injury. Exercise extreme caution when working with the coil springs.*

1. Raise the rear axle housing and support the body with jackstands. Leave the jack under the axle housing.

2. Remove the lower shock retaining nuts.

3. Unbolt the rear stabilizer bar support brackets (if so equipped) and pivot the bar down.

Correct lower insulator installation

4. Unscrew the bolt holding the lateral control arm to the axle housing and position the arm out of the way.

5. Using the jack, slowly lower the axle (lower control arm on IRS cars) until the coil springs and their insulators can be removed.

CAUTION: *While lowering the axle (or lower control arm), be careful not to put any stress on the brake lines and the parking brake cable.*

6. Installation is in the reverse order of removal. Please note the following:

—raise the axle housing until the body is free of the jackstands and then tighten the lateral control arm bolt to 26–39 ft. lbs. (solid-axle cars only).

NOTE: *Make sure the spring insulators are installed correctly as shown. If not, reinstall the coil spring.*

STEERING

Steering Wheel

REMOVAL AND INSTALLATION

Three-Spoke

CAUTION: *Do not attempt to remove or install the steering wheel by hammering on it. Damage to the energy absorbing steering column could result.*

1. Steer the wheels into the straight ahead position.

2. Disconnect the horn and turn signal connectors at the bottom of the steering column shroud.

3. Loosen the trim pad retaining screws from the back of the steering wheel.

4. Lift the trim pad and horn button assembly from the wheel.

5. Remove the steering wheel hub retaining nut.

6. Scribe match marks on the hub and the steering shaft to aid in proper installation.

7. Grasp the steering wheel with both hands and firmly pull it off the column.

NOTE: *If the wheel cannot be pulled off with your hands, use a steering wheel puller.*

8. Installation is in the reverse order of removal. Tighten the steering wheel hub retaining nut to 15–22 ft. lbs.

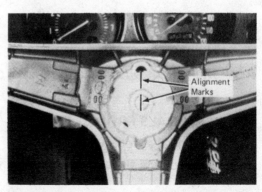

Matchmark the steering shaft and the hub

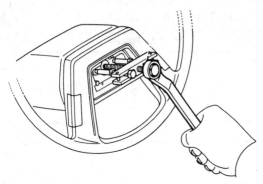

Use a steering wheel puller to remove the wheel

Four-Spoke

CAUTION: *Do not attempt to remove or install the steering wheel by hammering on it. Damage to the energy absorbing steering column could result.*

1. Steer the wheels into the straight ahead position.

2. Disconnect the horn and turn signal connectors at the bottom of the steering column shroud.

3. Remove the plastic center insert on the steering wheel pad. On GT models and Supras, use a small screwdriver to pry the insert out. On ST models, remove the wheel pad screws on the back of the wheel and pull the pad off.

4. Remove the steering wheel retaining nut.

5. Scribe match marks on the hub and the steering shaft to aid in proper installation.

6. Grasp the steering wheel with both hands and firmly pull it off the shaft.

NOTE: *If the wheel cannot be pulled off with your hands, use a steering wheel puller.*

7. Installation is in the reverse order of removal. Tighten the steering wheel retaining nut to 22–28 ft. lbs.

Two-Spoke

CAUTION: *Do not attempt to remove or install the steering wheel by hammering on it. Damage to the energy absorbing steering column could result.*

1. Steer the front wheels into the straight ahead position.

2. Disconnect the horn and turn signal connectors at the bottom of the steering column shroud.

3. Carefully pry off the steering wheel center pad.

4. Remove the steering wheel center nut.

5. Scribe match marks on the hub and the steering shaft to aid in proper installation.

6. Using a steering wheel puller, remove the wheel.

7. Installation is in the reverse order of removal. Torque the retaining nut to 22–28 ft. lbs.

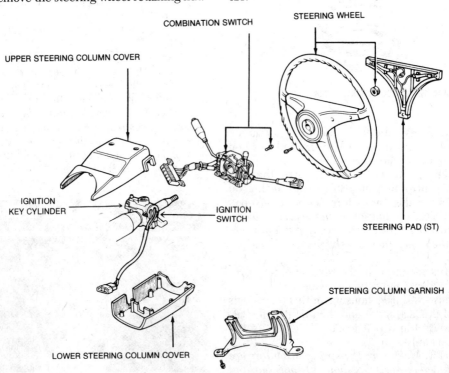

COMBINATION SWITCH

STEERING WHEEL

UPPER STEERING COLUMN COVER

IGNITION KEY CYLINDER

IGNITION SWITCH

STEERING PAD (ST)

STEERING COLUMN GARNISH

LOWER STEERING COLUMN COVER

Steering column assembly

Combination Switch

NOTE: *On some earlier models, the combination switch may only be the turn signal switch. Removal and installation procedures are the same for both.*

REMOVAL AND INSTALLATION

1. Disconnect the negative battery cable.
2. Unscrew the two retaining bolts and remove the steering column garnish.
3. Remove the upper and lower steering column covers.
4. Remove the steering wheel as detailed previously.
5. Trace the switch wiring harness to the multiconnector. Push in the lock levers and pull apart the connector.
6. Unscrew the four mounting screws and remove the switch.
7. Installation is in the reverse order of removal.

Ignition Lock/Switch
REMOVAL AND INSTALLATION

1. Disconnect the negative battery cable.
2. Unscrew the retaining screws and remove the upper and lower steering column covers.
3. Unscrew the two retaining screws and remove the steering column garnish.
4. Turn the ignition key to the 'ACC' position.
5. Push the lock cylinder stop in with a small, round object (cotter pin, punch etc.) and pull out the ignition key and the lock cylinder.
NOTE: *You may find that removing the steering wheel and the combination switch will facilitate easier removal.*
6. Loosen the mounting screw and withdraw the ignition switch from the lock housing.
To install:
1. Install the switch with the switch recess and the bracket tab positioned as shown in the illustration. Install the retaining screw.
2. Make sure that both the lock cylinder and the column lock are in the 'ACC' position. Slide the cylinder into the lock housing until the stop tab engages the hole in the lock.
3. Installation of the remaining components is in the reverse order of removal.

Tie Rod
REMOVAL AND INSTALLATION

1. Scribe alignment marks on the tie rod and rack end (rack and pinion cars only).
2. Working at the steering knuckle arm, pull out the cotter pin and then remove the castellated nut.
3. Using a tie rod end puller, disconnect the tie rod from the steering knuckle arm.
4. Repeat the first two steps on the other end of the tie rod (where it attaches to the relay rod).
To install (non-rack and pinion cars):
1. Turn the tie rods in their adjusting tubes until they are of equal lengths. They should be approximately 12.60 in. long.
2. Turn the tie rod ends so that they cross at 90°. Tighten the adjusting tube clamps so that they lock the ends in position.
3. Connect the tie rods and tighten the nuts to 37–50 ft. lbs.
4. Check the toe. Adjust if necessary.
Rack and pinion cars:

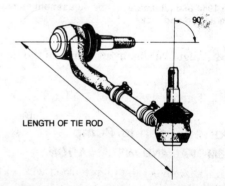

LENGTH OF TIE ROD

Make sure to position the tie rod properly before installation

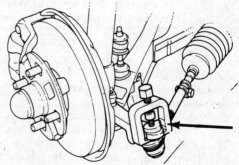

Remove the tie rod ends with a tie rod puller (arrow)

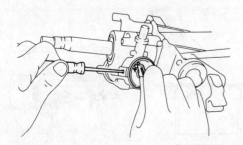

Push the lock cylinder stop in to remove the cylinder

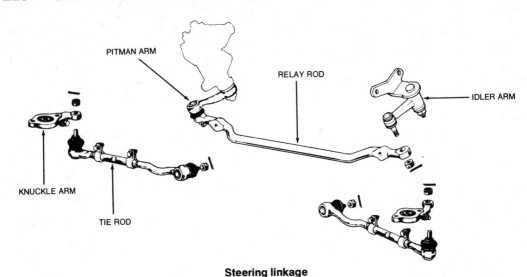

Steering linkage

MARKS

TAKE A NOTE OF THE DISTANCE

On 1982 and later cars, scribe adjustment marks on the tie rod and rack

1. Align the alignment marks on the tie rod and rack end.
2. Install the tie rod end.
3. Tighten the nuts to 11–14 ft. lbs.

Power Steering Pump

REMOVAL AND INSTALLATION

1. Disconnect the high tension wire to the distributor.
2. Tag and disconnect the air and return hoses at the pump.
3. Drain the steering fluid from the reservoir tank. Disconnect the pressure tube from the pump.
4. Push on the drive belt to hold the pump pulley in place, and remove the pulley set nut.
5. Loosen the pump drive belt adjusting bolt, and remove the drive belt. Remove the pulley and woodruff key.
6. Unbolt the pump mounting bolts, and remove the pump from the mounting bracket.
7. Installation is in the reverse order of removal. Torque the pump mounting bolts to 22–32 ft. lbs. Adjust pump drive belt tension, connect all hoses, and fill the power steering

reservoir with ATF Type Dexron® or Dexron:RM II. Bleed the power steering system (see below) and check for leaks.

BLEEDING

1. Jack up the front end of the car and safely support it with jackstands.
2. Check that the steering fluid is topped up to within the COLD LEVEL if cold, or the HOT LEVEL if the car has been running. Add fluid if necessary.
3. Start the engine and turn the steering wheel from lock to lock fully three or four times with the engine at idle.
4. Recheck the steering fluid level. Check that the fluid is not foamy or cloudy and does not rise over the maximum when the engine is stopped. With the engine running, the fluid should rise a maximum of 0.20 in. (5 mm).
5. Start the engine and let it idle. Turn the steering wheel from lock to lock two or three times.
6. Lower the car to the ground. With the engine idling, turn the steering wheel from lock to lock several times. Center the steering wheel.

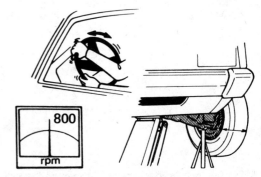

Bleeding the power steering pump

7. The bleeding is complete if the oil level in the reservoir has not risen excessively and there is no foaming or clouding of the fluid. If excessive rise and/or foaming is noticed, repeat step 6 until the fluid level and condition is correct.

Steering Gear

REMOVAL AND INSTALLATION

1971–81 All Models

1. Open the hood, and find the steering gearbox. Place matchmarks on the coupling and steering column shaft.
2. Disconnect the pitman arm from the relay rod using a tie rod puller on the pitman arm set nut.
3. Disconnect the steering gearbox at the coupling. Unbolt the gearbox from the chassis and remove.
4. Installation is in the reverse order of removal, with the exception of first aligning the matchmarks and connecting the steering shaft to the coupling before you bolt the gearbox into the car permanently.

1982 and Later (Rack and Pinion) Cars

1. Open the hood. Remove the two set bolts, and remove the sliding yoke from between the steering rack housing and the steering column shaft. On Supras, unbolt and remove the intermediate shaft (rack housing side first).
2. Remove the cotter pin and nut holding the knuckle arm to the tie rod end. Using a tie rod puller, disconnect the tie rod end from the knuckle arm.
3. Tag and disconnect the power steering lines if equipped. Remove the steering housing brackets and remove the housing.
4. Installation is the reverse of removal. Torque the rack housing mounting bolts to 29–39 ft. lbs., and the tie rod set nuts to 37–50 ft. lbs. *Use a new cotter pin.* On Supras, install the intermediate shaft column side first, then rack side. On power steering-equipped cars, bleed the power steering system and check for fluid leaks. Adjust toe-in on all models.

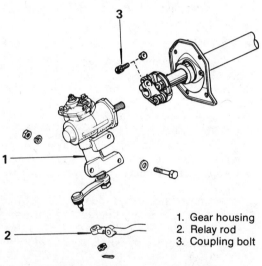

1. Gear housing
2. Relay rod
3. Coupling bolt

Typical steering gearbox, 1971–81 models

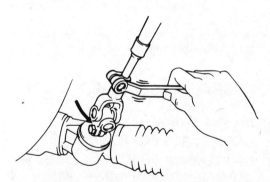

Removing the sliding yoke on 1982 and later cars

Brakes

ADJUSTMENTS

Disc Brakes

All disc brakes are inherently self-adjusting. No periodic adjustment is either necessary or possible.

Drum Brakes

The rear drum brakes used on Celicas are equipped with automatic adjusters actuated by the parking brake mechanism. No periodic adjustment of the drum brakes is necessary if this mechanism is working properly. If the brake shoe to drum clearance is incorrect, and applying and releasing the parking brake a few times does not adjust it properly, the parts will have to be disassembled for repair.

HYDRAULIC SYSTEM

Master Cylinder

REMOVAL AND INSTALLATION

CAUTION: *Be careful not to spill brake fluid on the painted surfaces of the vehicle; it will damage the paint.*
1. Unfasten the hydraulic lines from the master cylinder.
2. Detach the hydraulic fluid pressure differential switch wiring connectors. On models with ESP, disconnect the fluid level sensor wiring connectors, as well.
3. Loosen the master cylinder reservoir mounting bolt.
4. Then do one of the following:
   a. On models with manual brakes, remove the master cylinder securing bolts and the clevis pin from the brake pedal. Remove the master cylinder;
   b. On models with power brakes, unfasten the nuts and remove the master cylinder assembly from the power brake unit.
5. Installation is performed in the reverse order of removal. Note the following, however.
   • before tightening the master cylinder mounting nuts or bolts, screw the hydraulic line into the cylinder body, a few turns.
   • *after installation is completed, bleed the master cylinder and the brake system, as outlined following.*

OVERHAUL

1. Place the cylinder securely in a vise. Remove the reservoir caps and floats. Unscrew the bolts which secure the reservoirs to the main body.
2. Remove the pressure differential warning switch assembly. Then, working from the rear of the cylinder, remove the boot, snapring, stop washer, piston No. 1, spacer, cylinder cup, spring retainer, and spring, in that order.
3. Remove the end-plug and gasket from the front of the cylinder, then remove the front piston stop-bolt from underneath. Pull out the spring, retainer, piston No. 2, spacer, and the cylinder cup.
4. Remove the two outlet fittings, washers, check valves and springs.
5. Remove the piston cups from their seats only if they are to be replaced.

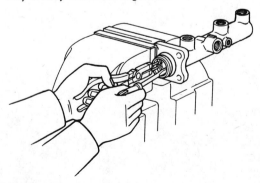

Removing the snap-rings

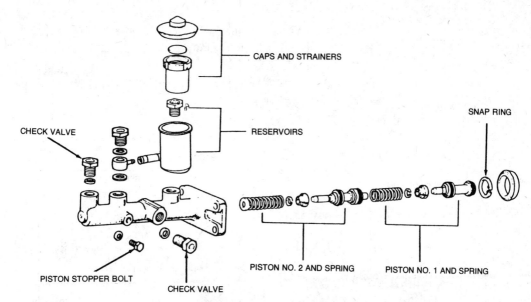

1980 master cylinder assembly (others similar)

After washing all parts in clean brake fluid, dry them with compressed air (if available). Drying parts with a shop rag can deposit lint and dirt particles inside the assembled master cylinder. Inspect the cylinder bore for wear, scuff marks, or nicks. Cylinders may be honed slightly, but the limits is 0.006 in. In view of the importance of the master cylinder, it is recommended that it is replaced rather than overhauled if worn or damaged.

6. Assembly is performed in the reverse order of disassembly. *Absolute cleanliness is essential.* Coat all parts with clean brake fluid prior to assembly.

Bleed the hydraulic system after the master cylinder is installed, as detailed following.

Vacuum Booster

NOTE: *Vacuum boosters can be found only on models equipped with power brakes.*

REMOVAL AND INSTALLATION

1. Remove the master cylinder as previously detailed.
2. Locate the clevis rod where it attaches to the brake pedal. Pull out the clip and then remove the clevis pin.
3. Disconnect the vacuum hose from the booster.
4. Loosen the four nuts and then pull out the vacuum booster, the bracket and the gasket.
5. Installation is in the reverse order of removal.

OVERHAUL

Aisin Type

1. Unscrew the nut at the front of the booster and remove the pushrod.
2. Loosen the retaining nut and then unscrew the clevis.

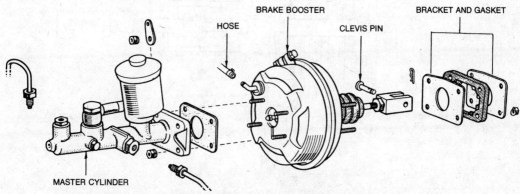

An exploded view of the master cylinder and vacuum booster assembly

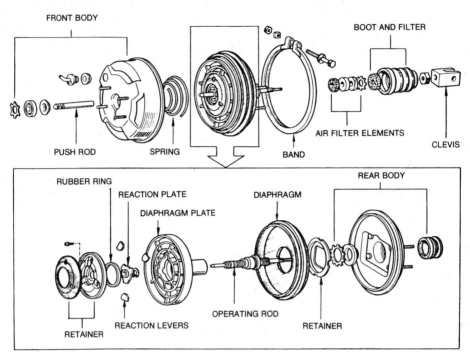

An exploded view of the AISIN-type vacuum booster

3. Pull off the rubber boot.

4. Use a screwdriver to pry out the air filter retainer from around the back of the booster and then remove the three filter elements.

5. Put an alignment mark across the front body, the band and the rear body.

6. Using Special Tool #09738-00010 or a few pieces of wood and some C-clamps, compress the rear body into the front body and remove the booster band. Separate the front and rear bodies from each other.

7. Carefully remove the spring retainers, the reaction plate, the reaction levers and the rubber ring.

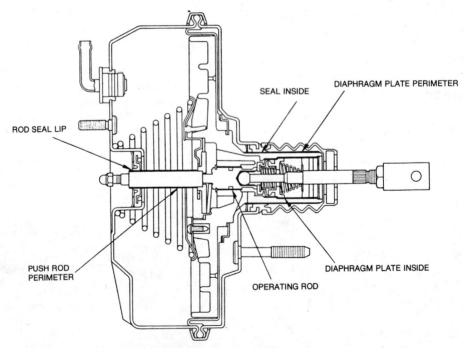

Apply silicone grease to these parts when assembling the AISIN vacuum booster

8. Use snapring pliers to remove the snapring in the diaphragm plate and then pull out the operating rod toward the rear.

9. Using a special retainer wrench, remove the retainer and then separate the diaphragm and the plate.

10. Assembly is in the reverse order of disassembly.

JKK Type

1. Loosen the retaining nut and unscrew the clevis. Remove the rubber boot.

2. Use a screwdriver to remove the air filter retainer and then pull out the two filter elements.

3. Put an alignment mark on the front and rear shells.

4. Use the Special Tool #09738-00010 or a few pieces of wood and some C-clamps to compress the rear shell into the front shell.

NOTE: *If the Special Tool is used, tighten its bolts to 35–52 ft. lbs.*

5. Turn the front shell clockwise to separate the two shells and then remove the pushrod and the spring.

6. Remove the diaphragm from the diaphragm plate.

7. Push the valve operating rod in and remove the stopper key.

8. Pull out the valve operating rod.

9. Assembly is in the reverse order of disassembly.

Proportioning Valve

Many of the early model Celicas use a proportioning valve to reduce the hydraulic pressure to the rear brakes because of weight transfer during high-speed stops. This helps to keep the rear brakes from locking up by improving front-to-rear balance. The proportioning valve can be found in the engine compartment, near the master cylinder.

REMOVAL AND INSTALLATION

1. Disconnect the brake lines from the valve unions.

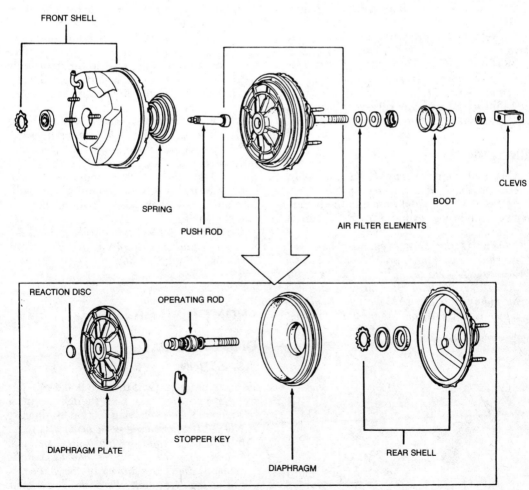

An exploded view of the JKK-type vacuum booster

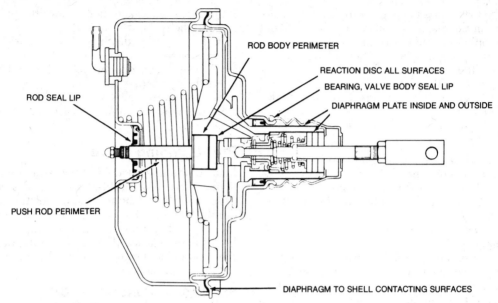

ROD BODY PERIMETER

REACTION DISC ALL SURFACES

BEARING, VALVE BODY SEAL LIP

DIAPHRAGM PLATE INSIDE AND OUTSIDE

ROD SEAL LIP

PUSH ROD PERIMETER

DIAPHRAGM TO SHELL CONTACTING SURFACES

Apply silicone grease to these parts when assembling the JKK vacuum booster

2. Unfasten the valve mounting bolt, if used.

3. Remove the proportioning valve assembly.

NOTE: *If the proportioning valve is defective, it must be replaced as an assembly; it cannot be rebuilt.*

4. Installation is the reverse of removal. Bleed the brake system after it is completed.

Bleeding

CAUTION: *Do not reuse brake fluid which has been bled from the brake system.*

1. Insert a clear vinyl tube into the bleeder plug on the master cylinder or the wheel cylinders.

NOTE: *If the master cylinder has been overhauled or if air is present in it, start the bleeding procedure with the master cylinder. Otherwise (and after bleeding the master cylinder), start with the wheel cylinder which is farthest from the master cylinder.*

Bleed the brakes into a half filled jar of brake fluid

2. Insert the other end of the tube into a jar which is half filled with brake fluid.

3. Have an assistant slowly pump the brake pedal several times. On the last pump, have the assistant hold the pedal to the floor (fully depressed). While the pedal is depressed, open the bleeder plug until fluid starts to run out, then close the plug.

NOTE: *If the brake pedal is depressed too fast, small air bubbles will form in the brake fluid which will be very difficult to remove.*

4. Bleed the cylinder before hydraulic pressure decreases in the cylinder.

5. Repeat this procedure until the air bubbles are removed and then go on to the next wheel cylinder.

CAUTION: *Replenish the brake fluid in the master cylinder reservoir, so that it does not run out during bleeding.*

FRONT DISC BRAKES

Disc Brake Pads

INSPECTION

For proper inspection, the disc brake cylinder (caliper) and the brake pads themselves must be removed. See following section for details.

NOTE: *If a squealing noise occurs from the front brakes while driving a 1982 or later Celica or Supra, check the pad wear indicator. If there are traces of the indicator contacting the rotor (disc), the brake pad must be replaced.*

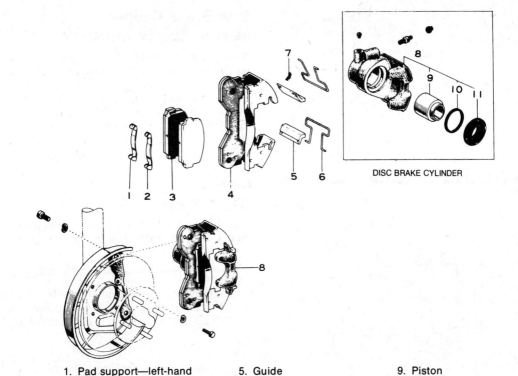

DISC BRAKE CYLINDER

1. Pad support—left-hand
2. Pad support—right-hand
3. Disc brake pad
4. Disc brake caliper mounting
5. Guide
6. Cylinder support spring
7. Clip
8. Caliper assembly
9. Piston
10. Ring
11. Cylinder boot

Front disc brake assembly, 1981 shown. Some clips and springs vary with different models years

REMOVAL AND INSTALLATION

1971–81 Models

1. Remove the hub cap and loosen the lug nuts.

2. Raise the front of the vehicle with a jack and support it with stands on the chassis pads provided.

CAUTION: *Be sure that the car is securely supported. Do not support the car by the lower control arm.*

3. Remove the lug nuts and the wheel.

4. Unfasten the four clips which secure the caliper guides and remove the guides.

5. Remove the disc brake cylinder assembly.

NOTE: *If only the brake pads are to be replaced, do not disconnect the brake line. Just wire the cylinder out of the way.*

6. Remove the brake pads, pad guide plates, anti-rattle springs and the pad support plates.

7. Inspect the pads for waer. If the grooves are worn out of the pads, they will require replacement. Check the pad thickness against the specifications given in the "Brake Specifications" chart later in this chapter. Check all guides and springs for any wear or deformation.

8. Installation is in the reverse order of removal. Bleed the brakes if necessary.

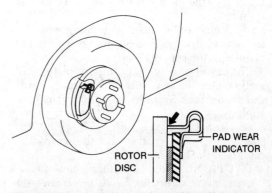

When the front brakes squeal on 1982 and later cars, check the wear indicators

1982 and Later

1. Remove the hub cap and loosen the lug nuts.

2. Jack up the front of the car and safely support it with jackstands.

3. Remove the lug nuts and the wheel.

4. Attach a clear vinyl tube onto the bleeder plug on the brake cylinder, and insert

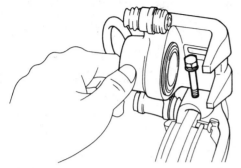

Insert a bolt into the torque plate to secure the cylinder

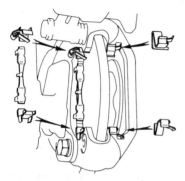

Pad support plate, guide plate and anti-rattle spring location, 1982 and later

the other end into a jar half filled with brake fluid. Bleed off a small amount of brake fluid.

5. Remove the caliper bolt by holding the sliding bushing. Lift up the caliper and insert a bolt into the torque plate hole to secure the cylinder.

6. Remove the brake pads along with the anti-squeal shim, anti-rattle springs, pad guide plates and the support plate.

7. Install a new pad support plate, pad guide plates and new anti-rattle springs. Push the piston back into the cylinder if it is protruding.

8. Install new pads onto each spring, installing the outside pad so that the wear indicator is at the top side.

CAUTION: *When installing new brake pads, make sure your hands are clean—do not allow any grease or oil to touch the contact face of the pads or the brakes will not stop the car properly.*

9. Install the anti-squeal shim toward the inside of the pad.

10. Remove the bolt from the torque plate and lower the brake cylinder.

NOTE: *Insert the cylinder onto the rotor carefully so that the boot is not wedged.*

Torque the cylinder installation bolt to 12–17 ft. lbs. Top up the master cylinder with fresh brake fluid.

Disc Brake Caliper
REMOVAL AND INSTALLATION

If you plan to overhaul the caliper, then you only need to remove the brake cylinder as detailed previously in the "Brake Pad Removal and Installation" section. If the whole assembly must be removed (such as to remove the brake disc), unscrew the two mounting bolts on the back of the caliper mounting frame and pull the whole assembly off of the disc.

OVERHAUL
1971–81 Models

1. Remove the caliper cylinder from the car. (See the appropriate preceding "Brake Pad Removal" procedure).

2. Carefully remove the dust boot from around the cylinder bore.

3. Apply compressed air to the brake line union to force the piston out of its bore. *Be careful: the piston may come out forcefully.*

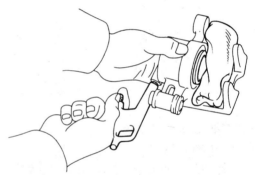

Use compressed air to force the piston out of the cylinder

4. Remove the seal from the cylinder. Check the piston and cylinder bore for wear and/or corrosion. Replace components as necessary.

Assembly is performed in the following order:

1. Coat all components with clean brake fluid.

2. Install the seal and piston in the cylinder bore, after coating them with the rubber lubricant supplied in the rebuilding kit. Seat the piston in the bore with your fingers.

3. Fit the boot into the groove in the cylinder bore.

4. Install the caliper cylinder assembly. Bleed the brake system.

1982 and Later

1. Remove the sliding bushing and boot.

2. Carefully remove the main pin boot with a chisel.

3. Apply compressed air to the brake line union to force the piston out of its bore. *Be careful: the piston may come out forcefully.*

4. Remove the cylinder boot and set ring from the cylinder.

5. Carefully pry the piston seal out of the cylinder bore. Check the piston and cylinder bore for wear and/or corrosion. Clean all metal components in clean brake fluid; replace any rubber part that is visibly worn or damaged.

6. Assembly is performed by following the above assembly procedure for 1971–81 cars. Install a new main pin boot by pressing it on with a 21 mm socket. When installing the cylinder onto the main pin, make sure the boot end is installed into the groove on the main pin.

Brake Disc

REMOVAL AND INSTALLATION

1. Remove the brake pads and the caliper, as detailed in the appropriate preceding section.

2. Check the disc run-out, as detailed following, at this point. Make a note of the results for use during installation.

3. Remove the grease cap from the hub. Remove the cotter pin and the castellated nut.

4. Remove the wheel hub with the brake disc attached.

Perform the disc inspection procedure, as outlined in the following section.

Installation is performed in the following order.

1. Coat the hub oil seal lip with multipurpose grease and install the disc/hub assembly.

2. Adjust the wheel bearing preload, as detailed following.

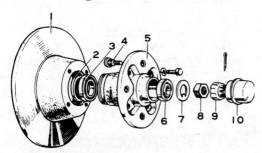

1. Disc
2. Oil seal
3. Tapered roller bearing
4. Hub bolt
5. Hub
6. Tapered roller bearing
7. Washer
8. Nut
9. Adjusting lock cap
10. Grease cap

Brake disc and hub assembly

3. Measure the disc run-out. Check it against the specifications in the "Disc and Pad Specifications" chart and against the figures noted during removal.

NOTE: *If the wheel bearing nut is improperly tightened, disc run-out will be affected.*

4. Install the remainder of the components as outlined in the appropriate preceding section.

5. Bleed the brake system.

6. Road-test the car. Check the wheel bearing preload.

INSPECTION

Examine the disc. If it is worn, warped or scored, it must be replaced. Check the thickness of the disc against the specifications given in the "Disc and Pad Specifications" chart. If it is below specifications, replace it. Use a micrometer to measure the thickness.

The disc run-out should be measured *before* the disc is removed and again, *after* the disc is installed. Use a dial indicator mounted on a stand to determine run-out. If run-out exceeds 0.0006 in. (all models), replace the disc.

NOTE: *Be sure that the wheel bearing nut is properly tightened. If it is not, an inaccurate run-out reading may be obtained. If different run-out readings are obtained with the same disc, between removal and installation, this is probably the cause.*

Wheel Bearings

REMOVAL AND INSTALLATION

1. Remove the caliper and the disc/hub assembly, as previously detailed.

2. If either the disc or the entire hub assembly is to be replaced, unbolt the hub from the disc.

NOTE: *If only the bearings are to be replaced, do not separate the disc and hub.*

3. Using a brass rod as a drift, tap the inner bearing cone out. Remove the oil seal and the inner bearing.

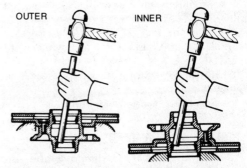

OUTER   INNER

Use a brass drift to tap out the bearing cones

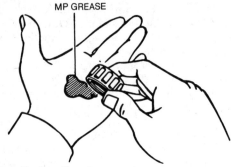

Pack the bearings thoroughly

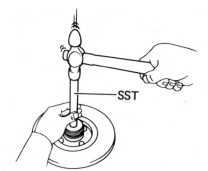

Tap the bearing in evenly with an old socket or bearing installation tool

NOTE: *Throw the old oil seal away.*
4. Drift out the inner bearing cup.
5. Drift out the outer bearing cup.
Inspect the bearings and the hub for signs of wear or damage. Replace components as necessary.

Installation is performed in the following order:

1. Install the inner bearing cup and then the outer bearing cup, by drifting them into place.

CAUTION: *Use care not to cock the bearing cups in the hub.*

2. Pack the bearings, hub inner well and grease cap with multipurpose grease.

3. Install the inner bearing into the hub, using Toyota tool 09608-20011 or an equivalent wheel bearing tool.

4. Carefully install a new oil seal with a soft drift.

5. Install the hub on the spindle. Be sure to install all of the washers and nuts which were removed.

6. Adjust the bearing preload, as detailed following.

7. Install the caliper assembly, as previously detailed.

PRELOAD ADJUSTMENT

1. With the front hub/disc assembly installed, tighten the castellated nut to the torque

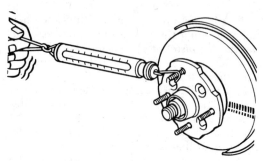

Tighten the nut firmly, then measure preload with spring scale

figure specified in the "Preload Specifications" chart.

2. Rotate the disc back and forth, two or three times, to allow the bearing to seat properly.

3. Loosen the castellated nut until it is only finger-tight.

4. Tighten the nut firmly, using a box wrench. Make sure the disc rotates smoothly.

5. Measure the bearing preload with a spring scale attached to a wheel mounting stud. Check it against the specifications given in the "Preload Specifications" chart.

Preload Specifications

Year	Initial Torque Setting (ft. lbs.)	Preload (oz)
1971-75	19-24	10-22
1976-77	19-24	10-24
1978-80	22	11-24
1981	22	11-24
1982-83	22	11-31

6. Install the cotter pin.
NOTE: *If the hole does not align with the nut (or cap) holes, tighten the nut slightly until it does.*
7. Finish installing the brake components and the wheel.

REAR DISC BRAKES

Disc Brake Pads
INSPECTION

For a quick, semi-accurate inspection of the rear brake pads, look through the hole in the top of the brake cylinder. This inspection will quickly give you a general idea of the condition of the brake pads; if you are in doubt, the disc brake cylinder and the brake pads them-

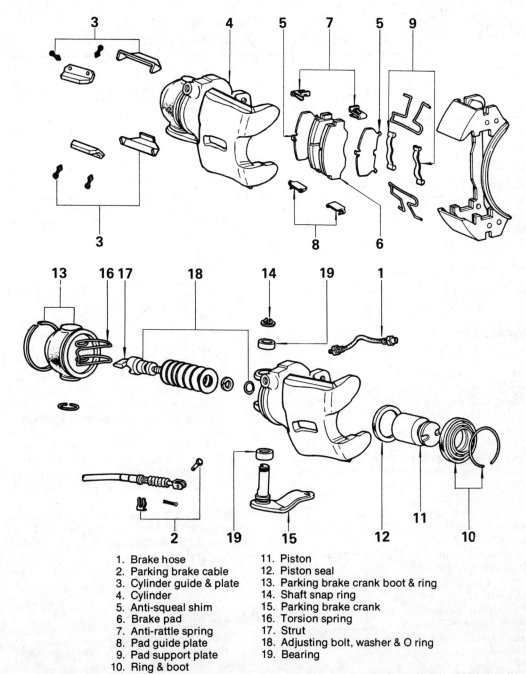

1. Brake hose
2. Parking brake cable
3. Cylinder guide & plate
4. Cylinder
5. Anti-squeal shim
6. Brake pad
7. Anti-rattle spring
8. Pad guide plate
9. Pad support plate
10. Ring & boot
11. Piston
12. Piston seal
13. Parking brake crank boot & ring
14. Shaft snap ring
15. Parking brake crank
16. Torsion spring
17. Strut
18. Adjusting bolt, washer & O ring
19. Bearing

An exploded view of the Supra rear disc brake assembly (top) and the brake cylinder (bottom)

selves will have to be removed for proper inspection.

REMOVAL AND INSTALLATION

1. Perform Steps 1–3 of the "Front Pad Removal" procedure.

2. Pull out the cotter pin and remove the parking brake cable on models up to 1981.

3. Perform Steps 4–8 of the "Front Pad Removal" procedure in the 1971–81 proce-

dure for cars of those years; and perform steps 4–10 in the "1982 and later" procedure for cars of those years.

Disc Brake Calipers
REMOVAL AND INSTALLATION

Removal and installation procedures for the rear calipers are the same as those given for

Brake Specifications

All measurements given are (in.) unless noted

Model	Lug Nut Torque (ft. lbs.)	Master Cylinder Bore	Brake Disc		Brake Drum			Minimum Lining Thickness	
			Minimum Thickness	Maximum Run-Out	Diameter	Max. Machine O/S	Max. Wear Limit	Front	Rear
Celica to 1981	65–86	0.813	0.35①	0.006	9.0	9.08	—	0.04	0.04
Supra to 1981	65–86	0.813	0.45②	0.006	—	—	—	0.04	0.04
Celica 1982–83	66–86	N.A.	0.75	0.006	9.0	9.08	—	0.118	0.039
Supra 1982–83	66–86	N.A.	0.75③	0.006	—	—	—	0.118	0.118

NOTE: Minimum lining thickness is as recommended by the manufacturer. Because of variations in state inspection regulations, the minimum allowable thickness may be different than recommended by the manufacturer.

N.A. Not Available ② Figure given for front disc only; rear is 0.35 in.
① 1978–81; 0.45 ③ Figure given for front disc only; rear is 0.67

the front calipers (don't forget to disconnect the parking brake cable on the rear calipers).

OVERHAUL

Pre-1982 Supras

1. Use a screwdriver to pry out the set ring and then remove the boot.
2. Using the Toyota Special Tool #09719-14010, remove the piston by turning it counterclockwise.
   NOTE: *If you cannot find the special tool, use a little ingenuity and fabricate something from tools which you already have.*
3. Use a screwdriver and carefully pry the piston seal out of the cylinder.
4. Use a screwdriver and remove the parking brake crank boot set ring. Remove the boot.
5. Remove the snap ring from the end of the parking brake shaft.
6. Use a gear puller and remove the parking brake crank.
7. Use a brass drift and punch out the needle roller bearing.
8. Assembly is in the reverse order of disassembly.

1982 and Later

The rear brake cylinder overhaul procedure for these models is the same as the front brake procedure.

REAR DRUM BRAKES

Brake Drums

REMOVAL AND INSTALLATION

1. Remove the hub cap (if used) and loosen the lug nuts. Release the parking brake.

2. Block the front wheels, raise the rear of the car, and support it with jackstands.
   CAUTION: *Support the car securely.*
3. Remove the lug nuts and the wheel.
4. Unfasten the brake drum retaining screws.
5. Tap the drum lightly with a mallet in order to free it. If the drum cannot be removed easily, insert a screwdriver into the hole in the backing plate and hold the automatic adjusting lever away from the adjusting bolt. Using another screwdriver, relieve the brake shoe tension by turning the adjusting bolt clockwise. If the drum still will not come off, use a puller; but first make sure that the parking brake is released.
   CAUTION: *Do not depress the brake pedal once the brake drum has been removed.*
6. Inspect the brake drum as detailed in the following section.
7. Installation is in the reverse order of removal.

INSPECTION

1. Clean the drum.
2. Inspect the drum for scoring, cracks, grooves and out-of-roundness. Replace the

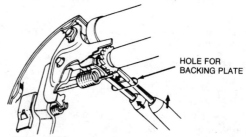

HOLE FOR BACKING PLATE

Backing off the brake shoes to remove the brake drum

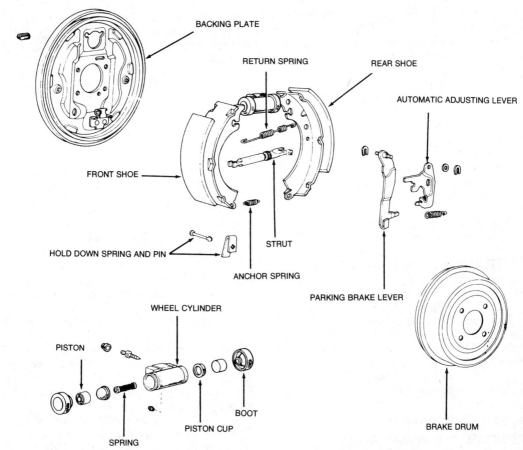

Exploded view of the rear drum brake assembly; '82 and later have a coil-type hold down spring

drum or have it "turned" at a machine or brake specialist shop, as required.

3. Light scoring may be removed by dressing the drum with *fine* emery cloth.

4. Heavy scoring will require the use of a brake drum lathe to turn the drum.

Brake Shoes

REMOVAL AND INSTALLATION

NOTE: *Most replacement brake lining (the friction material attached to the brake shoes) is bonded to the shoes; the replacements are purchased as a complete set. In some cases, you must exchange the old shoes for the new set.*

1. Perform the "Brake Drum Removal" procedure as previously detailed.

2. Unhook the shoe tension springs from the shoes with the aid of a brake spring removing tool.

3. Remove the brake shoe securing springs (pre-1982 models use a clip-type spring; 1982 and later use a coil spring).

4. Disconnect the parking brake cable at the parking brake shoe lever.

5. Withdraw the shoes, complete with the parking brake shoe lever.

6. Unfasten the C-clip and remove the adjuster assembly from the shoes.

Inspect the shoes for wear and scoring. Have the linings replaced if their thickness is less than 0.04 in.

Check the tension springs to see if they are weak, distorted or rusted.

Inspect the teeth on the automatic adjuster wheel for chipping or other damage.

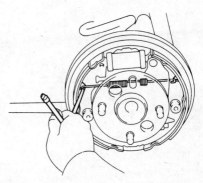

Use a brake spring tool to remove the tension spring

Installation is performed in the following order:

NOTE: *Grease the point of the shoe which slides against the backing plate. Do not get grease on the linings.*

1. Attach the parking brake shoe lever and the automatic adjuster lever to the rear side of the shoe.

2. Fasten the parking brake cable to the lever on the brake shoe.

3. Install the automatic adjuster and fit the tension spring on the adjuster lever.

4. Install the securing spring on the *rear* shoe and then install the securing spring on the *front* shoe.

NOTE: *The tension spring should be installed on the anchor, before performing Step 4.*

5. Hook one end of the tension spring over the rear shoe with the tool used during removal; hook the other end over the front shoe.

CAUTION: *Be sure that the wheel cylinder boots are not being pinched in the ends of the shoes.*

6. Test the automatic adjuster by operating the parking brake shoe lever.

7. Install the drum and adjust the brakes as previously detailed.

Wheel Cylinders

REMOVAL AND INSTALLATION

1. Plug the master cylinder inlet to prevent hydraulic fluid from leaking.

2. Remove the brake drums and shoes as detailed in the appropriate preceding section.

3. Working from behind the backing plate, disconnect the hydraulic line from the wheel cylinder.

4. Unfasten the screws retaining the wheel cylinder and withdraw the cylinder.

Installation is performed in the reverse order of removal. However, once the hydraulic line has been disconnected from the wheel cylinder, the union seat must be replaced. To replace the seat, proceed in the following manner:

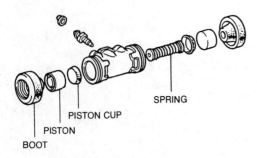

Typical wheel cylinder exploded

BOOT
PISTON
PISTON CUP
SPRING

1. Use a screw extractor with a diameter of 0.1 in. and having reverse threads, to remove the union seat from the wheel cylinder.

2. Drive in the new union seat with a $5/16$ in. bar, used as a drift.

Remember to bleed the brake system after completing wheel cylinder, brake shoe and drum installation.

OVERHAUL

It is not necessary to remove the wheel cylinder from the backing plate if it is only to be inspected or rebuilt.

1. Remove the brake drum and shoes. Remove the wheel cylinder only if it is going to be replaced.

2. Remove the rubber boots from either end of the wheel cylinder.

3. Withdraw the piston and cup assemblies.

4. Take the compression spring out of the wheel cylinder body.

5. Remove the bleeder plug (and ball), if necessary.

Check all components for wear or damage. Inspect the bore for signs of wear, scoring, and/or scuffing. If in doubt, replace or hone the wheel cylinder (with a special hone). The limit for honing a cylinder is 0.005 in. oversize. Wash all the residue from the cylinder bore with clean brake fluid and blow dry.

Assembly is performed in the following order:

1. Soak all components in clean brake fluid, and coat them with the rubber grease supplied in the wheel cylinder rebuilding kit.

2. Install the spring, cups (recesses toward the center), and pistons in the cylinder body, in that order.

3. Insert the boots over the ends of the cylinder.

4. Install the bleeder plug (and ball), if removed.

5. Assemble the brake shoes and install the drum.

Wheel Bearings

REMOVAL AND INSTALLATION

1971–81 Models

1. Remove the rear axle shaft as detailed in Chapter 7.

2. Use a grinder and grind down the bearing inner retainer.

3. Use a hammer and chisel to break the retainer and remove it from the axle shaft.

4. Use a press and press the bearing off the axle shaft.

To install:

1. Press a new bearing onto the axle shaft.

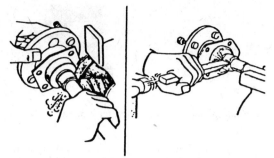

Grind down the bearing inner retainer and then break it off with a hammer and a chisel

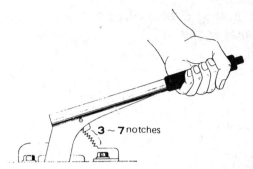

There should be 3–7 notches visable when the parking brake lever is all the way up

2. Heat the new bearing inner retainer to about 300°F (150°C) in an oil bath and then press it onto the axle shaft while it is still hot.

3. Replace the axle shaft.

PARKING BRAKE

Cable

ADJUSTMENT

1. Remove the rear console box and parking brake lever boot.

2. Slowly pull the parking brake lever upward without depressing the button on the end of it.

3. When the lever has reached the end of its travel, look beneath it and count the number of notches (teeth). There should be 3–7 notches visible between the bottom of the unit and the tang on the lever.

4. If the lever requires adjustment, loosen the lock nut and turn the adjusting nut clockwise to decrease the number of notches and counterclockwise to increase the number.

5. When the setting is correct, tighten the lock nut, using care not to disturb the setting of the adjusting nut.

6. Check that the rear wheels are not dragging when the wheels are turned.

7. Reinstall the rear console box and boot.

REMOVAL AND INSTALLATION

1. Remove the rear console box.

2. Remove the cable adjusting nut.

3. Unscrew the four mounting bolts and remove the parking brake lever.

4. Working under the car, disconnect the parking brake cable equalizer.

5. Remove the two cable clamps from each side of the drive shaft tunnel.

6. Remove the rear brakes and then disconnect the parking brake cable from the lever.

7. Remove the cable from the brake backing plate.

8. Installation is in the reverse order of removal.

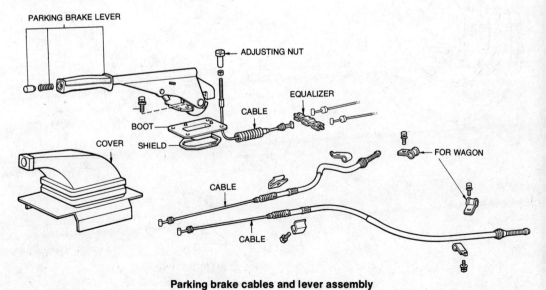

Parking brake cables and lever assembly

Parking Brake Shoes
REPLACEMENT

The parking brakes on rear disc brake-equipped Supras are actually small drum brakes which work inside the brake rotor/hub. Their design and construction is virtually identical to the rear drum service brakes found on the Celica models. Also, replacement shoes/linings are usually bought on an exchange basis, as are most drum-type service brake shoes.

1. Remove the rear disc brake assembly. Hang the caliper from the coil spring with a piece of string so the hose is not stretched.

2. Using pliers, remove the brake return springs. Remove the shoe strut with the springs.

3. Slide out the front brake shoe and remove the shoe adjusting screw set. Remove the tension spring, and remove the shoe.

4. Slide out the rear shoe, and disconnect the parking brake cable from the parking brake shoe lever. Remove the rear brake shoe.

5. Measure the brake shoe lining thickness. Standard thickness is 0.079 in., and minimum allowable thickness is 0.039 in. If the lining is thinner than minimum, replace the brake shoes on *both* wheels (to maintain even

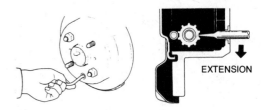

Adjusting parking brake shoe clearance

braking on both wheels). Maximum disc inside diameter is 6.61 in.

6. To reassemble the parking brake, apply non-melting type grease to the sliding surfaces on the back plate as shown. Apply the same grease to the adjusting screw threads.

7. Compress the cable spring and connect the parking brake lever to the cable.

8. Slide the rear brake shoe between the hold-down spring seat and the backing plate.

CAUTION: *Do not allow oil or grease to contact the faces of the brake linings.*

9. Install the tension spring to the rear shoe, and connect the front shoe to the tension spring. Install the shoe adjusting screw set betweeen the front and rear shoes. Slide in the front shoe between the shoe hold-down spring seat and the backing plate.

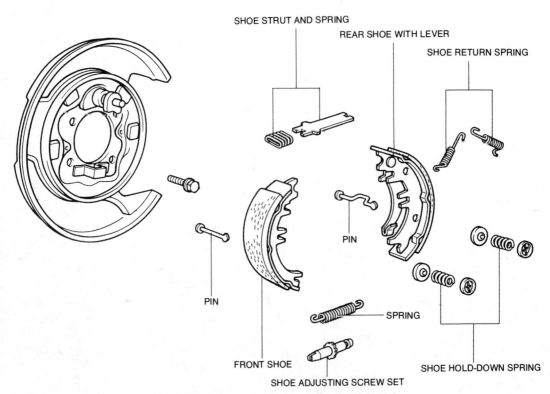

Parking brake assembly, 4-wheel disc brake models

10. Install the front shoe return spring, and also the strut with the spring.

11. Install the brake disc assembly by aligning the groove on the rear axle flange with the service hole on the disc. You may have to back off the adjuster to install the hub.

12. Temporarily install the disc hub nuts. From the front side of the hub, turn the adjuster star wheel and expand the shoes until the disc cannot be turned by hand. Back off the adjuster wheel about 8 turns.

13. Inspect and adjust the parking brake lever travel.

Troubleshooting

This section is designed to aid in the quick, accurate diagnosis of automotive problems. While automotive repairs can be made by many people, accurate troubleshooting is a rare skill for the amateur and professional alike.

In its simplest state, troubleshooting is an exercise in logic. It is essential to realize that an automobile is really composed of a series of systems. Some of these systems are interrelated; others are not. Automobiles operate within a framework of logical rules and physical laws, and the key to troubleshooting is a good understanding of all the automotive systems.

This section breaks the car or truck down into its component systems, allowing the problem to be isolated. The charts and diagnostic road maps list the most common problems and the most probable causes of trouble. Obviously it would be impossible to list every possible problem that could happen along with every possible cause, but it will locate MOST problems and eliminate a lot of unnecessary guesswork. The systematic format will locate problems within a given system, but, because many automotive systems are interrelated, the solution to your particular problem may be found in a number of systems on the car or truck.

USING THE TROUBLESHOOTING CHARTS

This book contains all of the specific information that the average do-it-yourself mechanic needs to repair and maintain his or her car or truck. The troubleshooting charts are designed to be used in conjunction with the specific procedures and information in the text. For instance, troubleshooting a point-type ignition system is fairly standard for all models, but you may be directed to the text to find procedures for troubleshooting an individual type of electronic ignition. You will also have to refer to the specification charts throughout the book for specifications applicable to your car or truck.

TOOLS AND EQUIPMENT

The tools illustrated in Chapter 1 (plus two more diagnostic pieces) will be adequate to troubleshoot most problems. The two other tools needed are a voltmeter and an ohmmeter. These can be purchased separately or in combination, known as a VOM meter.

In the event that other tools are required, they will be noted in the procedures.

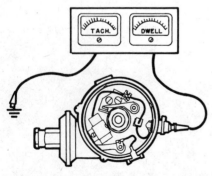

Tach-dwell hooked-up to distributor

Troubleshooting Engine Problems
See Chapters 2, 3, 4 for more information and service procedures.

Index to Systems

System	To Test	Group
Battery	Engine need not be running	1
Starting system	Engine need not be running	2
Primary electrical system	Engine need not be running	3
Secondary electrical system	Engine need not be running	4
Fuel system	Engine need not be running	5
Engine compression	Engine need not be running	6
Engine vacuum	Engine must be running	7
Secondary electrical system	Engine must be running	8
Valve train	Engine must be running	9
Exhaust system	Engine must be running	10
Cooling system	Engine must be running	11
Engine lubrication	Engine must be running	12

Index to Problems

Problem: Symptom	Begin at Specific Diagnosis, Number ___
Engine Won't Start:	
Starter doesn't turn	1.1, 2.1
Starter turns, engine doesn't	2.1
Starter turns engine very slowly	1.1, 2.4
Starter turns engine normally	3.1, 4.1
Starter turns engine very quickly	6.1
Engine fires intermittently	4.1
Engine fires consistently	5.1, 6.1
Engine Runs Poorly:	
Hard starting	8.1, 4.1, 5.1, 8.1
Rough idle	4.1, 5.1, 8.1
Stalling	3.1, 4.1, 5.1, 8.1
Engine dies at high speeds	4.1, 5.1
Hesitation (on acceleration from standing stop)	5.1, 8.1
Poor pickup	4.1, 5.1, 8.1
Lack of power	3.1, 4.1, 5.1, 8.1
Backfire through the carburetor	4.1, 8.1, 9.1
Backfire through the exhaust	4.1, 8.1, 9.1
Blue exhaust gases	6.1, 7.1
Black exhaust gases	5.1
Running on (after the ignition is shut off)	3.1, 8.1
Susceptible to moisture	4.1
Engine misfires under load	4.1, 7.1, 8.4, 9.1
Engine misfires at speed	4.1, 8.4
Engine misfires at idle	3.1, 4.1, 5.1, 7.1, 8.4

Sample Section

Test and Procedure	Results and Indications	Proceed to
4.1—Check for spark: Hold each spark plug wire approximately ¼″ from ground with gloves or a heavy, dry rag. Crank the engine and observe the spark.	If no spark is evident:	4.2
	If spark is good in some cases:	4.3
	If spark is good in all cases:	4.6

Specific Diagnosis

This section is arranged so that following each test, instructions are given to proceed to another, until a problem is diagnosed.

Section 1—Battery

Test and Procedure	Results and Indications	Proceed to
1.1—Inspect the battery visually for case condition (corrosion, cracks) and water level.	If case is cracked, replace battery:	**1.4**
	If the case is intact, remove corrosion with a solution of baking soda and water (**CAUTION**: *do not get the solution into the battery*), and fill with water:	**1.2**

DIRT ON TOP OF BATTERY

CORROSION

PLUGGED VENT

LOOSE CABLE OR POSTS

CRACKS

LOW WATER LEVEL

Inspect the battery case

1.2—Check the battery cable connections: Insert a screwdriver between the battery post and the cable clamp. Turn the headlights on high beam, and observe them as the screwdriver is gently twisted to ensure good metal to metal contact.	If the lights brighten, remove and clean the clamp and post; coat the post with petroleum jelly, install and tighten the clamp:	**1.4**
	If no improvement is noted:	**1.3**

TESTING BATTERY CABLE CONNECTIONS USING A SCREWDRIVER

1.3—Test the state of charge of the battery using an individual cell tester or hydrometer.	If indicated, charge the battery. **NOTE:** *If no obvious reason exists for the low state of charge (i.e., battery age, prolonged storage)*, *proceed to:*	**1.4**

°F

ADD THIS NUMBER TO THE HYDROMETER READING TO OBTAIN THE CORRECTED SPECIFIC GRAVITY

SUBTRACT THIS NUMBER FROM THE HYDROMETER READING TO OBTAIN THE CORRECTED SPECIFIC GRAVITY

Specific Gravity (@ 80° F.)

Minimum	Battery Charge
1.260	100% Charged
1.230	75% Charged
1.200	50% Charged
1.170	25% Charged
1.140	Very Little Power Left
1.110	Completely Discharged

The effects of temperature on battery specific gravity (left) and amount of battery charge in relation to specific gravity (right)

1.4—Visually inspect battery cables for cracking, bad connection to ground, or bad connection to starter.	If necessary, tighten connections or replace the cables:	**2.1**

Section 2—Starting System
See Chapter 3 for service procedures

Test and Procedure	Results and Indications	Proceed to

Note: Tests in Group 2 are performed with coil high tension lead disconnected to prevent accidental starting.

Test and Procedure	Results and Indications	Proceed to
2.1—Test the starter motor and solenoid: Connect a jumper from the battery post of the solenoid (or relay) to the starter post of the solenoid (or relay).	If starter turns the engine normally:	**2.2**
	If the starter buzzes, or turns the engine very slowly:	**2.4**
	If no response, replace the solenoid (or relay).	**3.1**
	If the starter turns, but the engine doesn't, ensure that the flywheel ring gear is intact. If the gear is undamaged, replace the starter drive.	**3.1**
2.2—Determine whether ignition override switches are functioning properly (clutch start switch, neutral safety switch), by connecting a jumper across the switch(es), and turning the ignition switch to "start".	If starter operates, adjust or replace switch:	**3.1**
	If the starter doesn't operate:	**2.3**
2.3—Check the ignition switch "start" position: Connect a 12V test lamp or voltmeter between the starter post of the solenoid (or relay) and ground. Turn the ignition switch to the "start" position, and jiggle the key.	If the lamp doesn't light or the meter needle doesn't move when the switch is turned, check the ignition switch for loose connections, cracked insulation, or broken wires. Repair or replace as necessary:	**3.1**
	If the lamp flickers or needle moves when the key is jiggled, replace the ignition switch.	**3.3**

Checking the ignition switch "start" position

STARTER RELAY (IF EQUIPPED)

Test and Procedure	Results and Indications	Proceed to
2.4—Remove and bench test the starter, according to specifications in the engine electrical section.	If the starter does not meet specifications, repair or replace as needed:	**3.1**
	If the starter is operating properly:	**2.5**
2.5—Determine whether the engine can turn freely: Remove the spark plugs, and check for water in the cylinders. Check for water on the dipstick, or oil in the radiator. Attempt to turn the engine using an 18″ flex drive and socket on the crankshaft pulley nut or bolt.	If the engine will turn freely only with the spark plugs out, and hydrostatic lock (water in the cylinders) is ruled out, check valve timing:	**9.2**
	If engine will not turn freely, and it is known that the clutch and transmission are free, the engine must be disassembled for further evaluation:	**Chapter 3**

Section 3—Primary Electrical System

Test and Procedure	Results and Indications	Proceed to
3.1—Check the ignition switch "on" position: Connect a jumper wire between the distributor side of the coil and ground, and a 12V test lamp between the switch side of the coil and ground. Remove the high tension lead from the coil. Turn the ignition switch on and jiggle the key.	If the lamp lights:	**3.2**
	If the lamp flickers when the key is jiggled, replace the ignition switch:	**3.3**
	If the lamp doesn't light, check for loose or open connections. If none are found, remove the ignition switch and check for continuity. If the switch is faulty, replace it:	**3.3**

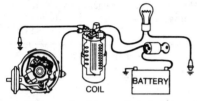

Checking the ignition switch "on" position

3.2—Check the ballast resistor or resistance wire for an open circuit, using an ohmmeter. See Chapter 3 for specific tests.	Replace the resistor or resistance wire if the resistance is zero. **NOTE:** *Some ignition systems have no ballast resistor.*	**3.3**

 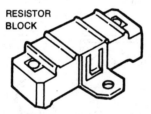

RESISTOR BLOCK

CALIBRATED RESISTANCE LEAD

Two types of resistors

3.3—On point-type ignition systems, visually inspect the breaker points for burning, pitting or excessive wear. Gray coloring of the point contact surfaces is normal. Rotate the crankshaft until the contact heel rests on a high point of the distributor cam and adjust the point gap to specifications. On electronic ignition models, remove the distributor cap and visually inspect the armature. Ensure that the armature pin is in place, and that the armature is on tight and rotates when the engine is cranked. Make sure there are no cracks, chips or rounded edges on the armature.	If the breaker points are intact, clean the contact surfaces with fine emery cloth, and adjust the point gap to specifications. If the points are worn, replace them. On electronic systems, replace any parts which appear defective. If condition persists:	**3.4**

Test and Procedure	Results and Indications	Proceed to
3.4—On point-type ignition systems, connect a dwell-meter between the distributor primary lead and ground. Crank the engine and observe the point dwell angle. On electronic ignition systems, conduct a stator (magnetic pickup assembly) test. See Chapter 3.	On point-type systems, adjust the dwell angle if necessary. **NOTE:** *Increasing the point gap decreases the dwell angle and vice-versa.*	**3.6**
	If the dwell meter shows little or no reading;	**3.5**
	On electronic ignition systems, if the stator is bad, replace the stator. If the stator is good, proceed to the other tests in Chapter 3.	

WIDE GAP   NARROW GAP

CLOSE   OPEN   SMALL DWELL   LARGE DWELL

NORMAL DWELL   INSUFFICIENT DWELL   EXCESSIVE DWELL

Dwell is a function of point gap

3.5—On the point-type ignition systems, check the condenser for short: connect an ohmeter across the condenser body and the pigtail lead.	If any reading other than infinite is noted, replace the condenser	**3.6**

Checking the condenser for short

3.6—Test the coil primary resistance: On point-type ignition systems, connect an ohmmeter across the coil primary terminals, and read the resistance on the low scale. Note whether an external ballast resistor or resistance wire is used. On electronic ignition systems, test the coil primary resistance as in Chapter 3.	Point-type ignition coils utilizing ballast resistors or resistance wires should have approximately 1.0 ohms resistance. Coils with internal resistors should have approximately 4.0 ohms resistance. If values far from the above are noted, replace the coil.	**4.1**

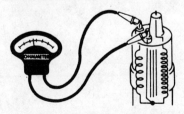

Check the coil primary resistance

Section 4—Secondary Electrical System
See Chapters 2–3 for service procedures

Test and Procedure	Results and Indications	Proceed to
4.1—Check for spark: Hold each spark plug wire approximately ¼″ from ground with gloves or a heavy, dry rag. Crank the engine, and observe the spark.	If no spark is evident:	**4.2**
	If spark is good in some cylinders:	**4.3**
	If spark is good in all cylinders:	**4.6**

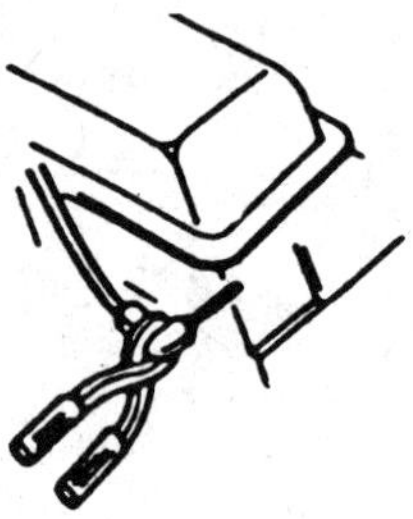

Check for spark at the plugs

4.2—Check for spark at the coil high tension lead: Remove the coil high tension lead from the distributor and position it approximately ¼″ from ground. Crank the engine and observe spark. **CAUTION:** *This test should not be performed on engines equipped with electronic ignition.*	If the spark is good and consistent:	**4.3**
	If the spark is good but intermittent, test the primary electrical system starting at 3.3:	**3.3**
	If the spark is weak or non-existent, replace the coil high tension lead, clean and tighten all connections and retest. If no improvement is noted:	**4.4**
4.3—Visually inspect the distributor cap and rotor for burned or corroded contacts, cracks, carbon tracks, or moisture. Also check the fit of the rotor on the distributor shaft (where applicable).	If moisture is present, dry thoroughly, and retest per 4.1:	**4.1**
	If burned or excessively corroded contacts, cracks, or carbon tracks are noted, replace the defective part(s) and retest per 4.1:	**4.1**
	If the rotor and cap appear intact, or are only slightly corroded, clean the contacts thoroughly (including the cap towers and spark plug wire ends) and retest per 4.1:	
	If the spark is good in all cases:	**4.6**
	If the spark is poor in all cases:	**4.5**

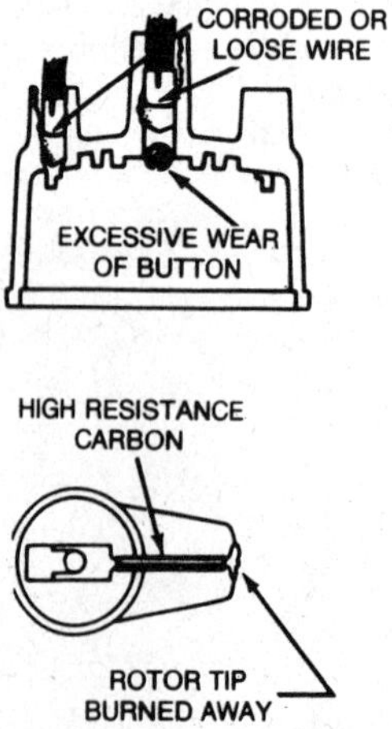

CORRODED OR LOOSE WIRE

EXCESSIVE WEAR OF BUTTON

HIGH RESISTANCE CARBON

ROTOR TIP BURNED AWAY

Inspect the distributor cap and rotor

CHILTON'S
AUTO BODY REPAIR TIPS

EASY STEP-BY-STEP TIPS FROM PROS

Tools and Materials • Step-by-Step Illustrated Procedures
How To Repair Dents, Scratches and Rust Holes
Spray Painting and Refinishing Tips

With a little practice, basic body repair procedures can be mastered by any do-it-yourself mechanic. The step-by-step repairs shown here can be applied to almost any type of auto body repair.

TOOLS & MATERIALS

You may already have basic tools, such as hammers and electric drills. Other tools unique to body repair — body hammers, grinding attachments, sanding blocks, dent puller, half-round plastic file and plastic spreaders — are relatively inexpensive and can be obtained wherever auto parts or auto body repair parts are sold. Portable air compressors and paint spray guns can be purchased or rented.

Auto Body Repair Kits

The best and most often used products are available to the do-it-yourselfer in kit form, from major manufacturers of auto body repair products. The same manufacturers also merchandise the individual products for use by pros.

Kits are available to make a wide variety of repairs, including holes, dents and scratches and fiberglass, and offer the advantage of buying the materials you'll need for the job. There is little waste or chance of materials going bad from not being used. Many kits may also contain basic body-working tools such as body files, sanding blocks and spreaders. Check the contents of the kit before buying your tools.

BODY REPAIR TIPS

Safety

Many of the products associated with auto body repair and refinishing contain toxic chemicals. Read all labels before opening containers and store them in a safe place and manner.

• Wear eye protection (safety goggles) when using power tools or when performing any operation that involves the removal of any type of material.

• Wear lung protection (disposable mask or respirator) when grinding, sanding or painting.

Sanding

1 Sand off paint before using a dent puller. When using a non-adhesive sanding disc, cover the back of the disc with an overlapping layer or two of masking tape and trim the edges. The disc will last considerably longer.

2 Use the circular motion of the sanding disc to grind *into* the edge of the repair. Grinding or sanding away from the jagged edge will only tear the sandpaper.

3 Use the palm of your hand flat on the panel to detect high and low spots. Do not use your fingertips. Slide your hand slowly back and forth.

WORKING WITH BODY FILLER

Mixing The Filler

Cleanliness and proper mixing and application are extremely important. Use a clean piece of plastic or glass or a disposable artist's palette to mix body filler.

1 Allow plenty of time and follow directions. No useful purpose will be served by adding more hardener to make it cure (set-up) faster. Less hardener means more curing time, but the mixture dries harder; more hardener means less curing time but a softer mixture.

2 Both the hardener and the filler should be thoroughly kneaded or stirred before mixing. Hardener should be a solid paste and dispense like thin toothpaste. Body filler should be smooth, and free of lumps or thick spots.

Getting the proper amount of hardener in the filler is the trickiest part of preparing the filler. Use the same amount of hardener in cold or warm weather. For contour filler (thick coats), a bead of hardener twice the diameter of the filler is about right. There's about a 15% margin on either side, but, if in doubt use less hardener.

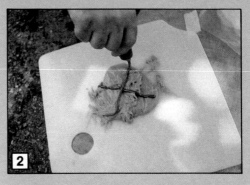

3 Mix the body filler and hardener by wiping across the mixing surface, picking the mixture up and wiping it again. Colder weather requires longer mixing times. Do not mix in a circular motion; this will trap air bubbles which will become holes in the cured filler.

Applying The Filler

1 For best results, filler should not be applied over ¼″ thick.

Apply the filler in several coats. Build it up to above the level of the repair surface so that it can be sanded or grated down.

The first coat of filler must be pressed on with a firm wiping motion.

Apply the filler in one direction only. Working the filler back and forth will either pull it off the metal or trap air bubbles.

REPAIRING DENTS

Before you start, take a few minutes to study the damaged area. Try to visualize the shape of the panel before it was damaged. If the damage is on the left fender, look at the right fender and use it as a guide. If there is access to the panel from behind, you can reshape it with a body hammer. If not, you'll have to use a dent puller. Go slowly and work the metal a little at a time. Get the panel as straight as possible before applying filler.

1 This dent is typical of one that can be pulled out or hammered out from behind. Remove the headlight cover, headlight assembly and turn signal housing.

2 Drill a series of holes ½ the size of the end of the dent puller along the stress line. Make some trial pulls and assess the results. If necessary, drill more holes and try again. Do not hurry.

3 If possible, use a body hammer and block to shape the metal back to its original contours. Get the metal back as close to its original shape as possible. Don't depend on body filler to fill dents.

4 Using an 80-grit grinding disc on an electric drill, grind the paint from the surrounding area down to bare metal. Use a new grinding pad to prevent heat buildup that will warp metal.

5 The area should look like this when you're finished grinding. Knock the drill holes in and tape over small openings to keep plastic filler out.

6 Mix the body filler (see Body Repair Tips). Spread the body filler evenly over the entire area (see Body Repair Tips). Be sure to cover the area completely.

7 Let the body filler dry until the surface can just be scratched with your fingernail. Knock the high spots from the body filler with a body file ("Cheesegrater"). Check frequently with the palm of your hand for high and low spots.

8 Check to be sure that trim pieces that will be installed later will fit exactly. Sand the area with 40-grit paper.

9 If you wind up with low spots, you may have to apply another layer of filler.

10 Knock the high spots off with 40-grit paper. When you are satisfied with the contours of the repair, apply a thin coat of filler to cover pin holes and scratches.

11 Block sand the area with 40-grit paper to a smooth finish. Pay particular attention to body lines and ridges that must be well-defined.

12 Sand the area with 400 paper and then finish with a scuff pad. The finished repair is ready for priming and painting (see Painting Tips).

Materials and photos courtesy of Ritt Jones Auto Body, Prospect Park, PA.

REPAIRING RUST HOLES

There are many ways to repair rust holes. The fiberglass cloth kit shown here is one of the most cost efficient for the owner because it provides a strong repair that resists cracking and moisture and is relatively easy to use. It can be used on large and small holes (with or without backing) and can be applied over contoured areas. Remember, however, that short of replacing an entire panel, no repair is a guarantee that the rust will not return.

1 Remove any trim that will be in the way. Clean away all loose debris. Cut away all the rusted metal. But be sure to leave enough metal to retain the contour or body shape.

2 Grind away all traces of rust with a 24-grit grinding disc. Be sure to grind back 3-4 inches from the edge of the hole down to bare metal and be sure all traces of paint, primer and rust are removed.

3 Block sand the area with 80 or 100 grit sandpaper to get a clear, shiny surface and feathered paint edge. Tap the edges of the hole inward with a ball peen hammer.

4 If you are going to use release film, cut a piece about 2-3″ larger than the area you have sanded. Place the film over the repair and mark the sanded area on the film. Avoid any unnecessary wrinkling of the film.

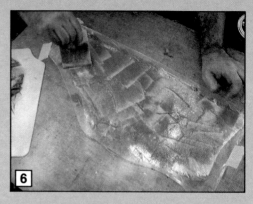

5 Cut 2 pieces of fiberglass matte to match the shape of the repair. One piece should be about 1″ smaller than the sanded area and the second piece should be 1″ smaller than the first. Mix enough filler and hardener to saturate the fiberglass material (see Body Repair Tips).

6 Lay the release sheet on a flat surface and spread an even layer of filler, large enough to cover the repair. Lay the smaller piece of fiberglass cloth in the center of the sheet and spread another layer of filler over the fiberglass cloth. Repeat the operation for the larger piece of cloth.

7 Place the repair material over the repair area, with the release film facing outward. Use a spreader and work from the center outward to smooth the material, following the body contours. Be sure to remove all air bubbles.

8 Wait until the repair has dried tack-free and peel off the release sheet. The ideal working temperature is 60°-90° F. Cooler or warmer temperatures or high humidity may require additional curing time. Wait longer, if in doubt.

9

9 Sand and feather-edge the entire area. The initial sanding can be done with a sanding disc on an electric drill if care is used. Finish the sanding with a block sander. Low spots can be filled with body filler; this may require several applications.

10

10 When the filler can just be scratched with a fingernail, knock the high spots down with a body file and smooth the entire area with 80-grit. Feather the filled areas into the surrounding areas.

11

11 When the area is sanded smooth, mix some topcoat and hardener and apply it directly with a spreader. This will give a smooth finish and prevent the glass matte from showing through the paint.

12

12 Block sand the topcoat smooth with finishing sandpaper (200 grit), and 400 grit. The repair is ready for masking, priming and painting (see Painting Tips).

Materials and photos courtesy Marson Corporation, Chelsea, Massachusetts

PAINTING TIPS

Preparation

1 SANDING — Use a 400 or 600 grit wet or dry sandpaper. Wet-sand the area with a 1/4 sheet of sandpaper soaked in clean water. Keep the paper wet while sanding. Sand the area until the repaired area tapers into the original finish.

2 CLEANING — Wash the area to be painted thoroughly with water and a clean rag. Rinse it thoroughly and wipe the surface dry until you're sure it's completely free of dirt, dust, fingerprints, wax, detergent or other foreign matter.

3 MASKING — Protect any areas you don't want to overspray by covering them with masking tape and newspaper. Be careful not get fingerprints on the area to be painted.

4 PRIMING — All exposed metal should be primed before painting. Primer protects the metal and provides an excellent surface for paint adhesion. When the primer is dry, wet-sand the area again with 600 grit wet-sandpaper. Clean the area again after sanding.

4

Painting Techniques

P aint applied from either a spray gun or a spray can (for small areas) will provide good results. Experiment on an old piece of metal to get the right combination before you begin painting.

SPRAYING VISCOSITY (SPRAY GUN ONLY) — Paint should be thinned to spraying viscosity according to the directions on the can. Use only the recommended thinner or reducer and the same amount of reduction regardless of temperature.

AIR PRESSURE (SPRAY GUN ONLY) — This is extremely important. Be sure you are using the proper recommended pressure.

TEMPERATURE — The surface to be painted should be approximately the same temperature as the surrounding air. Applying warm paint to a cold surface, or vice versa, will completely upset the paint characteristics.

THICKNESS — Spray with smooth strokes. In general, the thicker the coat of paint, the longer the drying time. Apply several thin coats about 30 seconds apart. The paint should remain wet long enough to flow out and no longer; heavier coats will only produce sags or wrinkles. Spray a light (fog) coat, followed by heavier color coats.

DISTANCE — The ideal spraying distance is 8″-12″ from the gun or can to the surface. Shorter distances will produce ripples, while greater distances will result in orange peel, dry film and poor color match and loss of material due to overspray.

OVERLAPPING — The gun or can should be kept at right angles to the surface at all times. Work to a wet edge at an even speed, using a 50% overlap and direct the center of the spray at the lower or nearest edge of the previous stroke.

RUBBING OUT (BLENDING) FRESH PAINT — Let the paint dry thoroughly. Runs or imperfections can be sanded out, primed and repainted.

Don't be in too big a hurry to remove the masking. This only produces paint ridges. When the finish has dried for at least a week, apply a small amount of fine grade rubbing compound with a clean, wet cloth. Use lots of water and blend the new paint with the surrounding area.

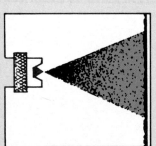

WRONG

Thin coat. Stroke too fast, not enough overlap, gun too far away.

CORRECT

Medium coat. Proper distance, good stroke, proper overlap.

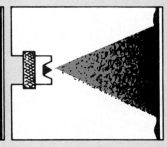

WRONG

Heavy coat. Stroke too slow, too much overlap, gun too close.

Test and Procedure	Results and Indications	Proceed to
4.4—Check the coil secondary resistance: On point-type systems connect an ohmmeter across the distributor side of the coil and the coil tower. Read the resistance on the high scale of the ohmmeter. On electronic ignition systems, see Chapter 3 for specific tests.	The resistance of a satisfactory coil should be between 4,000 and 10,000 ohms. If resistance is considerably higher (i.e., 40,000 ohms) replace the coil and retest per 4.1. **NOTE:** *This does not apply to high performance coils.*	

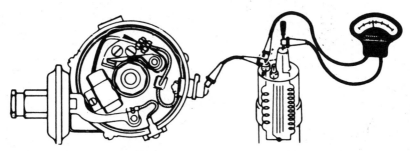

Testing the coil secondary resistance

4.5—Visually inspect the spark plug wires for cracking or brittleness. Ensure that no two wires are positioned so as to cause induction firing (adjacent and parallel). Remove each wire, one by one, and check resistance with an ohmmeter.	Replace any cracked or brittle wires. If any of the wires are defective, replace the entire set. Replace any wires with excessive resistance (over $8000\,\Omega$ per foot for suppression wire), and separate any wires that might cause induction firing.	**4.6**

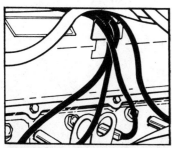

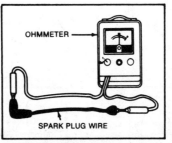

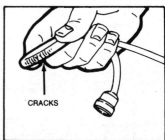

Misfiring can be the result of spark plug leads to adjacent, consecutively firing cylinders running parallel and too close together	**On point-type ignition systems, check the spark plug wires as shown. On electronic ignitions, do not remove the wire from the distributor cap terminal; instead, test through the cap**	**Spark plug wires can be checked visually by bending them in a loop over your finger. This will reveal any cracks, burned or broken insulation. Any wire with cracked insulation should be replaced**

4.6—Remove the spark plugs, noting the cylinders from which they were removed, and evaluate according to the color photos in the middle of this book.	See following.	**See following.**

Test and Procedure	Results and Indications	Proceed to

4.7—Examine the location of all the plugs.

The following diagrams illustrate some of the conditions that the location of plugs will reveal.

4.8

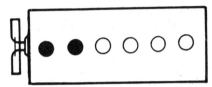

Two adjacent plugs are fouled in a 6-cylinder engine, 4-cylinder engine or either bank of a V-8. This is probably due to a blown head gasket between the two cylinders

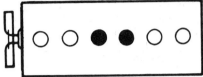

The two center plugs in a 6-cylinder engine are fouled. Raw fuel may be "boiled" out of the carburetor into the intake manifold after the engine is shut-off. Stop-start driving can also foul the center plugs, due to overly rich mixture. Proper float level, a new float needle and seat or use of an insulating spacer may help this problem

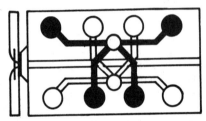

An unbalanced carburetor is indicated. Following the fuel flow on this particular design shows that the cylinders fed by the right-hand barrel are fouled from overly rich mixture, while the cylinders fed by the left-hand barrel are normal

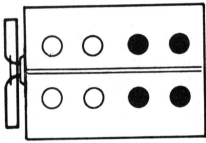

If the four rear plugs are overheated, a cooling system problem is suggested. A thorough cleaning of the cooling system may restore coolant circulation and cure the problem

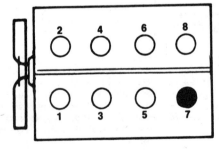

Finding one plug overheated may indicate an intake manifold leak near the affected cylinder. If the overheated plug is the second of two adjacent, consecutively firing plugs, it could be the result of ignition cross-firing. Separating the leads to these two plugs will eliminate cross-fire

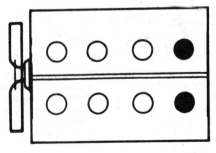

Occasionally, the two rear plugs in large, lightly used V-8's will become oil fouled. High oil consumption and smoky exhaust may also be noticed. It is probably due to plugged oil drain holes in the rear of the cylinder head, causing oil to be sucked in around the valve stems. This usually occurs in the rear cylinders first, because the engine slants that way

Test and Procedure	Results and Indications	Proceed to
4.8—Determine the static ignition timing. Using the crankshaft pulley timing marks as a guide, locate top dead center on the compression stroke of the number one cylinder.	The rotor should be pointing toward the No. 1 tower in the distributor cap, and, on electronic ignitions, the armature spoke for that cylinder should be lined up with the stator.	**4.8**
4.9—Check coil polarity: Connect a voltmeter negative lead to the coil high tension lead, and the positive lead to ground (**NOTE:** *Reverse the hook-up for positive ground systems*). Crank the engine momentarily. **Checking coil polarity**	If the voltmeter reads up-scale, the polarity is correct: If the voltmeter reads down-scale, reverse the coil polarity (switch the primary leads):	**5.1** **5.1**

Section 5—Fuel System
See Chapter 4 for service procedures

Test and Procedure	Results and Indications	Proceed to
5.1—Determine that the air filter is functioning efficiently: Hold paper elements up to a strong light, and attempt to see light through the filter.	Clean permanent air filters in solvent (or manufacturer's recommendation), and allow to dry. Replace paper elements through which light cannot be seen:	**5.2**
5.2—Determine whether a flooding condition exists: Flooding is identified by a strong gasoline odor, and excessive gasoline present in the throttle bore(s) of the carburetor. **If the engine floods repeatedly, check the choke butterfly flap**	If flooding is not evident: If flooding is evident, permit the gasoline to dry for a few moments and restart. If flooding doesn't recur: If flooding is persistent:	**5.3** **5.7** **5.5**
5.3—Check that fuel is reaching the carburetor: Detach the fuel line at the carburetor inlet. Hold the end of the line in a cup (not styrofoam), and crank the engine. **Check the fuel pump by disconnecting the output line (fuel pump-to-carburetor) at the carburetor and operating the starter briefly**	If fuel flows smoothly: If fuel doesn't flow (**NOTE:** *Make sure that there is fuel in the tank*), or flows erratically:	**5.7** **5.4**

Test and Procedure	Results and Indications	Proceed to
5.4—Test the fuel pump: Disconnect all fuel lines from the fuel pump. Hold a finger over the input fitting, crank the engine (with electric pump, turn the ignition or pump on); and feel for suction.	If suction is evident, blow out the fuel line to the tank with low pressure compressed air until bubbling is heard from the fuel filler neck. Also blow out the carburetor fuel line (both ends disconnected):	5.7
	If no suction is evident, replace or repair the fuel pump: NOTE: *Repeated oil fouling of the spark plugs, or a no-start condition, could be the result of a ruptured vacuum booster pump diaphragm, through which oil or gasoline is being drawn into the intake manifold (where applicable).*	5.7
5.5—Occasionally, small specks of dirt will clog the small jets and orifices in the carburetor. With the engine cold, hold a flat piece of wood or similar material over the carburetor, where possible, and crank the engine.	If the engine starts, but runs roughly the engine is probably not run enough. If the engine won't start:	5.9
5.6—Check the needle and seat: Tap the carburetor in the area of the needle and seat.	If flooding stops, a gasoline additive (e.g., Gumout) will often cure the problem:	5.7
	If flooding continues, check the fuel pump for excessive pressure at the carburetor (according to specifications). If the pressure is normal, the needle and seat must be removed and checked, and/or the float level adjusted:	5.7
5.7—Test the accelerator pump by looking into the throttle bores while operating the throttle.	If the accelerator pump appears to be operating normally:	5.8
	If the accelerator pump is not operating, the pump must be reconditioned. Where possible, service the pump with the carburetor(s) installed on the engine. If necessary, remove the carburetor. Prior to removal:	5.8
5.8—Determine whether the carburetor main fuel system is functioning: Spray a commercial starting fluid into the carburetor while attempting to start the engine.	If the engine starts, runs for a few seconds, and dies:	5.9
	If the engine doesn't start:	6.1

Check for gas at the carburetor by looking down the carburetor throat while someone moves the accelerator

Test and Procedure	Results and Indications	Proceed to
5.9—Uncommon fuel system malfunctions: See below:	If the problem is solved: If the problem remains, remove and recondition the carburetor.	**6.1**

Condition	Indication	Test	Prevailing Weather Conditions	Remedy
Vapor lock	Engine will not restart shortly after running.	Cool the components of the fuel system until the engine starts. Vapor lock can be cured faster by draping a wet cloth over a mechanical fuel pump.	Hot to very hot	Ensure that the exhaust manifold heat control valve is operating. Check with the vehicle manufacturer for the recommended solution to vapor lock on the model in question.
Carburetor icing	Engine will not idle, stalls at low speeds.	Visually inspect the throttle plate area of the throttle bores for frost.	High humidity, 32–40° F.	Ensure that the exhaust manifold heat control valve is operating, and that the intake manifold heat riser is not blocked.
Water in the fuel	Engine sputters and stalls; may not start.	Pump a small amount of fuel into a glass jar. Allow to stand, and inspect for droplets or a layer of water.	High humidity, extreme temperature changes.	For droplets, use one or two cans of commercial gas line anti-freeze. For a layer of water, the tank must be drained, and the fuel lines blown out with compressed air.

Section 6—Engine Compression
See Chapter 3 for service procedures

6.1—Test engine compression: Remove all spark plugs. Block the throttle wide open. Insert a compression gauge into a spark plug port, crank the engine to obtain the maximum reading, and record.	If compression is within limits on all cylinders: If gauge reading is extremely low on all cylinders: If gauge reading is low on one or two cylinders: (If gauge readings are identical and low on two or more adjacent cylinders, the head gasket must be replaced.)	**7.1** **6.2** **6.2**

Checking compression

6.2—Test engine compression (wet): Squirt approximately 30 cc. of engine oil into each cylinder, and retest per 6.1.	If the readings improve, worn or cracked rings or broken pistons are indicated: If the readings do not improve, burned or excessively carboned valves or a jumped timing chain are indicated: NOTE: *A jumped timing chain is often indicated by difficult cranking.*	**See Chapter 3** **7.1**

Section 7—Engine Vacuum
See Chapter 3 for service procedures

Test and Procedure	Results and Indications	Proceed to
7.1—Attach a vacuum gauge to the intake manifold beyond the throttle plate. Start the engine, and observe the action of the needle over the range of engine speeds.	See below.	**See below**

INDICATION: normal engine in good condition

Proceed to: 8.1

Normal engine
Gauge reading: steady, from 17–22 in./Hg.

INDICATION: sticking valves or ignition miss

Proceed to: 9.1, 8.3

Sticking valves
Gauge reading: intermittent fluctuation at idle

INDICATION: late ignition or valve timing, low compression, stuck throttle valve, leaking carburetor or manifold gasket

Proceed to: 6.1

Incorrect valve timing
Gauge reading: low (10–15 in./Hg) but steady

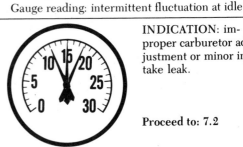

INDICATION: improper carburetor adjustment or minor intake leak.

Proceed to: 7.2

Carburetor requires adjustment
Gauge reading: drifting needle

INDICATION: ignition miss, blown cylinder head gasket, leaking valve or weak valve spring

Proceed to: 8.3, 6.1

Blown head gasket
Gauge reading: needle fluctuates as engine speed increases

INDICATION: burnt valve or faulty valve clearance. Needle will fall when defective valve operates

Proceed to: 9.1

Burnt or leaking valves
Gauge reading: steady needle, but drops regularly

INDICATION: choked muffler, excessive back pressure in system

Proceed to: 10.1

Clogged exhaust system
Gauge reading: gradual drop in reading at idle

INDICATION: worn valve guides

Proceed to: 9.1

Worn valve guides
Gauge reading: needle vibrates excessively at idle, but steadies as engine speed increases

White pointer = steady gauge hand

Black pointer = fluctuating gauge hand

Test and Procedure	Results and Indications	Proceed to
7.2—Attach a vacuum gauge per 7.1, and test for an intake manifold leak. Squirt a small amount of oil around the intake manifold gaskets, carburetor gaskets, plugs and fittings. Observe the action of the vacuum gauge.	If the reading improves, replace the indicated gasket, or seal the indicated fitting or plug: If the reading remains low:	**8.1** **7.3**
7.3—Test all vacuum hoses and accessories for leaks as described in 7.2. Also check the carburetor body (dashpots, automatic choke mechanism, throttle shafts) for leaks in the same manner.	If the reading improves, service or replace the offending part(s): If the reading remains low:	**8.1** **6.1**

Section 8—Secondary Electrical System
See Chapter 2 for service procedures

Test and Procedure	Results and Indications	Proceed to
8.1—Remove the distributor cap and check to make sure that the rotor turns when the engine is cranked. Visually inspect the distributor components.	Clean, tighten or replace any components which appear defective.	**8.2**
8.2—Connect a timing light (per manufacturer's recommendation) and check the dynamic ignition timing. Disconnect and plug the vacuum hose(s) to the distributor if specified, start the engine, and observe the timing marks at the specified engine speed.	If the timing is not correct, adjust to specifications by rotating the distributor in the engine: (Advance timing by rotating distributor opposite normal direction of rotor rotation, retard timing by rotating distributor in same direction as rotor rotation.)	**8.3**
8.3—Check the operation of the distributor advance mechanism(s): To test the mechanical advance, disconnect the vacuum lines from the distributor advance unit and observe the timing marks with a timing light as the engine speed is increased from idle. If the mark moves smoothly, without hesitation, it may be assumed that the mechanical advance is functioning properly. To test vacuum advance and/or retard systems, alternately crimp and release the vacuum line, and observe the timing mark for movement. If movement is noted, the system is operating.	If the systems are functioning: If the systems are not functioning, remove the distributor, and test on a distributor tester:	**8.4** **8.4**
8.4—Locate an ignition miss: With the engine running, remove each spark plug wire, one at a time, until one is found that doesn't cause the engine to roughen and slow down.	When the missing cylinder is identified:	**4.1**

Section 9—Valve Train
See Chapter 3 for service procedures

Test and Procedure	Results and Indications	Proceed to
9.1—Evaluate the valve train: Remove the valve cover, and ensure that the valves are adjusted to specifications. A mechanic's stethoscope may be used to aid in the diagnosis of the valve train. By pushing the probe on or near push rods or rockers, valve noise often can be isolated. A timing light also may be used to diagnose valve problems. Connect the light according to manufacturer's recommendations, and start the engine. Vary the firing moment of the light by increasing the engine speed (and therefore the ignition advance), and moving the trigger from cylinder to cylinder. Observe the movement of each valve.	Sticking valves or erratic valve train motion can be observed with the timing light. The cylinder head must be disassembled for repairs.	**See Chapter 3**
9.2—Check the valve timing: Locate top dead center of the No. 1 piston, and install a degree wheel or tape on the crankshaft pulley or damper with zero corresponding to an index mark on the engine. Rotate the crankshaft in its direction of rotation, and observe the opening of the No. 1 cylinder intake valve. The opening should correspond with the correct mark on the degree wheel according to specifications.	If the timing is not correct, the timing cover must be removed for further investigation.	**See Chapter 3**

Section 10—Exhaust System

Test and Procedure	Results and Indications	Proceed to
10.1—Determine whether the exhaust manifold heat control valve is operating: Operate the valve by hand to determine whether it is free to move. If the valve is free, run the engine to operating temperature and observe the action of the valve, to ensure that it is opening.	If the valve sticks, spray it with a suitable solvent, open and close the valve to free it, and retest. If the valve functions properly: If the valve does not free, or does not operate, replace the valve:	10.2 10.2
10.2—Ensure that there are no exhaust restrictions: Visually inspect the exhaust system for kinks, dents, or crushing. Also note that gases are flowing freely from the tailpipe at all engine speeds, indicating no restriction in the muffler or resonator.	Replace any damaged portion of the system:	11.1

Section 11—Cooling System
See Chapter 3 for service procedures

Test and Procedure	Results and Indications	Proceed to
11.1—Visually inspect the fan belt for glazing, cracks, and fraying, and replace if necessary. Tighten the belt so that the longest span has approximately ½″ play at its midpoint under thumb pressure (see Chapter 1).	Replace or tighten the fan belt as necessary:	11.2

Checking belt tension

Test and Procedure	Results and Indications	Proceed to
11.2—Check the fluid level of the cooling system.	If full or slightly low, fill as necessary:	11.5
	If extremely low:	11.3
11.3—Visually inspect the external portions of the cooling system (radiator, radiator hoses, thermostat elbow, water pump seals, heater hoses, etc.) for leaks. If none are found, pressurize the cooling system to 14–15 psi.	If cooling system holds the pressure:	11.5
	If cooling system loses pressure rapidly, reinspect external parts of the system for leaks under pressure. If none are found, check dipstick for coolant in crankcase. If no coolant is present, but pressure loss continues:	11.4
	If coolant is evident in crankcase, remove cylinder head(s), and check gasket(s). If gaskets are intact, block and cylinder head(s) should be checked for cracks or holes. If the gasket(s) is blown, replace, and purge the crankcase of coolant:	12.6
	NOTE: *Occasionally, due to atmospheric and driving conditions, condensation of water can occur in the crankcase. This causes the oil to appear milky white. To remedy, run the engine until hot, and change the oil and oil filter.*	
11.4—Check for combustion leaks into the cooling system: Pressurize the cooling system as above. Start the engine, and observe the pressure gauge. If the needle fluctuates, remove each spark plug wire, one at a time, noting which cylinder(s) reduce or eliminate the fluctuation.	Cylinders which reduce or eliminate the fluctuation, when the spark plug wire is removed, are leaking into the cooling system. Replace the head gasket on the affected cylinder bank(s).	

Pressurizing the cooling system

Test and Procedure	Results and Indications	Proceed to
11.5—Check the radiator pressure cap: Attach a radiator pressure tester to the radiator cap (wet the seal prior to installation). Quickly pump up the pressure, noting the point at which the cap releases.	If the cap releases within ± 1 psi of the specified rating, it is operating properly:	**11.6**
	If the cap releases at more than ± 1 psi of the specified rating, it should be replaced:	**11.6**

Checking radiator pressure cap

Test and Procedure	Results and Indications	Proceed to
11.6—Test the thermostat: Start the engine cold, remove the radiator cap, and insert a thermometer into the radiator. Allow the engine to idle. After a short while, there will be a sudden, rapid increase in coolant temperature. The temperature at which this sharp rise stops is the thermostat opening temperature.	If the thermostat opens at or about the specified temperature:	**11.7**
	If the temperature doesn't increase: (If the temperature increases slowly and gradually, replace the thermostat.)	**11.7**
11.7—Check the water pump: Remove the thermostat elbow and the thermostat, disconnect the coil high tension lead (to prevent starting), and crank the engine momentarily.	If coolant flows, replace the thermostat and retest per 11.6:	**11.6**
	If coolant doesn't flow, reverse flush the cooling system to alleviate any blockage that might exist. If system is not blocked, and coolant will not flow, replace the water pump.	

Section 12—Lubrication
See Chapter 3 for service procedures

Test and Procedure	Results and Indications	Proceed to
12.1—Check the oil pressure gauge or warning light: If the gauge shows low pressure, or the light is on for no obvious reason, remove the oil pressure sender. Install an accurate oil pressure gauge and run the engine momentarily.	If oil pressure builds normally, run engine for a few moments to determine that it is functioning normally, and replace the sender.	—
	If the pressure remains low:	**12.2**
	If the pressure surges:	**12.3**
	If the oil pressure is zero:	**12.3**
12.2—Visually inspect the oil: If the oil is watery or very thin, milky, or foamy, replace the oil and oil filter.	If the oil is normal:	**12.3**
	If after replacing oil the pressure remains low:	**12.3**
	If after replacing oil the pressure becomes normal:	—

Test and Procedure	Results and Indications	Proceed to
12.3—Inspect the oil pressure relief valve and spring, to ensure that it is not sticking or stuck. Remove and thoroughly clean the valve, spring, and the valve body.	If the oil pressure improves: If no improvement is noted:	— **12.4**
12.4—Check to ensure that the oil pump is not cavitating (sucking air instead of oil): See that the crankcase is neither over nor underfull, and that the pickup in the sump is in the proper position and free from sludge.	Fill or drain the crankcase to the proper capacity, and clean the pickup screen in solvent if necessary. If no improvement is noted:	**12.5**
12.5—Inspect the oil pump drive and the oil pump:	If the pump drive or the oil pump appear to be defective, service as necessary and retest per 12.1: If the pump drive and pump appear to be operating normally, the engine should be disassembled to determine where blockage exists:	**12.1** **See Chapter 3**
12.6—Purge the engine of ethylene glycol coolant: Completely drain the crankcase and the oil filter. Obtain a commercial butyl cellosolve base solvent, designated for this purpose, and follow the instructions precisely. Following this, install a new oil filter and refill the crankcase with the proper weight oil. The next oil and filter change should follow shortly thereafter (1000 miles).		

TROUBLESHOOTING EMISSION CONTROL SYSTEMS

See Chapter 4 for procedures applicable to individual emission control systems used on specific combinations of engine/transmission/model.

TROUBLESHOOTING THE CARBURETOR
See Chapter 4 for service procedures

Carburetor problems cannot be effectively isolated unless all other engine systems (particularly ignition and emission) are functioning properly and the engine is properly tuned.

Condition	Possible Cause
Engine cranks, but does not start	1. Improper starting procedure 2. No fuel in tank 3. Clogged fuel line or filter 4. Defective fuel pump 5. Choke valve not closing properly 6. Engine flooded 7. Choke valve not unloading 8. Throttle linkage not making full travel 9. Stuck needle or float 10. Leaking float needle or seat 11. Improper float adjustment
Engine stalls	1. Improperly adjusted idle speed or mixture **Engine hot** 2. Improperly adjusted dashpot 3. Defective or improperly adjusted solenoid 4. Incorrect fuel level in fuel bowl 5. Fuel pump pressure too high 6. Leaking float needle seat 7. Secondary throttle valve stuck open 8. Air or fuel leaks 9. Idle air bleeds plugged or missing 10. Idle passages plugged **Engine Cold** 11. Incorrectly adjusted choke 12. Improperly adjusted fast idle speed 13. Air leaks 14. Plugged idle or idle air passages 15. Stuck choke valve or binding linkage 16. Stuck secondary throttle valves 17. Engine flooding—high fuel level 18. Leaking or misaligned float
Engine hesitates on acceleration	1. Clogged fuel filter 2. Leaking fuel pump diaphragm 3. Low fuel pump pressure 4. Secondary throttle valves stuck, bent or misadjusted 5. Sticking or binding air valve 6. Defective accelerator pump 7. Vacuum leaks 8. Clogged air filter 9. Incorrect choke adjustment (engine cold)
Engine feels sluggish or flat on acceleration	1. Improperly adjusted idle speed or mixture 2. Clogged fuel filter 3. Defective accelerator pump 4. Dirty, plugged or incorrect main metering jets 5. Bent or sticking main metering rods 6. Sticking throttle valves 7. Stuck heat riser 8. Binding or stuck air valve 9. Dirty, plugged or incorrect secondary jets 10. Bent or sticking secondary metering rods. 11. Throttle body or manifold heat passages plugged 12. Improperly adjusted choke or choke vacuum break.
Carburetor floods	1. Defective fuel pump. Pressure too high. 2. Stuck choke valve 3. Dirty, worn or damaged float or needle valve/seat 4. Incorrect float/fuel level 5. Leaking float bowl

Condition	Possible Cause
Engine idles roughly and stalls	1. Incorrect idle speed 2. Clogged fuel filter 3. Dirt in fuel system or carburetor 4. Loose carburetor screws or attaching bolts 5. Broken carburetor gaskets 6. Air leaks 7. Dirty carburetor 8. Worn idle mixture needles 9. Throttle valves stuck open 10. Incorrectly adjusted float or fuel level 11. Clogged air filter
Engine runs unevenly or surges	1. Defective fuel pump 2. Dirty or clogged fuel filter 3. Plugged, loose or incorrect main metering jets or rods 4. Air leaks 5. Bent or sticking main metering rods 6. Stuck power piston 7. Incorrect float adjustment 8. Incorrect idle speed or mixture 9. Dirty or plugged idle system passages 10. Hard, brittle or broken gaskets 11. Loose attaching or mounting screws 12. Stuck or misaligned secondary throttle valves
Poor fuel economy	1. Poor driving habits 2. Stuck choke valve 3. Binding choke linkage 4. Stuck heat riser 5. Incorrect idle mixture 6. Defective accelerator pump 7. Air leaks 8. Plugged, loose or incorrect main metering jets 9. Improperly adjusted float or fuel level 10. Bent, misaligned or fuel-clogged float 11. Leaking float needle seat 12. Fuel leak 13. Accelerator pump discharge ball not seating properly 14. Incorrect main jets
Engine lacks high speed performance or power	1. Incorrect throttle linkage adjustment 2. Stuck or binding power piston 3. Defective accelerator pump 4. Air leaks 5. Incorrect float setting or fuel level 6. Dirty, plugged, worn or incorrect main metering jets or rods 7. Binding or sticking air valve 8. Brittle or cracked gaskets 9. Bent, incorrect or improperly adjusted secondary metering rods 10. Clogged fuel filter 11. Clogged air filter 12. Defective fuel pump

TROUBLESHOOTING FUEL INJECTION PROBLEMS

Each fuel injection system has its own unique components and test procedures, for which it is impossible to generalize. Refer to Chapter 4 of this Repair & Tune-Up Guide for specific test and repair procedures, if the vehicle is equipped with fuel injection.

TROUBLESHOOTING ELECTRICAL PROBLEMS

See Chapter 5 for service procedures

For any electrical system to operate, it must make a complete circuit. This simply means that the power flow from the battery must make a complete circle. When an electrical component is operating, power flows from the battery to the component, passes through the component causing it to perform its function (lighting a light bulb), and then returns to the battery through the ground of the circuit. This ground is usually (but not always) the metal part of the car or truck on which the electrical component is mounted.

Perhaps the easiest way to visualize this is to think of connecting a light bulb with two wires attached to it to the battery. If one of the two wires attached to the light bulb were attached to the negative post of the battery and the other were attached to the positive post of the battery, you would have a complete circuit. Current from the battery would flow to the light bulb, causing it to light, and return to the negative post of the battery.

The normal automotive circuit differs from this simple example in two ways. First, instead of having a return wire from the bulb to the battery, the light bulb returns the current to the battery through the chassis of the vehicle. Since the negative battery cable is attached to the chassis and the chassis is made of electrically conductive metal, the chassis of the vehicle can serve as a ground wire to complete the circuit. Secondly, most automotive circuits contain switches to turn components on and off as required.

Every complete circuit from a power source must include a component which is using the power from the power source. If you were to disconnect the light bulb from the wires and touch the two wires together (don't do this) the power supply wire to the component would be grounded before the normal ground connection for the circuit.

Because grounding a wire from a power source makes a complete circuit—less the required component to use the power—this phenomenon is called a short circuit. Common causes are: broken insulation (exposing the metal wire to a metal part of the car or truck), or a shorted switch.

Some electrical components which require a large amount of current to operate also have a relay in their circuit. Since these circuits carry a large amount of current, the thickness of the wire in the circuit (gauge size) is also greater. If this large wire were connected from the component to the control switch on the instrument panel, and then back to the component, a voltage drop would occur in the circuit. To prevent this potential drop in voltage, an electromagnetic switch (relay) is used. The large wires in the circuit are connected from the battery to one side of the relay, and from the opposite side of the relay to the component. The relay is normally open, preventing current from passing through the circuit. An additional, smaller, wire is connected from the relay to the control switch for the circuit. When the control switch is turned on, it grounds the smaller wire from the relay and completes the circuit. This closes the relay and allows current to flow from the battery to the component. The horn, headlight, and starter circuits are three which use relays.

It is possible for larger surges of current to pass through the electrical system of your car or truck. If this surge of current were to reach an electrical component, it could burn it out. To prevent this, fuses, circuit breakers or fusible links are connected into the current supply wires of most of the major electrical systems. When an electrical current of excessive power passes through the component's fuse, the fuse blows out and breaks the circuit, saving the component from destruction.

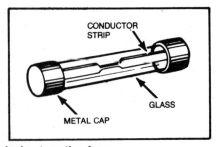

Typical automotive fuse

A circuit breaker is basically a self-repairing fuse. The circuit breaker opens the circuit the same way a fuse does. However, when either the short is removed from the circuit or the surge subsides, the circuit breaker resets itself and does not have to be replaced as a fuse does.

A fuse link is a wire that acts as a fuse. It is normally connected between the starter relay and the main wiring harness. This connection is usually under the hood. The fuse link (if installed) protects all the

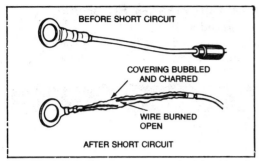

BEFORE SHORT CIRCUIT

COVERING BUBBLED
AND CHARRED

WIRE BURNED
OPEN

AFTER SHORT CIRCUIT

Most fusible links show a charred, melted insulation when they burn out

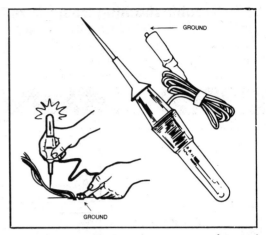

GROUND

GROUND

The test light will show the presence of current when touched to a hot wire and grounded at the other end

chassis electrical components, and is the probable cause of trouble when none of the electrical components function, unless the battery is disconnected or dead.

Electrical problems generally fall into one of three areas:

1. The component that is not functioning is not receiving current.

2. The component itself is not functioning.

3. The component is not properly grounded.

The electrical system can be checked with a test light and a jumper wire. A test light is a device that looks like a pointed screwdriver with a wire attached to it and has a light bulb in its handle. A jumper wire is a piece of insulated wire with an alligator clip attached to each end.

If a component is not working, you must follow a systematic plan to determine which of the three causes is the villain.

1. Turn on the switch that controls the inoperable component.

2. Disconnect the power supply wire from the component.

3. Attach the ground wire on the test light to a good metal ground.

4. Touch the probe end of the test light to the end of the power supply wire that was disconnected from the component. If the component is receiving current, the test light will go on.

NOTE: *Some components work only when the ignition switch is turned on.*

If the test light does not go on, then the problem is in the circuit between the battery and the component. This includes all the switches, fuses, and relays in the system. Follow the wire that runs back to the battery. The problem is an open circuit between the

battery and the component. If the fuse is blown and, when replaced, immediately blows again, there is a short circuit in the system which must be located and repaired. If there is a switch in the system, bypass it with a jumper wire. This is done by connecting one end of the jumper wire to the power supply wire into the switch and the other end of the jumper wire to the wire coming out of the switch. If the test light lights with the jumper wire installed, the switch or whatever was bypassed is defective.

NOTE: *Never substitute the jumper wire for the component, since it is required to use the power from the power source.*

5. If the bulb in the test light goes on, then the current is getting to the component that is not working. This eliminates the first of the three possible causes. Connect the power supply wire and connect a jumper wire from the component to a good metal ground. Do this with the switch which controls the component turned on, and also the ignition switch turned on if it is required for the component to work. If the component works with the jumper wire installed, then it has a bad ground. This is usually caused by the metal area on which the component mounts to the chassis being coated with some type of foreign matter.

6. If neither test located the source of the trouble, then the component itself is defective. Remember that for any electrical system to work, all connections must be clean and tight.

Troubleshooting Basic Turn Signal and Flasher Problems
See Chapter 5 for service procedures

Most problems in the turn signals or flasher system can be reduced to defective flashers or bulbs, which are easily replaced. Occasionally, the turn signal switch will prove defective.

F = Front   R = Rear   ● = Lights off   ○ = Lights on

Condition		Possible Cause
Turn signals light, but do not flash	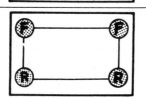	Defective flasher
No turn signals light on either side	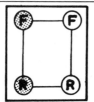	Blown fuse. Replace if defective. Defective flasher. Check by substitution. Open circuit, short circuit or poor ground.
Both turn signals on one side don't work	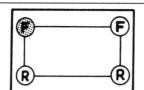	Bad bulbs. Bad ground in both (or either) housings.
One turn signal light on one side doesn't work	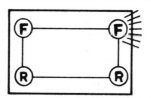	Defective bulb. Corrosion in socket. Clean contacts. Poor ground at socket.
Turn signal flashes too fast or too slowly		Check any bulb on the side flashing too fast. A heavy-duty bulb is probably installed in place of a regular bulb. Check the bulb flashing too slowly. A standard bulb was probably installed in place of a heavy-duty bulb. Loose connections or corrosion at the bulb socket.
Indicator lights don't work in either direction		Check if the turn signals are working. Check the dash indicator lights. Check the flasher by substitution.
One indicator light doesn't light		On systems with one dash indicator: See if the lights work on the same side. Often the filaments have been reversed in systems combining stoplights with taillights and turn signals. Check the flasher by substitution. On systems with two indicators: Check the bulbs on the same side. Check the indicator light bulb. Check the flasher by substitution.

Troubleshooting Lighting Problems
See Chapter 5 for service procedures

Condition	Possible Cause
One or more lights don't work, but others do	1. Defective bulb(s) 2. Blown fuse(s) 3. Dirty fuse clips or light sockets 4. Poor ground circuit
Lights burn out quickly	1. Incorrect voltage regulator setting or defective regulator 2. Poor battery/alternator connections
Lights go dim	1. Low/discharged battery 2. Alternator not charging 3. Corroded sockets or connections 4. Low voltage output
Lights flicker	1. Loose connection 2. Poor ground. (Run ground wire from light housing to frame) 3. Circuit breaker operating (short circuit)
Lights "flare"—Some flare is normal on acceleration—If excessive, see "Lights Burn Out Quickly"	High voltage setting
Lights glare—approaching drivers are blinded	1. Lights adjusted too high 2. Rear springs or shocks sagging 3. Rear tires soft

Troubleshooting Dash Gauge Problems
Most problems can be traced to a defective sending unit or faulty wiring. Occasionally, the gauge itself is at fault. See Chapter 5 for service procedures.

Condition	Possible Cause
COOLANT TEMPERATURE GAUGE	
Gauge reads erratically or not at all	1. Loose or dirty connections 2. Defective sending unit. 3. Defective gauge. To test a bi-metal gauge, remove the wire from the sending unit. Ground the wire for an instant. If the gauge registers, replace the sending unit. To test a magnetic gauge, disconnect the wire at the sending unit. With ignition ON gauge should register COLD. Ground the wire; gauge should register HOT.
AMMETER GAUGE—TURN HEADLIGHTS ON (DO NOT START ENGINE). NOTE REACTION	
Ammeter shows charge Ammeter shows discharge Ammeter does not move	1. Connections reversed on gauge 2. Ammeter is OK 3. Loose connections or faulty wiring 4. Defective gauge

Condition	Possible Cause

OIL PRESSURE GAUGE

Gauge does not register or is inaccurate	1. On mechanical gauge, Bourdon tube may be bent or kinked. 2. Low oil pressure. Remove sending unit. Idle the engine briefly. If no oil flows from sending unit hole, problem is in engine. 3. Defective gauge. Remove the wire from the sending unit and ground it for an instant with the ignition ON. A good gauge will go to the top of the scale. 4. Defective wiring. Check the wiring to the gauge. If it's OK and the gauge doesn't register when grounded, replace the gauge. 5. Defective sending unit.

ALL GAUGES

All gauges do not operate All gauges read low or erratically All gauges pegged	1. Blown fuse 2. Defective instrument regulator 3. Defective or dirty instrument voltage regulator 4. Loss of ground between instrument voltage regulator and frame 5. Defective instrument regulator

WARNING LIGHTS

Light(s) do not come on when ignition is ON, but engine is not started Light comes on with engine running	1. Defective bulb 2. Defective wire 3. Defective sending unit. Disconnect the wire from the sending unit and ground it. Replace the sending unit if the light comes on with the ignition ON. 4. Problem in individual system 5. Defective sending unit

Troubleshooting Clutch Problems

It is false economy to replace individual clutch components. The pressure plate, clutch plate and throwout bearing should be replaced as a set, and the flywheel face inspected, whenever the clutch is overhauled. See Chapter 6 for service procedures.

Condition	Possible Cause
Clutch chatter	1. Grease on driven plate (disc) facing 2. Binding clutch linkage or cable 3. Loose, damaged facings on driven plate (disc) 4. Engine mounts loose 5. Incorrect height adjustment of pressure plate release levers 6. Clutch housing or housing to transmission adapter misalignment 7. Loose driven plate hub
Clutch grabbing	1. Oil, grease on driven plate (disc) facing 2. Broken pressure plate 3. Warped or binding driven plate. Driven plate binding on clutch shaft
Clutch slips	1. Lack of lubrication in clutch linkage or cable (linkage or cable binds, causes incomplete engagement) 2. Incorrect pedal, or linkage adjustment 3. Broken pressure plate springs 4. Weak pressure plate springs 5. Grease on driven plate facings (disc)

Troubleshooting Clutch Problems (cont.)

Condition	Possible Cause
Incomplete clutch release	1. Incorrect pedal or linkage adjustment or linkage or cable binding 2. Incorrect height adjustment on pressure plate release levers 3. Loose, broken facings on driven plate (disc) 4. Bent, dished, warped driven plate caused by overheating
Grinding, whirring grating noise when pedal is depressed	1. Worn or defective throwout bearing 2. Starter drive teeth contacting flywheel ring gear teeth. Look for milled or polished teeth on ring gear.
Squeal, howl, trumpeting noise when pedal is being released (occurs during first inch to inch and one-half of pedal travel)	Pilot bushing worn or lack of lubricant. If bushing appears OK, polish bushing with emery cloth, soak lube wick in oil, lube bushing with oil, apply film of chassis grease to clutch shaft pilot hub, reassemble. NOTE: Bushing wear may be due to misalignment of clutch housing or housing to transmission adapter
Vibration or clutch pedal pulsation with clutch disengaged (pedal fully depressed)	1. Worn or defective engine transmission mounts 2. Flywheel run out. (Flywheel run out at face not to exceed 0.005″) 3. Damaged or defective clutch components

Troubleshooting Manual Transmission Problems
See Chapter 6 for service procedures

Condition	Possible Cause
Transmission jumps out of gear	1. Misalignment of transmission case or clutch housing. 2. Worn pilot bearing in crankshaft. 3. Bent transmission shaft. 4. Worn high speed sliding gear. 5. Worn teeth or end-play in clutch shaft. 6. Insufficient spring tension on shifter rail plunger. 7. Bent or loose shifter fork. 8. Gears not engaging completely. 9. Loose or worn bearings on clutch shaft or mainshaft. 10. Worn gear teeth. 11. Worn or damaged detent balls.
Transmission sticks in gear	1. Clutch not releasing fully. 2. Burred or battered teeth on clutch shaft, or sliding sleeve. 3. Burred or battered transmission mainshaft. 4. Frozen synchronizing clutch. 5. Stuck shifter rail plunger. 6. Gearshift lever twisting and binding shifter rail. 7. Battered teeth on high speed sliding gear or on sleeve. 8. Improper lubrication, or lack of lubrication. 9. Corroded transmission parts. 10. Defective mainshaft pilot bearing. 11. Locked gear bearings will give same effect as stuck in gear.
Transmission gears will not synchronize	1. Binding pilot bearing on mainshaft, will synchronize in high gear only. 2. Clutch not releasing fully. 3. Detent spring weak or broken. 4. Weak or broken springs under balls in sliding gear sleeve. 5. Binding bearing on clutch shaft, or binding countershaft. 6. Binding pilot bearing in crankshaft. 7. Badly worn gear teeth. 8. Improper lubrication. 9. Constant mesh gear not turning freely on transmission mainshaft. Will synchronize in that gear only.

Condition	Possible Cause
Gears spinning when shifting into gear from neutral	1. Clutch not releasing fully. 2. In some cases an extremely light lubricant in transmission will cause gears to continue to spin for a short time after clutch is released. 3. Binding pilot bearing in crankshaft.
Transmission noisy in all gears	1. Insufficient lubricant, or improper lubricant. 2. Worn countergear bearings. 3. Worn or damaged main drive gear or countergear. 4. Damaged main drive gear or mainshaft bearings. 5. Worn or damaged countergear anti-lash plate.
Transmission noisy in neutral only	1. Damaged main drive gear bearing. 2. Damaged or loose mainshaft pilot bearing. 3. Worn or damaged countergear anti-lash plate. 4. Worn countergear bearings.
Transmission noisy in one gear only	1. Damaged or worn constant mesh gears. 2. Worn or damaged countergear bearings. 3. Damaged or worn synchronizer.
Transmission noisy in reverse only	1. Worn or damaged reverse idler gear or idler bushing. 2. Worn or damaged mainshaft reverse gear. 3. Worn or damaged reverse countergear. 4. Damaged shift mechanism.

TROUBLESHOOTING AUTOMATIC TRANSMISSION PROBLEMS

Keeping alert to changes in the operating characteristics of the transmission (changing shift points, noises, etc.) can prevent small problems from becoming large ones. If the problem cannot be traced to loose bolts, fluid level, misadjusted linkage, clogged filters or similar problems, you should probably seek professional service.

Transmission Fluid Indications

The appearance and odor of the transmission fluid can give valuable clues to the overall condition of the transmission. Always note the appearance of the fluid when you check the fluid level or change the fluid. Rub a small amount of fluid between your fingers to feel for grit and smell the fluid on the dipstick.

If the fluid appears:	It indicates:
Clear and red colored	Normal operation
Discolored (extremely dark red or brownish) or smells burned	Band or clutch pack failure, usually caused by an overheated transmission. Hauling very heavy loads with insufficient power or failure to change the fluid often result in overheating. Do not confuse this appearance with newer fluids that have a darker red color and a strong odor (though not a burned odor).
Foamy or aerated (light in color and full of bubbles)	1. The level is too high (gear train is churning oil) 2. An internal air leak (air is mixing with the fluid). Have the transmission checked professionally.
Solid residue in the fluid	Defective bands, clutch pack or bearings. Bits of band material or metal abrasives are clinging to the dipstick. Have the transmission checked professionally.
Varnish coating on the dipstick	The transmission fluid is overheating

TROUBLESHOOTING DRIVE AXLE PROBLEMS

First, determine when the noise is most noticeable.

Drive Noise: Produced under vehicle acceleration.

Coast Noise: Produced while coasting with a closed throttle.

Float Noise: Occurs while maintaining constant speed (just enough to keep speed constant) on a level road.

External Noise Elimination

It is advisable to make a thorough road test to determine whether the noise originates in the rear axle or whether it originates from the tires, engine, transmission, wheel bearings or road surface. Noise originating from other places cannot be corrected by servicing the rear axle.

ROAD NOISE

Brick or rough surfaced concrete roads produce noises that seem to come from the rear axle. Road noise is usually identical in Drive or Coast and driving on a different type of road will tell whether the road is the problem.

TIRE NOISE

Tire noise can be mistaken as rear axle noise, even though the tires on the front are at fault. Snow tread and mud tread tires or tires worn unevenly will frequently cause vibrations which seem to originate elsewhere; *temporarily, and for test purposes only,* inflate the tires to 40–50 lbs. This will significantly alter the noise produced by the tires, but will not alter noise from the rear axle. Noises from the rear axle will normally cease at speeds below 30 mph on coast, while tire noise will continue at lower tone as speed is decreased. The rear axle noise will usually change from drive conditions to coast conditions, while tire noise will not. Do not forget to lower the tire pressure to normal after the test is complete.

ENGINE/TRANSMISSION NOISE

Determine at what speed the noise is most pronounced, then stop in a quiet place. With the transmission in Neutral, run the engine through speeds corresponding to road speeds where the noise was noticed. Noises produced with the vehicle standing still are coming from the engine or transmission.

FRONT WHEEL BEARINGS

Front wheel bearing noises, sometimes confused with rear axle noises, will not change when comparing drive and coast conditions. While holding the speed steady, lightly apply the footbrake. This will often cause wheel bearing noise to lessen, as some of the weight is taken off the bearing. Front wheel bearings are easily checked by jacking up the wheels and spinning the wheels. Shaking the wheels will also determine if the wheel bearings are excessively loose.

REAR AXLE NOISES

Eliminating other possible sources can narrow the cause to the rear axle, which normally produces noise from worn gears or bearings. Gear noises tend to peak in a narrow speed range, while bearing noises will usually vary in pitch with engine speeds.

Noise Diagnosis

The Noise Is:	Most Probably Produced By:
1. Identical under Drive or Coast	Road surface, tires or front wheel bearings
2. Different depending on road surface	Road surface or tires
3. Lower as speed is lowered	Tires
4. Similar when standing or moving	Engine or transmission
5. A vibration	Unbalanced tires, rear wheel bearing, unbalanced driveshaft or worn U-joint
6. A knock or click about every two tire revolutions	Rear wheel bearing
7. Most pronounced on turns	Damaged differential gears
8. A steady low-pitched whirring or scraping, starting at low speeds	Damaged or worn pinion bearing
9. A chattering vibration on turns	Wrong differential lubricant or worn clutch plates (limited slip rear axle)
10. Noticed only in Drive, Coast or Float conditions	Worn ring gear and/or pinion gear

Troubleshooting Steering & Suspension Problems

Condition	Possible Cause
Hard steering (wheel is hard to turn)	1. Improper tire pressure 2. Loose or glazed pump drive belt 3. Low or incorrect fluid 4. Loose, bent or poorly lubricated front end parts 5. Improper front end alignment (excessive caster) 6. Bind in steering column or linkage 7. Kinked hydraulic hose 8. Air in hydraulic system 9. Low pump output or leaks in system 10. Obstruction in lines 11. Pump valves sticking or out of adjustment 12. Incorrect wheel alignment
Loose steering (too much play in steering wheel)	1. Loose wheel bearings 2. Faulty shocks 3. Worn linkage or suspension components 4. Loose steering gear mounting or linkage points 5. Steering mechanism worn or improperly adjusted 6. Valve spool improperly adjusted 7. Worn ball joints, tie-rod ends, etc.
Veers or wanders (pulls to one side with hands off steering wheel)	1. Improper tire pressure 2. Improper front end alignment 3. Dragging or improperly adjusted brakes 4. Bent frame 5. Improper rear end alignment 6. Faulty shocks or springs 7. Loose or bent front end components 8. Play in Pitman arm 9. Steering gear mountings loose 10. Loose wheel bearings 11. Binding Pitman arm 12. Spool valve sticking or improperly adjusted 13. Worn ball joints
Wheel oscillation or vibration transmitted through steering wheel	1. Low or uneven tire pressure 2. Loose wheel bearings 3. Improper front end alignment 4. Bent spindle 5. Worn, bent or broken front end components 6. Tires out of round or out of balance 7. Excessive lateral runout in disc brake rotor 8. Loose or bent shock absorber or strut
Noises (see also "Troubleshooting Drive Axle Problems")	1. Loose belts 2. Low fluid, air in system 3. Foreign matter in system 4. Improper lubrication 5. Interference or chafing in linkage 6. Steering gear mountings loose 7. Incorrect adjustment or wear in gear box 8. Faulty valves or wear in pump 9. Kinked hydraulic lines 10. Worn wheel bearings
Poor return of steering	1. Over-inflated tires 2. Improperly aligned front end (excessive caster) 3. Binding in steering column 4. No lubrication in front end 5. Steering gear adjusted too tight
Uneven tire wear (see "How To Read Tire Wear")	1. Incorrect tire pressure 2. Improperly aligned front end 3. Tires out-of-balance 4. Bent or worn suspension parts

HOW TO READ TIRE WEAR

The way your tires wear is a good indicator of other parts of the suspension. Abnormal wear patterns are often caused by the need for simple tire maintenance, or for front end alignment.

Excessive wear at the center of the tread indicates that the air pressure in the tire is consistently too high. The tire is riding on the center of the tread and wearing it prematurely. Occasionally, this wear pattern can result from outrageously wide tires on narrow rims. The cure for this is to replace either the tires or the wheels.

This type of wear usually results from consistent under-inflation. When a tire is under-inflated, there is too much contact with the road by the outer treads, which wear prematurely. When this type of wear occurs, and the tire pressure is known to be consistently correct, a bent or worn steering component or the need for wheel alignment could be indicated.

Feathering is a condition when the edge of each tread rib develops a slightly rounded edge on one side and a sharp edge on the other. By running your hand over the tire, you can usually feel the sharper edges before you'll be able to see them. The most common causes of feathering are incorrect toe-in setting or deteriorated bushings in the front suspension.

When an inner or outer rib wears faster than the rest of the tire, the need for wheel alignment is indicated. There is excessive camber in the front suspension, causing the wheel to lean too much putting excessive load on one side of the tire. Misalignment could also be due to sagging springs, worn ball joints, or worn control arm bushings. Be sure the vehicle is loaded the way it's normally driven when you have the wheels aligned.

Cups or scalloped dips appearing around the edge of the tread almost always indicate worn (sometimes bent) suspension parts. Adjustment of wheel alignment alone will seldom cure the problem. Any worn component that connects the wheel to the suspension can cause this type of wear. Occasionally, wheels that are out of balance will wear like this, but wheel imbalance usually shows up as bald spots between the outside edges and center of the tread.

Second-rib wear is usually found only in radial tires, and appears where the steel belts end in relation to the tread. It can be kept to a minimum by paying careful attention to tire pressure and frequently rotating the tires. This is often considered normal wear but excessive amounts indicate that the tires are too wide for the wheels.

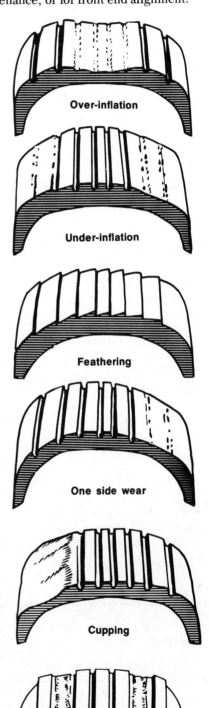

Over-inflation

Under-inflation

Feathering

One side wear

Cupping

Second-rib wear

Troubleshooting Disc Brake Problems

Condition	Possible Cause
Noise—groan—brake noise emanating when slowly releasing brakes (creep-groan)	Not detrimental to function of disc brakes—no corrective action required. (This noise may be eliminated by slightly increasing or decreasing brake pedal efforts.)
Rattle—brake noise or rattle emanating at low speeds on rough roads, (front wheels only).	1. Shoe anti-rattle spring missing or not properly positioned. 2. Excessive clearance between shoe and caliper. 3. Soft or broken caliper seals. 4. Deformed or misaligned disc. 5. Loose caliper.
Scraping	1. Mounting bolts too long. 2. Loose wheel bearings. 3. Bent, loose, or misaligned splash shield.
Front brakes heat up during driving and fail to release	1. Operator riding brake pedal. 2. Stop light switch improperly adjusted. 3. Sticking pedal linkage. 4. Frozen or seized piston. 5. Residual pressure valve in master cylinder. 6. Power brake malfunction. 7. Proportioning valve malfunction.
Leaky brake caliper	1. Damaged or worn caliper piston seal. 2. Scores or corrosion on surface of cylinder bore.
Grabbing or uneven brake action— Brakes pull to one side	1. Causes listed under "Brakes Pull". 2. Power brake malfunction. 3. Low fluid level in master cylinder. 4. Air in hydraulic system. 5. Brake fluid, oil or grease on linings. 6. Unmatched linings. 7. Distorted brake pads. 8. Frozen or seized pistons. 9. Incorrect tire pressure. 10. Front end out of alignment. 11. Broken rear spring. 12. Brake caliper pistons sticking. 13. Restricted hose or line. 14. Caliper not in proper alignment to braking disc. 15. Stuck or malfunctioning metering valve. 16. Soft or broken caliper seals. 17. Loose caliper.
Brake pedal can be depressed without braking effect	1. Air in hydraulic system or improper bleeding procedure. 2. Leak past primary cup in master cylinder. 3. Leak in system. 4. Rear brakes out of adjustment. 5. Bleeder screw open.
Excessive pedal travel	1. Air, leak, or insufficient fluid in system or caliper. 2. Warped or excessively tapered shoe and lining assembly. 3. Excessive disc runout. 4. Rear brake adjustment required. 5. Loose wheel bearing adjustment. 6. Damaged caliper piston seal. 7. Improper brake fluid (boil). 8. Power brake malfunction. 9. Weak or soft hoses.

Troubleshooting Disc Brake Problems (cont.)

Condition	Possible Cause
Brake roughness or chatter (pedal pumping)	1. Excessive thickness variation of braking disc. 2. Excessive lateral runout of braking disc. 3. Rear brake drums out-of-round. 4. Excessive front bearing clearance.
Excessive pedal effort	1. Brake fluid, oil or grease on linings. 2. Incorrect lining. 3. Frozen or seized pistons. 4. Power brake malfunction. 5. Kinked or collapsed hose or line. 6. Stuck metering valve. 7. Scored caliper or master cylinder bore. 8. Seized caliper pistons.
Brake pedal fades (pedal travel increases with foot on brake)	1. Rough master cylinder or caliper bore. 2. Loose or broken hydraulic lines/connections. 3. Air in hydraulic system. 4. Fluid level low. 5. Weak or soft hoses. 6. Inferior quality brake shoes or fluid. 7. Worn master cylinder piston cups or seals.

Troubleshooting Drum Brakes

Condition	Possible Cause
Pedal goes to floor	1. Fluid low in reservoir. 2. Air in hydraulic system. 3. Improperly adjusted brake. 4. Leaking wheel cylinders. 5. Loose or broken brake lines. 6. Leaking or worn master cylinder. 7. Excessively worn brake lining.
Spongy brake pedal	1. Air in hydraulic system. 2. Improper brake fluid (low boiling point). 3. Excessively worn or cracked brake drums. 4. Broken pedal pivot bushing.
Brakes pulling	1. Contaminated lining. 2. Front end out of alignment. 3. Incorrect brake adjustment. 4. Unmatched brake lining. 5. Brake drums out of round. 6. Brake shoes distorted. 7. Restricted brake hose or line. 8. Broken rear spring. 9. Worn brake linings. 10. Uneven lining wear. 11. Glazed brake lining. 12. Excessive brake lining dust. 13. Heat spotted brake drums. 14. Weak brake return springs. 15. Faulty automatic adjusters. 16. Low or incorrect tire pressure.

Condition	Possible Cause
Squealing brakes	1. Glazed brake lining. 2. Saturated brake lining. 3. Weak or broken brake shoe retaining spring. 4. Broken or weak brake shoe return spring. 5. Incorrect brake lining. 6. Distorted brake shoes. 7. Bent support plate. 8. Dust in brakes or scored brake drums. 9. Linings worn below limit. 10. Uneven brake lining wear. 11. Heat spotted brake drums.
Chirping brakes	1. Out of round drum or eccentric axle flange pilot.
Dragging brakes	1. Incorrect wheel or parking brake adjustment. 2. Parking brakes engaged or improperly adjusted. 3. Weak or broken brake shoe return spring. 4. Brake pedal binding. 5. Master cylinder cup sticking. 6. Obstructed master cylinder relief port. 7. Saturated brake lining. 8. Bent or out of round brake drum. 9. Contaminated or improper brake fluid. 10. Sticking wheel cylinder pistons. 11. Driver riding brake pedal. 12. Defective proportioning valve. 13. Insufficient brake shoe lubricant.
Hard pedal	1. Brake booster inoperative. 2. Incorrect brake lining. 3. Restricted brake line or hose. 4. Frozen brake pedal linkage. 5. Stuck wheel cylinder. 6. Binding pedal linkage. 7. Faulty proportioning valve.
Wheel locks	1. Contaminated brake lining. 2. Loose or torn brake lining. 3. Wheel cylinder cups sticking. 4. Incorrect wheel bearing adjustment. 5. Faulty proportioning valve.
Brakes fade (high speed)	1. Incorrect lining. 2. Overheated brake drums. 3. Incorrect brake fluid (low boiling temperature). 4. Saturated brake lining. 5. Leak in hydraulic system. 6. Faulty automatic adjusters.
Pedal pulsates	1. Bent or out of round brake drum.
Brake chatter and shoe knock	1. Out of round brake drum. 2. Loose support plate. 3. Bent support plate. 4. Distorted brake shoes. 5. Machine grooves in contact face of brake drum (Shoe Knock). 6. Contaminated brake lining. 7. Missing or loose components. 8. Incorrect lining material. 9. Out-of-round brake drums. 10. Heat spotted or scored brake drums. 11. Out-of-balance wheels.

Troubleshooting Drum Brakes (cont.)

Condition	Possible Cause
Brakes do not self adjust	1. Adjuster screw frozen in thread. 2. Adjuster screw corroded at thrust washer. 3. Adjuster lever does not engage star wheel. 4. Adjuster installed on wrong wheel.
Brake light glows	1. Leak in the hydraulic system. 2. Air in the system. 3. Improperly adjusted master cylinder pushrod. 4. Uneven lining wear. 5. Failure to center combination valve or proportioning valve.

Mechanic's Data

General Conversion Table

Multiply By	To Convert	To	
		LENGTH	
2.54	Inches	Centimeters	.3937
25.4	Inches	Millimeters	.03937
30.48	Feet	Centimeters	.0328
.304	Feet	Meters	3.28
.914	Yards	Meters	1.094
1.609	Miles	Kilometers	.621
		VOLUME	
.473	Pints	Liters	2.11
.946	Quarts	Liters	1.06
3.785	Gallons	Liters	.264
.016	Cubic inches	Liters	61.02
16.39	Cubic inches	Cubic cms.	.061
28.3	Cubic feet	Liters	.0353
		MASS (Weight)	
28.35	Ounces	Grams	.035
.4536	Pounds	Kilograms	2.20
—	To obtain	From	Multiply by

Multiply By	To Convert	To	
		AREA	
.645	Square inches	Square cms.	.155
.836	Square yds.	Square meters	1.196
		FORCE	
4.448	Pounds	Newtons	.225
.138	Ft./lbs.	Kilogram/meters	7.23
1.36	Ft./lbs.	Newton-meters	.737
.112	In./lbs.	Newton-meters	8.844
		PRESSURE	
.068	Psi	Atmospheres	14.7
6.89	Psi	Kilopascals	.145
		OTHER	
1.104	Horsepower (DIN)	Horsepower (SAE)	.9861
.746	Horsepower (SAE)	Kilowatts (KW)	1.34
1.60	Mph	Km/h	.625
.425	Mpg	Km/1	2.35
—	To obtain	From	Multiply by

Tap Drill Sizes

National Coarse or U.S.S.

Screw & Tap Size	Threads Per Inch	Use Drill Number
No. 5	40	39
No. 6	32	36
No. 8	32	29
No. 10	24	25
No. 12	24	17
1/4	20	8
5/16	18	F
3/8	16	5/16
7/16	14	U
1/2	13	27/64
9/16	12	31/64
5/8	11	17/32
3/4	10	21/32
7/8	9	49/64

National Coarse or U.S.S.

Screw & Tap Size	Threads Per Inch	Use Drill Number
1	8	7/8
1 1/8	7	63/64
1 1/4	7	1 7/64
1 1/2	6	1 11/32

National Fine or S.A.E.

Screw & Tap Size	Threads Per Inch	Use Drill Number
No. 5	44	37
No. 6	40	33
No. 8	36	29
No. 10	32	21

National Fine or S.A.E.

Screw & Tap Size	Threads Per Inch	Use Drill Number
No. 12	28	15
1/4	28	3
6/16	24	1
3/8	24	Q
7/16	20	W
1/2	20	29/64
9/16	18	33/64
5/8	18	37/64
3/4	16	11/16
7/8	14	13/16
1 1/8	12	13/64
1 1/4	12	1 11/64
1 1/2	12	1 27/64

Drill Sizes In Decimal Equivalents

Inch	Decimal	Wire	mm	Inch	Decimal	Wire	mm	Inch	Decimal	Wire & Letter	mm	Inch	Decimal	Letter	mm	Inch	Decimal	mm
1/64	.0156		.39		.0730	49			.1614		4.1		.2717		6.9		.4331	11.0
	.0157		.4		.0748		1.9		.1654		4.2		.2720	I		7/16	.4375	11.11
	.0160	78			.0760	48			.1660	19			.2756		7.0		.4528	11.5
	.0165		.42	5/64	.0768		1.95		.1673		4.25		.2770	J		29/64	.4531	11.51
	.0173		.44		.0781		1.98		.1693		4.3		.2795		7.1	15/32	.4688	11.90
	.0177		.45		.0785	47			.1695	18			.2810	K			.4724	12.0
	.0180	77			.0787		2.0	11/64	.1719		4.36	9/32	.2812		7.14	31/64	.4844	12.30
	.0181		.46		.0807		2.05		.1730	17			.2835		7.2		.4921	12.5
	.0189		.48		.0810	46			.1732		4.4		.2854		7.25	1/2	.5000	12.70
	.0197		.5		.0820	45			.1770	16			.2874		7.3		.5118	13.0
	.0200	76			.0827		2.1		.1772		4.5		.2900	L		33/64	.5156	13.09
	.0210	75			.0846		2.15		.1800	15			.2913		7.4	17/32	.5312	13.49
	.0217		.55		.0860	44			.1811		4.6		.2950	M			.5315	13.5
	.0225	74			.0866		2.2		.1820	14			.2953		7.5	35/64	.5469	13.89
	.0236		.6		.0886		2.25		.1850	13		19/64	.2969		7.54		.5512	14.0
	.0240	73			.0890	43			.1850		4.7		.2992		7.6	9/16	.5625	14.28
	.0250	72			.0906		2.3		.1870		4.75		.3020	N			.5709	14.5
	.0256		.65		.0925		2.35	3/16	.1875		4.76		.3031		7.7	37/64	.5781	14.68
	.0260	71			.0935	42			.1890		4.8		.3051		7.75		.5906	15.0
	.0276		.7	3/32	.0938		2.38		.1890	12			.3071		7.8	19/32	.5938	15.08
	.0280	70			.0945		2.4		.1910	11			.3110		7.9	39/64	.6094	15.47
	.0292	69			.0960	41			.1929		4.9	5/16	.3125		7.93		.6102	15.5
	.0295		.75		.0965		2.45		.1935	10			.3150		8.0	5/8	.6250	15.87
	.0310	68			.0980	40			.1960	9			.3160	O			.6299	16.0
1/32	.0312		.79		.0981		2.5		.1969		5.0		.3189		8.1	41/64	.6406	16.27
	.0315		.8		.0995	39			.1990	8			.3228		8.2		.6496	16.5
	.0320	67			.1015	38			.2008		5.1		.3230	P		21/32	.6562	16.66
	.0330	66			.1024		2.6		.2010	7			.3248		8.25		.6693	17.0
	.0335		.85		.1040	37		13/64	.2031		5.16	21/64	.3268		8.3	43/64	.6719	17.06
	.0350	65			.1063		2.7		.2040	6			.3281		8.33	11/16	.6875	17.46
	.0354		.9		.1065	36			.2047		5.2		.3307		8.4		.6890	17.5
	.0360	64			.1083		2.75		.2055	5			.3320	Q		45/64	.7031	17.85
	.0370	63		7/64	.1094		2.77		.2067		5.25		.3346		8.5		.7087	18.0
	.0374		.95		.1100	35			.2087		5.3		.3386		8.6	23/32	.7188	18.25
	.0380	62			.1102		2.8		.2090	4			.3390	R			.7283	18.5
	.0390	61			.1110	34			.2126		5.4		.3425		8.7	47/64	.7344	18.65
	.0394		1.0		.1130	33			.2130	3		11/32	.3438		8.73		.7480	19.0
	.0400	60			.1142		2.9		.2165		5.5		.3445		8.75	3/4	.7500	19.05
	.0410	59			.1160	32		7/32	.2188		5.55		.3465		8.8	49/64	.7656	19.44
	.0413		1.05		.1181		3.0		.2205		5.6		.3480	S			.7677	19.5
	.0420	58			.1200	31			.2210	2			.3504		8.9	25/32	.7812	19.84
	.0430	57			.1220		3.1		.2244		5.7		.3543		9.0		.7874	20.0
	.0433		1.1	1/8	.1250		3.17		.2264		5.75		.3580	T		51/64	.7969	20.24
	.0453		1.15		.1260		3.2		.2280	1			.3583		9.1		.8071	20.5
	.0465	56			.1280		3.25		.2283		5.8	23/64	.3594		9.12	13/16	.8125	20.63
3/64	.0469		1.19		.1285	30			.2323		5.9		.3622		9.2		.8268	21.0
	.0472		1.2		.1299		3.3		.2340	A			.3642		9.25	53/64	.8281	21.03
	.0492		1.25		.1339		3.4	15/64	.2344		5.95		.3661		9.3	27/32	.8438	21.43
	.0512		1.3		.1360	29			.2362		6.0		.3680	U			.8465	21.5
	.0520	55			.1378		3.5		.2380	B			.3701		9.4	55/64	.8594	21.82
	.0531		1.35		.1405	28			.2402		6.1		.3740		9.5		.8661	22.0
	.0550	54		9/64	.1406		3.57		.2420	C		3/8	.3750		9.52	7/8	.8750	22.22
	.0551		1.4		.1417		3.6		.2441		6.2		.3770	V			.8858	22.5
	.0571		1.45		.1440	27			.2460	D			.3780		9.6	57/64	.8906	22.62
	.0591		1.5		.1457		3.7		.2461		6.25		.3819		9.7		.9055	23.0
	.0595	53			.1470	26			.2480		6.3		.3839		9.75	29/32	.9062	23.01
	.0610		1.55		.1476		3.75	1/4	.2500		6.35		.3858		9.8	59/64	.9219	23.41
1/16	.0625		1.59		.1495	25			.2520		6.		.3860	W			.9252	23.5
	.0630		1.6		.1496		3.8		.2559		6.5		.3898		9.9	15/16	.9375	23.81
	.0635	52			.1520	24			.2570	F		25/64	.3906		9.92		.9449	24.0
	.0650		1.65		.1535		3.9		.2598		6.6		.3937		10.0	61/64	.9531	24.2
	.0669		1.7		.1540	23			.2610	G			.3970	X			.9646	24.5
	.0670	51		5/32	.1562		3.96		.2638		6.7		.4040	Y		31/32	.9688	24.6
	.0689		1.75		.1570	22		17/64	.2656		6.74	13/32	.4062		10.31		.9843	25.0
	.0700	50			.1575		4.0		.2657		6.75		.4130	Z		63/64	.9844	25.0
	.0709		1.8		.1590	21			.2660	H			.4134		10.5	1	1.0000	25.4
	.0728		1.85		.1610	20			.2677		6.8	27/64	.4219		10.71			

Index